The Gift of Active Empathy

SRLT

NORTHWESTERN UNIVERSITY PRESS

Studies in Russian Literature and Theory

The Gift of Active Empathy

Scheler, Bakhtin, and Dostoevsky

Alina Wyman

NORTHWESTERN UNIVERSITY PRESS / EVANSTON, ILLINOIS

Northwestern University Press
www.nupress.northwestern.edu

Printed in the United States of America

10 9 8 7 6 5 4 3 2 1

Library of Congress Cataloging-in-Publication Data

Names: Wyman, Alina, author.
Title: The gift of active empathy : Scheler, Bakhtin, and Dostoevsky / Alina Wyman.
Other titles: Studies in Russian literature and theory.
Description: Evanston, Illinois : Northwestern University Press, 2016. | Series: Northwestern University Press studies in Russian literature and theory
Identifiers: LCCN 2016005536| ISBN 9780810133365 (pbk. : alk. paper) | ISBN 9780810133372 (cloth : alk. paper) | ISBN 9780810133389 (e-book)
Subjects: LCSH: Dostoyevsky, Fyodor, 1821–1881—Criticism and interpretation. | Bakhtin, M. M. (Mikhail Mikhaæilovich), 1895–1975—Criticism and interpretation. | Scheler, Max, 1874–1928—Criticism and interpretation. | Empathy.
Classification: LCC PG3328.Z6 W96 2016 | DDC 891.73/3—dc23
LC record available at http://lccn.loc.gov/2016005536

♾ The paper used in this publication meets the minimum requirements of the American National Standard for Information Sciences—Permanence of Paper for Printed Library Materials, ANSI Z39.48–1992.

In memory of Leanila Martsinovich and Anna Lisa Crone

Contents

Acknowledgments

I owe a debt of gratitude to so many who have helped me bring this long-cherished project to fruition. I thank Caryl Emerson for her guidance, her many invaluable comments on the text and, most of all, for being a tremendous source of intellectual and personal inspiration for many years. Conversations with Gary Saul Morson and his provocative questioning of all things finalized have shaped much of my thinking on Bakhtin and Dostoevsky. The beginnings of this project were blessed by the intellectual brilliance and compassionate tutelage of the late Lisa Crone, whose influence on my way of thinking and being has only grown over the years.

I have benefited greatly from interactions with numerous Bakhtin scholars in the United States and abroad and would like to thank the many organizers and participants of the 12th, 13th, and 15th International Bakhtin Conferences, which proved extremely stimulating for my research. I am grateful for the steadfast support of my colleagues at New College of Florida, who helped me balance research and teaching as I was completing the book. Special thanks go to Jose Alberto Portugal, Amy Reid, and Maribeth Clark for their cheerful support during this busy period.

I thank Michael Levine and the staff of Northwestern University Press for their patience, good humor, and high professionalism in editing the manuscript.

Note on Translation and Transliteration

Mikhail Bakhtin's works are cited in their standard English translations, Vadim Liapunov's ("Author and Hero in Aesthetic Activity" and *Toward a Philosophy of the Act*) and Caryl Emerson's (*Problems of Dostoevsky's Poetics*), with my occasional emendations noted in the text. Translations of Max Scheler's works are my own, with the exception of *Ressentiment*, which is rendered in William H. Holdheim's translation throughout chapter 3, and two brief references to Peter Heath's translation of *The Nature of Sympathy*, clearly indicated as such in the text. I have used Michael Katz's translation of Dostoevsky's *Notes from Underground* in chapter 3, Jesse Coulson's translation of *Notes from the House of the Dead* in chapter 4, and David Magarshack's translation of *The Idiot* in chapters 4 and 5. In chapter 6, which demanded a meticulous, side-by-side analysis of *The Brothers Karamazov* and *The Idiot*, I have provided my own translations of the quoted passages, with all Dostoevsky citations in this final chapter referring to the standard collected edition of Dostoevsky's works, *Polnoe sobranie sochinenii v tridsati tomakh*.

Names of well-known authors (Dostoevsky, Bakhtin, Tolstoy) and Dostoevsky's literary characters (Alyosha, Smerdyakov, etc.) are given in their standard or most widely accepted English form. I have followed the Library of Congress transliteration system for text cited in Russian.

Abbreviations

"AH"	Mikhail Bakhtin. "Author and Hero in Aesthetic Activity." In *Art and Answerability: Early Philosophical Essays by M.M. Bakhtin*. Translated by Vadim Liapunov. Edited by Michael Holquist and Vadim Liapunov, 4–256. Austin: University of Texas Press, 1990.
GW	Max Scheler. *Gesammelte Werke*. Edited by Maria Scheler and Manfred Frings. 15 vols. Bern: Francke Verlag, 1954–97.
House of the Dead	Feodor Dostoevsky. *Memoirs from the House of the Dead*. Translated by Jessie Coulson. London: Oxford University Press, 1965.
Idiot	Feodor Dostoevsky. *The Idiot*. Translated by David Magarshack. London: Penguin Books, 1955.
Notes	Feodor Dostoevsky. *Notes from Underground*. Translated and edited by Michael R. Katz. New York: Norton, 1989.
PDP	Mikhail Bakhtin. *Problems of Dostoevsky's Poetics*. Edited and translated by Caryl Emerson. Introduction by Wayne C. Booth. Minneapolis: University of Minnesota Press, 1984.
PSS	Feodor Dostoevsky. *Polnoe sobranie sochinenii v tridtsati tomakh*. 30 vols. Edited by V. V. Vinogradov, G. M. Fridlender, and M. B. Khrapchenko. Leningrad: Nauka, 1972–90.
TPA	Mikhail Bakhtin. *Toward a Philosophy of the Act*. Translated by Vadim Liapunov. Edited by Vadim Liapunov and Michael Holquist. Austin: University of Texas Press, 1993.

WD	Feodor Dostoevsky. *A Writer's Diary*. Translated by Kenneth Lantz. Introduction by Gary Saul Morson. 2 vols. Evanston, Ill.: Northwestern University Press, 1993.

The Gift of Active Empathy

Dostoevsky's Philosophical Neighbors

MORE OFTEN THAN not, reading Dostoevsky is an excruciatingly visceral experience. Time and again, we are drawn to the site of the hero's execution, unable to avert our eyes from the spectacle of pain, as the text consistently demands the audience's participation in the suffering it so vividly depicts. We also suffer the discouraging failures of the heroes' spiritual quests and witness their repeated inability to respond to the others' pain in a helpful, morally authentic way demanded by the call of the hour. And yet, as the good perishes in yet another Dostoevskian catastrophe, we realize that the posited ideal, that of unacquisitive, active love for one's suffering neighbor, or agape, has survived the failures of its empirical realization: paradoxically, each work continues to gesture toward the ideal, even as its carriers are crushed on the level of the plot. This tantalizing spiritual engagement with the seemingly discredited or empirically unreachable ideal propels our interest in Dostoevsky's challenging metaphysics and draws us to reexamine those notorious "accursed" questions that populate his works.

How does faith in the value of human togetherness survive in Dostoevsky's world in the face of repeated failures of communication between his heroes? Can a Dostoevskian person enter the soul of the suffering other to gain intimate knowledge of her inner being, and if so, what can he "do" with his critical knowledge to make it ethically and spiritually productive? Does the disturbing fact that love and hatred may have virtually identical effects on its objects in the Dostoevskian universe have any bearing on the value of the agapeistic ideal posited in the texts?

It has become customary to turn to Mikhail Bakhtin's *Problems of Dostoevsky's Poetics* (1963) for answers to questions regarding communication in Dostoevsky's world, although most contemporary Dostoevsky scholars are reluctant to accept Bakhtin's once revolutionary argument wholesale. In that brilliantly insightful but eclectic and contradictory study, Bakhtin describes both the interaction between Dostoevsky's heroes and that between Dostoevsky-the-author and his heroes as a dynamic dialogue engaging all the parties as equally important, sovereign interlocutors. Bakhtin's groundbreaking monograph reveals the paramount significance of *the other* in Dostoevsky's ontology, hinting at the Christological basis of this important valuation, and highlights the profoundly active nature of interpersonal communication in his novelistic world. But is "dialogue" as described in *Problems of Dostoevsky's Poetics* and its earlier version, *Problems of Dostoevsky's Creative Art* (1929), necessarily a form of morally productive communication? Is it a normative or a descriptive concept, and can the communication between characters, which is the focus of my attention, be legitimately described with the help of the same conceptual apparatus as that between the author and his characters, as Bakhtin suggests? Finally, how effective is "dialogue" in examining the spiritual achievements and failures of Dostoevsky's ideal characters, whose fate is of special interest to this reader?

The first difficulty with employing "dialogue" for analyzing a Dostoevskian hero's response to another's suffering stems from the fact that it is a notoriously ambiguous, overburdened, and grossly overused concept, applied to vastly different types of communication. For example, in *Problems of Dostoevsky's Poetics* the same term describes such disparate relationships as Dostoevsky's (presumably minimal) authorial control over his heroes, the spiritually relevant, often morally productive communicative efforts of Tikhon, Prince Myshkin, and Alyosha Karamazov and the perverse, ultimately inconsequential "dialogue" perpetuated endlessly by the Underground Man with his invariably objectified, usually imaginary interlocutors. As many of Bakhtin's critics point out, the theorist places too few limitations on dialogue to meaningfully distinguish it from other, non-dialogical forms of speaking and being.[1] In G. Batishchev's view, at least two major types of "dialogue" are subsumed by the term in the Dostoevsky book: (1) spiritually relevant dialogue (profoundly *personal* communication correlated to a vertical hierarchy of values) and (2) "atomistic" dialogue (an inconsequential "bumping duel" between solipsistic selves, hopelessly closed off to any acquisition of value or spiritual growth).[2] In a similarly motivated, ethically minded critique, Ruth Coates also points to an apparent discrepancy in the definitions of dialogue, and of its sister concept, polyphony, as *normative concepts* in some instances and *descriptive* ones in others: in Bakhtin's Dostoevsky study two poorly compatible views of interpersonal and author-hero communication collide, Coates concludes, without achieving a synthesis.[3] Because, as readers from various critical camps have argued, Bakhtin's definition of dialogue is too broad and, for the most part, ethically neutral, his assessment of Dostoevsky's heroes' dialogical achievements is overly optimistic.[4]

Finally, for all its invaluable insights into the nature of communication in Dostoevsky, *Problems of Dostoevsky's Poetics* (hereafter, *PDP*) pays little attention to the "dialogical" life of the ideal in Dostoevsky's world. Nina Perlina, who has fruitfully extended Bakhtin's theory of dialogue to study (authoritative) quotation in *The Brothers Karamazov* (1985), notes that Bakhtin undervalues the significance of ideal teachers and the productive uses of their dialogically engaged authoritative discourse in Dostoevsky's novels.[5] According to Bakhtin's own repeated admissions, his concept of dialogue is largely irrelevant to the process of spiritual becoming or development (*stanovlenie*), which he overall denies to Dostoevsky's heroes.[6] "Not a single one of Dostoevsky's novels contains the process of dialectical development of a unified spirit, in fact, *there is no spiritual development at all* [*voobsche net stanovleniia, net rosta*], as there is no such development in tragedy," Bakhtin claims.[7] Although it is indeed impossible to speak of any kind of disembodied, abstractly conceived "spirit" in Dostoevsky, where spiritual life is always incarnated, rooted in a specifically defined, concretely embodied consciousness, nor describe the development of a Dostoevskian hero in terms of a strictly dialectical maturation, the fact of spiritual becoming is certainly not to be denied in Dostoevsky's prose altogether. While Dostoevsky is hardly a proponent of facile optimism nor a naively utopian thinker, his works routinely concern themselves with the process of personal maturation, even if this journey is a matter of tremendous difficulty for his many stumbling heroes. Clearly, Bakhtinian "dialogue" is not very useful in registering such moral-spiritual changes in Dostoevsky's characters.

PDP may not offer an adequate theoretical apparatus for tackling the question of spiritually relevant communication in Dostoevsky, but Bakhtin's earliest, philosophical works contain useful tools for addressing the issue. Using Bakhtin's "architectonic" concepts, grounded in his early phenomenology, offers the opportunity to focus on *productive* interpersonal contact, relevant to the process of spiritual maturation, and to highlight the crucial connection between the human *other* and the Divine *Other* in Dostoevsky's world, only marginally explored in the Dostoevsky book. Early Bakhtin's attention to what motivates spiritually meaningful interaction between consciousnesses will make it possible to avoid a popular critique launched against *PDP*, namely that Bakhtin has proposed an ambitious theory of communication without any account of motivation or desire,[8] while his broad focus in the pre-*PDP* works, that includes nonverbal communication, allows those relating his early reflections to Dostoevsky to account not only for the verbal output of Dostoevsky's ever-provocative ideologists but also for their no less significant deeds, often neglected in *PDP*.[9]

Overshadowed by "dialogue," still the most celebrated of his theoretical contributions, Bakhtin's early concept of active empathy (*vzhivanie*) has received relatively little attention among interpreters and those seeking to extend or apply the master's ideas.[10] And yet this important precursor of "dialogue," formulated in "Author and Hero in Aesthetic Activity" ("Avtor i geroi v esteticheskoi deiatel'nosti") and "Toward a Philosophy of the Act"

("K filosofii postupka"),[11] possesses a philosophical complexity that anticipates Bakhtin's mature concepts and avoids many of the inconsistencies inherent in *PDP*. In contrast to the well-studied but controversial concept of dialogue, active empathy opens vast possibilities for novel philosophical applications and offers useful insights for the ethical analysis of Dostoevsky's works. Unlike dialogue, which is largely irrelevant to the notion of personal becoming in Dostoevsky, active empathy is an expression of such ideal becoming—a spiritual maturation *through* and *with* the other. As, arguably, the most consistent and thorough consideration of spiritually *productive* communication in Bakhtin's oeuvre, *vzhivanie* is deeply relevant to Dostoevsky's ethical agenda.

With an eye to such potential uses in literary analysis, this study will explicate Bakhtin's early philosophy in light of its important source, Max Scheler's personalist phenomenology. In the theoretical portion of the book (chapters 1, 2), I focus on the largely neglected concept of *vzhivanie*, which is elucidated and polemically revised with the help of Scheler's relevant theories of Christian love and empathy. It is then used as a theoretical tool to examine empathetic encounters in Dostoevsky, an author whose *philosophical* influence on Bakhtin's early ethics is still underappreciated; this discussion comprises the application portion of the book (chapters 3–6).

In describing active empathy, a notion in many ways indebted to Max Scheler's *Mitgefühl*, Bakhtin emphasizes the creative aspect of understanding others. According to Bakhtin, empathy is most effective when it is both active and transformative. We may gain an ethically relevant insight into another's world, Bakhtin claims, only if we are able to enter his consciousness without completely losing our own "surplus of vision," the unique outside knowledge of the person, yielded by an external perspective. In other words, empathizing with the other is an undertaking that is emotionally richer, intellectually more complex, and spiritually more demanding than simply "becoming" the other. And ultimately, it is also more rewarding. Whence comes this surprising model that rings contrary to most theories of empathy contemporary to Bakhtin and Scheler?

In contrast to the reigning view of empathy as identification, questioned by few philosophers in their day, both thinkers pointed to the metaphor of Christ's paradoxical entry into the human world as an *active* alternative to the passive theories of empathy and compassion. Because the embodied divinity abandons its abstract position in Being, assuming a concretely individual, "dialogical" stance toward its human other, Incarnation is seen as a model of an *active* existential approach to one's neighbor. The active quality of the relationship, upon which human empathetic encounters are modeled, also stems from the fact that in Christ the divine interlocutor does not entirely coalesce with man but preserves His otherworldly divinity. Entering other souls through an act of loving empathy is then seen as a means of *embodying* the spiritual movement of love, of giving love a specific personal form, which brings us to Dostoevsky's problematics.

A concept of active empathy rooted in Incarnation is especially pertinent to Dostoevsky's world not only because in Dostoevsky a hero's relationship with his human other is always a reflection of his fundamental relationship with his Divine Other, but also because the key problem encountered by a Dostoevskian hero is precisely that of giving love an adequate *form*: to paraphrase one of the Underground Man's sarcastic utterances, the problem is not the intensity of love but its concrete "application." If in *PDP* Bakhtin proposes the role of dialogical partner to answer the question "What can one human being be to another in Dostoevsky's world?" his early investigation of active empathy suggests a more fundamental answer. Bakhtin's reflections on the ethical and aesthetic uses of love in "Author and Hero" and "Toward a Philosophy of the Act" allow one to define a Dostoevskian hero in terms of basic capacity for love and for its practical realization. In this sense, *vzhivanie* may be seen as the basic unit of emotional communication that underlies different forms of human togetherness in Dostoevsky, including dialogue. Making use of this largely unrealized theoretical apparatus, revised and enriched through Scheler's theory, I propose to answer the question: "How is an ethically productive entry into another soul possible in Dostoevsky's world?" By doing so I hope to narrow down Bakhtin's excessively broad definition of dialogue to spiritually relevant, loving dialogue—and to extend our understanding of Dostoevsky's means for registering "applied love."

It is important to stress that my critical framework is a secular and formal one. This study does not recruit Bakhtin as a believer, nor does it argue on the basis of revealed truths. But it does take seriously what manifestly nourished the worldviews of Scheler and Dostoevsky—a passionate if idiosyncratic Christianity—and strives to restore to Bakhtin the right to this same subtext, outlawed by the time and place of his writing.

The "marriage" of Bakhtin and Scheler is especially opportune because there is a remarkable kinship between the philosophers' worldviews, which makes their ethical theories mutually illuminating. Both philosophers reacted to the Nietzschean critique of empathy as a secondary, reactive feeling, rooted in ressentiment (i.e., deep-seated resentment), on the one hand, and to the early twentieth-century theories of passive empathy, on the other.[12] Both took an avid interest in religious themes and had modeled their depiction of the ideal interpersonal relationship on the notion of Christian love, agape. Both vehemently rejected depersonalizing approaches to the human sciences: Scheler criticized formal ethics in *Formalism in Ethics and Non-Formal Ethics of Values* (1913/1916) and, in *Ressentiment* (1912), took issue with contemporary altruism as a depersonalizing love that replaces the individual self with a generalized social image, adopting a stance remarkably similar to Dostoevsky's. Bakhtin consistently opposed Freudian psychology and the formal method in literary scholarship. Both Bakhtin and Scheler knew and valued the works of Dostoevsky's philosophical heir Vladimir Soloviev, although the extent of Scheler's familiarity with Soloviev's oeuvre, translated into German in the early twentieth century, is unclear. These shared philosophical concerns and Bakhtin's active use and extension of Scheler's ideas make the comparison especially fruitful.

Although by no means a blank page in literary and philosophical scholarship, the connection between Scheler and Bakhtin has not yet been explored in sufficient detail. The literature on the subject can be grouped into two categories: brief statements documenting similarities in the authors' use of a certain philosophical motif or a shared attitude toward a philosophical predecessor, and several relatively recent, more focused studies containing substantial discussions of the philosophical dialogue between the two thinkers. In the first category we should note Natalia Bonetskaia's extensive notes to "Author and Hero in Aesthetic Activity," where she states that for both philosophers the spirit is "an active individual 'I,' a subject," which cannot be objectified and is linked with the individual value center.[13] In a similar vein, O. B. Breikin points to Bakhtin's placement of the ultimate moral authority in the subject of a responsible act rather than in any concrete historical system of moral values as a debt to Scheler's personalism,[14] while Giovanni Palmieri notes that in both "Author and Hero" and in Scheler's theory of empathy, love is presented as a revealer of value.[15] Michael André Bernstein's intriguing study, *Bitter Carnival: Ressentiment and the Abject Hero* (1992),[16] which analyzes the nonproductive, negative "dialogue" in Dostoevsky, briefly links Bakhtin's dialogical theory with the theory of ressentiment, but focuses on Nietzsche's formulations, mentioning Scheler's study only in passing, as a less profound and inconsistent exposition of the same philosophical problem. In my study the concept of ressentiment in its Schelerian formulation will be linked with Bakhtin in the close readings of *Notes from Underground*.

In the thought-provoking study *Religion in the Thought of Mikhail Bakhtin* (2013), Hilary Bagshaw examines Western philosophical sources underlying Bakhtin's discussions of religion and faith, illuminating, among other topics, the similarities and differences between Bakhtin's and Scheler's concepts of confession, repentance, and grace and demonstrating Bakhtin's consistent pattern of transforming religious-philosophical concepts, creatively appropriated from his German source, into aesthetic ones in his innovative theories of verbal creation.[17] Although, in contrast to Bagshaw's substantially broader topic, I focus exclusively on the personalist concepts of loving empathy in Scheler and Bakhtin, I also take the religious context of the thinkers' ideas seriously, adopting a similar stance to Bagshaw's wisely chosen "middle course between those who would neglect and disregard any reference to religious themes in [Bakhtin's] texts as irrelevant to a basically secular enterprise, and those who would read the texts as theological at their foundation."[18] Like Bagshaw, I refrain from looking at Bakhtin's religious references in the narrow context of Russian Orthodoxy and read his Christian metaphors as an expression of a broadly defined "sense of faith," nourished in equal measure by the religious themes in the works of his favorite Western philosophers and by Russian religious thought of the early twentieth century.[19]

In his seminal work, *The Bakhtin Circle: Philosophy, Culture and Politics* (2002), Craig Brandist acknowledges Scheler's influence on Bakhtin's early concept of interpersonal understanding and credits the Russian philosopher with adding to Scheler's theory by discovering the "aesthetic moment" in co-experiencing.[20] Brandist also convincingly links Bakhtin's notion of *krugozor* (purview) with Scheler's "milieus," overlapping fields of vision, and argues for the influence of Scheler's *Wesen und Formen der Sympathie* (*The Nature of Sympathy*, 1913) on Bakhtin's Dostoevsky study.[21] Using Brandist's insights as a starting point for discussion, I will shift the focus from sociological relevance of the thinkers' ideas, explored by Brandist, to their ethical significance in the service of the distinctly personalist philosophies.

The two major articles addressing the relationship between Scheler and early Bakhtin in considerable detail are Vladimir Nikiforov's "First Philosophy as Philosophy of Individual *Postupok*" (1999–2001)[22] and Brian Poole's "From Phenomenology to Dialogue: Max Scheler's Phenomenological Tradition and Mikhail Bakhtin's Development from 'Toward a Philosophy of the Act' to his Study of Dostoevsky" (2001). While Nikiforov's article, which illuminates Bakhtin's selection of "the Act" (*postupok*) and not "the Person," as was Scheler's choice, as the foundation of his philosophy, does not directly pertain to the present inquiry, Poole's research provides a historical basis for it. Poole establishes Bakhtin's familiarity with the third edition of Scheler's *The Nature of Sympathy* (*Wesen und Formen der Sympathie*, 1926) and explores the links between Scheler's theory of sympathetic feelings and "Toward a Philosophy of the Act," "Author and Hero," and *Problems of Dostoevsky's Art* (*Problemy tvorchestva Dostoevskogo*, 1929), citing archival materials, such as a detailed summary of the 1926 edition of *The Nature of Sympathy* made for Bakhtin by his wife, to argue for a clear case of influence. While Poole regards Bakhtin's use of Scheler's theoretical apparatus as largely passive and appropriative, he does credit Bakhtin with enriching Scheler's thought by developing the implicit suggestion contained in Scheler's work to create a comprehensive ethical theory of communication, a path Scheler himself did not take.[23] In my study, I will accentuate the communicative aspects of active empathy in Bakhtin's rendering of the concept, shedding more light on the Russian thinker's *extension* of Scheler's ideas.

Now that it has been documented, Bakhtin's use of Scheler needs to be explored in greater detail. In contrast to the previously published literature, this book does not only attempt a more comprehensive examination of the two related concepts of empathy, but also includes an important context, largely omitted by the comparative scholarship on empathy, namely, the central significance of Christological motifs in both theories. Unlike most critics, I refrain from looking at Scheler exclusively or even primarily as a *source* of Bakhtin's architectonic. Instead, I reveal several divergences between the two theoreticians in the course of my analysis. In Bakhtinian fashion, I treat Scheler as a member of a related "chronotope," as Bakhtin's philosophical neighbor, who shares many of the thinker's ethical concerns and possesses a kindred worldview, rooted in the twentieth-century phenomenological tradition. An important goal of this study is to showcase the fruitfulness, sophistication, and utility of the doubly authored concept of active empathy as an analytical tool, by using it to illuminate the lapses and successes of communication in the diverse social universe of Dostoevsky's novels.

In chapter 1, I focus on the early, religious-philosophical period in Bakhtin's oeuvre ("Author and Hero in Aesthetic Activity" [probably between 1924 and 1927]; *Toward a Philosophy of the Act* [probably between 1918 and 1922]) and on Scheler's "Catholic" period (*The Nature of Sympathy* [1913], *Formalism* [1913/1916], *On the Eternal in Man* [1921], and *Ressentiment* [1912]) and examine the two concepts of empathy in the context of the prominent theological motifs that permeate these works. In my interpretation, the fundamental affinity between the two theories of intersubjectivity, as yet not fully acknowledged in scholarship, is the centrality of the Incarnation motif for both philosophers. Both Bakhtin and Scheler see the model of an *active* approach to another being, indeed to Being in general, in Christ's "dialogical" act of enfleshment. Scheler states that after Christ's Incarnation "the summum bonum of the new world is no longer the value of a thing but that of an *act*," that is, the value of the quintessential love-act performed by the self-sacrificing Christ.[24] In a similar vein, for Bakhtin, the Incarnation of Christ, who assumes an individual position in being by abandoning the sphere of pure potentiality, becomes the supreme symbol of activity. For both, the act of Incarnation signifies leaving behind pure inwardness. It is a movement from the sphere of abstract potentiality toward that of responsible individual action, which implies a profoundly personal approach to another self, who is now treated as a "Thou," a uniquely positioned "Individual-Ineffable," addressed by us as another subject. The "ontological gulf," an irreducible existential distance between individual selves, is a precondition of any ethically productive act for both philosophers. On the other hand, the multiplicity of selves is an essential feature of *personal* love, which distinguishes it from pathological cases of emotional infection, where one consciousness becomes fully consumed by another.

How is the ambitious task of live-entering achieved practically? The first stage of active empathy, mental penetration into another consciousness, receives little attention in either theory. Both Scheler and Bakhtin see the assignment as achievable; neither is truly interested in the mechanics of projection. Building up on the findings of the first chapter, which provides a theoretical definition of active empathy as an ontological concept, chapter 2 reflects on the means of its concrete *realization* in the world of ethical action: I critically reevaluate Bakhtin's vision of intersubjectivity and polemically revise it with the help of Scheler. In this chapter, I propose to restore the much needed balance to the concept of agapeistic dialogue by introducing a "usable" *surplus of the self*, which will complement but not replace the equally productive *surplus of the other* in Bakhtin's system, and to rehabilitate the concept of positive *consummation* (*zavershenie*), abandoned by Bakhtin in his dialogical period.

In the final analysis, Bakhtin's system is flawed by his neglect of the concealed part of the other's psyche. Unacknowledged by Bakhtin, this largely monological core of the self inevitably faces inward, away from the partner in dialogical exchange, and may be related to what Scheler calls the region of absolute privacy. Paradoxically, this incommunicable residue of the self actually creates the dialogical tension necessary for a productive interaction. By positing the ultimate limit of projection into another personality, this Schelerian entity guarantees the non-coincidence of consciousnesses, so crucial for the Bakhtinian vision of human communication. Because the other's inner world can never be completely encompassed in the empathizer's consciousness, the early Bakhtinian concept of *consummation,* rejected by the later Bakhtin, may now also be revised and rehabilitated for use in philosophical analysis. If the region of absolute privacy is acknowledged, the empathizer's completion of the other's spiritual image is not a dead end, but rather an opening, I argue.

Chapter 3 considers the applicability of such Schelerian-Bakhtinian concepts as "the ontological gulf," "the surplus of the self," and "consummation" to Dostoevsky's fictional world and examines the failure of empathy in *Notes from Underground*, the novel that introduces us to an important Dostoevskian type, that of an underground "dialogist." The character's peculiar way of relating to his ephemeral, depersonalized others is examined in light of Scheler's theories of active empathy and ressentiment, a life strategy synonymous with anti-empathy in Scheler. The Underground Man's imprisonment in the realm of empty potentiality is seen as a crisis of incarnation: his refusal to inhabit an individual place in Being, to find a stable domicile for his inwardly deconstructing self results in tragic inability to fathom the inner world of his fellow human beings; failure to grant individuality to others results in the practical loss of the hero's own, theoretically affirmed, sense of personal uniqueness.

The "dialogical challenge" posed by the Underground Man, who makes an interlocutor indispensable to his very existence but denies him the status of ontological, and ontic, reality, is answered by Dostoevsky's agapeistic characters. Chapter 4 discusses important, if short-lived, victories of loving empathy, a life strategy that becomes an alternative to underground aggression in *Notes from the House of the Dead* and *The Idiot*. In my related close readings of Prince Myshkin's and Goryanchikov's efforts to "enter" another soul, I make use of Bakhtin's insights about the mechanics of live-entering in "Author and Hero," with its gentle use of one's surplus of vision to establish one's "strongholds" within another psyche and a delicate labor of consummating the knowledge attained in the process of *vzhivanie*.

In chapter 5, I take a more critical look at the "consummating" activity of a Dostoevskian saint, discussing the challenges of Prince Myshkin's spiritual journey in *The Idiot*. The novel's tragic finale has polarized critics, who continue to debate whether the Christlike character's crashing defeat results from the world's bitter hostility to Christ's revolutionary mission or from the deeply flawed actions of an imperfectly conceived, or perhaps imperfectly incarnated Christ figure. I suggest that *the challenges* faced by Myshkin are precisely those of Christ as defined in the Schelerian-Bakhtinian theory of intersubjectivity, highly relevant to Dostoevsky's worldview, and use the concept of active empathy as a measure of the hero's successful Incarnation. But, having accepted these binding challenges, does this spirited imitator of Christ prove equal to the ambitious tasks entailed by the assumed role?

I argue that Myshkin largely fails in his role as a (Christlike) communicator, unable to empathetically support others without relinquishing his own individual place in Being. As a failed brother-in-Christ, whose impatient clairvoyance compels him to articulate Rogozhin's murderous intentions before the latter is fully aware of them himself, on the one hand, and someone who loses all productive distance to Nastiasia Filippovna's pain, on the other, the hero succumbs to both "temptations" of active empathy specified by Bakhtin and Scheler in "Author and Hero" and *The Nature of Sympathy*. As a result, (a) another consciousness is finalized and objectified, becoming a function of Myshkin's master consciousness, or (b) Myshkin's own individual voice becomes extinguished, eclipsed by the voice of his interlocutor. From the point of view of the Schelerian-Bakhtinian philosophy, the twofold failures of the hero's communicative efforts reflect the challenges of Christ: through Christ, God actively "lives into" a human being, yet retains

His otherworldly divinity. In the context of the later, dialogical Bakhtin, the model communicator withstands the two principal dangers that threaten *dialogue*, preserving both the divine and the human "surplus of vision." In this sense, the novel does not only illustrate the difficulty of *choosing* Christ, a point often stressed by critics, but also that of *being* Christ (and being Christlike)—which entails an arduous commitment to practicing active love, whose hopeful surplus may not be lost either "from above" or "from below."

In chapter 6, I demonstrate that Dostoevsky returns to the problem of *imitatio Christi* in his last and most celebrated novel, making Alyosha Karamazov revisit some of the same interpersonal scenarios he had devised for Prince Myshkin more than a decade earlier. I argue that Alyosha's empathy for Dmitry, Ivan, Grushenka, and Captain Snegiryov is truly *active* (and thus dialogical in my narrowed definition of the word) because, unlike Myshkin, Alyosha does not over-identify with others. Instead, this differently conceived Christlike empathizer remains firmly *outside* of those he counsels, productively using his *surplus of vision* to support their inner renewal without doing their moral-spiritual work for them. Analyzing Alyosha's interpersonal ethics with the help of early Bakhtin, I underscore the role of productive closure (*consummation*) in the character's less dramatic, at times prosaically routine, but no less life-changing interactions with others. Because Alyosha resists the temptation to coalesce with his interlocutors, he is able to deliver hope and help as gifts ushering from the *outside* of their hopeless selves, and for that reason Dostoevsky's beloved hero is also more successful than Myshkin at opening those around him to Divine *Otherness*.

Thus in the two concluding chapters we will come full circle in our consideration of active empathy, returning to the image of the "Divine Empathizer," central in all three models of intersubjectivity examined in this study. Let us now turn to Bakhtin, Scheler, and Dostoevsky as acknowledged experts on the ethics of human togetherness. The three thinkers answer the question "What makes emotional co-experiencing ethically and spiritually productive?" in individual ways, while sharing a fundamental appreciation for the value of *active* communication. Each will contribute a uniquely valuable insight to the discussion: Bakhtin points out the significance of the formal structure inherent in agapeistic love and empathy, Scheler places it in the context of a thoroughly developed ontology, while Dostoevsky's intriguing case studies help us answer a seminal question: in what *form* does the Christian ideal survive in the challenging world of modernity?

Chapter One

Bakhtin and Scheler: Toward a Theory of Active Empathy

Nam ne dano predugadat',
Kak slovo nashe otzovetsia,
I nam sochuvstvie daetsia,
Kak nam daetsia blagodat'.

We have no power to foretell
How our word will resonate with others.
And precious sympathy is granted to us,
As grace is granted to us.
—Feodor Tiutchev

THE FOLLY OF PASSIVE EMPATHY

In the field of twentieth-century ethical philosophy the connection between two seminal thinkers, two passionate crusaders for the sovereignty of the unique and uniquely perceived Person in the human sciences, deserves greater scholarly attention.[1] Max Scheler and Mikhail Bakhtin stand out sharply among their philosophical contemporaries, distinguished not only by the sheer power and longevity of their ideas but also by the extraordinary intellectual affinity with each other, which exceeds the bounds of simple influence.

In their search for the appropriately dynamic definition of an acting spiritual being within the sphere of traditional philosophy, the two phenomenologists faced the paradoxical task of creating a philosophical system for formulating an essentially anti-systematic concept of human individuality, and both the intriguing achievements and the equally remarkable shortcomings of their theories are linked with the challenges of rising to this Herculean task. Both were drawn to religious themes and took a special interest in the concept of Incarnation, offering original, often thoroughly unorthodox interpretations of biblical events from the standpoint of traditional theology. However, what joins the two original, at times eccentric thinkers in the most powerful way is not the similarity in specific philosophical themes but the impressive, perhaps even hubristic magnitude of their inquiry: each boldly attempted to solve the most essential metaphysical problems, be it the question of man's position in Being that had occupied Scheler throughout his life or the ambitious task of formulating "a first philosophy," as was the goal of Bakhtin's early writings.

In this context, the philosophers' interest in the problem of interpersonal understanding, in defining the essential means of communication between spiritual selves is an example of this ever-present concern with the central questions of Being, for in both Scheler and Bakhtin, the nature of Being is personal. How can one bridge the enormous chasm between one's own private self and the other's elusive, externally perceived inner world? Can a self transgress its psychic boundaries and enter another self in order to reach authentic understanding of another's inner life without objectifying this life in the process? What is the most personal way (a) of relating to God as ultimate Other and (b) of making an ethically meaningful connection between my love for God and my regard for fellow human beings? These and other central questions, essential to understanding the social context of personhood, are raised by Bakhtin and Scheler in their efforts to situate the human subject among its all-important *others*, both in the human and in the divine sphere. They lead the philosophers to develop the notion of ideal interpersonal communication, which, without becoming a reified norm or an abstractly conceived "standard" of ethical conduct, would best represent their commitment to preserving human individuality.

Both thinkers advocate an *active* understanding of one's fellow men and women as the most productive way of "entering" other selves. As an alternative to the purely empathetic, duplicating understanding resulting from a passive merging with another's psyche, recommended by many of their philosophical contemporaries, the two thinkers propose a creative approach to another consciousness. Such an approach is grounded in the empathizer's sovereignty as an active subject, whose unique individuality is not dissolved in the process of empathizing. "In what way would it enrich the event if I merged with the other, and instead of two there would be only one?" Bakhtin asks emphatically in "Author and Hero in Aesthetic Activity":

> And what would I myself gain by the other's merging with me? If he did, he would see and know no more than what I see and know myself; he would merely repeat in himself that want of any issue out of itself which characterizes my own life. Let him rather remain outside of me, for in that position he can see and know what I myself do not see and do not know from my own place, and he can essentially enrich the event of my own life. If all I do is merge with the other's life, I only intensify the want of any issue from within

> itself that characterizes his own life, and I only *duplicate his life numerically*. ("Author and Hero," 8; hereafter "AH"; here and throughout, italics added unless otherwise indicated)[2]

Bakhtin rejects passive co-experiencing of another's suffering, however intense, on the grounds of its ethical inefficacy. Not only is losing one's unique place outside the sufferer during the process of empathizing ineffective from the standpoint of practical action, it is ethically irresponsible, for the moral subject, no longer possessing an individual "address" in Being, cannot be located to assume personal responsibility. We find the same intolerance of the identification ethics in Scheler, who deems complete fusion of selves pathological, claiming that such a depersonalizing view of another's suffering is incompatible with true empathy.

Bakhtin's reference to the "numeric duplication" of another's inwardly hopeless emotional image in the event of passive understanding evokes Scheler's concern with the purely mechanical reproduction of the sufferer's experience, wrongly identified with empathy. In *The Nature of Sympathy*, a work carefully examined by Bakhtin,[3] Scheler responds to the Nietzschean evaluation of pity, the "instinct" that results in "*multiplying misery* quite as much as in preserving all that is miserable" by infecting the sympathizer's consciousness with the sufferer's emotional state (quoted in Scheler, *Gesammelte Werke* [hereafter *GW*], 7:28).[4] Taking this criticism very seriously, Scheler begins his defense of empathy by revealing the legitimacy of Nietzsche's disapproval of infectious pity, adding the charge of ethical irrelevance to Nietzsche's accusations of hypocritical passivity. He then proceeds to separate himself from his mentor's point of view by questioning the final conclusions of Nietzsche's otherwise lucid analysis. According to Scheler, Nietzsche is entirely correct in his penetrative evaluation of emotional infection as a symptom of psychological pathology, but not in his ultimate diagnosis, which identifies this moral malady with empathy. While recognizing Nietzsche as an effective critic of passive understanding, whose investigative work he vigilantly continues, Scheler identifies the problematic behavior not with empathy but rather with instances of its perversion (*The Nature of Sympathy*, hereafter *Sympathy*, *GW*, 7:28; see also *Ressentiment*, *GW*, 3:70, 75). Scheler's rehabilitation of empathy, based on the fact that authentic, active fellow-feeling respects the sovereignty of the other's suffering and thus *prevents* rather than spreads emotional infection, is echoed by Bakhtin, who emphasizes the importance of experiencing the other's suffering "precisely as his—in the category of the other"[5] ("AH," 26).

Besides Nietzsche, Scheler was facing a group of perhaps less formidable but newly authoritative intellectual opponents among the contemporary philosophical community. His polemics with the "projective theories" of empathy, depicting the phenomenon as a mere transfer of intellectual and emotional content between subjects, reveal the absurdly circular, utterly unproductive movement of passive understanding. According to such prominent advocates of the projective approach as Theodor Lipps and Gustav Störring,[6] the act of empathizing consists in the reproduction of the other's feeling, or rather in the evocation of a similar feeling within the empathizer's own emotional realm (either immediately so or by means of imitating the sufferer's expressive gestures), followed by a mental projection of this artificially manufactured feeling into the other's psyche (*Sympathy*, *GW*, 7:56–57). If this is indeed the operative strategy behind empathetic understanding, then at the moment of actual co-experiencing I encounter nothing more than my very own emotions, previously ascribed to the other and now "returning" to me in the guise of *his* true feelings, Scheler argues (*Sympathy*, *GW*, 7:58).

Scheler's analysis foregrounds the thoroughly solipsistic nature of projective empathy, revealing its profound impotence and ultimate inability to break through the vicious circle of inauthentic, endlessly "recycled" feelings to the *real* other, whose equally real, unassuaged suffering remains beyond its grasp. The philosopher contends that those reproductive theories of understanding that do not rely on the projection technique but nevertheless make the "numeric duplication" of *one* subject's emotional state an essential component of empathy are no closer to capturing its moral and ethical significance. For Scheler, only the recognition of the empathizer and the empathized as *two* sovereign subjects, which, in turn, leads to the recognition of two distinctly separate emotional functions, the empathized feeling and empathy itself, results in a truly intentional, morally significant attitude toward the other. Indeed,

> any theory that does not acknowledge the phenomenologically posited distinctiveness of the two processes: that of co-suffering and of the other's suffering as well as the intentional directedness of the former toward the latter is wrong, and . . . every such theory misjudges the ethical value of empathy. (*Sympathy*, *GW*, 7:50)

Those who identify empathy with passive, duplicating understanding impoverish its value by denying its ethical productivity, for, as Scheler notes, a mere reproduction of another's feeling is not yet a morally relevant act (see, for example, *Sympathy*, *GW*, 7:20).

Revealing the covert similarity between contemporary reproductive ethical theories and Nietzsche's concept of pity, Scheler argues that what reproductive theories explain is not the workings of empathy but rather the psychological mechanics of mere emotional infection, brought about by the residual herd instincts (*Sympathy*, *GW*, 7:23). Those who experience fellow-feeling only as emotional infection are motivated not by loving regard for their suffering neighbor but by the squeamish fear of contamination: they may help the sufferer only to be rid of his suffering, to extinguish the menacing source of contagion. Such "help" is hardly an example of a spontaneous existential attitude from Nietzsche's point of view, nor is it an ethically significant gesture from the standpoint of Scheler's value system.

Bakhtin, who draws a parallel between a genuinely active, creative attitude toward a fellow human being and aesthetic creation,[7] criticizes the "impoverishing theories" of empathy and empathetic aesthetics for similar reasons. According to the Russian philosopher, such theories fail to recognize the individual nature either of the aesthetic event or of its participants, assuming that creation in general and cultural creation in particular are based on "participation in one unitary consciousness" ("AH," 88). He groups the theories of aesthetic empathy into *expressive* (Volkelt, Wundt, Lipps, E. von Hartmann) and *impressive* (Fiedler, Witasek, the Formalists) aesthetics.[8] Both reduce the essentially interactive empathetic process to *one* participant: *expressive* aesthetics passively assumes that the (aesthetic) object's exterior is the self-sufficient expression of its inner state, neglecting the empathizer's impact on the creative process, while *impressive* aesthetics confines creation to the author's or empathizer's sole activity[9] (see "AH," 61–81, 91–92).

For Bakhtin, as for Scheler, what makes sympathy ethically relevant is its profoundly active nature. "It is only from within my participation [in the act of aesthetic contemplation, as in any unitary event that links me with another subject in a responsible way] that the function of each participant can be understood," Bakhtin writes. "In the place of another, just as in my own place, I am in the same state of senselessness" ("Toward a Philosophy of the Act," 18, hereafter *TPA*). According to Bakhtin, "becoming" the sufferer in the process of complete merging with his ego is just as ineffective and morally unrewarding as remaining utterly unconnected with his private self, unmoved by his suffering within the impenetrable domicile of one's own all-important sensations. If my act of compassion with the other ends in assuming his position in Being, I simply trade the limitations of my own solipsistic point of view for those of another's equally unsatisfying, fragmentary outlook on the world, finding myself "in the same state of senselessness" and paralyzing helplessness that characterizes the sufferer's own existence in its unmitigated solitude. For that reason, "what should be emphasized [in describing the act of active co-experiencing] is the absolutely incremental, *excessive, productive and enriching character of sympathetic understanding*. . . . The point is a transposition of another's experience to an entirely different axiological plane, into a new category of valuation and affirmation" ("AH," 102). Indeed, as Scheler notes, the phenomenon of true empathy, ultimately misunderstood by Nietzsche, is necessarily "*additional* to the other's experience, which is already grasped and understood" (*Sympathy*, *GW*, 7:19).

The "additional" element in empathy is love: only if bolstered by love does it acquire its active, value-oriented quality and its capacity for absolute affirmation (see, for example, *Sympathy*, *GW*, 7:146–47). So much so, that "the only thing that makes pity bearable is love that it betrays," Scheler states in response to Nietzsche's critique, which portrays both love and empathy as equally reactive, non-spontaneous emotions (*Sympathy*, *GW*, 7:148). When empathy is steeped in love, it does not reduce the empathized to his suffering, a gesture that would be offensive to his sense of self. Rather, love directs the empathetic emotional current beyond the co-experienced sensation of pain, toward the sufferer himself, actively affirming his entire, deeply valuable person. It is the sufferer's individual face, whose expressive wrinkles tell the unique tale of his anguish, and not the depersonalizing masks of a generalized social type, such as "the abused" or "the downtrodden," that loving empathy warmly acknowledges, while mere emotional identification would "look past" its object as an immediately present individuality, drawn only to the menacing sight of the wound.

Bakhtin, too, speaks of sympathy accompanied by love or of "love-like sympathy" as a genuinely active force and the primary source of creativity in aesthetic production[10] ("AH," 82), emphasizing the dynamic, enriching nature of love as a movement, which is lost if love is defined in a narrowly psychological sense (*TPA*, 64). This careful qualification evokes Scheler's distinction between *emotional functions* (empathy, joint feeling), which, as such, have a receptive, passive quality and are, at least partially, subject to psychological laws, and *emotional acts* (love, hatred), described as entirely spontaneous, value-oriented movements independent of psychology (see, for example, *Sympathy*, *GW*, 7:156, 191; *Formalism*, *GW*, 2:266–67). Only if inspired by love can empathy become a truly dynamic emotional force capable of staying emotional infection and preventing the pathological merging of selves that Nietzsche wrongly identifies with Christian compassion, Scheler argues. For Bakhtin, too, only love allows one to apprehend the infinite diversity of Being, guarding against the dissolution of individual consciousnesses within an abstractly conceived, schematized "matrix" of the surrounding world (*TPA*, 64).

The special reverence for the subject's sovereignty as an active "I" in the process of dialogical exchange, evident in both concepts of empathetic understanding, stems from the philosophers' awareness of the fundamental asymmetry between individual experiences, accepted as an a priori phenomenological fact. In *The Nature of Sympathy* and *Formalism in Ethics and Non-Formal Ethics of Values*, Scheler speaks of the irreducible differences between all human beings, rooted in the "individual diversity of their central personalities" (*Personzentren*) (*Sympathy*, *GW*, 7:45). These fundamental discrepancies would not be obliterated even if all physical differences associated with the functions of the vital body, specifically situated in time and space, and all the differences in objectifiable contents of consciousness[11] were eliminated. The stern guardians of human individuality, these original and irreconcilable differences are a source of ultimate division between persons. For that reason, a loving individual always stands before an ontological gulf,[12] an "intentional existential distance" (*Daseinsdistanz*) separating him from the beloved (see, for example, *Sympathy*, *GW*, 7:45). But love does not simply "put up" with the challenging conditions encountered on its journey across the ontological gulf—it celebrates them, directing the full force of its intentionality toward affirming the beloved as *other*. And it finds value precisely in discovering the entirely new, previously unencountered qualities in the beloved during the course of its movement, all the while completely aware of its ultimate inability to make these palpable, if partially grasped, qualities *fully* apparent. In fact, if the essential and fundamental differences between persons were an illusion, love, too, would be an illusion, Scheler claims (*Sympathy*, *GW*, 7:82). Like a bird in flight that needs the resistance of the air even as it strives to overcome it, love utilizes the traction-producing spiritual disparity between the lover and his beloved in its ceaseless movement, deriving its very dynamics from the potent asymmetry of their individual personalities. And, according to love's true ambition, this powerful yet infinitely gentle movement never aspires to fuse the selves together but rather to connect their spiritual centers in a loving encounter.

The challenging, yet ultimately productive, non-coincidence between myself and other is but a logical consequence of the profoundly asymmetrical relationship between myself and the Ultimate Other, the absolutely or "wholly different" of God. According to Scheler, even the so-called mystical union with the absolute does not imply a total coalescence between the human and the divine participants but rather signifies only the grasping of the essential affinity between God and man, grounded in their shared *personal* identity[13] (*Sympathy*, *GW*, 7:44–45). As the ultimate and thus the most complete person in Scheler's scheme of the world,[14] God preserves His perfect individuality within His loving union with man. Man's personal, read: individual, identity also remains intact if he is to maintain his common bond with the Deity by preserving this, most Godlike, core of his being. Thus the relationship between God and Man, the participants in the ultimate process of communication sharing the attributes of personhood but separated by the original ontological gulf, constitute a model of dialogue, positing the final limits of penetrating another consciousness.

Bakhtin's metaphysics also rests on the presumption of something akin to an ontological gulf between persons, but its location is different from that assigned to Scheler's "Daseinsdistanz." In his archival study of Bakhtin's reception of Scheler, Brian Poole points out that the distance between the empathizer and the empathized is a prerequisite for a genuinely empathetic encounter in both Scheler and Bakhtin, citing Bakhtin's synopsis of what he calls Scheler's "theory of distance."[15] Poole notes that Bakhtin adds "the uniqueness of place in the experience of 'co-being' and the position of being located outside" to Scheler's concept.[16] But there are more fundamental differences in the philosophers' understanding of distance between personal beings. While Scheler postulates the general uniqueness of each person as such, Bakhtin emphasizes the asymmetry between *my experience of myself* and *my experience of others*, situating the existential gulf between the two major categories of selfhood, the "I-for-myself" and the "other-for-me."

"As the leading actor in my own life, actual as well as imagined, I experience myself on a plane that is fundamentally different from the one on which I experience all other active participants in my life and in my imagining," Bakhtin writes ("AH," 32). What makes my perception of self radically different from my perception of others is the fact that the other "I" presents itself to me largely as an object. While I apprehend my own deeply subjective inner self as the yet unfinalized and in principle unfinalizable personality that can be identified only with the *act* of becoming and not with its one-time product, the other is given to me as an essentially complete, both inwardly and outwardly "compact" being. I am inwardly so immense and infinite that I defy not only the limitations of a specific space but also those of time: because of the protean quality of my conscious self-experience, I perpetually deconstruct or destroy my own present for the sake of the all-redeeming, as it were, absolute future. By contrast, the other exists for me within the specific, shape-giving dimensions of space and time (see, for example, "AH," 45). Indeed, for Bakhtin,

> everything inward that I know and in part co-experience in him I put into the outward image of the other as into a vessel which contains his *I*, his will, his cognition. For me, the other is gathered and fitted as a whole into his outward image. My own consciousness, on the other hand, I experience as encompassing the world, as embracing it, rather than as fitted into it [indecipherable]. In other words, the outward image of a human being can be experienced as consummating and exhausting the *Other*, but I do not experience it as consummating and exhausting *myself*. ("AH," 39, italics in text)

This phenomenologically given asymmetry has to be struggled with and at least partially overcome in my endeavor to apprehend and address my interlocutor as another subject, but can also be used productively in helping to "complete" the other's inwardly fragmented, hopelessly inchoate self-image by providing her with an enriching external perspective of herself.

Applying Bakhtin's terminology to Scheler, one could say that Scheler proclaims the general uniqueness and non-coincidence of the "I-for-myself" and the "other-for-himself," while Bakhtin sees the division between the "I-for-myself" and the "other-for-me" as more basic, as it were, encapsulating the whole world within a single viewpoint, that of the perceiving "I." If Scheler defines each person's uniqueness autonomously, for the early Bakhtin, whose emerging worldview already contains the germs of a future dialogical theory, personal uniqueness as such comes into being and can be defined only *in the process* of interpersonal interaction, within the identity-shaping relationship with others.

Like Scheler, Bakhtin locates the model for the interpersonal ontological gulf in the theological sphere, naming Christ as the supreme example of the "I-for-myself," lovingly embracing humanity as "others-for-me" ("AH," 56). Just as, for me, existence is inevitably divided into myself as "the one and only *subiectum* and the rest of the world as an object," for Christ, the supreme "I-for-myself," the world is rigidly separated into "himself as unique one—and all other human beings" ("AH," 38 and 56). For Christ, the universe is split into "himself as the one bestowing loving mercy—and all others as receiving mercy, into himself as the savior—and all others as the saved, into himself as the one assuming the burden of sin and expiation—and all others as relieved of this burden and redeemed" ("AH," 56). Here the fundamental divide between the savior and the saved epitomizes the ontological gulf precisely in its Bakhtinian definition, as following the prominent border between the *I-for-myself* and the *Other-for-me*, for, according to Bakhtin, "in all of Christ's norms, the *I* and the *other* are contraposed" ("AH," 56). As we shall see later, this daring metaphorical connection will lead Bakhtin to a highly original concept of Incarnation, resonant with Scheler's interpretation of this central biblical event.

THE PROGRAM OF ACTIVE UNDERSTANDING: "LIVING INTO" ANOTHER SELF

Regardless of its specific "location," the existence of the ontological gulf has to be acknowledged in order to ensure a lucid, ethically mature outlook on the world and a properly active attitude toward one's fellow human beings. If one does not recognize the individuality principle as the major consequence of the ontological gulf—whether by perceiving and treating the other as oneself, or oneself as the other—one succumbs to a fundamental delusion that perverts the entire worldview, affecting not only the sphere of human contact but also the realm of the absolute. According to Bakhtin, the abnegation of my unique position in Being leads to the denial of the uniqueness of Being as a whole:

> Pure empathizing, that is, the act of coinciding with another and losing one's own unique place in once-occurrent Being, presupposes the acknowledgment that my own uniqueness and the uniqueness of my place constitute an inessential moment that has no influence on the character of the essence of the world's being. But this acknowledgment of one's own uniqueness as inessential for the conception of Being has the inevitable consequence that one also loses the uniqueness of Being, and, as a result, we end up with a conception of Being only as possible Being, and not essential, actual, once-occurrent, inescapably real Being. (*TPA*, 15)

Because the fate of individual *beings* is inseparably linked with the welfare of *Being*, perceived as equally individual and once-occurrent in Bakhtin's system, the dissolution of essential personal differences threatens the unique and irreplaceable status of Being as a whole. And conversely, that which may rescue myself or my neighbor from the depersonalizing fate of empty potentiality, be it an identity-shaping act of authentic empathy or a simple gesture of assuming personal responsibility, is equally beneficial for my conception of the uniquely meaningful, ultimately real universe.

Scheler, too, observes that failure to recognize the existential gulf between individual selves leads to major distortions in one's perception of the world: "Whenever I apprehend and treat another 'as if' he were essentially identical with myself," Scheler writes, "it means that I succumb to a double illusion. I have an illusory view of his reality status [*Realitätstäuschung*], on the one hand, and of his spiritual status [*Soseinstäuschung*] on the other" (*Sympathy*, *GW*, 7:81). The other's reality status is not recognized because his otherness is denied ontic reality: if the other is merely an aspect of my own being that alone has a claim to ultimate reality, love of others also loses its independent meaning, becoming merely a special case of self-love. The other's *spiritual* status is misinterpreted, because he is not recognized as an individual spiritual being. Although this implication is not specifically explored by Scheler, ultimately, such a depersonalizing view of both myself and the other would compromise the spiritual status of God, who in Scheler's theory is an individual, a Person par excellence. If my neighbor, my immediate other in the human sphere, is devoid of individuality, so, too, is my absolute other. From Scheler's point of view, such an unsettling conclusion, utterly incompatible with his profoundly personal concept of the universe, would signal the onset of a global, indeed, of an ontological delusion.

An active, loving approach to another human being results in the recognition of the beloved as both *real* and *spiritually autonomous*. Scheler, who, at times, tends to present empathy and love as consecutive stages of one, progressively more spontaneous and morally significant emotional movement,[17] ascribes to empathy the function of granting the other the status of ultimate reality, while crediting love with discovering the full measure of his otherness. The natural man, in possession of only his innate cognitive faculties, as yet uneducated by the enlightening experience of empathy, harbors a "natural delusion" concerning the status of his own and the other's reality, Scheler suggests. While, on the cognitive level, *homo naturalis* acknowledges the existence of fellow spiritual beings, on the level of fundamental belief and value, he grants those fellow humans only a relative reality, limiting the sphere of the absolutely real to his own existence.

> What is overcome [if natural solipsism is dispelled through empathy] is precisely the ontic egocentric tendency to relate the other to one's own self as *seemingly absolutely real*, which, as long as the illusion obtains, is characterized by the lack of *conscious awareness* of this connection: motivated by an egocentric and solipsistic attitude, we take the existence of this fellow man, in actuality completely dependent on our own being and sphere of interests, to be his ultimate and absolute reality—and precisely herein lies the "metaphysical illusion." (*Sympathy*, *GW*, 7:70, italics in text)

Through authentic fellow-feeling I overcome the natural illusion: by freeing the other from the unconsciously present, pernicious dependence on my own ego and value system, I for the first time become truly aware of the pure and simple fact of his existence.[18] Empathy steeped in Christian love elevates the other's reality level to that of one's own in God, uniting the two selves within the realm of absolute reality and thus creating the opportunity for their first true encounter. Such, according to Scheler, is the profound meaning of the love commandment: "Love God above all and thy neighbor as thyself" (*Sympathy*, *GW*, 7:88, 109). As it were, born into ultimate existence through the life-affirming power of empathy, the other is no longer a shadowy presence on the periphery of my all-encompassing psyche but another spiritual self, a true neighbor in the shared domicile of Being: he is cherished and valuable, for *he is*.[19] Thus, together with the "discovery" of the other's existence, comes that of his "ontically real," sovereign value. What is immediately and pre-rationally apprehended by the empathizing consciousness is that "the other is equal in value to you as a human being, as a vital self, he exists as truly as you do; the other's value is equal to your own," Scheler writes (*Sympathy*, *GW*, 7:71).

But although the other's value "qua person" is equal to mine, he is valued and affirmed precisely as *other*. If empathy "maps out" the location of the other personality by recognizing his equally real position in being, love makes use of this specific "address" to make its call. According to Scheler, it is the task of love to follow the direction indicated by empathy and to discover the full extent of the neighbor's otherness, merely approximated by empathetic understanding. Building up on the foundation of equal reality status, already achieved by empathy, love penetrates ever deeper into the core of the other's personal being, until it discovers the ultimate border between selves, signaling the inaccessible sphere of absolute privacy (*Sympathy*, *GW*, 7:82). Remarkably, the "otherness" of the beloved is not merely a prerequisite for love, but a phenomenological fact discovered in the very process of loving. "Granting and accepting freedom, independence and individuality is essential to love," Scheler writes. "In the phenomenon of love the conscious awareness of two *different* persons, gradually emerging from emotional identification [*Einsfühlung*], is given clearly and distinctly; and this consciousness does not simply precede love but for the first time fully emerges only in the course of its movement" (*Sympathy*, *GW*, 7:81, italics in text).

And so it is when love is directed toward or issues forth from the Ultimate Other: in the course of love's movement both the absolute *reality* and the absolute *otherness* of God come to the fore. In *On the Eternal in Man*, Scheler describes revelation, an act in which God's love of man meets man's love of God, as a means of communicating the reality of the divine essence to the believer (*GW*, 5:249). The reality of God is the concrete spiritual reality of a person, for, in Scheler's view, only the specific can be ultimately real:

> *If* something of the divine essence does really exist, there is only *one* way in which its reality can be given to finite persons: that it [the divine essence] *offers itself spontaneously for their discovery* (or for the discovery of the select number) or it makes itself apprehensible through receptive or reactive acts. If this reality is that of a *person*—as it must be, as it is supposed to be in accordance with the idea of divinity—then this giving-itself-to-the-other's-discovery-as-real can only be a *self-revelation* of that person. ("Absolutsphäre und Realsetzung der Gottesidee," *GW*, 10:185, italics in text)

Thus God's ultimate revelation is that of His personal substance (*Person-Substanz-Offenbarung*) through Christ ("Vorbilder und Führer," *GW*, 10:278, 279). This divine emergence on the scene of ultimate reality, which exposes the *other*'s critical role in the knowledge- and value-producing work of love, becomes the highest example of "Realsetzung," the acknowledgment of the other's ontic existence, crucial for the development of loving dialogue. It is equally important that the ultimately real supreme Being is recognized as the absolute *Other*, "das ganz Andere," as Scheler describes him on multiple occasions.

As we have seen, Scheler insists on recognizing both the *otherness* of the beloved and his or her ultimate *reality* as another personal being, the two essential components of what I would like to call the Schelerian "Thou" principle. For Scheler, only such a sovereign, as it were, spiritually "voluminous" person can become an object of a truly intentional emotional act. For Bakhtin, who endorses both components of the "Thou principle," only such a self can be addressed by another consciousness; and for the later, post-architectonic Bakhtin, only such a self can be addressed *dialogically*. True empathy implies outsideness, Bakhtin states, claiming that it is "the author's loving removal of himself from the field of the hero's life" that signifies his "compassionate understanding" of this life and makes for its most productive transfiguration on the plane of aesthetic activity ("AH," 14–15). Like Scheler, who rejects the view of aesthetic empathy as a merging between the participants of the aesthetic process (*Sympathy*, *GW*, 7:29),[20] Bakhtin asserts that two distinct, non-coinciding consciousnesses are necessary for a successful aesthetic event ("AH," 22), just as the presence of two separate selves is a prerequisite for an ethically productive event.

However, it is not only the subject's otherness, but also his status as another, ultimately real *self*, not a flattened object, that is important for a properly active empathetic relationship. According to Bakhtin, compassion grounded in love guarantees precisely that kind of affirmation by another human being:

> Sympathetic co-experiencing of the hero's life means to experience that life in a form completely different from the form in which it was, or could have been, experienced by the *subiectum* of that life himself. . . . A sympathetically co-experienced life is given form not in the category of the *I* but in the category of the *other*, as the life of *another* human being, another *I*. ("AH," 82, italics in text)

Assuming an active empathetic stance toward the other means consciously approaching him from a specifically defined and intentionally utilized external perspective, as it were, initially examining his life "in profile," enjoying a view in principle inaccessible to the other himself. Yet, as a compassionate empathizer, I should not abuse my privileged position by reducing the other to a mere thing, knowing that the "object" can always turn around and return my stare, approaching me "en face," as an equal subject.

Both thinkers conceptualize active understanding as an entry into another self fundamentally different from a passive projection into an alien psyche. A loving subject approaches the other not to become one with him in the process of ecstatic psychic fusion. He penetrates the other's inner world not to usurp the other's identity or to impose his own, but to become enlightened by the invaluable, if inevitably incomplete knowledge of the other's private realm in order to affirm his reality as truly personal. "Love implies such an understanding 'entry' into *another* individuality, essentially different from the entering 'I,' precisely as another and different one, [that is] nevertheless an emotionally warm, total affirmation of 'its' reality and 'its' spiritual existence," Scheler writes (*Sympathy*, *GW*, 7:81).

Bakhtin also contemplates the ethical and aesthetic implications of entering other psyches in a responsible way, developing a concrete "mechanics" of the empathetic process. In "Toward a Philosophy of the Act" and "Author and Hero in Aesthetic Activity," Bakhtin proposes a three-step program of *vzhivanie*, literally, "living into" another consciousness (also translated as "live-entering"), a mental operation that aims to avoid the dangers of complete absorption of one consciousness by another. *Vzhivanie* consists of (1) the moment of mental projection (pure empathizing); (2) a return into oneself with the newly acquired knowledge of the other's inner world; and (3) the "consummation" of the other, which consists in the creative use of both the external and the internal points of view on the subject of active empathy[21] (see, for example, "AH," 25; *TPA*, 14). This "program" should not be viewed as a chronological sequence of separate stages, Bakhtin warns. Rather, it should be interpreted dynamically, as a series of synchronic, often virtually inseparable "moments" of one continuous emotional process ("AH," 27; *TPA*, 15).

Bakhtin structures his concept of live-entering in such a way that "pure empathizing," the moment of temporarily coinciding with the other, becomes merely one of the components in the complex process of understanding. Having returned into himself and resumed his individual position in being, the subject concerns himself with "shaping and objectifying the blind matter obtained through empathizing" (*TPA*, 15). "Referring what I myself have experienced to the other is an obligatory condition for a productive projection into the other and cognition of the other, both ethically and aesthetically," Bakhtin observes. "Aesthetic activity proper actually begins at the point when we *return* into ourselves, when we *return* to our own place outside the suffering person, and start to form and consummate the material we derived from projecting ourselves into the other and experiencing him from within himself" ("AH," 26, italics in text). The "shaping" and "objectifying" of the other's emotional content is accomplished through my intentional and consistent utilization of the "surplus of vision," a visual advantage I possess in relation to the other by virtue of my external position in the process of empathizing. While on the level of personal relationships, I have an "excess" of information in respect to the less privileged other, on the aesthetic level, the author "sees and knows something that is in principle inaccessible to [the hero]" ("AH," 12). The fruitful interaction between the two "surpluses" or points of view, my original external stance and the internal perspective obtained during my "projection" into his inner world, results in the act of *consummation*, my loving completion of the other's inwardly incoherent and fragmented spiritual image.

After penetrating into the other's inner world, I resume my position outside him, emerging with invaluable insights about his inner being, which will become "externalized" in my return movement, shaped into a tangible, but not reified, *image* of the other's inner world, so that it can be "viewed" on the same plane as his plastically expressive exterior. I may now enframe it by my own field of vision, creating a "consummating environment for him out of this excess of my own seeing, knowing, desiring and feeling" ("AH," 25). By consummating another self, I impose shape-giving limits on the internally chaotic, infinite stream of the other's experience, calling into being those unrealized, dormant values that have only a yet-to-be reality from within the other's consciousness and thus saving him from the fate of empty potentiality. From my value-revealing position I affirm the other's absolute worth, so that he, too, may gradually become assured of his palpable identity with that cherished personality that I embrace so completely. By witnessing my consummating efforts, he may become aware of his own beneficent reality as other in respect to me and may use this newly gained awareness as a stable platform for further spiritual growth.

THE VALUE-REVEALING WORK OF LOVE

In Scheler, the act of consummation is paralleled by the gradual emergence of the "individual ineffable," the indescribable but ultimately apprehensible inner person, the carrier of the individual core of values, summoned by the value-revealing voice of agape. Like the consummating work of *vzhivanie*, in Scheler's theory, love's creative labors result in the actualization of those inherently present but initially inert spiritual qualities that might have forever remained within the realm of potentiality, were they not awakened by the call of love. "'Become, empirically, what you are by virtue of your individual nature,' so calls the non-cosmic personal love to every man, extending to him precisely this image of his individual vocation in the act of its movement and not a 'generalized' standard of conduct as his original 'ideal,'" Scheler proclaims (*Sympathy*, *GW*, 7:136). Because in the non-cosmic sphere of the metaphysical order human beings are irreplaceable, though they may vary in individual value, their intrinsic ideal, revealed to the penetrating gaze of love, is equally unique and irreplaceable. It is this deeply personal ideal, which is akin to one's spiritual countenance, invisible to the loveless gaze, and not a defaced social standard or an impersonal pattern of excellence, that love points to in its spontaneous movement toward the ultimately real. One may say that in the lover's eyes the ultimately real exercises a "tug" on the empirically real: because the lover perceives the beloved dynamically, already in movement toward the other, better self, this ideal image is apprehended as the only real, true image (*Sympathy*, *GW*, 7:156–57). In Bakhtinian terms, we may say that the beloved's ultimate spiritual countenance, gradually revealed to the lover, is not a *given* but a *posited*: it is imposed as a task, as a calling forth or a challenge announced by love, which spontaneously brings into existence ever higher values but remains entirely independent of these values. For that reason, "love always loves and sees more in the course of loving than . . . what it has 'on hand'" ("Ordo Amoris," *GW*, 10:358), pointing to values that cannot yet be "felt" or "confirmed" as real on the empirical level. Indeed,

> love does not simply gape approval, so to speak, at a value lying ready to hand for inspection. It does not reach out toward given objects (or real persons) merely on account of the positive values inherent in them and already "given" *prior* to the coming of love . . . Love only occurs when, upon the values already acknowledged as "real" there supervenes a *movement* and intention toward potential values still higher than those already given and presented.[22] (italics in text)

In its effortless, entirely spontaneous motion, love makes palpable those deeply cherished individual values that can never be defined or evaluated in conceptual terms, eventually revealing, albeit partially, the most personal and thus the least "describable" core of the spiritual self, the elusive but immanently present "individual ineffable."

As we have seen, for Scheler, love is not a reaction to an "offer" of given values, but rather a potent, productive force that both reveals and creates value in the process of its joyful vocation of the "individual ineffable." Bakhtin also emphasizes love's non-reactive, unmotivated, and profoundly affirmative character.[23] In aesthetic love, as in any loving relationship, the act of loving valuation (but not of evaluation) precedes any conceptual apprehension of value. Thus the other is not lovingly cherished because he is valuable; instead he is valuable precisely because he is so cherished. "In aesthetic seeing you love a human being not because he is good, rather a human being is good because you love him [*ne po khoroshu mil, a po milu khorosh*]," Bakhtin asserts, quoting a popular Russian proverb (*TPA*, 62). Thus a loving relationship of the author to the hero is "the relationship of an unmotivated valuation to the object of such valuation ('I love him, whatever he may be; and only after the act of valuation comes the active idealization, the gift of form)" ("AH," 90).[24]

For Bakhtin, a thoughtful student of Scheler, love can be conceived only dynamically, as an act and a movement, and, as such, it is creative and not merely reproductive of value. For that reason an aesthetic consciousness—be it that of a literary author or of any creatively minded individual "authoring" his relationships with fellow men—is a "loving and value-positing consciousness" ("AH," 89). But this by no means implies "projecting" or ascribing one's own values to the other, a depersonalizing gesture that is utterly incompatible with loving valuation, against which Scheler warns in *The Nature of Sympathy* (*GW*, 7:162). In Bakhtin's opinion, such a transfer would signify a mere duplication of the ready-made, "frozen" value content, and not an embracing of an entirely new value, enriching to my life and, in its turn, enriched and induced to grow by my consummating challenge. That is why reproductive interpretations of empathy impoverish its ethical and aesthetic significance, for the reproduced emotional and spiritual content is not enhanced by any "transgredient [i.e., external] values" ("AH," 80). For Bakhtin,

> sympathetic understanding is not a mirroring, but a fundamentally and essentially new valuation, a utilization of my own architectonic position in being outside another's inner life.[25] Sympathetic understanding recreates the whole inner person in aesthetically loving categories for a new existence in a new dimension of the world. ("AH," 103)

While both Scheler and Bakhtin acknowledge the revelation and growth of value in the course of love's movement, Bakhtin's architectonic emphasizes the bestowal of value from the outside by the loving *other*, not a necessary condition for the enhancement of value in Scheler's phenomenology. The divergence between Bakhtin's and Scheler's views on value-realization stems from the differences in the philosophers' concepts of the ontological gulf. If Scheler posits the discrepancy in value between all individual persons, independently of the I/other division,[26] Bakhtin proclaims the radical difference between *my self-value* and *my valuation of others*. Though the very possibility of my being in the world is predicated upon my survival and well-being, "I am not [my own life's] valuable hero," Bakhtin asserts decisively ("AH," 106). Simply put, for Bakhtin, the absence of self-value is an a priori condition of human existence, a phenomenological given that does not require any additional explanation.[27] "I myself cannot be the author of my own value, just as I cannot lift myself by my own hair," Bakhtin claims. "The biological life of an organism becomes a value only in another's sympathy and compassion with that life" ("AH," 55). For that reason the bestowal of value is precisely that, a bestowal, an unsolicited yet precious gift from the privileged other in Bakhtin's architectonic.[28]

We find a more balanced approach to self and other in Scheler's work. Contrary to Bakhtin's categorical assumption that from within a self there can only be a negation of value, Scheler contends that my own value can be revealed in the process of genuine self-love (see, for example, *Sympathy*, *GW*, 7:130, 146). In this case, we may say that love itself is the ever-novel and value-revealing *other* that creates an external challenge necessary for spiritual growth and enrichment of value. In the instance of self-regard, the ontological gulf traversed by love, which both challenges and enables its movement, is not between two different empirical personalities but between my empirical self and my potential, purely personal self. It results from the fact that I am as unknown and often as alien to myself as pure person, the elusive and entirely individual being within, as the other may be to me. Authentic self-love then itself becomes the principal, externally positioned actor that calls forth this alien other within me, momentarily bridging but never completely eliminating the internal ontological gulf. This better other, as it were, united with me in the act of self-love in a single embrace, is not a given but a posited—a task achieved through the rare but invaluable instances of *ingatherdness* (*Sammlung*), when I actively "gather" and raise myself to a new spiritual level for an encounter with my inner person, momentarily experiencing my act-center freely (see, for example, *On the Eternal in Man*, *GW*, 5:23). If one defines personal identity as that implied in the concept of salvation or the membership in the kingdom of God, as Scheler does on several occasions, the value division between self and other becomes less essential, for, as Scheler argues, my own salvation should be as valuable to me as that of the other (see, for example, *Ressentiment*, *GW*, 3:105).[29]

An important consequence of embracing the ethically valid appreciation of self-value for social relationships, such as loving empathy, is a more balanced, interactive concept of dialogue, in which the other does not merely receive value but participates in its revelation and creation. A relevant reflection on self-love by Søren Kierkegaard may serve as a less obtrusive "correction" of Bakhtin's architectonic. Because, like Bakhtin, Kierkegaard is often hesitant to assign spiritual or ethical value to self-love, his cautious attempts to reconcile the last part of the love commandment with the demand for self-renunciation, implicit in Christ's sacrifice, may be more compatible with Bakhtin's worldview than Scheler's direct endorsement of self-regard. According to Kierkegaard, he who loves himself "in the truth and earnestness of eternity" learns the infinite value of his own eternally cherished life from Christ, whose sacrificial gesture did not only transfigure all neighbor-love but changed the very character of self-love.[30] For indeed, "no one lived with him [with Christ] who loved himself as deeply as Christ loved him," Kierkegaard proclaims.[31] What deserves Kierkegaard's cautious approval is self-love whose spontaneous movement aspires to meet Christ's saving gesture of absolute affirmation with a truly affirmative act of accepting and celebrating His sacrificial love. Thus one may say that Christ's world-transforming love takes root in the heart of the believer not only in the form of neighbor-love but also in the form of Christian self-love, a less obvious but equally holy way of *imitatio Christi*.

This self-love, introduced into the "context of eternity" through Christ's gift of salvation and radically different from any "natural," essentially egoistic instincts of self-preservation, is akin to Scheler's love for oneself as a member of the kingdom of God. Although initially such self-love receives its value "from the outside," through Christ's love of others, it enjoys a sovereign status in Scheler's value-system. Once affirmed by the Supreme Other in "truth and earnestness of eternity," I no longer depend on the affirmation of immediate others for ultimate value. He who has learned to love from Christ uses his initial education in value to continue the value-enhancing work of Christian love both in relation to self and others. A human being who loves himself as a member of the kingdom of God does not negate his own value but cherishes it with the same reverence and solemnity as that of his fellow men and women. Thus, evaluating Scheler's concept of active understanding in light of Bakhtin's criteria for the production of value, we may say that, in Scheler's world, Christ is the only *other* whose presence is necessary for the revelation and growth of value, a fundamentally productive outcome that is as intrinsic to genuine self-love as it is to the love of others.

INCARNATION AS A MODEL *ACT*

It is the presence of Christ, the original "person" or the original "I-for-myself," as Bakhtin puts it, that authenticates an act of love by placing it in the context of Incarnation. Furthermore, it is Christ's fundamentally active existential stance that posits the highest model of *active* understanding for both Scheler and Bakhtin. Scheler's somewhat cryptic definition of a concrete spiritual self, a person, as "a being of acts" becomes less puzzling if one remembers that for the German philosopher the highest, as it were, "the most active act," is that of love, as exemplified in the event of Christ's life. A fundamentally active human being, a person, then becomes synonymous with a loving human being, *ens amans* or *homo amans*. After Incarnation, Scheler writes, "there is no longer any 'highest good' independent of and beyond the *act* and *movement* of love" (*Ressentiment*, *GW*, 3:73). Now it is no longer the objective value of some impersonal standardized goodness that governs the ethical realm but the highly "subjective" force of love, issuing forth from a loving subject and itself becoming the source of all value.

> [Thus] *the summum bonum is no longer the value of a thing, but of an act*, the value of love itself as love—not for its results and achievements. Indeed,

> the achievements are only symbols and proofs of its presence in the person. And thus God Himself becomes a "person," who has no "idea of the good," no "form and order," no logos above Him, but only below Him—through the deed of love. (*Ressentiment*, *GW*, 3:73)

Bakhtin, too, sees "the descent of Christ" as the supreme example of assuming an active stance in being, a "great *symbol of self-activity*" (*TPA*, 16).

It is consistent with Scheler's concept of the active loving self, the "act-person," that the most personal and thus the least objectified image of the other can be apprehended in the act of his love, compassionately co-experienced by me (see, for example, *Sympathy*, *GW*, 7:169). Consequently, the infinite loving person of God, the absolute Other, can best be grasped in the highest act of God's love, Incarnation, which bridges, albeit incompletely, the chasm between God's absolute transcendence and man's finite existence.

In Bakhtinian terms, we may call this model of dealing with the ontological gulf the original act of *vzhivanie*, a divine "living into" the human sphere. The Russian philosopher, whose discourse is less overtly theological than Scheler's, uses Incarnation as an effective metaphor of interpersonal understanding.[32] In the incarnated Christ Bakhtin hails an empathizer who is utterly different from the one endorsed by the proponents of projection theories. Instead of a complete fusion between participants in dialogue, the original live-entering results in the profoundly meaningful encounter between two distinct spiritual entities, the human and the divine.

For Bakhtin, Incarnation becomes synonymous with the highly responsible act of abandoning a purely theoretical position toward the indefinite, as it were, abstractly conceived other. Instead, Christ both enters the dialogue as a uniquely defined self and approaches his human interlocutors as concrete individuals: having abandoned the divine heights, he encounters them as neighbors, whose distinct countenances are clearly visible from this new, personable distance. And, just like Christ's original act of affirmation, every genuine act of love bestows value on the fully embodied, uniquely individual beloved from a concrete place in being. "Any valuation is an act of assuming an individual position in being," Bakhtin writes, "even God had to incarnate himself in order to bestow mercy, to suffer and to *forgive*—had to descend, as it were, from the abstract standpoint of justice ("AH," 129, italics in text). Because in Bakhtin's theology the body is presented as God's other, the "transfiguration of the body in God," achieved by Christ, is the "transfiguration of that which is the Other for God" ("AH," 57).

Thus, for Bakhtin, Christian spirituality is a spirituality of turning toward the other, of incarnating and transfiguring oneself *in the other* and thus inextricably linking one's own personal becoming with that of another.

> [After Incarnation] God is no longer defined essentially as the voice of my conscience, as purity of my relationship to myself (purity of my penitent self-denial of anything *given* within myself), as the one into whose hands it is a fearful thing to fall and to see whom means to die (immanent self-condemnation). God is now the heavenly father who is *over me* and can be merciful to me and justify me, whereas I, from within myself, cannot be merciful to myself and cannot justify myself in principle. ("AH," 56, italics in text)

Therefore, God is no longer pure interiority—He is above and beside me; He himself is a relationship and His voice tends toward a dialogue.[33]

This depiction of spiritual and ethical becoming in the act of "stepping out" of the solipsistic, inevitably hopeless interior self resonates with Scheler's concept of personal emergence (*Personwerdung*), based on the Christian model of Incarnation.[34] In Heinz Leonardy's eloquent summary of Scheler's notion of "incarnated" personhood, the striking affinity between the philosophers' symbolic visions comes to the fore:

> The [Schelerian] person can realize itself only through a deed, that is, through leaving behind pure inwardness, in a gesture of active turning toward the world and the other. Granted, in the beginning there was Logos, reason, but reason has become flesh! The creative act arises from reason, together with reason we are born for an active existence. And the act leads us beyond ourselves—toward the world and toward the Thou.[35]

Both Scheler and Bakhtin see the realization of the spirit, epitomized in the idea of Incarnation and present in every genuine act of personal becoming, as a somewhat paradoxical movement away from pure potentiality that nevertheless does not destroy or exhaust one's potential. For Scheler, the spirit reaches its highest realization in the form of a person, a belief that remains unchanged throughout his life. But already in his so-called Catholic period Scheler begins to expose the insufficiency of pure spirit, a trend that will become more prominent in his later years. In *The Nature of Sympathy*, Scheler describes "the absolute individual" as an "X," referring to our elusive knowledge of the other's personal being, which is present in our consciousness as an empty or partially filled slot: we know and even immediately "feel" that it exists, but fail to understand it, to endow it with any ultimate conceptual content ("letzter Verständnisgehalt") (*Sympathy*, *GW*, 7:78). The pure person is so dynamic, so deeply steeped in the potential realm that no last word can be said about it. This largely potential mode of existence obtains for *my own* ultimate person as well. "Man's spiritual 'person' is not a substantial thing and not being that is objective in form," Scheler writes in "Philosophische Weltanschauung" ("Philosophical Worldview"). "Man can only 'gather' himself to his inner 'person'" (*GW*, 9:83). For the older Scheler, pure spirit is necessarily passive and helpless: "The spirit cannot be independent and self-sufficient. The spiritual person is not an effective reality; it is only an X to which one can 'gather oneself' from the standpoint of its given reality" ("Der Sphärenunterschied vom Psychischen und Physischen" ("The Difference between the Psychic and the Physical Spheres") *GW*, 12:160).

Thus, to use Bakhtin's terms, for Scheler the spirit is always a *posited*, a yet to be achieved reality, to which one aspires, as it were, actively lifting or "gathering" oneself from the position of a *given* existence. And yet, paradoxically, but perhaps not in contradiction with the biblical paradigm, the very act of "Sammlung," of reaching toward one's spiritual center in search of its momentary realization (or incarnation?) is achieved with the help of non-spiritual, vital faculties:

> Ontically it [spirit] [is] only that which determines itself and only itself and which manifests itself in us through acting. It is the real causa sui, if by causa we mean the basis of being and not the ability to act (creatia continua!). The person and the act can realize themselves only through the activity and functions of the vital centers, which are, in their turn, directed and "led" by the former. ("Der Sphärenunterschied vom Psychischen und Physischen," *GW*, 12:160)

The more mature Scheler reinterprets the active essence of incarnation, evident in every event of personal emergence, as the dynamic *interpenetration* of the spiritual and the vital forces (*Durchdringung*) that results in the spiritualization of life and the vitalization of the spirit[36] (see, for example, "Manuskripte zur Lehre vom Grunde aller Dinge" ("Manuscripts toward a Theory of the Foundation of All Things"), *GW*, 11:209). Although fully developed only in Scheler's later years, the concept of interpenetration is already present in *The Nature of Sympathy* in the discussion of Saint Francis of Assisi's profoundly open worldview, which embraces both the non-cosmic, personal Christian neighbor-love and the cosmic feeling of innermost unity with the entire created world, seen by Scheler as pagan in origin. In the person of Francis two qualitatively different kinds of love, the deeply spiritual agape, directed at the individual core of value, and the vital, impulsive but boundlessly energetic eros, meet and, as Bakhtin would put it, "live into" each other, transforming and enriching each other in the process:[37]

> [Here one witnesses] a *unique movement on the part of both "eros" and "agape"* (agape deeply steeped in both *amor Dei* and *amor in Deo*) in an innately holy soul of a genius—and finally a case of complete *interpenetration* [*Durchdringung*] of the two, which constitutes the greatest and the most

sublime example of synchronic "spiritualization of life" and "vitalization of the spirit" known to me. (*Sympathy*, *GW*, 7:103, italics in text)

What Scheler has in mind here is the fact that Saint Francis's energetic, ever cheerful love for all of God's creation, be it a strayed bird or a nearby mountain, is not only compatible but thoroughly consistent with his equally warm, indiscriminate personal love; that in fact the two emotional currents have grown and matured in the process of their intimate contact with each other. The kind of inspired reevaluation of natural phenomena as warmly affirmed love-objects that takes place in Francis's worldview is seen by Scheler as a "vitalization of God," as yet another means of making Him corporeal ("Verleiblichung Gott"), an event analogous to Christ's Incarnation and sacrifice that in fact continues the original process of creation (*Sympathy*, *GW*, 7:101).[38] Seen from this perspective, Francis's affirmation of creation in light of Christ's sacrifice reveals the profoundly creative nature of Christ's gesture in Scheler's view: it is implied in Scheler's interpretation of Francis's Weltanschauung that it is only through Incarnation, the quintessentially creative act, that the true, "embodying" significance of the earlier, natural creation becomes fully apparent.

In Bakhtin we also detect the notion that the solipsistic spirit is powerless or, as Bakhtin puts it, necessarily "hopeless" from within itself. The Russian philosopher describes one of the two major categories of selfhood in his system, the "I-for-myself," as the yet unincarnated spirit in its pure inwardness. The soul is then "*spirit-that-has-not-actualized-itself* as it is reflected in the loving consciousness of another (another human being, God); it is *that which I myself can do nothing with*, that in which I am passive or receptive (from within itself, the soul can only be ashamed of itself; from without, it can be beautiful and naive)" ("AH," 111). In its pure interiority spirit is ineffective and unutilized ("I can do nothing with [it]"), hence the notorious hopelessness of the "I for myself" in Bakhtin's world. Consummation, the other's loving bestowal of form on my externally perceived inner world, becomes a means of "representing" the spirit, a temporary incarnation of my internally shapeless private self in the other's shape-giving consciousness. In contrast to the Schelerian "Sammlung," an act of "gathering" oneself to the other's or one's own inner person that can also be described as a temporary incarnation, consummation is always performed by the *other* in early Bakhtin.

It will be recalled that the incarnated Christ of the Gospels now represents the new "I-for-myself," qualitatively different from the self-absorbed and self-sufficient model of being that Bakhtin associates with the world prior to the Incarnation and that he identifies with the purely spiritual, inwardly locked, part of each personality. Thus, on the one hand, Christ symbolizes the bitter division along the Bakhtinian ontological gulf (we may recall that for both Christ and the "I" the world is rigidly separated into "Himself" and "the rest of the world" or "all others" ["AH," 38 and 56]). On the other hand, he epitomizes both the partial transcendence and the productive use of this division, which results in the creation of the profoundly novel concept of self:

> In Christ we find a synthesis of unique depth, the synthesis of *ethical solipsism* (man's infinite severity toward himself, i.e., an immaculately pure relationship to oneself) with *ethical-aesthetic kindness* toward the other. For the first time, there appeared an infinitely deepened *I-for-myself*—not a cold *I-for-myself*, but one of boundless kindness toward the other; an *I-for-myself* that renders full justice to the other as such, disclosing and affirming the other's axiological distinctiveness in all its fullness. ("AH," 56, italics in text)

If Christ indeed represents the new model of self, as it were, compassionately open to the world and to the other, he can no longer view the world merely as an "object," in the sense of a self-identical, reified given, the way the old, solipsistic self did. Thus, what Bakhtin describes as the essential characteristic of the "aesthetic standpoint," namely, "the living correlation of me—the one-and-only *subiectum*, and the rest of the world as an object not only of my cognition and my outer senses, but also of my volition and feeling" ("AH," 38, italics in text), may be interpreted as merely a given, or a starting point of the creative situation, which is not necessarily identical with its final point. Although Christ's predicament in some ways mirrors the ontological gulf between self and other, his sacrificial gesture of "boundless kindness toward the other" becomes a means of (partially) bridging this fundamental divide. By way of analogy, in the context of the Incarnation model, my consummating efforts in relation to the other must be understood as a movement away from the old, rigidly separated "I-for-myself" toward the new, Christlike one and from the old, as it were, terminally objectified "other-for-me" toward the entirely new, gentle, and non-reifying means of creative objectification.

For Bakhtin, Incarnation provides a structural model for acquiring knowledge in a responsible way, for "living into" any kind of alien intellectual or emotional content. "Theoretical cognition of an object that exists by itself, independently of its actual position in the once-occurrent world from the standpoint of a participant's unique place, is perfectly justified. But it does not constitute ultimate cognition," Bakhtin warns (*TPA*, 48). Rather, it represents merely one component of the cognitive process:

> My abstracting [myself] from my own unique place in Being, my *as it were* disembodying of myself, is itself an answerable act or deed that is actualized from my own unique place, and all knowledge with a determinate content (the possible self-equivalent givenness of Being) that is obtained in this way must be *incarnated* by me, must be translated into the language of participative (unindifferent) thinking, must submit to the question of what obligation the given knowledge imposes upon me—the unique me—from my unique place. . . . Thus knowledge *of* [*znanie*] the content of the object in itself becomes a knowledge of *it for me*—becomes a *cognition* [*uznanie*] *that answerably obligates me*. (*TPA*, 48–49, italics in text)

Understanding an object is a complex, multi-dimensional process, Bakthin argues. It includes two essential steps or "moments": that of penetrating into the object, necessarily leaving my own stable position outside of it, and, upon my return into the self, that of personalizing the material obtained in the process of projection by immersing it in my own consciousness, now firmly rooted in a specific place in Being. Similarly, when I enter another consciousness, I temporarily abandon my individual address in Being, as it were, becoming a homeless spirit possessing the other's inner self, only to come back and incarnate the acquired knowledge in my own psyche, informing it by my unique surplus of vision. On its way to its new domicile, once it has been "extracted" from the personalizing context of the other's psyche, the obtained knowledge about the other is impersonal and abstract: it is as reified and self-equivalent as an object, and as such it is a *given*. This given data, which has little merit on its own, becomes one of the building blocks in the process of constructing a dynamic, living portrait of the other; it becomes part of the work in progress, or as Bakhtin would put it, a *posited*.

The gesture of embodying the gathered knowledge signals the beginning of a truly creative activity, for, as Bakhtin explains, (aesthetic) creation begins only with the return into the self ("AH," 26). In contrast to abstract cognition, the active, incarnated knowledge carries the mark of my participation in the emotionally warm, responsible relationship with the object. It becomes meaningful precisely in the act of its compassionate appropriation, of making it the uniquely individual "knowledge for me" by incorporating my emerging response to the object into this carefully shaped cognitive material. And as such, it contributes to our understanding of Being not as a static, self-equivalent entity but as an ongoing event.

So powerful is the message of Incarnation for Bakhtin and Scheler that it ceases to be merely a philosophical motif in their oeuvre but becomes something akin to a worldview and an active life strategy: both consistently postulate the need for daily embodiment, or, to use Scheler's vocabulary, personalization of knowledge, experience, and value. The all-important lesson of Incarnation is that for a genuinely active, read: loving consciousness, there can be no abstractly conceived, disembodied knowledge or good. "There is no acknowledged self-equivalent and universally valid value, for its acknowledged validity is conditioned *not* by its content, taken in abstraction, but by its being *correlated* with the unique place of a participant. It is from this unique place that all values and any other human being with his values can be acknowledged," Bakhtin writes (*TPA*, 48, italics in text). Scheler also emphasizes the importance of "the good for me" as for any "concrete spiritual act-center" that has to realize or bring into being its individually assigned value-content[39] (see "Vorbilder und Führer" ["Role Models and Leaders"], *GW*, 10:264, 302, quoted in Leonardy, *Liebe und Person* [*Love and the Person*], 213). The uniquely individual yet objective "good for me" is that specific value which helps me achieve personhood in the purest form.[40] Thus the person is the central locus of value-actualization and apprehension. Bakhtin agrees: "The center of value in the event-architectonic of aesthetic seeing is man as a lovingly affirmed concrete actuality, and not as something with self-identical content" (*TPA*, 63).

Scheler also reminds us that love does not reach for some kind of self-standing, disembodied value but is drawn to individual value incarnated in a (personal) being: "I love not value but always something that is valuable," Scheler observes (*Sympathy*, *GW*, 7:151). Consequently, any particular qualities and achievements of the beloved receive their full value only through his or her person as a concrete spiritual reality[41] (see *Sympathy*, *GW*, 7:152).

Indeed, it would be absurd to attempt to "distill" or extract pure value by removing it, like a garment, from the valuable person or from the act of love, which lies at the foundation of personhood in Scheler's system. For such is the ever-novel spiritual achievement of Christianity that through Christ's revolutionary sacrificial gesture value is posited not as a thing with "self-identical content" but as a personal act, that of unconditional and empowering love. That is why Scheler adamantly proclaims that there can be no love of goodness, because there could be no self-standing, abstract goodness separate from love, and counsels his readers not to love God for His Heaven and Earth, His abstractly conceived, so to speak, "marketable" value, but rather to love Heaven and Earth because they are God's and thus embody His infinite love (see *Sympathy*, *GW*, 7:164–67 and *Ressentiment*, *GW*, 3:80).

Intellectual and spiritual kinsmen occupied with similar ethical concerns and responding to a shared canon of philosophical texts, Scheler and Bakhtin have developed mutually illuminating concepts of empathy. In their largely rehabilitative efforts to redefine the compassionate worldview as a profoundly active existential position, both thinkers turn to the event of Christ's life for a model of empathetic understanding. As a result of this far-reaching analogy, both postulate existential distance between subjects as a necessary precondition of loving empathy and describe such empathy as a value-affirming and value-revealing event. Electing incarnation as a model of interpersonal communication results in the vision of dialogue in which my own spiritual growth is inextricably linked with the other's personal becoming. This striking choice of metaphor posits an ideal that is both decidedly otherworldly and uniquely "mine," personalized and reincarnated by my individual act of faith. But it also opens the door to criticism by those who may be skeptical of such an elusive standard of personal interaction. Because both theories rely on a *paradoxical* concept of dialogue, whose original participant is no less than the mighty God-Man himself, the philosophers' opponents could argue, with Dostoevsky's Ivan Karamazov, that such a model of compassion imposes enormous, indeed, impossible demands on human empathizers.

Chapter Two

Empathy as a Task: Problems and Solutions

> . . . he tried, as always and everywhere, to imagine the inner, transparent movement of another person, carefully seating himself inside his interlocutor, as in an armchair, so that the other's elbows served as arm rests and his soul would slip into another's soul—and then the lighting of the world would change . . .
> —Vladimir Nabokov, *The Gift*

"LIVE-ENTERING" WITHOUT AN ENTERING? ACTIVE EMPATHY AND THE PHENOMENOLOGICAL METHOD

In their mutually illuminating theories of intersubjectivity, Scheler and Bakhtin arrive at compatible concepts of loving empathy, whose ideal nature is readily apparent. Modeled on the original act of love, Incarnation, creative empathy is a tribute to the communicative achievement of the supreme dialogist, the God-Man Christ, in both theories. But how can this lofty ideal be implemented in daily life? While chapter 1 provides a theoretical definition of active empathy as a major ontological concept, the present chapter considers the means of its *realization* in the challenging world of ethical action. Exploring practical implications of empathetic co-experiencing, we shall uncover problematic elements in both philosophical constructs and suggest some viable solutions.[1]

As we have seen, in the early Bakhtin, the creative use of the surplus of vision brings about one's "consummation" (*zavershenie*), the loving completion of one's inwardly inchoate spiritual image by the privileged other. In Scheler, the act of love results in the gradual emergence of the "individual ineffable," the elusive but ultimately apprehensible inner person. The individual's consummation and revelation of value occur upon the empathizer's return into the self, after the projection into another consciousness has been successfully completed. But how is the Herculean task of live-*entering* achieved?

The first stage of empathy, mental penetration into another consciousness, receives little attention in either theory: both Scheler and Bakhtin see the assignment as essentially achievable. "There can be no doubt that, phenomenologically, co-experiencing of another being's inner life does occur, whatever the unconscious technique of its actualization might be," Bakhtin writes, betraying his sources ("AH," 62). Scheler affords somewhat more consideration to the problem of approaching the other's experience by acknowledging the represented nature of the other's feelings within the emotional structures of our own consciousness, once these feelings have already been apprehended, but promptly moves on to the discussion of the opposite problem, namely, the dangers of penetrating the other's psyche too deeply (*GW*, 7:20–21). Because neither author is truly interested in the "unconscious techniques" or the mechanics of co-experiencing with others, the obstacles to the first "stage" of active empathy are largely ignored.

The poverty of detail in Scheler's depiction of active empathy as a practical undertaking, which may indeed involve unconscious or unarticulated methods or techniques, could be due to the fact that the philosopher never developed a consistent theory of moral-ethical praxis, as Eugene Kelly argues.[2] Another, methodological, reason for dismissing the problem of obtaining emotional data is that, for Scheler, the question of *how* any knowledge is possible could not be posed at the outset of a philosophical inquiry. According to Scheler's analytic strategy, one's investigation must begin directly with that which is given (*das Gegebene*) without first questioning how it can be given. For, as Kelly explains, the question of the criteria of knowledge may arise only *after* some knowledge is already given to us.[3] In this context, our knowledge of the other's inner world is seen by Scheler as "that which is already given" to the empathizing self, while the question of *how* this knowledge is obtained becomes peripheral.[4]

This restrictive focus on the given elements of the empathetic process, also discernable in Bakhtin's treatment of active empathy, is consistent with the specifics of Scheler's phenomenological method, linked with the notion of religious revelation. Scheler may not be especially interested in the actual process of gleaning and assembling the knowledge of the other's inner life because this knowledge, achieved through intuitive contemplation of his personal essence, is presumed to be largely direct and immediate.[5] Indeed, for Scheler, knowledge of essences in general is participative and direct, because we are able to partake of the Absolute Being (*das absolute Sein*) through emotional acts. In this sense, a phenomenologist's inspired movement toward the essential in Being is first and foremost a participative act of a *loving* consciousness directed at the yet unrealized value of the surrounding universe, which unveils its deepest meaning as it becomes personally significant to him. As such, this act is fundamentally similar to the lover's spiritual discovery of the beloved.

Because Scheler makes an implicit analogy between the (immediate) way a phenomenologist and an empathizer each capture and exhibit the essential in their respective objects, phenomenological methodology is not only "externally" but also "internally" relevant to the phenomenon of empathy. For Scheler, phenomenological contemplation is not only a preferred intellectual *tool* used for analyzing empathetic experiences but also *a structuring force* behind them: it is instrumental in the very act of "calling forth" the other's essential individuality.

Just as a loving person overcomes the "natural delusion" of seeing another human being only in terms of his or her utility for the perceiving ego, liberating this satellite other for a sovereign existence,[6] a phenomenologist overcomes a natural, egocentric deficiency of sight in respect to Being as a whole. He learns to look beyond the sphere of mere environment (*Umweltsein*), with its narrowly utilitarian significance, which is so often confused with the whole of Being (*Sein*) (see *GW*, 7:70; *GW*, 5:90). In both cases, through overcoming the illusions inherent in the natural worldview, the object of knowledge (another person; Being as a whole) is revealed in its essence as truly *other*, joyfully and productively independent from the viewer's distanced self.

This crucial liberation of meaning is achieved through what Bakhtin would later call one's "loving removal" from the field of contemplated experience,[7] an act clearly endowed with religious significance in Scheler's world. "This way of *finding oneself in God* through *sacrificing* one's ego completely is called 'Humility' in moral terms and pure 'Intuition' in intellectual terms," Scheler writes in "On the Rehabilitation of Virtue," establishing an important connection between the work of phenomenological reduction and the daily accomplishments of those spontaneous phenomenologists whose "humble" love reveals the hidden essence of its human objects (*GW*, 3:23, italics in text).[8] Indeed, "philosophical love" is akin to Christian love, Scheler contends, for both liberate us from the biases of the exclusively vital view of the world, opening our eyes to the timeless essence of Being and to the eternal essence of our fellow men and women (*GW*, 6:91).[9] Thus, the knowledge of Being is inextricably linked with the knowledge of (personal) beings in Scheler's work, while the process of phenomenological and philosophical investigation[10] is often shown to be analogous to one's life-investigation, in so far as both are inspired and enabled by love. In a similar vein, the fruits of both investigations are often perceived as grace-like revelations, largely independent from any deliberate investigative techniques.[11]

As we have seen, for Scheler, every human being is a spontaneous phenomenologist in so far as she is an *ens amans*, a loving being. This parallel system of reference obtains for Bakhtin as well. If Scheler draws an analogy between a phenomenologist intuiting the essence of *Being* and a loving individual intuiting the essence of a fellow *human being*, Bakhtin makes an implicit connection between the author's intuition of the hero's essential unity and any act of real-life "authoring" or consummation, which allows a loving person to perceive the individualizing unity of the beloved.[12] Because both thinkers see the spiritual-ethical act of accessing and creatively exhibiting the other's inner world as a special case of phenomenological reduction, it may be useful to examine their discussion of active empathy in the context of the phenomenological method.

FROM CONTEMPLATION TO CREATION: PROBLEMATIC ASPECTS OF BAKHTIN'S *VZHIVANIE*

The lack of detail in depicting empathy as an actual, real-life process, somewhat disappointing to the lay reader, is indeed partly due to the particular "phenomenological bias" inherent in Scheler's thought. True to his philosophical worldview, which, unlike Husserl's approach, was characterized not by "method" but by the so-called intuitional attitude ("Einstellung, nicht Methode") (*GW*, 10:380), Scheler begins his analysis of interpersonal relationships by simply identifying rather than specifically describing what he perceives as self-given, directly apprehended phenomena of man's emotional life. According to Scheler's "Einstellung" (attitude) and in contrast to Husserl's "Methode" (method) to endow a phenomenological analysis with meaning, these self-given phenomena should be posited *before* a scientific inquiry takes place. Because the phenomena in question are not considered empirically observable but rather made palpable or "grasped" (*erfasst*) in one direct mental act of intuition, such eloquent "pointing" to their existence and interconnections with each other is deemed to be a more fitting approach than an empirically based description. And since (Scheler's) phenomenology deals with self-evident, if at times partially concealed essences, its goal is not to prove a logically induced truth but rather to bring this partially obscured knowledge of essences to the fore by means of focused intuitive contemplation.[13]

Such, for example, is Scheler's phenomenologically consistent intuitive assessment of the general cognitive and emotive preconditions that enable an empathetic experience. According to Scheler:

> That we cannot be aware of an experience without being aware of a self is something which is directly based upon the intuitable essential connection between individual and experience, there is no need of empathy on the part of the perceiving self. That is why we can also have it *given* to us that the other has an individual self, different from ours, steeped as it is in its psychic experience, and that we can never adequately grasp this individual self but only an aspect of it, conditioned by our own individual essence. (*GW*, 7:20–21)

Pursuing the phenomenological inquiry into the structures formed by the intuitively grasped self-given phenomena, Scheler defines a fundamental connection between *experience* and *self*, central in his theory of intersubjectivity. "That the other—like we ourselves—has a sphere of absolute privacy [*eine absolute Intimsphäre*], which can never be given to us, is contingent upon this essential link [*Wesenszusammenhang*]," Scheler continues. "But the fact that experiences take place in that sphere is given to us through expressive phenomena" (*GW*, 7:21). Indeed, for Scheler, *emotional experience* and its *expression* form another essential link, which obtains universally in spite of the cultural differences between the expressive languages in question.

Bakhtin often presents his reader with a similar approach. For example, the "I"'s intuited insight into the other's turbulent, eternally unconsummated inner realm, somewhat reminiscent of Scheler's private sphere, becomes one of the starting points for a phenomenological discussion of the other's fruitful consummation. Bakhtin claims: "I know that in the other as well there is the same insanity of not coinciding (in principle) with himself [as in myself], the same unconsummatedness of life" ("AH," 128). As in the case of Scheler's analogy, this insight into the other's psychic interior is inseparable from my initial self-knowledge. As in Scheler's text, a self-evident link between the "I"'s inner experience and that of another is posited by the author.

However, for all of their methodological similarity, the two accounts of active empathy differ in one important way: Scheler's discussion of interpersonal communication raises the question of its ultimate limits, while Bakhtin's does not. In this context, the German scholar's mention of the least accessible part of another consciousness in the opening pages of his treatise on fellow-feeling is instructive (*Sympathy*, *GW*, 7:21). Such thorough delineation of boundaries is also consistent with the goals and objectives of a phenomenological investigation, aimed at describing things as they are given to us, within the limits of their "givenness."[14] In this context, the less boundary-conscious Bakhtin appears to be a less consistent phenomenologist than Scheler. Scheler's attention to the ultimate limits of approach in human relations, unparalleled in Bakhtin's early work, also indirectly opens up the important question of obstacles to active empathy, neglected by Bakhtin and only implicitly addressed in Scheler.

According to Scheler, our knowledge of the other's sphere of absolute privacy, which "can never be *given* to us," is nevertheless more than *nihil*: it amounts to the simple but crucially important fact of its existence (see, for example, *Sympathy*, *GW*, 7:21). Even in the case of maximum closeness, such as perhaps presumed in the process of Bakhtinian *live-entering*, all one knows about the absolutely personal core of the other's being ("die absolut intime Person") is that it is there ("Daß sie *da ist*") (*Sympathy*, *GW*, 7:77). An analogous probing of the limits of interpersonal contact is undertaken by Scheler in *Problems of a Sociology of Knowledge*, where he names the *Thou / I* sphere as a primary region of consciousness and imagines a hypothetical consciousness where this region remains vacant, having no concrete representation (*GW*, 8:57). Because for Scheler the *Thou* is part of an a priori structure of consciousness, the basic apprehension of the other's existence would obtain even if one sole consciousness existed in a world devoid of concretely represented others. In other words, even an absolute Robinson Crusoe, an imaginary person who has no contact with or empirical knowledge of other human beings, would intuitively know that the other "I," dialogically contraposed to him as a "Thou," though not immediately present, exists (*Sympathy*, *GW*, 7:230; *Formalism*, *GW*, 2:511). Paradoxically, even in absentia, the other "is there," experienced as a palpable void.[15]

This essentially optimistic premise is countered by Scheler's cautious assessment of our apprehension of the other's inner life. Although the existence of another, spiritually voluminous self is given to us in one mental act of intuition, our actual "view" of his inner experiences is conditioned by our own individual essence, as it were, filtered through our individual perceptual apparatus (*Sympathy*, *GW*, 7:22).

In his creative adaptation of Scheler's theory of intersubjectivity, Bakhtin emphasizes the visual aspect of this challenging process, making the Schelerian connection (*den phänomenologischen Wesenszusammenhang*) between expressive phenomena and the expressed emotional and psychic experience a starting point of what may be called his theory of "plastic" consummation. In "Author and Hero" Bakhtin considers a compassionate observer's reaction to the other's suffering. Because "the person suffering does not experience the fullness of his own outward expressedness in being," I possess an essential surplus of vision in relation to the suffering person, Bakhtin claims ("AH," 25). "He [the sufferer] experiences this expressedness only partially, and then in the language of his inner sensations of himself. He does not *see* the agonizing tensions of his own muscles, does not *see* the entire, plastically consummated posture of his own body" ("AH," 25). But *I* can observe this meaningfully expressive exterior among other "visible objects," and my privileged transgredient position following the interior moment of co-experiencing allows me to unify his entire cherished being as a "concretely *viewable* whole" ("AH," 30). And conversely, because "my inner sensation of myself and my life for myself remain present in me as the one who is imagining and seeing . . . [and] not present in me as the one who is imagined and seen," I rely on the invaluable assistance of the other's consummating eye to obtain a moment of positively objectifying wholeness, issuing from outside ("AH," 30).

Thus in Bakhtin's work we observe a shift from the self's role as a sensitive observer and interpreter of the expressive, "pantomimic," language of the other's emotional experience, to its active aesthetic function of bestowing form in the very process of this predominantly visual contemplation. This is a promising elaboration on the master's model, and yet, in Bakhtin's system of communication the other self is too obviously and, at times, shamelessly displayed before the nearly omniscient consummating consciousness.

Bakhtin's analysis is especially flawed by the neglect of the concealed part of the other's personality, the region of absolute privacy, acknowledged by Scheler, which is essentially monological in Bakhtinian terms and remains inaccessible to the dialogist's grasp. This "ineffable" knowledge possessed by the *self in relation to the self* also constitutes a surplus of sorts, although it lacks the visual, "plastic" qualities characteristic of the other's surplus, which allow Bakhtin to call the latter "izbytok *videniia*" (the *excess* or *surplus of vision*). Although at times Bakhtin does implicitly acknowledge the existence of something akin to Scheler's "surplus" of absolute privacy,[16] it is the Other who has a *useful* "surplus of vision" in relation to myself, while I possess no essential inward knowledge that may be utilized in the process of consummation. Such a "utilitarian" approach to self-knowledge leads Bakhtin to a neglect and, at times, to a downright denial of the self's ultimate interior. For instance, regarding the complete and utter penetration of the other's psyche, "[videnie] dannogo cheloveka *naskvoz'*," as an insufficient basis for a productive interaction in "Toward a Philosophy of the Act," Bakhtin nevertheless sees it as a given in the process of active empathy (*TPA*, 17; *Sobranie sochinenii*, 1:20). In a similar fashion, in "Author and Hero," he endows the author, who is an equivalent of the "I" category on the level of personal relationships, with such an enormous surplus in regards to the hero that the authorial vision encompasses not only the hero's actual, but also his "potential" consciousness ("AH," 13).

This textual evidence calls into question the popular suggestion that Bakhtin proposes an "apophatic" approach to human consciousness, which consists in acknowledging the ultimate mystery of God and, consequently, of man, as created in His image.[17] "The apophatic framework fits Bakhtin very well because it rests on the conviction that the human person cannot be, and ought not to be, theoretically determined or finalized," Randal Poole argues.[18] Poole's thesis can be accepted as valid with one essential reservation, namely, that in early Bakhtin the apophatic approach is one-sided: humans are unknowable to themselves only in the "I" category, while the other has an almost unlimited surplus of knowledge in respect to me.[19] In other words, the God-Man Christ, the incarnated divine dialogist, who completes the perfect act of consummation, is seen primarily as a model of the *consummating Other*, utilizing his divine surplus of "seeing, knowing and valuing" in order to forgive, to absolve, and to save his human neighbors.[20] In Bakhtin, Christ does not become a model of the *consummated Self*, as the son of God dispatched into the world, in whom the divine self-knowledge is enriched and partially realized in the very act of its revelation in the flesh. In this context, it may be argued that Scheler, who is more interested in the opposite direction of the divine-human communication, assessing man's loving understanding of God, complements Bakhtin's vision of the "dialogizing" Christ and offers a way of correcting the apparent imbalance inherent in Bakhtin's theory.

In his article "Bakhtin and the Tropes of Orthodoxy," Charles Lock further develops the apophatic theme by examining Bakhtin's work in the context of both Kantian theory and the writings of church fathers. An apophatic formulation of the post-Kantian philosophical stance serves as a point of departure in Lock's analysis: the rejection of Kantian transcendentalism, which implied a strictly symmetrical relationship between self and other, resulted in a post-Kantian statement, "I cannot know an other in any way adequate to the other's self-knowledge."[21] It is the necessary corollary of this statement, "I cannot know myself in any way adequate to the other's knowledge of me," that Bakhtin would choose as the foundation of his ethical theory, rejecting or at best ignoring the first proposition. Following Lock's argument, one may concede that, as a means of directing attention to the importance of exterior knowledge, neglected by the Kantians, Bakhtin's attack on interiority is understandably vehement. However, denying interiority *any* place in Bakhtin's system does not only render empathy and dialogue senseless, but also threatens the sanctity of his divine model of communication, Christ's Incarnation. According to Lock, "dialogism is the discourse whose trope is outsideness and whose moment is Incarnation," for, just as [novelistic] writing is exterior to language, Incarnation is outside of God.[22] Lock's reading of the Incarnation image in Bakhtin's theory is at best an exaggeration of Bakhtin's position: God's *inner* essence, external to man, should also be recognized in Christ to ensure the meaningfulness of his sacrifice.

If no essential inner knowledge exists, the result of a dialogical exchange is a consummation that penetrates not only the dialogically addressed part of the other's psyche but also the sphere of the absolute future, the region Bakhtin calls "potential consciousness" (*AH*, 13), leaving the other no private sphere at all. Such a consummation can only be deemed unloving, and essentially un-dialogical. Indeed, the apparent transparency of the object of live-entering eliminates any need for "entering" his inner world, except, perhaps, in an effort to procure part of the other's surplus of vision in respect to *my own* self. If the door to my innermost private region is perpetually open, exposing even my "deepest point of contact with the spirit" ("AH," 128), why would I need to speak, to address the other dialogically, or to probe my own potential through personal interaction?[23] What would

I possibly have to impart to the other in respect to myself, except my impatient wish that he share his all-encompassing vision with me?

Interpreted by such scholars as R. Poole, Lock, and notable others,[24] whose choice of Bakhtin's textual material highlights and at times magnifies the palpable imbalance between the exterior and the interior elements of communication characteristic of his early theories, the philosopher is especially vulnerable to the criticism launched by some of his Russian readers. G. Batishchev's insightful article,[25] that censures Bakhtin's neglect of the interior self and criticizes his theory of communication for lacking a "vertical hierarchy of values,"[26] something akin to Scheler's order of love, or *ordo amoris*, may serve as a link to Scheler's phenomenology as a possible resource for expanding and revising Bakhtin's architectonic.

SCHELER'S APOPHATIC ALTERNATIVE

Bakhtin's system may be revised and conceptually sharpened with the help of Scheler, who advocates a more balanced relationship between the exterior and the interior components of the communication process. In *Ressentiment*, Scheler criticizes the popular infatuation with otherness, with pure exteriority he believes to be inherent in contemporary altruism (*GW*, 3:82, 104–5). In *Sympathy* and *On the Eternal in Man* he emphasizes the role of self-disclosure in the process of interpersonal understanding (*GW*, 7:220; *GW*, 5:331–32). Indeed, for Scheler, the Godlike essence of each individual personality may never be completely uncovered even under the revealing gaze of agape (see, for example, "Absolutsphäre und Realsetzung der Gottesidee" ("The Sphere of the Absolute and the Positing of the Idea of God as Real") [*GW*, 10:186–87] and *Sympathy* [*GW*, 7:130]). This apophatic quality of Scheler's thought, instructive in view of Bakhtin's arguable shortcomings, will become fully apparent if we examine Scheler's theory of active empathy in the context of his philosophy of religion.

If the phenomenologically peripheral question of *how* knowledge of others is possible is not asked in the beginning of Scheler's treatise on intersubjectivity, it is eventually addressed in the concluding section of the book. "Two . . . real spiritual substances or, for example, two minds certainly cannot 'enter' each other in a literal sense or cross over into each other's inner territory," Scheler concedes, acknowledging that common conception of interpersonal understanding which has necessitated the interpretation of empathy as a "transfer" of emotional experience from one self to another (*Sympathy*, *GW*, 7:239). And yet, if one approaches the problem from a purely phenomenological perspective, it becomes clear that such "entries" are made on a daily basis, Scheler argues (*GW*, 7:239). What makes our understanding of another's inner world possible is the fact that we have not come into the world as isolated psychic beings with a ready-made, separate emotional life, but had initially shared our psychic-emotional experiences with others.

According to Scheler, a self is initially immersed in a stream of experiences as yet undifferentiated with respect to the *I / other* division. Only gradually does a child emerge from the primordial pool of anonymous or unclaimed psychic events, slowly consolidating an individual emotional world out of the appropriated "particles" of communal co-experiencing, eventually taking leave of the shared domicile and learning to "live in himself" and not in the other (*Sympathy*, *GW*, 7:240).[27] Because the emotionally warm, if dormant, memory of this common origin is kept alive on the unconscious level, the others' inner life is not inaccessible to us, although, as an adult, one may not reenter the original, as yet impersonal, channel of communication.[28] Once the ontological gulf between individual personalities has thus emerged, one has to rely largely on the other's expressive efforts, that is, on the conscious or unconscious acts of self-disclosure to grasp the elusive dynamic of his emotional life.[29]

It is implicit in Scheler's phenomenology of religion that the *essential* ontological gulf between man and God arises through the Fall. Christ's descent into the world, seen as the quintessential gesture of self-disclosure, then presents a spiritually mature response to the ontological division. For Scheler, this participation in the spiritual life of the Divine Other through Christ is by no means a return to the naive sharing of the undifferentiated primordial knowledge, as it were, entirely contained in the pre-personal global "Thou," characteristic of humanity's spiritual childhood. On the contrary, because this archetypal communicative act bridges the essential ontological gulf between man and God only partially, man's divine Other retains the incommunicable but palpable spiritual "surplus"[30] in respect to the rediscovered humanity. A notable "surplus" is also achieved in man's spiritual makeup after Incarnation. Incarnation is not simply a restoration of the former "status quo," returning humanity to the spiritual condition of the pre-Fall Adam, but a deeply transformative act initiating man into a completely new fellowship with God that is infinitely more profound and enduring than the one that had existed between God and Adam, Scheler suggests (see *GW*, 5:57). Man's naive, as yet impersonal, bond with God is now replaced by a mature relationship deeply respectful of both parties as individual beings. We may say that humanity's spiritual "surplus" partially revealed by the act of Incarnation is that of "Homo Personalis" over "Homo Naturalis,"[31] whose return to the scene as a spiritually unchanged, if rehabilitated, Adam would render Incarnation a mere act of reproductive empathy, denying it its creative essence.

If, on the interpersonal level, an emotionally and psychically mature human being cannot resume an impersonal mode of communication without lapsing into an "ontological delusion,"[32] on the level of God-man relationship, the post-Fall humanity cannot communicate with the divine without a reference to Christ. It is this reliance on the other's voluntary self-disclosure, exemplified by Incarnation, which partially reveals but by no means exhausts the divine spiritual "surplus" that becomes the new, emotionally mature means of communication. And this novel way of approaching the personal divine Other dictates a similar reverence for the concealed "surplus" of individuality in one's human interlocutor. For that reason, Scheler never tires of emphasizing the importance of self-revelation in the challenging world of personhood, whose inhabitants, unlike purely vital beings, are not objects of entirely spontaneous knowledge (see, for example, *Sympathy*, *GW*, 7:220). In this context, it is not surprising that the distinguishing characteristic of the Person of Persons, or God, is self-revelation. And yet this deeply affirmative act cannot be a real choice unless there is an equally real possibility of an utterly silent God, a frightening but necessary alternative entertained by Scheler in *On the Eternal in Man* to highlight the fundamentally *active* nature of the divine revelation (*GW*, 5:332).

The spiritual life of a human person also unfolds between these two characteristic expressions of personhood, silence and self-disclosure. Discussing the limits of personal closeness, "given" to us in the very concept of empathy, Scheler introduces the notion of "double transcendence" as a measure of one's spiritual penetration into another individuality. This hypothetical notion describing the full "distance" to one's ultimate inner being traversed by a potential empathizer presupposes not one but two "gulfs" separating us from the beloved person. The first divide is the basic qualitative difference between self and other partially transcended through the other's free self-disclosure, while the second one, the ultimate obstacle barring one's entry into the absolutely intimate territory, can be transcended only by God (*GW*, 7:77, 215). While man's greatest grasp of the other's personality stops at apprehending his "ordo amoris" (*GW*, 10: 348), the acknowledgment of the yet deeper levels of his spiritual inner being, paradoxically "present" to us only in absentia, as it were, encompassed only in God's privileged gaze, inspires our ceaseless movement toward the other and endows our love for him with the quality of faith.

Because the ultimate "destination" of this spiritual quest can be reached only by God, we conclude that human empathy always remains a posited (*das Aufgegebene*) in Scheler. It is a never-ending project, a challenging effort at interpreting the inconclusive melody of the soul, as it were, composed of rhythmically alternating utterances and silences. And yet, a Schelerian listener does not despair, for he knows that the daunting silences that frustrate our understanding of the beloved are in some way more telling about her personal essence than her most eloquent confessions.

It is this deeply respected capacity for silence, distinctly different from simply not speaking, the notion that would attract Bakhtin's interest toward the end of his career, when he contemplated a reworking of his earlier theories,[33] that seems an appropriate addition to the Bakhtinian concept of active empathy. The proposed concept of "the Surplus of the Self" will include both, a region possessing inward information that can be communicated and thus can also be silenced, and a region of absolute privacy that is essentially monological, immanently silent, rather than silenced.

If, as Bakhtin suggests, individuality is created by borders, the complex process of personal becoming must be affected by multiple psychic and spiritual boundaries. If the *external border* imposed by the other through the act of consummation productively limits the self's potential by acknowledging its concrete realization, the *internal boundary* limits this very realization. This essential limit, which saves us from utter "exteriorization," from utterly exhausting our potential in self-actualization, is perceived by the self even as it partially transcends it in the process of self-disclosure. Stimulated by these productive boundaries, one does not simply endure the other's consummating efforts but actively responds to the consummating challenge, "gathering" oneself for the other in an act of inspired self-unfolding toward her.

This Schelerian revision of Bakhtin, with its emphasis on the self's responsiveness to the other's individualizing gaze, is consistent with the active, largely existentialist concept of God embraced by Scheler at the end of his Catholic period. In Scheler, the image of the divine person is perceived dynamically, in movement, and is hailed as the supreme example of a spiritually active being at the very moment of self-expression, as it boldly engages its human other in the act of its own personal becoming through Incarnation.[34] Because for Scheler the moment of authentic self-expression (*Ausdruck*) always yields a powerful and novel understanding of *one's own* self in the very act of disclosing it to the other,[35] it is implicit in Scheler's theory that the divine self-knowledge becomes enriched and deepened through its spontaneous expression in Christ. It is far-reaching implications of this kind that allow Manfred Frings to conclude that in Scheler "a religious act opens doors, as it were, for God to enter us and for Him to the disclosed Himself."[36] It seems that just as man is profoundly transformed by the act of Incarnation, having partaken of God's "surplus" and thus surpassed Adam's spiritual status, so is the Schelerian God forever changed by His self-expression through Christ. In this sense, the "Surplus of the Self" is not simply retained but enriched in the course of this mutually productive personal realization. Put in Bakhtinian terms, this interpretation of God-Man Christ acknowledges his dialogical role as both a *consummating* and a *consummated* person.[37] This dynamic concept of the deity, inflected as it is by the ethical tenor of the emerging existentialist philosophy, anticipates Scheler's later, panentheist, vision of the ever-changing God, who looks upon man as an active co-creator, as "that unique point in being, in which and through which the original Being apprehends and acknowledges Itself" (*Philosophische Weltanschauung*, *GW*, 9:83).[38]

Scheler's paradigmatic examples demonstrate the many uses of the communicable part of the self's surplus, but this privileged region of being plays an important role in interpersonal relations even when it is not being "used." The largely concealed region of human consciousness, which corresponds to the seat of the *individual ineffable* in Scheler's theory, is by definition excluded from dialogue. And yet, this incommunicable residue of the self actually creates the dialogical tension necessary for a productive interaction, for, by positing the ultimate limit of projection into another consciousness, it guarantees the non-coincidence of selves, so crucial for the Bakhtinian *vzhivanie*. Thus, the surplus of the self both limits the extent of dialogical interaction and ensures its productivity. This insight may be helpful in analyzing empathetic efforts of literary characters: for instance, it may sharpen our understanding of Dostoevsky's fundamental disagreement with some of his reluctant interlocutors, who, like Ivan Karamazov, see the profound asymmetry between selves, the inability to grasp the other's intimate experience from within, as the basis for rejecting agape and compassion. It also points to a larger thesis, often neglected by Bakhtinian scholars, namely, that monologue does play a positive, productive role in ensuring the well-being of dialogue as its value-bestowing Other.

THE CHALLENGE OF PERSONAL BECOMING: BAKHTIN'S CONCEPT OF *CONSUMMATION*

Closely linked with the "surplus of vision" is the Bakhtinian "consummation" (*zavershenie*)—another problematic concept that may benefit from partial revision before it is used in a philosophical or ethical analysis. In the early Bakhtin, *consummation* is the creative outcome of live-entering. It is the gift of form bestowed on the internally fragmented, protean self by the beneficent other, whose distinctly unique, external position vis-à-vis the object of live-entering allows him to utilize his surplus of vision in the process of empathetic understanding. By consummating another self, I affirm the very act of his personal becoming, acknowledging those unifying moments of his inner life, clearly visible only from my external perspective, in which his potential has reached realization. This actualization of value resulting from the act of *vzhivanie* is parallel to the revelation and creation of value in the process of loving understanding in Scheler.

While unquestionably positive in early Bakhtin, the concept of consummation undergoes a dramatic reevaluation in Bakhtin's Dostoevsky book. If for the author of "Toward a Philosophy of the Act" and "Author and Hero" the self escapes consummation in the "I" category but may be fruitfully consummated by the loving *other*, in *Problems of Dostoevsky's Poetics*, Bakhtin rejects the possibility of consummating a human subject in either category of personhood. Not only am *I* incapable of completing my own spiritual image from within, but the *other* is equally incompetent and ethically unjustified in his efforts to consummate me.[39] Moreover, the concept of consummation is incompatible with dialogue as defined in the Dostoevsky book. This is so, in part, because the other no longer has a *productive* surplus of vision in relation to me, which may be used in the process of creative consummation.[40]

The act of consummation (*zavershenie*)[41] now becomes associated exclusively with unfair, deliberately cruel objectification of the other's living self, reified and flattened in the process. For instance, a "consummating definition" given to the hero by a traditional monological author is synonymous with a secondhand definition, entirely divorced from dialogue ("zaochnoe opredelenie") (see, for example, *Sobranie sochinenii*, 6:80–81; *PDP*, 68). Thus, as a profoundly dialogical artist, Dostoevsky consistently refrains from such impoverishing characterizations, Bakhtin concludes, while the essentially monological Tolstoy makes full use of the "consummating function of the author's privileged purview" (*izbytochnyi krugozor*) (*Sobranie sochinenii*, 6:104–5, 84–85; *PDP*, 92, 72–73). On the whole, in Bakhtin's Dostoevsky book *zavershenie* becomes a defining attribute of the monological novel and of any "monologizing" consciousness that shuns interactive engagement with others, apprehending another consciousness entirely as an object. This objectified (consummated) consciousness may be utterly exhausted by an externally imposed definition, as a hero's consciousness is exhausted by the act of authorial penetration into its innermost regions. It is as if the word "live-" had been eliminated from "live-entering" in this sobering depiction of authoring the ephemeral, less than personal others. Indeed, to quote Ruth Coates, in the absence of positive consummation, in *PDP* Bakhtin "[affirms] the hero's exclusive right to his own definition, however hopeless."[42]

If in the early works the other's surplus of vision in relation to the self is enormous, in *PDP* it is eliminated altogether. It is as if, taken aback by the *author*itarian bias of his own earlier model of intersubjectivity, Bakhtin hastens to compensate for his shortcomings in his next major work and . . . lapses into the opposite extreme. Instead of introducing a "usable" surplus of the self, which complements but does not replace the equally productive surplus of the other, Bakhtin seems to endow each subject with an enormous, virtually unobstructed field of vision in respect to both itself and the world, which essentially eliminates the need for knowledge-bestowing others. Or, at least, such is Bakhtin's assessment of human relations in Dostoevsky's novels.[43] What emerges from Bakhtin's provocative analysis of Dostoevsky's fictional communities is then a kind of polytheistic universe, in which every godlike, unhappily omniscient self, burdened by its painful, often unusable knowledge, strives for the status of a single deity.

The most fundamental question that arises in response to this view of human togetherness in Dostoevsky is not whether it does justice to the complexity of the novelist's vision,[44] but whether such coexistence of consciousnesses is compatible with the values of agapeistic communication and with *dialogue* understood as a form of such communication, for, aside from occasional implicit references to negative dialogue (*durnoi dialog*), whose outcomes are clearly predetermined,[45] the relationships between Dostoevsky's heroes are generally characterized as truly, that is, openly, dialogical in *PDP*. This question is especially relevant, because the book does not limit itself to an analysis of Dostoevsky's artistic achievement but, rather, actively puts forth a (prescriptive) philosophy of dialogue, presenting the challenging but ultimately productive "multi-voicedness" of Dostoevsky's novels as a model of genuinely pluralistic communication, most conducive to individual freedom and personal sovereignty.

The apparent discrepancy between the conflicting definitions of dialogue in *PDP* may be partly resolved by suggesting that in Dostoevsky's novels Bakhtin sees (agapeistic) dialogue triumph on the level of the author/hero relationship and fail on the level of interpersonal communication between heroes.[46] Still, questions remain whether Bakhtin has denied himself this very loophole by suggesting too strong a parallel between the way Dostoevsky authors his heroes and the way his heroes "author" each other, or whether the (presumably dialogical) way Dostoevsky's heroes are *given* to the reader is not influenced or even ultimately negated by the (less dialogical) way they are *given* to each other, and, finally, if Bakhtin makes enough of an effort to distinguish between these different forms of "givenness" in Dostoevsky's narratives.[47]

Answering these questions is the topic of another inquiry: here it suffices to show how these issues relate to Bakhtin's "consummation" and "surplus of vision," the two early concepts that were essentially abandoned by the thinker in the Dostoevsky book but could, I believe, be used productively as tools of general ethical analysis and in the study of Dostoevsky. It is apparent that Bakhtin's rejection of *consummation* in *PDP* is as much a result of serious inconsistencies inherent in the early rendition of the concept as it is a reflection of the philosopher's changing value system. For instance, while the active aspect of *vzhivanie* was consistently emphasized in the early works, the consummated self did not participate in the act (see, for example, "AH," 14). The self's passivity in the process of consummation, which likened one's aesthetic transformation to a death, became highly problematic in view of such newly embraced values of active (dialogical) communication as *addressivity* and *freedom* in Bakhtin's second, dialogical, period.

In this context, Konstantin Isupov's observation, in "Smert' drugogo" ("The Death of the Other"), that the actual fate of the "I" and the "Other" is of no interest to Bakhtin after the process of consummation, an aesthetic death, has taken place, may be used to initiate our revision of the concept and to clarify its development throughout Bakhtin's philosophical career. In Isupov's view, Bakhtin often treats his "material"—a literary text, a doctrine, or a type of worldview under discussion—the same way his Other treats the interlocutor after consummation, namely, he simply casts it aside upon reaching a "consummating" conclusion of any sort,[48] a paradigm evident in the fate of Bakhtin's inquiries, many of which were abandoned for good after certain theoretical questions had been "finalized."[49] The early Bakhtin is tellingly silent about what happens to the mutually engaged "I" and the "Other" after the value-bestowing act of live-entering has taken place, for "the act of consummation-salvation is a death and a resurrection of the aesthetically perfect creatures, whose fate has no connection to the linear empirical reality," Isupov argues.[50] Perhaps Bakhtin's reevaluation of consummation is not as radical as it seems, for, even in the early works, where consummation clearly appears in positive light, it is already a peripheral concept, as it were, located beyond the true boundaries of Bakhtin's philosophical inquiry. It takes only a small step in the same direction to eliminate this concept from his system altogether. In this context, the much-discussed conceptual shift occurring in Bakhtin's worldview in the late 1920s may be seen as a logical consequence of his neglect to acknowledge the *reality* of consummation in the first place, to accept its rightful place within the temporal continuum.

In my interpretation of this important Bakhtinian concept I will seek middle ground between the two extreme definitions of consummation given in "Author and Hero" and the Dostoevsky book. Since the ultimate goal of this study is assessing the success of active empathy in Dostoevsky's world, abandoning the characters after a consummating presence has graced their lives in Bakhtinian fashion would do poor service to our analysis. Thus the proposed adjustments to the concept of *zavershenie* will aim at emphasizing the "mechanics" of consummation, affirming its earthly, practical aspect alongside the transcendent, ideal one. Some of the changes in the concept will follow from my revision of the Bakhtinian concept of surplus of vision. Namely, the introduction of the Schelerian surplus of the self will eliminate the need to do away with the Other's surplus of vision, as was Bakhtin's choice in *PDP*, for the interlocutor's profound respect for the other's surplus of the self will safeguard against unfair, reifying consummation. The Other's surplus will then become an "open surplus," dialogically revealed to the interlocutor in the process of open-minded and honest exchange, as the later Bakhtin himself suggests in the notes toward a reworking of the Dostoevsky book (*PDP*, 299).

If the main "prerequisite" for consummation, the productive surplus of vision, is preserved, positive consummation is possible and, indeed, desirable. It is beyond doubt that, for Bakhtin, positive revelation of value, whether it was called consummation or dialogical exchange, was modeled on the "communicative" acts of Christ, a cherished ideal that remained a measure of dialogical achievement throughout Bakhtin's career. The early Bakhtin's highly symbolic depiction of consummation as well as his occasional use of the terms "svershenie" and "zavershenie" (fulfillment and consummation) interchangeably[51] suggests that consummation could be read as a parable of both Incarnation and Resurrection in the philosopher's early oeuvre.[52] Indeed, the two-stage process of live-entering may be seen as a reference to Christ's Incarnation (projection) and subsequent "return into the self" (Resurrection). While in the early works Incarnation seems to be the leading motif, Resurrection is implicitly present in the Dostoevsky book, with its consistent evocation of "threshold moments," symbolically anticipating but never actually yielding the eye-opening revelation of the resurrected Christ in Dostoevsky's novels. In view of our intended use of the concept, it seems to be most beneficial to interpret consummation as a dual signifier, pointing to these two possible referents of the biblical *fulfillment* (*svershenie*).

Interpreted in this context, consummation is not a dead end, but rather an opening: the incarnating movement that appoints a concrete position in being for the consummated personality also places it "in the context of eternity," as Kierkegaard might have put it.[53] Such an interpretation is respectful of both the empirical and the transcendent elements of the Bakhtinian consummation, affirming the reality of consummation *in time*, while also recognizing its function as a highly symbolic act, a sign pointing beyond the finite sphere, toward extra-temporal, apocalyptic reality. True, Christlike, consummation does not reify the other; it does not exhaust his vital potential, as Christ's Incarnation does not exhaust his divine surplus, which enables him to perform the creative act of Resurrection. By using the revised concept of consummation, one could also avoid Isupov's critique: there is no need to abandon the hero after the act, for, as an active participant in the process of live-entering, he, unlike the hero in early Bakhtin, will survive the consummating moment. For, indeed, such an instance will be one of many—an incarnating moment in a self's spiritual journey toward Resurrection.

In light of our revised formulation of *zavershenie*, the central question is no longer whether consummation is a negative or a positive concept but, rather, whether a particular act of consummation is positive (an example of true, Christlike consummation), or negative (false consummation that perverts the Christian ideal) in Dosotevsky's world.[54] While positive consummation brings about the production of value resulting from the loving vocation of the ideal other, the often dormant higher self Dostoevsky calls "man in man" or "Christ in man," negative consummation results in the depletion of value and in the ressentiment "revaluation of values," a process thoroughly explicated by Nietzsche and Scheler and implicitly defined in Bakhtin's Dostoevsky study.[55]

It is relevant to our discussion that in Dostoevsky's world, the acts of negative consummation, which freeze the self's spiritual image, as it were, taking it out of the context of eternity, are usually linked with a special kind of mentality shared by such diverse characters as the Underground Man, Stavrogin, Ivan, and, at times, even Alyosha Karamazov. The "either-or" mentality of Dostoevsky's negative consummators, revealed in the Underground Man's deliberately limited choice between the "*true* Crystal Palace" of absolute affirmation and the absolute negation of the Underground or in Stavrogin's extreme slogan in notebooks for *The Devils*: "one should either believe [with perfect faith] or burn everything,"[56] constitutes a rejection of the necessity of Incarnation, of the value of transitional spirituality, developed and tested *in time*, in the imperfect world between Incarnation and the second coming. It is a kind of impatient or premature apocalypticism that Dostoevsky finds objectionable. In this sense, the characters' rejection of the necessity of enfleshment *in time* is similar to Bakhtin's own rejection of the temporal reality of incarnation-consummation in "Author and Hero." Bakhtin's revolt against any finalization during his second period, apparent in the Dostoevsky book, may then be seen as a curious parallel to the underground rebellion of numerous Dostoevskian characters who, unable to attain or apprehend the absolute value of Christian Incarnation, crusade against false finalization symbolized by the de-animating power of the "stone wall" of natural laws or by the coerced, terminal bliss of the ominous Crystal Palace.

READING BETWEEN THE LINES: THE PRACTICE OF ACTIVE EMPATHY

Whether their reluctance to discuss the practical aspects of active empathy results from their strictly phenomenological approach to the problem or from their failure to accept the reality of Incarnation, in spite of modeling their concepts of intersubjectivity on this seminal biblical event, both Bakhtin and Scheler fall short of demonstrating just how the delicate work of empathy is achieved. Nevertheless, a pragmatic reader will discern something akin to a "program" of active empathy in the works of both thinkers, although its formulation may entail some imaginative reading between the lines. Let us examine the most descriptive depictions of loving empathy in Bakhtin and Scheler and explore some implicit suggestions latent in their texts in search of those elusive empathetic "techniques" that, perhaps, had appeared too obvious to the two thinkers to be discussed at length.

A practical guide to active empathy must begin with establishing the basic order of mental and emotional experiences: in both Scheler and Bakhtin, love necessarily precedes knowledge.[57] "The fundamental precondition of any cognition . . . is taking interest [in the subject]," Scheler writes (*GW*, 10:370), claiming that our loving apprehension of the other's general value as a person is followed by the gradual revelation of her individual spiritual essence, the order of love, or *ordo amoris*. Like the Schelerian *homo amans*, drawn to the value of what is to be known, the Bakhtinian person is directed to the yet-unknown other by love. The Bakhtinian self can begin to understand the other and to shape her spiritual image in the process of consummation only *after* the other's unique and prominent place in being is revealed by love: the initial act of "unmotivated valuation" is followed by the gift of knowledge-bestowing form ("AH," 90).

The process of gleaning and assimilating this crucial knowledge about the beloved is not emotionally neutral: it is continually guided and, as it were, monitored, by love. Some of the emotive techniques used in the act of such loving cognition, achieved through partial identification with the other, become apparent in Scheler's description of one's "entry" into the person of a spiritual leader. "[The belief in a charismatic person] is that which we call the spiritual-practical self-identification with a person," Scheler writes, "a complete putting oneself in his place and at his disposal" (*GW*, 7:96).

> Such an entry into the other's personal substance entails an immediate identity of thought, will and feeling—and hence a reshaping and modeling of one's own self in the image and according to the essence of the master: a continuous dynamic sequence of constantly arising visions of the master's spiritual image produced from the material of one's own psychic life. . . . It resembles a transverse wave-motion, in which the wave pattern is continuously transferred to new regions of the water. (*GW*, 7:96)

Although an entry into the inner world of a spiritual leader is a special case of emotional communion and is not entirely relevant to empathetic understanding between more equal partners, some specific features of the inspired co-experiencing described here are pertinent to a discussion of active fellow-feeling in general. After all, any active entry into the other's privileged inner world is a reverent dwelling in his "personal substance," which entails a constant, "practical" relation of these spiritual discoveries to one's own individual mission in the world. On the other hand, the careful crafting of the other's continually evolving inner image from the fragile material of *one's own* psychic life, so utterly unlike any mechanical reproduction of the other's experience, is a complex, yet partly imitable, emotive strategy that allows us a glimpse into the daily labors of empathy as a "spiritual-practical" undertaking.

For personalist thinkers the central question of empathy, "How does the other feel?" is inseparable from the question "Who is he?," that is, "What is the *personal*, deeply individual aspect of his suffering or joy?" For Scheler, the process of assessing the other's essential inner being, "Soseins-Setzung," which ultimately results in the "dwelling in his personal substance," begins with a kind of hypothesis:

> The content of this "hypothesis" about his essence is put forth in different variations, tested and corrected through observation of his temporal states and their real and abstract constituents . . . . It must be confirmed in these temporal states—but in such a way that we are constantly guided by an a priori "blueprint" of man's essential nature that can also be revealed in ourselves (as opposed to that of "the Frenchman," "the German," "the shopkeeper," "the soldier" etc.). Precisely in the process of this progressive journey of discovery the content of this hypothesis becomes more and more individual, less and less expressible ("individuum est ineffabile"), but at the same time more and more certain. (*GW*, 7:130)

What guides our progressive movement toward the other's innermost core of being is that ineffable intuition of his individual spiritual vocation that is never limited to the sphere of mere actuality, always aware of the unexpressed "surplus" beyond a revealed character trait or a psychological peculiarity. On the other hand, although our practical "hypothesis" about the other may be informed by this emerging intuitive image, it is not identical with it, formed as it is in the "here and now" of the temporal, empirical sphere. Here it is constantly pitied against other "hypotheses," those attempting to explain one's identity by means of objectifying labels of a political group, a social type, a profession, and so on. Because for Scheler a spiritual being can and does reveal itself in the temporal realm as a psychophysical unity (*Sympathy*, *GW*, 7:130), one need not reject *all* empirically based insights. Instead, one is constantly on the lookout for the "essential moments," when the somewhat otherworldly reality of pure personhood "shines through," illuminating the sometimes deceptive world of space and time. It is during our search for these precious essential moments, when man, as it were, resembles himself the most, that our hypothesis about the other's fundamental individuality is tested, gradually refined and, finally, confirmed.

Becoming more and more familiar with a person, we gradually penetrate through the various levels of his emotional and mental life: the vital, the psycho-vital, the psychic, and, finally, the personal levels of his inner world become to some degree accessible to our knowledge (see, for example, *Sympathy*, *GW*, 7:131). And while this formidable system is clearly a hierarchy in Scheler's view, with the personal sphere comprising its highest level, this hierarchy is not "sealed": constant communication and negotiation take place between the different levels of our lived experience, often blurring the boundaries between them.

When the various hypotheses about the other's essential identity emerge, each offering "data" about some level of his existence, we may benefit from knowing that he is a government official, a "timid soul," or a convinced pacifist, although only that poorly communicable information which ultimately resists objectification, pointing to the ineffable level of being, may vie for the status of an essential definition. Nevertheless, even the largely "statistical" information about one's typical qualities or character traits is not entirely without value: it may have a mediating function, facilitating one's approach to the person within.[58] As we attempt to define the other's personal position in the world, we are presented with a succession of imperfect "drafts" of his probable identity, some more individual than others: is he an "amiable chap"? "a lover of nature"? or "the one who loves deeply"? But, as we try to grasp his ultimate being, we realize, time and again, that the latest "fit" is inadequate, that that which we, so to speak, have in hand, is not and cannot be his personal essence, and so we continue our search. Always looking beyond the inadequate signifiers, we eventually move closer to the genuine seat of personality. Thus moments of temporary objectification are a part of the empathetic process, although they may threaten the sanctity of one's personal identity if they are allowed to last, that is, if an objectifying, necessarily *provisional*, definition is taken for the person's ultimate definition.

In this context, it is important that in Bakhtin's theory of live-entering, where objectifying moments also attain a positive, mediating significance during the process of consummation, special care is taken to ensure the survival of the temporarily objectified person as an active *subject*.[59] There is a danger of completely destroying the other's uniquely personal, sovereign self both during my mental "entry" into his inner world and during my "exit" from it, Bakhtin suggests. For that reason, my potentially dangerous, objectifying surplus of vision must be used sparingly both "on the way in" and "on the way out" of the other's temporarily invaded and eventually consummated inner being. During the time when I project myself into the other, Bakhtin notes, I must virtually renounce my surplus of vision, not to overwhelm the less informed other: "I must detach myself from the independent significance of all these features that are external to his consciousness and *I must utilize them merely as a directive . . . , the path by which I penetrate him and almost merge* and become one with him from within" ("AH," 26). It is equally important to protect the other from the complete loss of "subjectivity" on the way out, when I complement his limited purview with my own finalizing surplus vision (*izbytochnym videniem*): "I . . . must render his horizon complete without at the same time forfeiting his distinctness," Bakhtin warns ("AH," 25).

In the final analysis, for both Scheler and Bakhtin, an active contemplation of another personal being, a "living into" its personal substance is a dynamic and often arduous process of negotiating and unifying the diffuse elements of external and internal, vital and spiritual, intuitive and empirical knowledge. For Scheler, empathetic understanding entails using the directive of love, the radar of individuality, to bring the person's external expression and his active efforts of self-revelation into the context of his intuitively recognized *ordo amoris*, the essential order or structure of his love for the world, God, and other human beings.[60] With the help of the largely nonempirical, loving cognition, which takes the form of a spiritual-practical "hypothesis" about one's defining essence, I begin to apprehend the inner unity of one's being, gradually situating one's expressive gestures, actions, and lived experiences, perceived externally, *within* this emerging unity. A similar objective is posed before Bakhtin's ideal empathizer, who realizes that love must "unit[e] one's own *directedness* with a *direction* and one's own *horizon* with an *environment*" ("AH," 83, italics in text). Indeed, for Bakhtin, as for Scheler, a loving, aesthetically active consciousness apprehends the beloved in such a way that the internal information about her is constantly examined and reevaluated in the context of one's external knowledge. Love enables us to perceive the productive unity of the beloved personality, so that the boundless potentiality of one's inner self, characterized as it is by abstract "directedness," encounters a possibility of realization in the eyes of others, who may suggest a concrete and unifying "direction" for the beloved's spiritual movement. Of course, here, in contrast to Scheler's model, the phenomenologically intuited unity of the beloved person necessarily issues from *without*, bestowed on it by others, from their privileged, external position in Being.

Thus, active empathy emerges from our revisionist analysis as a dynamic, widely applicable theoretical tool, whose practical aspects are somewhat more fully developed than in the original theories. The critical explication of the concept suggested in this chapter aimed both at understanding its specific meaning within the sphere of phenomenological theory and at revealing its more general significance, enabling its use in other disciplinary contexts. Ultimately, the practice of active empathy involves a sophisticated negotiation between psychological, vital, and spiritual levels of knowledge, obtained through various strata of human experience. For both Bakhtin and Scheler, living into another personality is a complex and heterogeneous process: guided by phenomenological contemplation, it incorporates elements of empirical observation as well as insights gained by means of inductive reasoning.

Chapter Three

The Value of Resentment: A Sideward Glance at Empathy

> If two things don't fit, but you believe both of them, thinking that somewhere, hidden, there must be a third thing that connects them, that's credulity.
>
> —Umberto Eco, *Foucault's Pendulum*

"THERE IS AN *OTHER*, MY IDEAL, WHO IS BEAUTIFUL, SAINTLY AND BLESSED": INTERSUBJECTIVITY IN DOSTOEVSKY

Dostoevsky's fictional world provides many intriguing case studies that could be productively illuminated through the lens of the Schelerian-Bakhtinian theory of intersubjectivity.[1] The relevance of these phenomenological reflections to Dostoevsky's ethical concerns, only partly explained by the authors' common philosophical heritage,[2] is due to the *personalist* agenda shared by all three thinkers and to the crucial importance of the Christological ideal in their respective models of the world. Such concepts as "ontological gulf," "surplus of vision," "individual ineffable," and "consummation" are especially useful in describing the spiritual movements of a Dostoevskian hero, that profoundly social being who always lives *in* the other, *for the sake of* the other, or *in spite of* the other.

A Dostoevskian character is deeply and often painfully aware of the profound divide between himself and others, lamenting that unavoidable asymmetry between individual experiences that makes complete self-revelation to the other impossible. This distinct intellectual and moral discomfort at the existence of something akin to Scheler's "ontological gulf" is expressed in the Underground Man's tragicomic exclamation: "I am alone, and they are *everyone*!" ("Ia-to odin, a oni-to *vse*") (*Polnoe sobranie sochinenii*, hereafter *PSS*, 5:125, italics in text),[3] in Ippolit's indignation at being unable to communicate "the most vital point" of his notorious "Necessary Explanation" to his audience, because "in every serious human idea born in anyone's brain, there is something that cannot possibly be conveyed to others" (*PSS*, 8:328), and in Ivan Karamazov's bitter acknowledgment of one's inability to fully understand another's suffering: "Suppose I, for example, suffer intensely, but another will never be able to know how much I suffer, because he is *another* and not I" (*PSS*, 14:216; italics here and throughout added, unless otherwise indicated). The extreme sensitivity of many Dostoevskian heroes about the recognition of their pain as uniquely individual, their wish, so to speak, to "copyright" their emotional experiences, recalls Scheler's concern with addressing another's suffering as *his*, in the category of the other. Such is Ivan Karamazov's insistence that the mother of a tortured child may not forgive the child's murderer on the child's behalf and Stavrogin's morbid anxiety about his interlocutors usurping his, and only his, identity in the notebooks for *The Devils*. Attempting a confession to a priest at a nearby monastery, the character that would eventually become Stavrogin in the final version of the novel, tentatively called "the Prince" in the notebooks, is offended by his interlocutor's mocking use of the inclusive "we" and immediately makes a point about observing the ontological gulf:

> "How could *we* possibly attain such lofty understanding?" (Gde zhe *nam* takoe vysokoe ponimanie?) says [Father] Tikhon.
>
> "Say, 'How could *I*.' Say it, please!" (Skazhite: "gde zhe *mne*." Skazhite, pozhaluista!) says the Prince.
>
> "Why do you want me to say that?" . . .
>
> *"When one says 'we,' it's as if one wants to hide behind everyone, say it simply about yourself: 'How could I?'"*
>
> "How could *I* attain such understanding!" Tikhon repeated. (*PSS*, 11:266)

Obsessed with accountability, the ur-Stavrogin insists on separating his own experience from the others'. He refuses to share in the others' transgressions, even if this sharing is merely figurative, demanded by the structure of a linguistic idiom, a conventional turn of phrase, as in the passage above. In return, he will not burden his Father-confessor with his own sins, for which he does not wish to be forgiven.

In contrast to this scornful closure of the self in the face of a non-identical and thus non-communal other, Father Tikhon's notion of the ontological gulf, shared with all Christ-oriented characters in Dostoevsky, is quite different. It resembles the "intentional existential distance" in its Bakhtinian definition, as the fundamental asymmetry between the "infinite severity toward the self [and infinite] kindness toward the other" ("AH," 56). In the ultimately excised chapter "At Tikhon's," Father Tikhon discusses Stavrogin's plans to confess his crimes of child molesting publicly, warning his uncompromising visitor about the likelihood of a less than charitable reception of his confession:

> "The horror will be general and, of course, more feigned than sincere. People fear only what directly threatens their personal interests. I'm not talking about pure souls: they will be horrified and will accuse themselves, but they will not be noticed. But the laughter will be universal."
>
> "And don't forget the philosopher's observation that there's always something that pleases us in the other's misfortune."
>
> "A sound observation."
>
> "But how is it that you . . . you yourself . . . *I'm surprised at how low your opinion of people is, with what disgust you regard them,*" Stavrogin said with some apparent irritation.
>
> "Believe it or not, *I actually judged more by my own behavior than by other people's!*" Tikhon exclaimed.
>
> "Did you really? Could there possibly be something in your soul as well that is amused by my misfortune?
>
> "Who knows, perhaps there is. Oh, perhaps there is!" (*PSS*, 11:26–27)

Like those "pure souls" who would be horrified and shaken by Stavrogin's revelation, blaming themselves for the other's transgressions, Tikhon must subject his own soul to a stern examination, admitting shameful callousness in his own reception of the scandalous confession, and thus vindicate the momentarily accused others. In a similar exchange, Alyosha Karamazov vindicates his guilt-ridden brother, who is planning an escape from an undeserved prison sentence, only to hear Dmitry's fervid self-condemnation:

> "Of course, bribing is dishonest . . . , but I can't possibly take it upon myself to judge this [*sudit' ni za chto ne voz'mus'*], because, in fact, if, for instance, Ivan and Katya decided to put me in charge of this business [of preparing Mitya's escape], I know I would go and give bribes. I must tell you the whole truth here. And so I can't judge you, you must make your own decision. *But know that I will never judge you [for it]* [*No znai, chto i tebia ne osuzhu nikogda*]. . . .
>
> "*But I will judge myself!*" [*No zato ia sebia osuzhu!*] (*PSS*, 15:185–86)[4]

This juxtaposition of self and other is, of course, modeled on Christ's merciful stance toward "all others" and thus suggests a way out of the seemingly absolute solipsism associated by many characters with the reality of the "ontological gulf." The identification of Christ with the ultimate other, or "the innermost other in me" ("chelovek v cheloveke"), results in a special appreciation of *otherness* as an ontological category in Dostoevsky's world.

For all the horrendous abuses inflicted by Dostoevsky's characters on each other in the course of their existential struggles, the *other* ("drugoi"; "drugoi chelovek") is ultimately a source of grace and hope for the Dostoevskian hero. He becomes a sacred refuge where a spiritual ideal may reside when it can no longer be fulfilled, or even believed in, by the self. This profound existential need for a (better) other is expressed by characters in various states of moral development, obtaining throughout the entire spectrum of Dostoevskian souls, located as they are at different points of his spiritual hierarchy. From Zosima's authoritative admonitions, to Mitya Karamazov's uncertain hopes of renewal through the "hymn" to his perfect Other, to Stavrogin's impossible dreams of redemption—all these gestures bespeak the value of *otherness* in Dostoevsky's world. When Alyosha explains Father Zosima's unwavering popularity among the town folk, his spokesmanship for one of Dostoevsky's cherished ideas hardly surprises us:

> [Alyosha] understood that for the humble soul of the Russian commoner . . . there was no greater need and no greater comfort than to find someone or something holy to fall down before and worship: "If there is sin, injustice and temptation among us, nevertheless *somewhere on earth, in such-and-such a place, there is someone holy and exalted.* He is true and just [to vse ravno *est' na zemle tam-to, gde-to sviatoi i vyshii*, u togo zato pravda]; he knows the truth, so it is not dead on this earth; therefore, one day it will come to us, too, and reign over the earth, as had been promised." (*PSS*, 14:29)

It is more provocative when the same idea emerges from the lips of that lovable demagogue, a caricaturized westernizer Stepan Trofimovich Verkhovensky, who seems infinitely removed from "the humble soul of the Russian commoner" and his tenacious beliefs. "I am worse than you, I have disgraced this earth, but *you are better than me, and I rejoice*," the hero pronounces on the eve of his dubious conversion in Dostoevsky's plans for a "poetic chapter" that describes the hero's tragicomic last pilgrimage in "Notebooks for *The Devils*" (*PSS*, 11:176). As we shall see in our analysis of *Notes from Underground*, this kind of comparison yields an apprehension of value radically different from the one resulting from ressentiment, with its constant, anxious pitting of the self against the all-important, at once indispensable and intolerable others. The use of the second person ("*You are* better than me") imparts a dialogical poignancy to this important slogan: also communicating the more general meaning of "Thou art," it affirms the ontological reality of the grace-bestowing other.[5]

Stavrogin's version of the same motto in the notebooks is even more intriguing, because his very essence proclaims the opposite of the propagated ideal both in the notebooks for *The Devils* and in the finished novel. In a conversation with Shatov, that anticipates Stavrogin's controversial preaching to the character in the final version of the novel, "the Prince" declares: "If I am imperfect, nasty and mean, I still know that *there is an other, my ideal, who is beautiful, saintly and blessed.* If there is at least a tiny spark of greatness and magnanimity in me, this idea alone gives me comfort." ("Esli ia ne sovershenen, gadok i zol, to ia znaiu, chto *est' drugoi, ideal moi, kotoryi prekrasen, sviat i blazhen*. Esli vo mne khot' na iskru velichiia i velikodushiia, to uzhe odna eta ideia otradna mne" [*PSS*, 11:189].) The necessary evocation of the divine *Other* in the human *other* inherent in this statement comes to the fore when it is read in the context of Stavrogin's earlier utterance in the notebooks: "Man is incapable of saving himself alone, but is saved through revelation and then through Christ, that is, through God's immediate involvement in man's life—that is, through a miracle in both cases" (*PSS*, 11:182).

For the Stavrogin of the notebooks this kind of salvation is predicated on absolute faith, which, as we learn from the adjacent notes, he lacks. Ironically, this very argument will eventually lead the hypothetical character to pillage and burn, for "it is better to burn everything" if one does not believe with one's whole soul: "[the choice is] either faith or arson" ("ili vera ili zhech'"), the character declares in the notebooks (*PSS*, 11:182, see also *PSS*, 11:179, 180). The pernicious logic of Stavrogin-like characters turns the argument for the need of the redeeming Other on its head: "I cannot be saved alone, yet I *am* alone (for I don't believe in the Savior)," the character seems to reason, "so I shall destroy myself and others. If I cannot take credit for my salvation, I shall take credit for my own destruction." In the final version of the novel, such is the torturous logic of the ideological suicide Kirillov, Stavrogin's tragically faithful disciple. It is also echoed in Ippolit's and Ivan Karamazov's related philosophies of despair.

The Prince's relationship to Dostoevsky's cherished motto may be defined with the help of Scheler's insights about the ontological validity of the Absolute. Here we see an intriguing illustration of Scheler's statement that "the Absolute" is an original, a priori sphere of consciousness: it is *given* to us (just like the sphere of the other, or the "Thou") even if it remains vacant—not filled with any positive content—throughout our lives (see, for example, *Problems of a Sociology of Knowledge*, *GW*, 8:57). "The Prince" experiences the absence or the impossibility of the Divine Other as a palpable void precisely because he experiences the *givenness* of the Absolute as such, as a necessary sphere of his personal being, which remains painfully empty. In this context, Kirillov's enigmatic description of God's reality status: "He does not exist, but He is" ("Ego net, no on est'") (*PSS*, 10:94) may be read as the unavoidable admission of God's ontological presence in His "allotted" space in the primary region of consciousness, on the one hand, and of His *absence* as a positive spiritual content, directly and personally "available" to the hero as an affirmative answer to his metaphysical quest, on the other.

The first kind of "He is" (or rather "He is there") is always a given in Dostoevsky's world, while the second affirmation ("He exists [*for me*"]) is often highly problematic. For that reason, it is not inconsistent that Stavrogin-like characters can recognize the ideal of divine Otherness and its absolute value, even if they are unable to take possession of this value and to apprehend it fully through faith and love. Those who, like the Underground Man, Stavrogin and, to a certain extent, Ivan Karamazov, denigrate and reject the other (and the Absolute Other) nevertheless recognize his crucial significance as an *other*.[6] In this context, the close connection between the a priori given spheres of the other and of the Divine Other in Scheler's phenomenology, also registered but not explicitly acknowledged in the works of the early Bakhtin, is very relevant to Dostoevsky's world.

This is why in Dostoevsky's novels the religiously based significance of otherness is affirmed even in the most secular spheres of experience, for example, in Feodor Karamazov's metaphysical yearning for "another person," necessarily unlike himself, honest, kind, and forgiving:

> Depraved and often cruel in his lust, like some vicious insect, Feodor Pavlovich was sometimes, in moments of drunkenness, seized by spiritual terror and moral convulsions . . . At such moments *he liked to feel that there was next to him, near at hand* . . . a loyal, strong-willed person, *completely unlike himself* [*sovsem ne takoi, kak on*], not depraved, who had seen all his debauchery and knew all his secrets, but would be ready in his loyalty to overlook all that, not to object, above all, not to reproach him or threaten him with anything, neither in this life, nor in the next, and, if need be, to defend him . . .
>
> The point was precisely that it should be *another* person [nepremenno *drugoi* chelovek] [italics in text], an old, familiar friend, so that he might summon him at a painful moment just to look at his face, or, perhaps, exchange some insignificant words with him. And if the other were all right with it, not angry, his heart felt lighter, and if he were angry, well, then he felt more despondent. (*PSS*, 14: III, I, 86–87)

In this ludicrous inversion of the Christological theme, the self-serving Dostoevskian buffoon uses the better other as a spiritual tranquilizer: the "sovsem drugoi chelovek" becomes an alibi for his own spiritual sluggishness and moral inertia. Nevertheless, this inexplicable thirst for redeeming otherness manifests a certain spiritual alertness even in such an unlikely

God-seeker as Feodor Pavlovich. Foreshadowing the novel's major themes, Feodor Pavlovich's wish anticipates the kind of other (or neighbor) that Alyosha will become for him and Ivan will not.

Because the ultimate prototype of the better other, Christ, also posits a model of bridging the natural ontological gulf between persons, an entry into another's inner world is always possible in Dostoevsky. Hence the significance of *proniknovenie* (a mental, or rather soulful, penetration into another self) in Dostoevsky's world[7] and the exceptional ability of his heroes to grasp the logic of the other's inner life, even if they rarely use that knowledge productively. There is a path from one "I" to another in Dostoevsky's world, no matter how far removed these beings (*sushchestva*) may be from each other class-wise, intellectually, or temperamentally. This is why it is quite consistent with Dostoevsky's notion of dialogical openness that a city prostitute Sonya Marmeladov and an aristocratic landowner Svidrigailov find themselves in such "unrealistic" proximity not only as neighbors at a dingy hostel, but also as partners in dialogue over the fate of Raskolnikov's soul. By the same token, it is not surprising that, on the eve of the trial, Ivan Karamazov understands Mitya's at once rapturous and anguished "hymn" to his Divine *Other*, God the Father, even as he refuses to join in it (*PSS*, 15:35), or that Rogozhin is said to comprehend Ippolit's existential dilemmas, as different as they are from his own immediate concerns. This latter ability is hinted at in the final version of *The Idiot* and emphasized in the preparatory notes for the novel: "It's strange—this man lives with all the intensity of life that is possible in this world, but, I think, he's able to understand my situation too [sposoben ponimat' i moe delo]," Ippolit observes with amazement in Dostoevsky's notes for *The Idiot* (*PSS*, 9:223).[8]

But although an entry into another consciousness is a common event in the emotional life of a Dostoevskian hero, he is often unable or unwilling to make use of the critical knowledge obtained through such an entry. Befuddled by "what to do" with his empathy (in the words of the Underground Man: "I, most likely, wouldn't be able *to make use* of my magnanimity [*nichego by ne sumel sdelat'* iz moego velikodushiia]" (*PSS*, 5:103), or with its emotionally conquered object, the hero is often unable to make a productive transition from mere co-experiencing to an ethically and morally relevant action. "I . . . couldn't even imagine *what to do* with the person I won over [*chto delat'* s pokorennym predmetom]," the Underground Man offers with bitter self-mockery (*PSS*, 5:176). This question of making use of *proniknovenie* is equally relevant to the dilemmas of Dostoevsky's egoists and to the challenges of his saintly communicators, who, like the tragically ineffective Prince Myshkin, do not lack love or the ability to see into another soul, but often have trouble utilizing or *consummating* their "data" about the suffering other.

This is where Schelerian and Bakhtinian insights about the *mechanics* of active empathy are extremely useful precisely because these theories address the process of making emotional co-experiencing ethically and spiritually productive. In the application part of this study we shall examine problems of intersubjectivity in *Notes from Underground*, *Notes from the House of the Dead*, *The Idiot*, and *The Brothers Karamazov*, using the concepts of *consummation*, *surplus of vision* (including *surplus of the self* and *the other's surplus*), *ontological gulf*, and *value acquisition*. The present chapter opens the discussion with an analysis of *Notes from Underground*, a seminal text that introduces Dostoevsky's reader to an important and prolific character type, that of an underground "dialogist." Embodying many features of such future characters as Ippolit, Ivan Karamazov, and Stavrogin, the underground type represents the philosophy of anti-empathy and will be relevant to our subsequent discussions of Myshkin's, Goryanchikov's, and Alyosha Karamazov's spiritual missions, as a major opponent of the Dostoevskian "saint."

Because the hero's relationship with his ephemeral, invariably objectified others is a curious inversion of empathy, the novel will be analyzed with the help of Scheler's concept of ressentiment, a psycho-spiritual phenomenon describing a peculiar corruption of the empathetic instinct, leading to a fundamentally passive existential attitude and a deliberate denigration of the *value* of otherness.

THE SEEDS OF *RESSENTIMENT* IN *NOTES FROM UNDERGROUND*

Dostoevsky's Underground Man is petty, malicious, and utterly devoid of those noble virtues that are traditionally associated with an author's mouthpiece, and yet he expresses some of Dostoevsky's most cherished convictions. An ardent spokesman for the sovereignty of human will, he seizes every opportunity to dominate the wills of those vulnerable enough to succumb to his petty tyranny. An enemy of every kind of determinism, whose life is a relentless struggle against the "stone wall" of natural necessity, he becomes hopelessly entrapped in the circular logic of underground revenge. Caught in the pattern of seeking external acknowledgment in deliberately provoked hurt, finding masochistic satisfaction in savoring his pain in memory and then validating his old injuries by provoking new ones, the Underground Man becomes subject to psychological laws no less rigid and menacing than the formidable "laws of nature."

The Underground Man's ambivalent position in Dostoevsky's hierarchy of values as both the author's mouthpiece and an anti-hero, a seeker of absolute freedom and an actor in a predictable play of vanity, has received substantial critical attention. The question of the underground's "value status" becomes central in the works of those critics who consider Dostoevsky's problematics in the light of Nietzsche's concepts of ressentiment and the *revaluation of values*. In his *Bitter Carnival: Ressentiment and the Abject Hero* and "The Poetics of *Ressentiment*," Michael André Bernstein treats the Underground Man as one of Dostoevsky's abject heroes, whose concept of freedom is fundamentally flawed and whose entire worldview is imperceptibly distorted by ressentiment. On the contrary, in "Dostoevsky and Nietzsche: The Philosophy of Tragedy," Lev Shestov, who argues for a complete identification between Dostoevsky and his hero, interprets the Underground Man's passionate rejection of the "humanitarian" ideals, propagated by the socialist utopians of the 1840s and the socialist materialists of the 1860s, as a sign of psychological and ideological maturity. According to Shestov, the Underground Man (read: Dostoevsky himself) has overcome the ressentiment delusion inherent in both systems of values.[9] Having liberated himself from the sham ideals of compassionate ministering to the ungrateful masses, the hero was able to rise to a vantage point beyond good and evil, Shestov argues.

Although both studies offer seminal insights into the character of the Underground Man, the critics' analyses of ressentiment-like processes in Dostoevsky's work leave room for further inquiry. While Bernstein's description of the psychological mechanisms of underground revenge is perceptive and precise, the Underground Man's psychology cannot be *fully* identified with ressentiment processes. On the other hand, although Shestov is correct in acknowledging a kind of "revaluation of values" that takes place in the novel, he fails to notice to what great extent the rejected values continue to dominate the Underground Man's life. I propose to reexamine the relationship between underground psychology and ressentiment, supplementing Nietzsche's concept with a more elaborate theory by Max Scheler, whose endorsement of Christian love as a means of overcoming ressentiment suggests an affinity with Dostoevsky's own deeply religious worldview.[10]

In *Genealogy of Morals* and *Beyond Good and Evil*, Nietzsche defines ressentiment as a peculiar psychological reaction to situations of coercion, in which the subject's immediate emotive responses, such as the impulse for revenge, anger, and rage against the oppressor, are silenced and, as it were, turned inwards. Barred from external expression by the consciousness of utter impotence in the face of the injuring power, these venomous feelings penetrate deep into the injured self, finding no other target but one's own anguished pride, already lacerated by the oppressor. This repeatedly frustrated craving for power, this cold malice, which gradually becomes dissociated from its object, does not dissipate with time but grows ever stronger as external resistance to oppression weakens. It is situations of such extreme powerlessness that condition the most sublimated form of revenge, accomplished through the radical revaluation of values, which Nietzsche associates with the "slave revolt in morality." In a gesture of covert defiance, whose subtlety is incomprehensible to a noble consciousness, the oppressed embraces his own debasement, proclaiming his very powerlessness to be his highest and most cherished value, thus devaluing the desired but unattainable values of power, self-respect, and contentment. Such a crafty, if ingenious, act of intellectual and spiritual manipulation directed at the *self* with the far-reaching intention of gradually affecting the psyche of the powerful *other* is utterly contemptible to Nietzsche, who finds the spectacle of sheer necessity masquerading as virtue distasteful (compare, for example, his assessment of Christian values as the fruit of Jewish psychological revenge against the Gentile oppressor).[11] Although Nietzsche acknowledges the superiority of master morality over slave morality, he does not advocate a return to the former. Rather, his plan of action includes the debunking of the slave values, prevalent in the contemporary bourgeois morality, followed by the creation of an entirely new value system, free from the influence of either master, slave, or herd mentality.

Scheler, whose diagnosis of ressentiment as a psychic phenomenon essentially agrees with Nietzsche's, sees the origin of this moral malady in the *perversion* of Christ's teachings rather than in his original message, as Nietzsche does.[12] Contrary to Nietzsche, who counts Christian love among the perverted slave values, largely responsible for the spread of the disease, Scheler proposes agape as a remedy effective against the ressentiment delusion, which alone is capable of restoring the sacred "order of the heart," inverted by ressentiment.

The opening paragraph of *Notes from Underground*, narrated by a speaker both blindly aggressive toward his imaginary audience and morbidly sensitive to its reaction to his unsolicited confession, seems to offer some evidence of a ressentiment attitude. "I refuse to get medical treatment out of spite," the Underground Man asserts in that inherently unstable, sneering tone that is always on the verge of breaking into genuine pathos:

> Now then, that's something you probably won't understand. Well, I do. Of course, I won't really be able to explain to you precisely who will be hurt by my spite in this case; I know perfectly well that I can't possibly "get even" with doctors by refusing their treatment; I know better than anyone that all this is going to hurt me alone, and no one else. Even so, if I refuse to be treated, it's out of spite. My liver hurts? Good, let it hurt even more! (*Notes*, 3; *PSS*, 5:99).[13]

"The world has subjected me to pain—well, I shall take the most appropriate measures against such an affront," the Underground Man announces; "namely, I will exacerbate my own pain, making the world suffer the disgusting spectacle of my half-real, half-theatrical agony." As in classic ressentiment, the suffering ostensibly inflicted on the self is at the same time used as a weapon against others. Here it is the reader who becomes the most obvious target of such passive-aggressive retaliation. Such profound confusion between external and internal aggression as well as his extraordinary sensitivity to insult, which makes the peculiar sensual enjoyment of pain possible, are telling signs of the Underground Man's predisposition to ressentiment. As Bernstein notes in regards to Dostoevsky's "underground" characters:

> One of the central dilemmas of abjection is the impossibility of distinguishing between inner and outer pressures, between self-loathing and social humiliation, cunning mockery and a pathetic need for attention. Irrespective of its origin, Dostoevskian abjection functions as a weapon of global aggression, whose sting is all the more venomous for continually traversing the complex passage between internal and external targets.[14]

According to Nietzsche, the vector of ressentiment aggression points both in the direction of *self* and *other*, because the original, outward-oriented impulse of revenge is denied a direct outlet of expression and thus seeks roundabout ways of reaching its target: hurt is visited upon the self in order to hurt the oppressor.[15] In *Notes from Underground* the whole universe assumes the role of the omnipotent oppressor, who has denied the Underground Man every possible outlet of action. In this context, the use of Bernstein's expression "*global* aggression" in relation to the Underground Man is especially apt because of the universal or existential character of oppression in *Notes from Underground*. The Underground Man's aggression is *global* because it is directed against an omniscient enemy—the totalitarian universe of natural laws that reduces human will to a mechanical function of its mighty apparatus. And since such an opponent is truly ubiquitous, the hero's very self becomes part of the enemy territory and is regarded as a legitimate target of assault in his struggle with the global Other.

It is precisely the Underground Man's radically *objective* conception of the universe that denies him what Scheler considers the most effective preventive remedy against ressentiment—forgiveness. Indeed, in such a universe, the victim's search for the guilty party, to whom he could extend his generous pardon, is predictably futile. In the absence of the very notion of subjectivity, forgiveness proves as ineffective as revenge in assuaging the pain of the injured self, for both of these "noble" reactions to injury imply a recognition of the offender's guilt. But neither the Underground Man's desire for revenge, nor his magnanimous impulses find a justifiable object in his fatalistic universe, condemning him to a life of hyper-conscious inertia: "I probably wouldn't have been able to make use of my magnanimity," the

Underground Man confesses, "*neither to forgive*, as the offender, perhaps, had slapped me in accordance with the laws of nature, and there's no way to forgive the laws of nature; *nor to forget*, because even if it is because of the laws of nature, it's offensive nonetheless" (*Notes*, 7; *PSS*, 103).

According to Scheler, the outward-oriented impulse of revenge tends to be transformed into the passive-aggressive, inward-directed energy of ressentiment in "lasting situations which are felt to be injurious but beyond one's control—in other words, *the more the injury is experienced as a destiny*" (*Ressentiment*, 50).[16] One can hardly find a more fitting definition of the Underground Man's "existential injury," perceived as a global joke at his expense, a painful but inevitable blow dealt by the anonymous forces of the fatalistic universe. "You look—and the object vanishes, the arguments evaporate, a guilty party can't be identified," the Underground Man complains, "*the offense ceases to be one and becomes a matter of fate*, something like a toothache for which no one's to blame" (*Notes*, 13; *PSS*, 108–9). But while the culprit is envisioned as a mathematically objective force, the injury is experienced as a deeply personal insult, directed at the very core of the hero's being. "It's the laws of nature that *hurt* me [*obizhali*] the most my entire life," the Underground Man exclaims, as if, by interpreting his hurt as a deliberate offense and by thus personalizing his relationship with the blind powers of nature, he attempts to preserve his own anguished sense of subjectivity in the mute world of objects (*Notes*, 12; *PSS*, 107). The Underground Man's desperate insistence on the possibility of a subjective response to the tyranny of a subjectless universe reveals a tragic inconsistency in his worldview, which results in the painful conflict between the most potent will to freedom and the most lucid realization of its empirical impossibility.

From Scheler's point of view, such a discrepancy between the conceptual and the empirical levels of reality may trigger the most powerful *ressentiment* reaction. He observes, for example, that social ressentiment is strongest not in a political structure with a legal code explicitly sanctioning social inequality but rather in a society with sufficiently developed *concepts* of freedom and equality, where the constitutional status of a group may be at odds with its factual power (*Ressentiment*, 50). In other words, the likelihood of a ressentiment revolt is greater in a subject capable of *conceiving of* and even educated to *believe in* his own sovereignty but repeatedly confronted with opposite proofs in reality. Existential despair, fraught with *ressentiment*, is most cruel when the long-cultivated appetite for power finds no satisfaction in the world of actuality.

Read from a Schelerian point of view, Shestov's study supplies a plausible socio-historical explanation of what may be called a ressentiment situation in *Notes from Underground*.[17] According to Shestov, the fundamental ideological inconsistency underlying the worldview of a progressive "intelligent" of the 1860s, reflected in the Underground Man's dilemma, results from the simultaneous affirmation of two mutually exclusive ideas: (1) the proclamation of man's rights before society and (2) the whole-hearted acceptance of the laws of natural necessity.[18] The first postulate, championed by the utopian socialists of the 1840s and inherited by the succeeding socialist movements of the 1860s, came into a sharp contradiction with the central component of the materialist ideology—the belief in determinism. Thus, as Shestov puts it, the declaration of man's rights before humanity was negated by the simultaneous declaration of his lack of rights before the greater, ultimately, all-pervasive, authority of nature.[19] Unrecognized by the myopic theoreticians of Russian socialist materialism, this profound contradiction was masterfully dramatized by Dostoevsky, Shestov argues. In terms of Scheler's ressentiment theory, the Underground Man's conflict may then be described as that between the lofty *conception of freedom*, cultivated by the socialist idealists of the 1840s, and the negation of individual will, expressed as the *empirical impossibility of freedom* in the materialist doctrines of the 1860s.

This painful contradiction comes to the fore in the Underground Man's refusal to surrender his high-minded vision of human sovereignty in exchange for the "ideal" of sanctioned happiness in the Crystal Palace. "What do I care if it [the Crystal Palace] is *impossible* and if I must settle for some apartments?" the hero exclaims, rejecting the argument of the empirical unfeasibility of the "true Crystal Palace"—a place where joyful affirmation is compatible with individual freedom—as an excuse for abandoning his irrational striving for the realm of the truly ideal. "Then why was I made with such desires? Can it be that I was made this way only in order to reach the conclusion that my entire way of being is a fraud? Can this be the whole purpose? I don't believe it" (*Notes*, 26; *PSS*, 121).[20] The hero brilliantly exposes the complacent blindness of those naive proponents of the stone wall who presume that its supreme law does not only tolerate but solicits the assertion of individual will. Such "liberal determinists" deliver the most impudent insult to the lofty notion of personal sovereignty by asserting that each individual will must be brought into correspondence with the superior will of nature through a process of rational education. The Underground Man, who cannot tolerate an act of such crude ideological manipulation, asks his imaginary interlocutor to spare him the despicable charade of parading sheer necessity in the guise of free choice. "But gentlemen, what sort of free choice will there be when it comes down to tables and arithmetic, when all that's left is two times two makes four?" the Underground Man exclaims with bitter sarcasm: "Two times two makes four even without my will. Is that what you call free choice?" (*Notes*, 22; *PSS*, 117).

In a word, if the Underground Man succeeds at proving anything conclusively, it is the fact that the notion of individual freedom and the concept of natural determinism represent two mutually exclusive realities. As Edward Wasiolek points out, one of the contesting systems has to be an illusion, or, perhaps, a private dream, while the other represents the ultimate reality in *Notes from Underground*.[21] We have seen that the simultaneous affirmation of the two "truths" leads to the relentless torment of ressentiment, as in the case of a man torn between the theoretically sound belief in his sovereign rights and the empirically "proven" impossibility of their satisfaction. To avoid the ressentiment entrapment between two conflicting value systems, one has to make a decisive choice of an existential position.[22] One may wholeheartedly acknowledge the reality of personal freedom (as does the faithful idealist of the 1840s) or that of natural necessity (as do the more consistent followers of socialist materialism). A third, much more emotionally costly and spiritually demanding solution, chosen by the Underground Man, entails accepting the natural laws on the rational level and then rejecting them on the level of belief in a kind of Kierkegaardian leap of faith. This difficult spiritual undertaking becomes a challenge the Underground Man is not always capable of meeting. We shall see that when the hero courageously "leaps" into his belief head first, irrationally suspending the laws of nature, he succeeds at overcoming ressentiment. But when, like the hesitant Orpheus, he stealthily looks back at the oppressive realm he is attempting to escape, he compromises his freedom, exhibiting ressentiment-like responses.

A CRISIS OF AFFIRMATION: REACTIVE ASPECTS OF THE UNDERGROUND PROTEST

When a self is unable either to sustain a transcendent faith in freedom or to resign to its powerless position through the equally stabilizing belief in determinism, the acute inner tension between desire and impotence is resolved by means of the psychological resources of ressentiment. According to Nietzsche, the ultimate consummation of the ressentiment worldview, the decisive transition from the passive despair of powerlessness, *fraught with* ressentiment, to the passive-aggressive strategy of softening the underlying conflict, characteristic of ressentiment proper, consists in the act of the radical revaluation of values. Nietzsche thus describes what he sees as the daring reversal of the aristocratic value system undertaken by the Jews to avenge their Gentile oppressors, whose once coveted but unattainable values they successfully denigrate:

> It was the Jews who, in opposition to the aristocratic equation (good = aristocratic = beautiful = happy = loved by the gods), dared with a terrifying logic to suggest the contrary equation, . . . namely, "the wretched are alone the

> good; the suffering, . . . the needy, the sick, the loathsome, are the only ones who are pious, the only ones who are blessed, for them alone is salvation—but you, on the other hand, you aristocrats, you men of power, you are to all eternity the evil, the horrible, the covetous, the insatiable, the godless.[23]

It is tempting to interpret the Underground Man's endorsement of pain as a classic example of the ressentiment strategy. But does the Underground Man's apology of suffering indeed amount to the cunning phrase: "[The suffering] are alone the good"? The relationship between the underground masochism and the positive valuation of pain characteristic of ressentiment ideology may be clarified by analyzing the Underground Man's digression apropos the toothache and his critique of the Crystal Palace in light of the Nietzschean-Schelerian theory.

Responding to his imaginary interlocutor, the "normal man," incapable of appreciating some of life's finer pleasures, such as the masochistic savoring of pain, the Underground Man ventures to explain his peculiar predilection for suffering. "Well, what of it? There is some enjoyment even in a toothache," the hero replies:

> In this instance, of course, people don't rage in silence; they moan. But these moans are insincere; they are malicious, and malice is the whole point. . . . In the first place, these moans express all the aimlessness of the pain which consciousness finds so humiliating, the whole system of natural laws about which you really don't give a damn, but as a result of which you're suffering nonetheless, while nature isn't. They express the consciousness that while there's no real enemy to be identified, the pain exists nonetheless; the awareness that, in spite of all possible Wagenheims, you're still a complete slave of your teeth; that if someone so wishes, your teeth will stop aching, but that if he doesn't so wish, they'll go on aching for three more months; and finally, that if you still disagree and protest, all there's left to do for consolation is flagellate yourself or beat your fist against the wall as hard as you can and absolutely nothing else. (*Notes*, 10–11; *PSS*, 106)

The character uses the deliberately low toothache metaphor to enact yet another scandalous confrontation with "the wall," dramatizing a situation of extreme coercion. Here the character's suffering, "[the humiliatingly aimless] pain," is precisely the tangible locus of un-freedom, the shameful evidence of Nature's "lawful" domination over its trembling creatures. In other words, it is *the given* in the obscure equation of the natural law, whose authority the Underground Man attempts to undermine. The underground protest consists precisely in the subtle transformation of this posited element within the limits of underground freedom. If man cannot suspend the pain inflicted on him by mother nature, he can accept it on his own terms, declares the underground hero. The hideously groaning toothache sufferer, who makes an artful spectacle out of his torment, introduces a deliberately "unnatural" element into his "natural" pain. Through self-laceration he takes persecution into his own hands; by turning the play of fate into a theatrical production of his own, he imperceptibly changes the rules of the game, defying his tormentor by his repulsive parody of suffering.

In its general structure the toothache sufferer's protest resembles that of ressentiment: the character *reacts* to a situation of extreme impotence; he embraces injury inflicted upon him, hurting himself with the intention of hurting others. It is also clear that suffering as such is not affirmed as a value in the toothache episode. Rather, it is insincere suffering, suffering as a pose that is embraced in defiance of "natural" suffering. Instead of wholeheartedly complying with the natural law, the character, as it were, suffers half-heartedly, thus defying the terms of the supreme legislation. No matter how skeptical he may be about the effectiveness of the underground revolt, Dostoevsky makes it clear that even in a situation of ostensible powerlessness the hero finds a way of asserting his will. Subjected to pain, he *chooses* his suffering, opting for the kind that scandalizes the injurer.

In the case of the Nietzschean slave revolt the slaves also accept their lot on different terms from the ones envisioned by the masters, but Nietzsche, disgusted by the very notion of "slave mentality," downplays the significance of this *choice*, emphasizing the *reactive* nature of the underlying ideological strategy instead. While Nietzsche depicts the powerlessness of the Jews in order to expose the slavish conditions that gave rise to what he deems to be a slavish ideology, Dostoevsky dramatizes situations of maximum necessity with the contrary purpose of emphasizing the extraordinary vitality of the human will to freedom. Even under the conditions of extreme coercion, the Dostoevskian hero irrationally strives to preserve his idea of selfhood, finding loopholes of freedom—no matter how small—to assert his will. And even though both the hero's choices and his concept of freedom, in which they find inspiration, are often fundamentally flawed, the very inclination toward liberty, the indestructible desire to "prove oneself a man and not an organ stop" (*Notes*, 22; *PSS*, 117), constitutes an independent value in Dostoevsky's world. Thus we may say that a situation analogous to that of the Nietzschean ressentiment receives a different authorial evaluation in the Russian novel. To use Bakhtin's terminology, the passages depicting a ressentiment protest are differently "accentuated" in Dostoevsky's work. However, as we shall see, this, more positive, evaluation of the underground revolt does not eliminate the author's concern about its fundamentally reactive quality, which is implicitly contrasted with the affirmative essence of *freedom in faith* in *Notes from Underground.*

If in the toothache episode suffering was forcibly inflicted on the self by the oppressor and accepted on the sufferer's own terms, in the Crystal Palace passage it is freely chosen as an alternative to the mandatory happiness of the utilitarian utopia. Here the initial conditions of the hero's value judgment are distinctly different from those characteristic of the Nietzschean revaluation of values: suffering is affirmed as a value not because the truly coveted value of happiness is out of reach. Indeed, the impossibility of attaining the utilitarian bliss in the Crystal Palace is clearly not the reason for its rejection. On the contrary, a permanent lease granting the Underground Man the right of residing in the "capital building" is ceremoniously extended to him, with a special provision of the dentist Wagenheim to put an end to his embarrassing toothache. It is rather the impossibility of resisting the seductive comforts of the Crystal Palace that the Underground Man fears. "And, perhaps, I'm so afraid of this building precisely because it's made of crystal and it's eternally indestructible, and because it won't be possible to stick one's tongue out at it even on the sly," the hero complains (*Notes*, 25; *PSS*, 120). In the rigidly finalized quality of the utopian edifice the Underground Man sees a sign of totalitarianism: its indestructible walls seem to be impenetrable from within, and the hero's permanent lease threatens to become an order of confinement. Thus the specter of *coerced happiness* in the Crystal Palace episode is no less objectionable to Dostoevsky's lucid hero than the *coerced suffering* of the toothache passage. And the underground protest against such benevolent tyranny is strategically similar to that against the tyranny of terror: it consists in scandalizing the tyrant. Indeed, the spiteful, theatrical groans of the toothache sufferer belong to the same paradigm of signs as the clownish gesture of sticking out one's tongue at the Crystal Palace.

The Underground Man thus stands outside the Crystal Palace, irreverently sneering at its formidable façade and honoring its authority with obscene gestures. The ideological space outside the realm of ready-made happiness, delineated by the crystal walls, in which the hero places himself, is the space of militant opposition to the Crystal Palace values. If inside the elegant walls reigns the sterile order of natural necessity, outside bustles the dynamic chaos of "zhivaia zhizn'" (literally: "the living life"). And, if inside the palace the "Hosanna!" of eternal affirmation announces the coming of the secular apocalypse, then outside, the struggling self is continually renewed through suffering and negation. Located "on this side" of the crystal wall, in the same ideological space as *consciousness* and *free will*, *suffering* becomes a code word for freedom by virtue of a metonymic shift. Once again, as in the toothache episode, it is not suffering as such that is affirmed. Rather suffering as doubt, as unceasing psychic movement and spiritual rejuvenation becomes an antithesis of happiness as psychic and spiritual atrophy. In this sense, like the slaves' reactive acknowledgment of their own value, merely as a weapon against the values of the oppressor, the Underground Man's endorsement of suffering in freedom is a negation rather than an affirmation. Indeed, by proclaiming his choice to continue his painful struggle outside the Crystal Palace, rather than to exchange his personal freedom for its slavish comforts, the character primarily seeks to negate the value of such ready-made happiness. Hence the important disclaimer explaining the provisional value of suffering: "*I'm not actually standing up for suffering* here . . . I'm standing up for . . . my own whim and for its being guaranteed to me whenever necessary" (*Notes*, 24; *PSS*, 119).

Thus, the similarity between the underground critique of the Crystal Palace and the process of *revaluation of values* consists precisely in the reactive or secondary character of both value judgments. The hero's denouncement of the utopian paradise is not motivated by sheer necessity, as in the case of the slaves' "rejection" of the oppressor's coveted happiness, but rather by the fully justified belief in its deficiency. And yet his negation is not reinforced by a positive affirmation of an intrinsically meaningful value. As the slaves' suffering *receives* its value by virtue of its structural opposition to the combated value of happiness, so, in the Crystal Palace passage, suffering is "positively coded" as a counter-value in relation to the passionately rejected totalitarian bliss. It may be argued that, since in the cited passage suffering is essentially a code word for freedom, *freedom* is the intrinsically positive value affirmed by the hero. But, paradoxically, the fundamentally negative nature of the underground concept of freedom makes any absolute affirmation, even the affirmation of freedom itself, impossible.

The Underground Man's anguished professions of faith in the sovereignty of human consciousness are often followed by gestures of involuntary tribute to the belief in the supremacy of "the wall." The hero concludes his philosophical digression apropos the Crystal Palace by declaring his decision to remain outside its restrictive walls, but, if his earlier estimates of its authority are to be taken seriously, it is questionable whether this choice is even available to him. He prides himself on defying the values of the totalitarian utopia by sticking out his tongue at the crystal edifice (his irreverent attack on the utilitarian ideals on the pages of *Notes* has been just that). And yet, at the outset of his theoretical discussion, he had himself admitted that, by virtue of its very nature, the "eternally indestructible building" would simply not tolerate such self-willed acts of protest: "*it won't be possible to tease it* [the Crystal Palace] *by sticking out one's tongue at it*, nor by secretly giving it the finger in one's pocket" ([khrustal'nomu dvortsu] *nel'zia budet* ni *iazyka ukradkoi vystavit'*, ni kukisha v karmane pokazat'") (*PSS*, 120).[24] Could it be that the Underground Man's own obscene gesturing in front of his rationalist reader has not been an act of spontaneous self-assertion but rather a prescripted event, sanctioned by the very authority he has attempted to undermine? The Underground Man exclaims, perhaps, anticipating the fate of his own revolt against the authoritarian universe:

> If, for example, someday they calculate and demonstrate to me that I gave so-and-so the finger[25] because I couldn't have done otherwise and that I had to do it precisely with the hand I used, what part of me could possibly be considered *free* then, especially if I am an educated man and have completed a course of study somewhere? (*Notes*, 19–20; *PSS*, 114, italics in text).

The gnawing suspicion that the transparent walls of the Crystal Palace have imperceptibly encircled the hero, gradually subsuming the salutary space of opposition and rendering his protest an illusion, is always palpable behind the Underground Man's militant anti-totalitarian rhetoric.

Combating this, his greatest, fear, Dostoevsky's character conceives of an ultimate loophole to freedom—an underground emergency exit, which would provide a costly but honorable means of escaping such extreme tyranny. The Underground Man contends that, if man discovered that even his most spontaneous movements of self-assertion had been acts of sheer necessity, he would resort to self-inflicted insanity. In other words, man would deliberately extinguish his own consciousness to preclude rational comprehension of the triumph of rational determinism. Quite intentionally, Dostoevsky renders this escape strategy highly problematic even from the point of view of the underground ideology: in his self-delusion the hero resembles the despised man of action, who bows before the wall but remains blind—albeit through no choice of his own—to the all-pervasive effects of its totalitarian authority.

The Underground Man hastens to assure the reader that this chilling vision of a mechanistic universe is merely a hypothesis, a purely theoretical speculation, used to expose the ultimate implications of a popular belief, to which the speaker himself does not subscribe. On the contrary, in response to the reigning cult of natural necessity, the hero professes a counter-belief in the unique and irreducible nature of human will. "I believe in it," the Underground Man proclaims,

> I vouch for it, because, after all, the whole of man's work seems to consist only in proving to himself constantly that he's a man and not an organ stop! Even if he has to lose his own skin, he'll prove it; even if he has to become a troglodyte, he'll prove it. Now, having said that, *how can one resist mentioning that all this hasn't yet come to pass and that desire still depends on the devil knows what*. (*Notes*, 22; *PSS*, 117)

But the Underground Man's fervor is that of a preacher who has yet to convince himself of the validity of his professed creed. An analysis of the narrator's use of the lexeme "вер-," designating belief or conviction, often in a negative or attenuated meaning ("*ne* verit'," "*chut' ne* poverit'," "*polu*vera" /

"*not* to believe," "to *almost* believe," "*half*-faith"), reveals a consciousness painfully suspended between negation and affirmation.

Having acknowledged "the wall" as an obstacle on the path of free activity, the hyper-conscious hero immediately casts doubt on the validity of his alibi for inaction, so suspiciously convenient is the popular excuse of natural necessity: "For us, those who think and therefore do nothing, [the wall] . . . is an excuse to turn aside from the path, an excuse in which our fellow thinker *doesn't believe himself* [predlog, v kotoryi nash brat obyknovenno *i sam ne verit*], but one for which he's always extremely grateful" (*Notes*, 7–8; *PSS*, 103). The secret, partially repressed doubt in the omnipotence of the wall also torments the conscious mouse, who lives under the fragile shield of self-created illusion, "in that *laboriously created*, yet *somewhat dubious hopelessness* of its predicament" ("v etoi *usilenno sozdannoi* i vse-taki *otchasti somnitel'noi* bezvykhodnosti svoego polozheniia") (*PSS*, 105; *Notes*, 9). But this gnawing disbelief in the omnipotence of the natural law does not translate into a wholehearted affirmation of human freedom. The conscious mouse may fantasize about revenge, but it regards its timid dreams of willful action with as much skepticism as its complacent visions of a fatalistic universe. It avenges itself timidly, stealthily, "*not believing* [*ne veria*] in its right to be revenged, nor in the success of its own revenge, and knowing in advance that from all its attempts to take revenge it will suffer a hundred times more than the object of its vengeance" (*Notes*, 9; *PSS*, 104–5). On the other hand, its human counterpart, the hyper-conscious Underground Man, confesses his flirtation with the belief in determinism when he describes his fits of debauchery as the *normal* state of affairs, perhaps dictated by the natural law: "I *almost came to believe* (*perhaps I really did believe*) [Ia *chut' ne poveril* (*a mozhet i v samom dele poveril*)] that this [depravity] might really have been my normal condition" (*Notes*, 6; *PSS*, 102).

The negative spirit of doubt contaminates all faculties of cognition, thwarting every genuine movement of faith. So great is the Underground Man's fear of everything positive, firmly rooted, and final—the qualities he perceives as epitomized by the ominous Crystal Palace—that his negation is guided by a peculiar methodology, intended to prevent any "slippages" into affirmation. Instead of the consistent and thus essentially positive *un*-belief in the determinist universe, which would signify an affirmation of personal responsibility, the Underground Man expresses a thoroughly ambiguous *dis*-belief in the supremacy of the wall, which does not imply a commitment to any positive affirmation. Because, paradoxically, only incomplete, or, so to speak, "unfinalized" negation may be thoroughly negative (in the sense that it may not engender a positive belief in the opposite value), the Underground Man's *disbelief* in the wall is necessarily half-hearted, mixed in with the superstitious fear of its menacing power. (Using Bakhtinian terminology, we may describe it as "*disbelief with a loophole.*") And it engenders an equally unstable, timid, and inconsistent *belief* in human freedom.

Thus, in his flight from the tyranny of finalization, the Underground Man constantly oscillates between negation and affirmation, living in the intermediary realm of "half-faith," "half-despair" (note the characteristic use of attenuating particles: "*polu*-otchaianie," "*polu*-vera," "*chut'* ne poveril" / "*half*-despair," "*half*-faith," "*almost* believed," etc.). This constant fluctuation between the belief in the power of human volition and the acknowledgment of impotence before the forces of necessity is comparable to the internal struggle of the man of ressentiment. The shifting modality of the Underground Man's argument often resembles that of the ressentiment discourse in its crucial phase of *revaluation of values*. Compare the following characteristic passages from *Notes from Underground*:

PASSAGE 1

Ia ne tol'ko zlym, no dazhe i **nichem ne sumel sdelat'sia**: ni zlym, ni dobrym, ni podletsom, ni chestnym, ni geroem, ni nasekomym. Teper' zhe dozhivaiu v svoem uglu, draznia sebia zlobnym i ni k chemu ne sluzhashchim utesheniem, chto umnyi chelovek i **ne mozhet** ser'ezno **chem-nibud' sdelat'sia**, a delaetsia chem-nibud' tol'ko durak. Da-s, umnyi chelovek deviatnadtsatogo stoletiia **dolzhen i nravstvenno obiazan byt' sushchestvom po preimushchestvu beskharakternym**; chelovek zhe s kharakterom, deiatel'—sushchestvom po preimushchestvu ogranichennym. Eto sorokaletnee moe ubezhdenie. (*PSS*, 100)

Not only **did I fail to become spiteful**, I failed to become anything at all: neither spiteful nor good, neither a scoundrel nor an honest man, neither a hero nor an insect. Now I live out my days in my corner, taunting myself with the spiteful and entirely useless consolation that an intelligent man **cannot** seriously **become anything** and that only a fool becomes something. Yes, sir, an intelligent man in the nineteenth century **must be and is morally obliged to be mainly a characterless creature**; while a man possessing character, a man of action, must be fundamentally a limited creature. That's my conviction at the age of forty. (*Notes*, 4)

PASSAGE 2

Mozhet byt', tol'ko **mne** odnomu vo vsei kantseliarii postoianno **kazalos', chto ia byl trus i rab**; imenno potomu i kazalos', chto ia byl razvit. No ono **ne tol'ko kazalos', a i deistvitel'no tak i bylo v samom dele: ia byl trus i rab**. Govoriu eto bez vsiakogo konfuza. Vsiakii poriadochnyi chelovek nashego vremeni **est' i dolzhen byt' trus i rab**. **Eto—normal'noe ego sostoianie**. V etom ia ubezhden gluboko. **On tak sdelan i na to ustroen**. I ne v nastoiashchee vremia, ot kakikh-nibud' tam sluchainykh obstoiatel'stv, a voobshche vo vse vremena poriadochnyi chelovek **dolzhen byt' trus i rab**. **Eto zakon prirody vsekh poriadochnykh liudei na zemle**. Esli i sluchitsia komu iz nikh pokhrabrit'sia nad chem-nibud', to pust' etim ne uteshaetsia i ne uvlekaetsia: vse ravno pered drugim sbrendit. Takov edinstvennyi i vekovechnyi vykhod. Khrabriatsia tol'ko osly i ikh ubliudki, no ved' i te do izvestnoi steny. (*PSS*, 125)

Perhaps **I** was the only one in the whole office who constantly **thought of himself as a coward and a slave**; it seemed to me this way precisely because I was so cultured. But **it didn't only seem so, it actually was so: I was a coward and a slave**. I say this without any embarrassment. Every decent man of our time **is and ought to be a coward and a slave. This is his normal condition**. I'm deeply convinced of it. **This is how he's made and what he's meant to be**. And not only at the present time, as a result of some accidental circumstance, but in general at all times, a decent man **must be a coward and a slave. This is a law of nature for all decent men on earth**. If one of them happens to put on a brave face about something or other, they shouldn't be comforted by it: he'll still lose his nerve about something else. Only jackasses and their mongrels put on a brave face, and only until they come up against a wall. (*Notes*, 30)

PASSAGE 3

. . . naslazhdenie bylo tut imenno ot slishkom iarkogo soznaniia svoego unizheniia; ottogo, chto uzh sam chuvstvuesh', chto do poslednei steny doshel; chto **i skverno eto**, no chto i **nel'zia tomu inache byt'; chto uzh net tebe vykhoda, chto uzh nikogda na sdelaesh'sia drugim chelovekom**; chto esli b dazhe i ostavalos' eshche vremia i vera, cthob peredelat'sia vo chtonibud' drugoe, to, naverno, **sam by ne zakhotel peredelyvat'sia; a zakhotel by, tak i tut by nichego ne sdelal, potomu chto na samom-to dele i peredelyvat'sia-to, mozhet byt', ne vo chto**. A glavnoe i konets kontsov, chto vse eto proiskhodit po normal'nym i osnovnym zakonam usilennogo soznaniia i po inertsii, priamo vytekaiushchei iz etikh zakonov, a sledstvenno, tut ne tol'ko ne peredelaesh'sia, da i prosto nichego ne podelaesh'. (*PSS*, 102)

. . . the pleasure resulted precisely from the overly acute consciousness of one's own humiliation; from the feeling that one had reached the last limit (literally: the last wall); that **it was bad** but that **it couldn't be otherwise; you had no other way out, you would never become a different person**; and that even if there were still time and faith enough for you to change into something else, most likely **you wouldn't even want to change**, and **if you did, you wouldn't have done anything, perhaps because there**

> **really was nothing for you to change into**. But the main thing and the final point is that all of this was taking place according to normal and fundamental laws of overtly acute consciousness and of the inertia which results directly from these laws; consequently, not only couldn't one change, one simply couldn't do anything at all. (*Notes*, 6–7)

In all three passages the narrator contemplates the notion of "becoming," of self-evaluation and self-creation in accordance with an established system of values. In each case the process of change, "peredelyvanie," is thwarted in favor of conscious inertia: the Underground Man remains a characterless slug, "sushchestvom po preimushchestvu beskharakternym" (passage 1), persists in his petty acts of depravity (passage 3), and masochistically rejoices in his reputation as "a coward and a slave" (passage 2). And, somewhat like the man of ressentiment, who confuses events conditioned by necessity with deliberate acts of will, the Underground Man makes it unclear whether the values that might have been gained through an act of "peredelyvanie" are deliberately rejected or simply remain out of reach for reasons beyond the hero's control.

The psycho-ideological progression from a belief in personal freedom and responsibility to its negation and then to a further re-conceptualization of an act of destiny as that of free choice, reflected in all three passages, is illustrated in table 1.

Notes of guilt and self-condemnation are discernable in the Underground Man's description of his nightly adventures in the Petersburg brothels (passage 3) and in the anguished confession of his own cowardice (passage 2). The use of the verb "sumet'" in passage 1 ("Ia ne tol'ko zlym, no dazhe i nichem *ne sumel* sdelat'sia" / "I *failed* to become anything at all, let alone spiteful"), which communicates a strong sense of responsibility for the success or failure of the undertaken task, also suggests that the hero's inability to attain a definable character is initially perceived as a failed opportunity rather than an impossibility. The Underground Man's wish to attain a sense of personal identity ("to become something" / "chem-nibud' sdelat'sia"), to break free from the rut of routine depravity, and to achieve a position of genuine sovereignty and power ("not to be a coward and a slave" / "ne byt' trusom i rabom") is not fulfilled. In a universe governed by free will such an outcome is interpreted in terms of personal responsibility (note the Underground Man's initial self-evaluation: ("I *failed* to become anything," *"it's bad"* / *"ne sumel* nichem sdelat'sia," *"skverno eto"*). But once the formidable theory of natural necessity is taken into account, a personal failure is immediately transformed into a predestined event ("an intelligent man simply *cannot* seriously become anything," "it *couldn't be* otherwise" etc. / "umnyi chelovek i *ne mozhet* ser'ezno chem-nibud' sdelat'sia," "i *nel'zia* tomu inache byt'" etc.). However, the most intriguing conceptual shift takes place when the hero seeks to empower himself by transforming his failures into victories through an act of psychological self-manipulation.[26] Once again, he claims responsibility for the act of "non-becoming," but now it is presented as a laudable achievement rather than a regrettable shortcoming: by so doing, the hero is said to fulfill a moral obligation to his underground conscience (see table 1, column 3). Through such a psychological shift, the very current of desire seems to be reversed: the hero no longer reproaches himself for failing to become anything ("nichem ne sumel sdelat'sia"), but rather congratulates himself on achieving the desired non-identity ([sumel nichem ne sdelat'sia]).

A reader of Scheler may be struck by a resemblance between this peculiar logic and the psychological strategy used by the man of ressentiment, as it is defined in the philosopher's analysis of Aesop's famous fable "The Fox and the Grapes" (see *Ressentiment*, 73–74). Failing to reach the much desired grapes, an object of unquestionable value, the fox leaves, having convinced itself that the grapes are sour; now its surrender is perceived not as an act of necessity but that of free will. For Scheler, this partial revaluation of values is only the beginning stage of the ressentiment process, for the fox falsifies only the value of an individual object, continuing to appreciate the general quality of "sweetness." But although the ressentiment reversal of values is complete only when the entire value structure becomes fundamentally perverted (i.e., sourness is preferred over sweetness), the fox does employ a reactive strategy of easing the tension between desire and impotence by means of the deliberate falsification of worldview. After all, the difference between the fox's cunning and a fully developed ressentiment attitude may be defined in quantitative terms: for a man of ressentiment, *all goodness* is permanently "denigrated in a massive sour grapes gambit," as David Booth puts it.[27]

If the Underground Man is to be likened to Scheler's fox, thwarted in his striving for the sweet grapes of power and socio-moral identity, it should be concluded that he rejects these highly desirable values out of sheer impotence to attain them. Indeed, in spite of the Underground Man's ostensible pride in "not becoming anything," there is a perceptible sense of frustration in the character's accounts of his pathetically uneventful, lethargic existence, governed by the laws of conscious inertia. And yet, for all their apparent similarity, the Underground Man cannot be fully identified with Scheler's fox. In order to both ascertain the specifics of the Underground Man's case and to explain *ressentiment*-like patterns in his behavior, it would, perhaps, be helpful to distinguish between different horizons of desire in Dostoevsky's novel.

When the Underground Man passionately defends his rejection of the Crystal Palace as a poor substitute for the genuine happiness of "the real Crystal Palace," in which affirmation is compatible with freedom, he

Table 1: The Modality of the Underground Man's Argument

Admission of failure "to change," "to become something," "not to be a coward and a slave" / *Acknowledgment of personal responsibility for the act of failure* (**"I could . . . but failed"**)	*Reconceptualization of failure as an act of destiny / Suspension of personal responsibility* ("**I could not**")	*Further reconceptualization of an act of destiny as that of free choice / Renewed acknowledgment of personal responsibility* ("**I could . . . but chose not to**")
PASSAGE 1 "Ia ne tol'ko zlym, no dazhe i **nichem ne sumel sdelat'sia** . . ."	"umnyi chelovek **i ne mozhet** ser'ezno **chem-nibud' sdelat'sia**, a delaetsia chem-nibud' tol'ko durak."	"umnyi chelovek deviatnadtsatogo stoletiia **dolzhen i nravstvenno obiazan byt' sushchestvom po preimushchestvu beskharakternym . . .**"
PASSAGE 3 "uzh sam chuvstvuesh', chto do poslednei steny doshel; chto **i skverno eto** . . ."	"no chto i **nel'zia tomu inache byt'** "	"uzh sam chuvstvuesh' . . . chto esli b dazhe ostavalos' eshche vremia i vera, chtob peredelat'sia vo chto-nibud' drugoe, to naverno, **sam by ne zakhotel peredelyvat'sia** . . ."
PASSAGE 2 "mne odnomu vo vsei kantseliarii postoianno **kazalos', chto ia byl trus i rab** . . ."	"No ono ne tol'ko kazalos', a i deistvitel'no **tak i bylo** v samom dele: ia byl trus i rab. **Eto normal'noe . . . sostoianie** [poriadochnogo cheloveka]. . . . On tak sdelan i na to ustroen."	"Vsiakii poriadochnyi chelovek nashego vremeni **est' i dolzhen byt' trus i rab** . . ."

expresses his irrational loyalty to the highest horizon of desire. Hence, the fact that this sublime horizon is unattainable ("so far, there is not a single building out of all you've offered at which one wouldn't want to stick out one's tongue" [*Notes*, 26; *PSS*, 120]) does not compel the Underground Man to lower his spiritual appetite to the level of the palatial "chicken coop," advertised by the proponents of utilitarian utopia. In fact, the hero

Table 2: Translation of Table 1

Admission of failure "to change," "to become something," "not to be a coward and a slave" / *Acknowledgment of personal responsibility for the act of failure* (**"I could . . . but failed"**)	*Reconceptualization of failure as an act of destiny / Suspension of personal responsibility* ("**I could not**")	*Further reconceptualization of an act of destiny as that of free choice / Renewed acknowledgment of personal responsibility* ("**I could . . . but chose not to**")
PASSAGE 1 "Not only **did I fail to become spiteful, I failed to become anything at all . . .**"	"an intelligent man **cannot** seriously **become anything** and only a fool can become something."	"an intelligent man in the nineteenth century **must be and is morally obliged to be mainly a characterless creature** . . ."
PASSAGE 3 "you feel yourself that you have reached the last limit, that **it is bad** . . ."	"but **it couldn't be otherwise** . . . "	"you know yourself . . . that even if there were still time and faith enough for you to change into something, most likely **you wouldn't want to change** . . ."
PASSAGE 2 "**it** constantly **seemed** to me . . . **that I was a coward and a slave** . . ."	"But it didn't only seem so, **it actually was so**: I **was** a coward and a slave. . . . **This is [the] normal condition** [of a decent man]. . . . This is how he's made and meant to be."	"Every decent man of our time **is and ought to be a coward and a slave** . . ."

makes it clear that, if "the true Crystal Palace" is unavailable to him, he will sooner take refuge in the underground than settle for an apartment in the crystal "tenement building." "I won't accept as the crown of my desires a large building with rooms for poor tenants to be rented for a thousand years and, just in case, with the name of the dentist Wagenheim on the sign," the Underground Man declares. "Destroy my desires, eradicate my ideals, show me something better and I'll follow you. . . . And if you don't grant me your attention, I won't beg for it. *I have my underground*" (*Notes*, 25; *PSS*, 120).

Similarly, the notes of regret in the Underground Man's admission of failure "to become anything" may be attributed to the discrepancy between reality and the supreme desire for what may be called positive finalization. Indeed, it is the highest consummation of the self, which does not limit but paradoxically expands one's freedom, possible in the true Crystal Palace, that the hero secretly longs for. This supreme horizon of desire remains out of reach, leaving the character with a number of attainable but unsatisfying alternatives. In the restrictive universe of natural laws, the only "models of becoming" available to the hero are the despised men of action and the worshippers of the sublime and the beautiful. It is these available but ultimately unacceptable identities that the Underground Man rejects when he exclaims with bitterness: "In reality, there is probably nothing worthwhile to change into" (*Notes*, 6; *PSS*, 102). Thus the Schelerian scene of the fox's striving for the grapes should be modified to include the truly sweet grapes of ultimate desire, suspended at an unreachable altitude, but still visible, at least to our extraordinarily lucid fox, above the clusters of cheap substitutes, hanging at an arm's length from the hero. The values that comprise the lower tier—those of the bull's illusory power and ignorant bliss behind the impenetrable wall of natural laws—are justly considered deficient; they are, so to speak, not worth jumping for. Here the rejected grapes *are* indeed sour.

Thus the ressentiment element in the Underground Man's behavior consists not in his distrust of the natural man's compromised values of happiness and power, as Weisberg claims in *The Failure of the Word*,[28] but rather in his capitulation before the impossibility of attaining the truly satisfying values of the "real Crystal Palace." Frustrated in his attempts to break through to the transcendent values of the higher tier and terrified by the prospect of digesting the impostor values of the lower tier by mistake, Dostoevsky's fox stops jumping altogether. He thus gives implicit acknowledgment to the natural law, which hinders him from attaining his ideal of being, that elusive "something I long for but cannot find." (Hence the significant shift from "failed to become" [*ne sumel sdelat'sia*] to "could not become" [*ne mozhet nichem sdelat'sia*].) Instead of affirming, albeit by virtue of the absurd, the sweet grapes of freedom, the Underground Man devotes all his energies to battling the opposing values of natural necessity, epitomized by the despicable "man of action." In this reactive aspect of his struggle, he resembles Nietzsche's slave, whose creative word is not the affirmation of his own deed (A is embraced as a value) but the negation of the hostile deeds of his oppressor (anti-A is rejected as a value).

Yet, the Underground Man's painful lucidity during the very process of psychological self-manipulation distinguishes him from Scheler's man of ressentiment, whose delusion eventually prevents him from any critical self-evaluation. The hero realizes that his acknowledgment of the natural law as an alibi for inaction is an unforgivable concession to the wall (hence the narrator's distrust of his own rhetoric of consolation: "Now I live out my days in my corner, *taunting myself with the spiteful and entirely useless consolation* that an intelligent man cannot seriously become anything" (*Notes*, 4; *PSS*, 100). He understands only too clearly that his underground protest, which takes the form of lucid inertia, is as ineffective in undermining the hegemony of the natural law as the bull's pretense of action. In fact, he anticipates his Nietzschean critics[29] in realizing that, by mechanically negating the enemy values, he has simply reproduced the abhorred image of the wall in reverse, creating a no less menacing ideological structure. Hence the telling similarity between the vocabulary designating the despised laws of natural necessity ("*the natural laws*" / "*zakony prirody*") and that describing the psychic processes guiding the underground protest *against* these laws ("*normal and fundamental laws* of hyper-consciousness"; "a *natural law* of all decent people" / "*normal'nye i osnovnye zakony* usilennogo soznaniia" [*Notes*, 6; *PSS*, 102]; "*zakon prirody* vsekh poriadochnykh liudei" [*Notes*, 30; *PSS*, 125], see the passages analyzed above).

Another complication introduced into the classic fable in its Dostoevskian version is that Dostoevsky's fox does periodically succumb to the temptation posed by the sour grapes. The hero passionately rejects the natural man's complacent acceptance of the natural laws, and yet he secretly envies his Olympian calm in the face of the tyrannical universe, to whose blows the "bull's" coarse hide is simply insensitive. "I'm green with envy at such a man [the son of nature]," the Underground Man confesses (*Notes*, 8; *PSS*, 104). And although the Underground Man realizes that it is precisely the "normal man's" innate blindness to the truly sweet grapes of desire that allows him to embrace his illusory power as a value, he often longs for the lasting sense of fulfillment afforded by this "natural" deficiency of vision. When the Underground Man eyes his abhorred enemy and offender, the officer, with a mixed feeling of resentment and admiration or covets the obtuse but handsome face of the popular Zverkov, he does acknowledge the rejected values on the level of desire. But these "base" longings are an expression of the lowest, least individuated level of desire, whose mimetic character is fully apparent to the Underground Man himself. The hero's momentary wish to join the mediocre majority by procuring its cherished values: obtaining the officer's petty powers or Zverkov's vulgar charms—in no way validates or redeems these fundamentally corrupt values. Indeed, no matter how much the Underground Man may wish to be in their shoes, the paltry Zverkov and his ingratiating retinue are hardly the personification of "splendor, power and happiness," as some critics have suggested.[30] To put it in terms of the Schelerian conflict, the grapes have remained sour, but the frequent attention of other foxes has inspired the Underground Man's superficial desire for them.

But, no matter how attractive the natural man's terminal bliss may seem at a moment of weakness, the Underground Man is simply incapable of sustaining the delusion for any substantial length of time: his field of vision eventually expands beyond the zone of safety, delineated by the stone wall, revealing the loftier horizons of desire and thus exposing the glaring inadequacy of the sour grapes ideal. Having thus caught himself in the act of flirting with the enemy values, the hyper-conscious hero cringes with shame, and the painful realization of his own "ideological depravity" throws him into a frenzied fit of self-loathing. The episode of the Underground Man's preparation for Zverkov's farewell dinner is a remarkable example of the hero's seduction by the paltry values of the "bulls."

Feverishly awaiting the appointed hour, the Underground Man is both terrified and intoxicated by the thought of his inevitable humiliation. He pictures the scene of the impending catastrophe with merciless precision characteristic of a masochistic consciousness, experiencing hurt well in advance. He then seeks to compensate for this anticipated injury by means of hallucinatory revenge. The unsentimental realism of his initial visions gives way to fantasy, as the hero drifts into a sweet dream of power. "I desperately wanted to prove to all this 'rabble' that I really wasn't the coward I imagined myself to be," the Underground Man confesses (*Notes*, 48; *PSS*, 141). The hero's daydream begins with a fervent attack on his offenders, but, in the heat of battle, the current of passion seems to change its direction, and the blows dealt to "all that rabble" imperceptibly turn into love caresses. As the Underground Man makes the characteristically Freudian, seamless transition from warrior to lover ("I dreamt of gaining the upper hand, of conquering them, of carrying them away, of compelling them to love me"), he casts a sideward glance at his own dream, catching himself in the very act of wooing the despicable Zverkov (*Notes*, 48; *PSS*, 141). And, in the tradition of that peculiar emotional synchrony that contributes to the piquant flavor of the underground, the hero's fantasy is accompanied, but not obliterated, by the most lucid realization of its absurdity. In the midst of his reverie, the Underground Man realizes, not on the intellectual level, but on the fundamental level of desire, that Zverkov's friendship, or even his very identity, are worthless possessions. As appealing as they may be to the superficial impulses of vanity, they are unable to satisfy the hero's deep-seated desire for that transcendent "something I long for but cannot find," which may be identified with the "true Crystal Palace": "I knew even then, I knew perfectly well and for sure that *I didn't need any of it at all*; that in fact *I didn't want* to crush them, conquer them, or attract them" (*Notes*, 48; *PSS*, 141).

The Underground Man's seduction by another set of sham values, those championed by the worshippers of "the sublime and the beautiful," triggers a similar recognition of emotional and ideological falsity on the hero's part, followed by a masochistic celebration of his fall. Just as his dream of conquering Zverkov's heart is accompanied by the realization of its mimetic character, so are the utopian visions of ready-made happiness with Liza accompanied by a shameful recognition of their obvious literary source. Like the "wooing" of Zverkov, which is not motivated by an authentic wish for his friendship, the Underground Man's wooing of Liza is divorced from the current of individual desire. Rather, his brilliantly banal plan of Liza's rescue is inspired by that highly abstract "love of mankind," nourished by the sentimental narratives of the 1840s, that is utterly "inapplicable to anything human" (*Notes*, 39; *PSS*, 133). Once again, Dostoevsky's lucid hero realizes that he has been wishing "according to a logarithm"—indeed, relying on the catalogue of literary desires proves as restricting as using the notorious table of natural laws. In this context, it is significant that the Underground Man reacts to his own fantasies of instant happiness à la George Sand with the same ideologically marked gesture he used to defy the ready-made bliss of the Crystal Palace: in the middle of his daydream the hero suddenly awakens and scornfully sticks out his tongue at his own reflection in the mirror.

> "For instance, I'd save Liza, precisely because she'd come to me, and I'd talk to her . . . I'd develop her mind, educate her. At last I'd notice that she loved me, loved me passionately. I'd pretend I didn't understand (for that matter, I didn't know why I'd pretend; most likely just for the effect). At last, all embarrassed, beautiful, trembling, and sobbing, she'd throw herself at my feet and declare that I was her savior and she loved me more than anything in the world. . . .
>
> Then we'd begin to live happily ever after, travel abroad etc., etc. In short, it began to seem despicable even to me, and I ended it all by sticking my tongue out at myself. (*Notes*, 75–76; *PSS*, 166–67)

Thus the Underground Man is occasionally tempted by the impostor values, whose deficiency he has so brilliantly exposed. But, unlike the Schelerian man of ressentiment, he does not reach the stage of "organic mendacity," when the sham values completely eclipse the values of the first order, so that the sour grapes are perceived as sweet even on the deepest level of the psychic processes. It is contrary to the hero's hyper-conscious nature that his analytic faculties should be off guard long enough for the falsification not to register on the conscious level. As a result, every recognition of emotional and ideological falsity on the hero's part becomes a new wound on his massively lacerated pride, and the moral-psychic discomfort caused by that constantly reopened lesion prevents him from reaching the unreflective state of moral complacency, associated with the "organic" phase of ressentiment.

Far from being a complacent "bull," the Underground Man becomes enslaved by the values of natural necessity in a less direct manner. As we have seen, the thoroughly negative methodology of his protest prevents him from affirming any value, even the "truly sweet" value of freedom, the longing for which propels his desperate struggle. Shestov is wrong in asserting that, having exposed the deficiency of the existing ideals, including the romantic lie about "the sublime and the beautiful," the Underground Man proceeds to create "[his] own concept of the sublime and the beautiful."[31] On the contrary, haunted by the terror of spiritual enslavement, the Underground Man directs all his energies *against* the formation of such an ideal. The vague image of "the true Crystal Palace" dimly shimmers on the horizon of his desire, against which the ludicrousness of the stone-wall "ideal" becomes immediately apparent. But this mysterious value is not affirmed on the level of faith. Thus the hero devotes his life to battling the sham values of the natural man, failing to proclaim his own credo. As a result, he honors the paltry ideal of natural necessity with his repeated acknowledgment, resembling the Nietzschean man of ressentiment, who constantly looks back at the negated value.

RESSENTIMENT AS A RHETORICAL STRATEGY

The reactive quality of the underground revolt is reflected in the peculiar narrative structure of the *Notes*. As Bakhtin insightfully pointed out, the underground narrator desperately tries to free himself from the influence of the other's consciousness, but his obsessive efforts to retain the final word in the confessional dialogue only reveal his fundamental dependency on the other's opinion (*PDP*, 229–32). The terminology used in Bakhtin's interpretation of the Underground Man's reactive discourse resonates with that employed by Nietzsche to describe the phenomenon of ressentiment. In *Beyond Good and Evil* and *Genealogy of Morals*, Nietzsche states that the subject's inability to ascribe value to himself is one of the most characteristic features of ressentiment psychology. According to Nietzsche, the man of ressentiment passively *receives* value from the all-important others, slavishly submitting to their judgment. His anguished pride relies on external props, and his envious gaze seeks to penetrate into the most private regions of the other's psyche, anxiously anticipating his judgment. Nietzsche's description of the man of ressentiment as "squinting" or "cross-eyed" ("seine Seele *schielt*")[32] seems to refer to the character's covert desire to invade another's field of vision, to catch a glimpse of himself from the other's perspective, stealing his enemy's secret weapon. "The man of *ressentiment* is never sincere nor naïf nor honest and candid with himself," Nietzsche writes. "His soul squints, his mind loves hidden crannies, tortuous paths and backdoors."[33] (Incidentally, Scheler also uses the root "Scheel—" in his discussion of ressentiment: in his study, "Scheelsucht," the impulse to detract from another's value in order to compensate for one's own spiritual bankruptcy, is described as one of the emotional preconditions of ressentiment [*GW*, 3:38].)[34] Bakhtin seems to be describing a similar phenomenon, albeit in the realm of verbal communication, when he ascribes to the underground narrator a special kind of discourse, the so-called word with a sideward glance (*slovo s ogliadkoi*), which is charged with intense anticipation of the interlocutor's response and partially reflects the listener's perspective in its double-voiced utterance. Both metaphors are used to describe a pathological duality of vision associated with the profound crisis of identity, when the fullness of the self is habitually reduced to its externally perceived image.

Nietzsche continues his disdainful portrayal of the man of ressentiment by depicting his dark dwellings: his antihero seeks out tortuous paths and dusty corners and exits inconspicuously through secret "backdoors."[35] The image of the backdoors ("Hintertüren") has sometimes been read as a metaphor for repression. But it may also be interpreted as a reference to a more conscious means of escaping external judgment when it becomes too burdensome, somewhat like Bakhtin's "loopholes" ("lazeiki"), a term coined after one of the Underground Man's colorful expressions. When Nietzsche's oppressed Jews reverse the judgment of the Gentiles by embracing their own lowly state as their greatest value, they use a psychological "emergency exit," escaping the ultimate enslavement through the back door of the ressentiment protest. Bakhtin discusses a similar problematic strategy, when he describes the Underground Man's use of "words with loopholes," which allow for the *post factum* alteration of the utterance's meaning, providing the narrator with a means of escaping the reader's finalizing judgment. Both double vision ("Scheeläugigkeit"/ "sideward glances") and the predilection for psychological backdoors ("Hintertüren"/ "loopholes") are characteristic of the Underground Man's relationship with the invariably inimical *others* in *Notes from Underground*.

Like the man of ressentiment, who perceives value only in comparative situations, the Underground Man considers "relation [to be] the selective precondition for apprehending any value" (Scheler, *Ressentiment*, 55). This habitually squinting character constantly measures himself against his fellow clerks, his schoolmates, and even the prostitute Liza, all of whom are described by means of comparative adjectives as "worse," "better," "loftier / than me." "Of course, I hated all my fellow clerks and despised every one of them, yet, at the same time I was somehow afraid of them," the Underground Man writes. "At times I would suddenly even treat them as *superior to me* [*stavil ikh vyshe sebia*]. It happened quite abruptly with me: one moment

I despised them and another I saw them as *superior to me* [*stavliu vyshe sebia*]" (*Notes*, 30; *PSS*, 125). The Underground Man's frantic oscillation between self-elevation and self-abasement is a symptom of the "Scheelsucht" pathology. With mortal anguish, the character pictures himself in another's field of vision, and then, inevitably insulted by the unsightly view revealed to his imagination, retaliates for the presumed belittling of his ego ("stav[lenie ikh] vyshe [menia]")[36] by placing himself high above the "despised" others in his own hierarchy of values.

This reactive social behavior mirrors the Underground Man's metaphysical struggle: on the social level, his desperate striving for independence from the constricting authority of "the wall" translates into an effort to free himself from the objectifying judgment of his peers, who come to personify the hated laws of nature (Compare, for example, Zverkov's description as "a man favored by the gifts of nature" [*Notes*, 42; *PSS*, 136]). A temporary (and ultimately illusory) escape from the influence of another's value judgment may be accomplished by passing a negative judgment on oneself to forestall the other's critique. "I hated them [my schoolmates] terribly," the Underground Man asserts, and, anticipating the reader's retort, concludes his utterance with a concessive clause, taking the words right out of the reader's mouth: "although, perhaps, I was *even worse than they were*" (*Notes*, 46; *PSS*, 139). Once in the character's possession, such "stolen" judgments can be easily reversed. Indeed, they are usually followed by a self-justifying remark, which reverses the original guilty verdict, providing the narrator with a convenient loophole. For instance, the pathos of self-condemnation in the Underground Man's remark: "I'm *the nastiest, most ridiculous, pettiest, stupidest, most envious* worm of all those living on earth" is undercut, just as it seems to reach its crescendo, by the very next clause: "who're *not at all better than me*, but who, the devil knows why, never get embarrassed" (*Notes*, 84; *PSS*, 174), which cancels the categorical meaning of the preceding superlatives.

This underground strategy of forestalling the other's negative judgment in order to reverse it is most apparent in the hero's manipulative game with Liza. As he begins his cynical sermon on love and compassion, only minutes after enjoying Liza's professional services, the Underground Man resorts to demonstrative self-condemnation to win the sympathy of his reluctant interlocutor. "Pay no attention to the fact that I'm here, I'm no role-model for you. *I may be even worse than you,*" the Underground Man says, only to revert to blatant self-justification in the concluding part of his double-voiced utterance: "Then again, I was drunk when I came here—*I hastened nonetheless to defend myself*'" (*Notes*, 63; *PSS*, 155). Although not immediately effective, the Underground Man's tactics eventually yield the desired results: deceived by his play at compassion, Liza accepts his severe judgment of herself, acknowledging his moral authority. And when, overwhelmed and humiliated by Liza's visit to his shabby dwelling, the hero retaliates by disclosing the unsightly motives of his psychological experiment, the mechanics of the underground power struggle become fully apparent to the reader. "I'd been humiliated, so I wanted to humiliate someone else," the Underground Man explains with merciless candor,

> I'd been treated like a rag, and I wanted to exert some power . . . That's what it was; you thought that I'd come there on purpose to save you, right? Is that what you thought? Is that it? . . . To save you?— . . . to save you from what? *Why, I may myself be worse than you*. When I recited that sermon to you, why didn't you throw it back in my face? You should have said to me, "Why did you come here? To preach morality or what?" (*Notes*, 83; *PSS*, 173).

The deficiency of the Underground Man's memory is remarkable here. In actuality, during the conversation in the brothel, Liza did not throw the all-too-obvious argument of the Underground Man's own moral bankruptcy ("you are perhaps worse than me") into his face, because he had articulated it *himself*. (Compare: Sermon in the Brothel: "Ty ne smotri na menia, chto ia zdes', ia tebe ne primer. Ia, *mozhet, eshche tebia khuzhe*"; Confession in the Underground: "*Da ia, mozhet, sam tebia khuzhe*. Chto ty mne togda zhe [etogo] ne kinula v rozhu, kogda ia tebe ratsei-to chital" [see above for translation].) Having thus usurped her judgment, he has disarmed his naive interlocutor by using her potential weapon against himself. A similar reactive strategy of using "words with a sideward glance" followed by "loopholes" is employed throughout the whole narrative against the reader, whose arguments against the major tenets of the underground philosophy are cleverly anticipated by the narrator.

A REJECTED SOLUTION: AGAPE AS A REMEDY FOR RESSENTIMENT

And yet, for all his reactive behavior, the Underground Man is not identical with the man of ressentiment described by Scheler and Nietzsche in one essential aspect. According to both Nietzsche and Scheler, ressentiment does not only cause the subject to embrace a counter-value B with the sole purpose of denigrating the hated value A, but also eventually obliterates the traces of this original motivation from consciousness, fostering a delusional belief in the intrinsically positive quality of B[37] (see Nietzsche's reflections on the origins of the Christian faith in *Genealogy of Morals* or Scheler's analysis of the apostate mentality in *Ressentiment* [66–67]). The fundamental problem of Scheler's "squinting" hero is not the fact that he estimates the relative value of things but rather that this relative value is perceived as absolute. For instance, Scheler's arriviste is utterly unconcerned with the extent of his personal accomplishment, as long as he is esteemed as *more* accomplished, happier, or more powerful than the others: for him, "better" becomes synonymous with "good" (see *Ressentiment*, 55–56).

What distinguishes the Underground Man's psychic condition from mature or "organic" ressentiment is precisely his lucidity about the provisional nature of the underground protest. As we have seen, already in his polemics against the Crystal Palace the Underground Man recognizes the *conditional* value of willful suffering as a weapon against the mandatory bliss of the "eternally indestructible building." He makes it clear that the underground is by no means a recipe for salvation but rather the only acceptable solution in the absence of the "truly sweet" values. "If you will not show me a truly satisfying ideal [i.e., the genuine Crystal Palace]," the hero in effect says to his utopian interlocutors in chapter X, "I will have to resort to the underground [i.e., the eternal negation of the false Crystal Palace]" (see *Notes*, 25; *PSS*, 120). Like the superior "values" possessed by Scheler's arriviste, the lucid inertia of the underground is, perhaps, "better" than the bull's complacent delusion of freedom behind the wall of natural laws,[38] and yet, the Underground Man refuses to absolutize the relative value of his existential position. "No, no, in any case, the underground is more advantageous!" the Underground Man begins, with somewhat exaggerated enthusiasm, but suddenly interrupts himself in mid-sentence: "At least there one can . . . Hey, but I'm lying once again! I'm lying, for I know myself, as surely as two times two, that *it isn't the underground that's better but something different, entirely different, something I long for but can't find!*" (*Notes*, 26; *PSS*, 121).

Just what is this absolute value that constitutes the supreme horizon of the Underground Man's desire is left unspecified, although we know that the original, uncensored version of the preceding chapter contained an explicit mention of the need for religious faith. The present version of chapter 11 also contains a reference to faith, although here the narrator uses the word "verit'" ("to believe") in its broader sense, as it were, emancipating it from its narrowly religious meaning. "Why, here's what would be better: if I myself were to *believe* even a fraction of everything I've written [esli b ia *veril* sam khot' chemu-nibud' iz vsego togo, chto teper' napisal]," the Underground Man exclaims in the very next paragraph (*Notes*, 26; *PSS*, 121). This inconspicuous sentence perhaps contains a better answer to the Underground Man's existential dilemma than the one provided in the original version of chapter 10, because it draws the reader's attention to the tragic implications of faithlessness in the most secular spheres of human experience without forcing the underground narrator into the unlikely role of a religious propagandist. The first part of the utterance ("here's what would be better: if I myself were to *believe* [esli b ia *veril*"]) may be read as the hero's diagnosis of his own spiritual malady—that of the fundamental crisis of affirmation, which affects every aspect of his underground existence. With admirable subtlety, the author suggests that the unattainable "something" the Underground Man desperately needs is faith, not in the narrow sense of "allegiance to a religious doctrine," but rather faith as the fundamental capacity for affirmation. Victim to his own thoroughly negative ideology, the hero finds it impossible to believe in the sanctity of his own right to protest ("[the hyperconscious mouse] *doesn't believe* in its own right to revenge nor in the success of its revenge" [*Notes*, 9; *PSS*, 104–5]), in the truth-value of the underground rhetoric ("*I don't believe* a single word, not one word of what I've just scribbled!" [*Notes*, 26; *PSS*, 121]), or in the authenticity of his own suffering ("In the depths of your soul *you don't believe* that you are suffering; there is a stir of mockery, and yet you do suffer, and in the most real way" [*Notes*, 12; *PSS*, 108]). And yet he realizes, with tragic lucidity, that only the wholehearted affirmation of his freedom on the level of belief, incompatible with the negative essence of the underground doctrine, could endow his protest with meaning.

If in part 1 the author merely hints at the meaning of "the true Crystal Palace," in part 2 the question of the transcendent value, capable of affecting the hero's spiritual resurrection from the underground, is answered in no uncertain terms in the story of Liza's unconditional love for the Underground Man. In an uncharacteristically positive, single-voiced passage, the hero acknowledges the redemptive quality of Liza's feeling, even as he fails to reciprocate it:

> She [Liza] had come not to hear "the words of pity" at all but to love me, because it's in that kind of love that a woman finds her resurrection [*voskresenie*], all her salvation from whatever kind of ruin, and her rebirth [*vozrozhdenie*], as it can't appear in any other form. (*Notes*, 86; *PSS*, 176)

The notion of resurrection—"voskresenie," "vozrozhdenie"—suggests a spiritual leap upward from a depth, evoking the haunting image of the underground, which has been consistently associated with both the hero's and Liza's symbolic space.[39] Liza's deeply affirmative love becomes a means of emerging from the spiritual underground, a channel leading to "zhivaia zhizn'," suddenly opened before the befuddled hero, but eventually rejected by him.

Scheler, who seems to be Dostoevsky's intellectual kinsman, proposes essentially the same remedy for the pathology of reactive behavior. In

Ressentiment and *The Nature of Sympathy*, he places Christian love, agape, on the opposite end of the spiritual spectrum from ressentiment. Love in the service of ressentiment is merely a trump card against a hated thing, Scheler writes. When an apostate rapturously embraces his new faith, his fervid passion is directed not toward the newly elected values but rather toward his old beliefs, whose denigration becomes the primary purpose of his conversion: A is "loved" to offset B. Scheler complements Nietzsche's classic example of ressentiment "love" for one's abject *self* in order to turn away from the hated and secretly desired *other* (the slave's sublime revenge against the master) with an example of the equally reactive "love" for the *other* with the secret intention of turning away from one's own hated and spiritually impoverished *self*. "Turning toward others is but the secondary consequence of this urge to flee from oneself," Scheler writes. "This love is not directed at a previously discovered positive value, nor does any such value flash up in the act of loving: there is nothing but the urge to turn away from oneself and to lose oneself in other people's business" (*Ressentiment*, 95). Unlike this fundamentally negative, reactive feeling, agape is an expression of absolute affirmation. Its open gaze, immediately directed at the beloved object, is quite different from the squinting countenance of ressentiment. As Anders Nygren puts it, "*agape* love is directed to the neighbor himself, with no further thought in mind and no side-long glances at anything else."[40] Modeled on Christ's sacrificial love, agape is not motivated by a coveted value, as is its Hellenic counterpart, eros, but itself constitutes the highest possible value. We shall recall that for Scheler, after Christ's revolutionary sacrifice, "the summum bonum" is no longer the value of a thing but of a deed, "the value of love itself as love, and not its results and achievements" (*Ressentiment*, 87). Not only does agape not depend on the recognition of a valuable quality in its object, but value is continually created in the act of loving (*GW*, 7:156, 160).

In his analysis of the agape formula, "love thy neighbor *as* thyself," Scheler discusses the crucial balance in the relationship between self and other, touching upon a number of ethical issues also central in Dostoevsky's work. Unlike Nietzsche, who sees in the nineteenth-century altruism an apotheosis of Christianity, Scheler denounces the contemporary egalitarian ethic as a dangerous misinterpretation of the message of Christian love, which leads to *ressentiment*. According to Scheler, standing before the depersonalized global *other*, the socialist altruist has replaced the living object of his love with a faceless "entity." His motto, the corrected version of Christ's message: "love thy neighbor *more* than thyself," may engender nothing but escapist "love" of otherness for the sake of otherness, with which he desperately tries to conceal his abhorrence of his own self, Scheler argues. The inability to appreciate the integrity of one's own self, to experience the vital potential of one's own "*I*," revealed only through an act of "loving myself," ultimately results in the objectification of the *other*. "If I am not worthy of love, why should the 'other' be?" Scheler asks. "As if he were not also an 'I' for himself and I another for him?" (*Ressentiment*, 125). And conversely, the replacement of the other's unfinalized individual self with an objectified "social personality" or type, characteristic of the altruist "love" for the poor, the downtrodden, and the unfortunate, inevitably undermines the sovereignty of the "I." Only through agape does genuine subjectivity emerge, inducing the revelation of that inexpressible essence of individuality in both the lover and the beloved that Scheler calls "*Individual Ineffable*" (*GW*, 7:136).

Scheler's analysis of self-evaluation in both ressentiment "love" and agape is highly relevant to our discussion of the concept of selfhood in *Notes from Underground*. We have seen how the Underground Man's objectification of the global *other* threatens his own zealously guarded sense of subjectivity. The officer, Zverkov, and the Underground Man's nameless colleagues and clients all wear the uniforms of easily identifiable social types, which deny them any sense of individuality, let alone the revelation of the *individual ineffable*. Liza is the only "other" in the Underground Man's narrative whose individuality shines through the constricting shell of her "social personality." But his relationship with the heroine is terminated at the very moment when her spontaneous movement of love affects a transcendence of the fixed codes of behavior attributed to "that sort of woman." By paying for Liza's visit in the tale's finale, the hero attempts to reverse the individualizing effects of agape, interpreting Liza's deeply personal gesture of compassion as a prostitute's service call. But the arrows of objectification, aimed at others, return to the Underground Man like boomerangs. In his quest to become the only subject in the mute world of human objects, he disregards the law of reciprocity between giving and receiving freedom, attempting to establish a monopoly on selfhood. But his futile attempts to crystallize the essence of subjectivity in his own person by utterly separating himself from the others only demonstrate the fundamentally social nature of the self, its threshold location between the "I for myself" and the "I for another."

Far from liberating himself from another's authority by constructing a grotesquely flat, objectified image of his neighbor, the Underground Man is haunted by the fear of his reciprocal, equally depersonalizing gaze. As we have seen, the Underground Man's humiliating self-abasement under the gaze of his colleagues is but the reverse side of his own objectifying judgment of others. Similarly, in his romance with Liza, whose unconditional love offers an alternative to the stifling symmetry of reactive relationships, the hero is unable to separate his self-image as *a beloved* from the slavish image he himself projects on his erotic object as *a lover*. As Wasiolek insightfully points out, the Underground Man can receive love and pity "only as he has given them"—as a sophisticated weapon in the struggle for power, a means of gaining the upper hand over the pitied *object*.[41]

In the Underground Man's utterly abstract "love of mankind," which inspires his literary romance with "the fallen woman," Dostoevsky ridicules the same ressentiment altruism that comes under a sharp attack in Scheler's work. Like the Schelerian altruist, the Underground Man uses the utopian dream of all-encompassing love, "stolen from the poets and novelists [of the 1840s]," to conceal the painful sensation of homelessness within his own pathologically fragmented self. Here, love for the universal other is merely a means of disguising a deep-seated feeling of self-loathing, an escape into the salutary space of elsewhere: a "[salvation] through the sublime and the beautiful" ("[spasenie] vo vse prekrasnoe i vysokoe") (*Notes*, 39; *PSS*, 133). Directed away from the self, in search of the ultimate elsewhere, the underground love flows past its alleged objects, loving only the impenetrable otherness of the beloved and embarking for a more distant goal as soon as she reveals her individual essence at a moment of intimacy, as it happens with Liza. Anticipating Ivan Karamazov, who will realize that the more he loves the anonymous humanity, the less he loves his neighbor,[42] the Underground Man admits that his "fantastic" love of the world is simply "inapplicable" to any specific human object ("[love] that in practice has never been applied to anything human" / "nikogda ni k chemu chelovecheskomu na dele ne prilagavsh[aia]sia [liubov']" [*Notes*, 39; *PSS*, 133]).

Like the notorious philosophy of "the sublime and the beautiful," in which the Underground Man locates the source of his objectless "love," the hero's "compassion" toward Liza deserves to be put in quotation marks. The reactive nature of his psychological assault on the heroine is fully apparent: in Liza, the insulted hero finds a target for his displaced aggression against Zverkov. Thus, in Schelerian terms, the primary significance of the Underground Man's gesture is not in *turning toward Liza* but in *turning away* from the discomforting reality of his own shameful humiliation before Zverkov and his cronies. A telling detail at the beginning of the brothel scene demonstrates the arbitrary nature of the underground aggression, also characteristic of ressentiment violence. Having realized that his offenders left before his arrival at the brothel, and so the ultimate confrontation has been happily avoided, the character breathes a sigh of relief. He even experiences a sudden rush of power as he approaches a brothel girl, when he notices a mirror reflection of his own "utterly abject" face, distorted by cowardly joy, and maliciously congratulates himself on reaching the ultimate limit of depravity: "I happened to glance in a mirror. My overwrought face appeared extremely repulsive: it was pale, spiteful, mean and with disheveled hair. 'Good, I'm glad,' I thought. 'In fact, I'm especially glad that I'll seem so repulsive to her [Liza]" (*Notes*, 59; *PSS*, 151). Here a masochistic impulse

("[*I* am repulsive]—good, I'm glad") immediately turns into a sadistic one ("I'm especially glad that I'll seem repulsive to *her*"), as self-laceration becomes a means of assaulting others.

The hero's aggressive preaching to Liza is another exercise at turning his own acute sense of injury into a sophisticated weapon against his interlocutor. Insulted and humiliated by Zverkov, the Underground Man finds momentary relief in the compensatory aggression of sex, but, roused from his post-coital stupor by the prostitute's hostile stare, the hero is rudely awakened from his dream of power. Newly wounded both by Liza's silent defiance of his authority and by the gnawing sensation of guilt under her censuring gaze, he challenges himself to secure a complete victory over the "young soul," to force emotional intimacy where physical intimacy was forced an hour earlier. The tactics employed in pursuit of this goal vary from soft-spoken pleading (the sugary sermon on love in the tone of sentimental novels) to overt intimidation (the grim prophecy of Liza's death in the slums of Petersburg made in the graphic style of naturalism).

In what may be interpreted as the Underground Man's parody of the Sermon on the Mount, the hero mocks all of the essential values of active love, agape: its spontaneity, its fundamentally affirmative tone, and its creative disregard for the empirical value of its object. When the Underground Man delivers his didactical tirades on the dangers of a negative worldview, the profound divergence between the preached values and the preacher's own thoroughly negative existential position results in powerful ironic tension. "As long as there's love, one can live even without happiness. Even in sorrow life is good; it's good to be alive, no matter what befalls you," the Underground Man remarks sententiously, as if mimicking the authoritative voice of his own critics (*Notes*, 63; *PSS*, 155). He continues to dispense his ready-made wisdom, amusing his readers by his pseudo-affirmative tone: "There's something else, Liza. Man only likes to count his troubles; he doesn't calculate his happiness. If he figured as he should, he'd see that everyone gets his share" (*Notes*, 65; *PSS*, 157). The courageous optimism of agape, the joyful certainty of its voice, grounded in the absolute affirmation of the beloved object, is here turned into an empty form and used as a means of psychological entrapment.

The value-creating role of love is also mocked in the Underground Man's hypocritical sermon. If ressentiment love is "love for the sake of" a coveted value, agape is fundamentally unconcerned with the objective value of the beloved. The gaze of true agape is directed at the beloved's potential, penetrating beyond the limiting boundaries of the empirical realm and liberating the beloved from the objectifying effects of her finalized social image. By sharing his "surplus of vision" with the beloved, the lover inspires her faith in her yet unrealized potential, inducing her self to grow. In the first part of *The Idiot* such is Myshkin's influence on Nastasia Filippovna, whose self-esteem seems to benefit from the Prince's "surplus of vision." When, in response to Totsky's efforts to sell her to the highest bidder, Nastasia Filippovna scandalizes her offenders by deliberately parading her status of a "kept woman" in front of the Ivolgin family, Myshkin exclaims with reproach: "You are not the sort of woman you pretend to be!" ("Razve vy *takaia*, kakoiu teper' predstavlialis'!") (*PSS*, 8:99), and his faith in "the other," magnanimous and high-minded Nastasia affects a genuine, if short-lived, change in the masochistic heroine. At first glance, the Underground Man's assertion that Liza's employment at the brothel must have been an involuntary one, because she is "not that sort of woman" ("a *girl like you* wouldn't come here of her own free will" [*Notes*, 64] / "*takaia* devushka, kak ty, verno, ne s okhoty svoei siuda popadet" [*PSS*, 156]) may seem to be of the same order as Myshkin's compassionate utterance. But, as is often the case in Dostoevsky, the external similarity only sharpens the profound contrast between the two statements. While Myshkin's reproach is inspired by his irrational knowledge of Nastasia Filippovna's inner "I," revealed to him in the act of loving, the Underground Man possesses no insight into Liza's *individual ineffable*; he merely tries to provoke the heroine's emotional intimacy by claiming the knowledge of her private self. It is not surprising that his manipulative remark meets with distinct, if timid, protest on Liza's part: "*What kind* of girl am I?" ("Kakaia *takaia* ia devushka?")—she whispers uncomfortably, resenting the stranger's attempt to "peer into her soul" (*Notes*, 64; *PSS*, 156).

If Myshkin's compassion is grounded in his staunch belief in Nastasia Filippovna's capacity for change, the Underground Man's empathy with Liza is fundamentally passive; it is directed not at liberating her individual "I" from the objectifying influence of her social image, nor at saving her from the banal fate awaiting "that sort of woman," but rather at perpetuating the existing status quo. Indeed, it is consistent with the Underground Man's thoroughly negative worldview that he is simply incapable of using positive concepts, even as tools in a power game: as he fails to move Liza with his mediocre sermon on love, he opts for a much more familiar strategy of emotional laceration. To awaken Liza's emotional response, the underground masochist can now utilize his exceptional capacity for cultivating one's sense of injury, perfected by years of conscious self-wounding. As a result, unlike the ready-made images of familial bliss in his lifeless sermon, his "scenes from the life of a prostitute" are both emotionally poignant and artistically powerful, for here the depiction of suffering is animated by the delicious memory of the underground author's own injuries, often no less fictional than the ones featured in his tale.

Both terrified and inspired by the hero's apocalyptic preaching, Liza does not realize that the underground dweller has no stake in her resurrection: the proponent of "soznatel'noe slozha-ruki-sidenie" has as little interest in affecting her spiritual transformation as he does in "becoming something" or in achieving closure after an emotional trauma. Under the guise of "tough love" he merely lacerates Liza's wounds. Both sharpening her sensitivity to pain ("There is no greater insult for a girl, don't you understand?" [*Notes*, 68; *PSS*, 159]) and emphasizing the inevitability of her tragic fate ("Don't you see that you'll end up just the same [as the dying prostitute from Haymarket Square]?" [*Notes*, 69; *PSS*, 160]), he seems to be preparing her for a life of lucid inertia in a totalitarian universe, where every injury is an insult, and insults can be neither prevented nor forgotten. "And won't it be better if she carries away the insult with her forever?" the Underground Man exclaims upon Liza's final departure: "An insult, after all, is purification; it's the most caustic and painful form of consciousness" (*Notes*, 87; *PSS*, 177). The unfading memory of one's own humiliation, the unforgiving consciousness of pain and the insatiable impulse to injure, which feeds on one's own anguished pride in the absence of an available external target—such is the notorious legacy of the underground education.

In the closing scene, the hypocrisy of the hero's earlier phrase: "You are not that sort of woman," which epitomizes the underground sympathy, becomes fully apparent, for his final gesture—that of paying Liza for her "professional" visit—communicates precisely the opposite: "You *are* that sort of woman! In fact, to me, you can never be anything else but *that sort of woman*!" As the Underground Man struggles with the painful feeling of guilt for his transgression against love, he consoles himself with yet another determinist excuse—the fact that he is "by nature" incapable of loving anything but the sweet sensation of power over another being. Not unlike the "squinting" man of ressentiment, the hero finds *relative* value in his despicable deed: his hurtful gesture has liberated Liza from the tyranny of his oppressive will, whose long-term effects on her spiritual being would prove much more damaging than this single destructive blow. As unsatisfying as this explanation may seem from the point of view of the philosophy of agape, it foregrounds an important implication of the underground worldview: since Dostoevsky's hero can conceive only of a negative freedom *from* others, the only freedom he can grant others is the equally negative freedom *from* himself.

Thus the Underground Man emerges from our analysis as a character whose psychological makeup is similar to, but not fully identical with, that of the man of ressentiment. Like the tactics of "the sublime revenge," the strategy of the underground revolt is essentially reactive, for no affirmative movement toward an intrinsically positive value underlies the hero's negation. Like the man of ressentiment, the Underground Man is engaged in an uneven and emotionally exhausting battle with the values of his ideological opponents, but his rejection of the "bull's" illusory power or the totalitarian happiness of the Crystal Palace is motivated not by sheer impotence to attain these socially validated "goods," but by the fully justified belief in their deficiency. Nevertheless, in the absence of an intrinsically meaningful ideal, the negated values attain primary status—indeed, not the affirmation of the true Crystal Palace but the rejection of its powerful impostor becomes the Underground Man's creative deed. Paraphrasing Scheler, we may say that the underground protest is laden with ressentiment in as much as any negative existential strategy that ascribes creative power to sheer negation is laden with ressentiment.

Unlike the Schelerian hero, the Underground Man never enters the final, "organic" stage of the ressentiment process, when the *conditional quality* of the provisionally affirmed values (such as the conditional value of the slave's suffering embraced as an antithesis of the master's abhorred happiness) is no longer transparent to the subject. As we have seen, the ultimate goal of "the sublime revenge"—the complete "naturalization" of the reversed value system, can never be achieved in the case of the hyperconscious hero, who remains lucid about the relative value of his protest. Thus, for the Underground Man, the tension between impotence and desire is never completely relieved, as it is for the natural man, who elevates the necessary (the laws of nature) to the level of the ideal (the stone-wall "ideal") without much reflection and remains blissfully unconcerned about this obvious falsification of values. On the other hand, the very lucidity of the Underground Man's vision becomes a prop for his injured pride, paraded as the measure of the hero's superiority over the "duped" others. Having congratulated himself on his lucid assessment of the wall's authority, the Underground Man is soon overcome with self-loathing, painfully ashamed of his own complacency, only to celebrate this new lucidity about the alleged lucidity a moment later, and so on ad infinitum. Dostoevsky's bitterly conscious hero is thus forever suspended in the first, caustic, stage of ressentiment, during which self-consciousness is indissolubly linked with suffering, for the self is experienced precisely as the painful locus of unfreedom.

As we have seen, in the absence of an intrinsically meaningful ideal underlying the Underground Man's protest, his struggle, which amounts to the painfully ineffective "bumping duel" with the stone wall of natural necessity, is propelled by the negative energy of despair. And yet, paradoxically, it is this vaguely delineated ideal, experienced by the character as a palpable void, that is accountable for the intense emotional torment of the underground, because its very existence, albeit beyond the realm of the empirically possible, forever "sours" the enjoyment of the natural man's "grapes" for the spiritually anguished hero. The ideal in question is that murky and elusive concept of Christian love that transcends the normative ethics of the Law, the ideal that is never fully attainable, for it is "contrary to man's nature," as Dostoevsky's notebook of 1864 tells us (*PSS*, 20:175). Unlike the fulfillment of the Law, whose prescriptive ethic aims at the achievement of moral satisfaction, the uncertain path of *imitatio Christi* may lead to ressentiment, if the striving for the unattainable, "non-Euclidean" ideal of agape is not grounded in faith. In this context, it is possible to read *Notes from Underground* as an early statement of the problem of Christian freedom in Dostoevsky's work, an interpretation that links the Underground Man's confession with Ivan's monologue and the Legend of the Grand Inquisitor in *The Brothers Karamazov*.[43]

The Underground Man's existential despair, fraught with ressentiment, epitomizes the fate of a consciousness unable to break through to the sublime ideal of Christ but equally incapable of finding spiritual solace in a world forever transformed by its exposure to his perplexing truth. His predicament is in some ways akin to that of the ressentiment-ridden Grand Inquisitor, a man unwilling to affirm Christ's "pitiless" ideal of freedom on the level of faith but also incapable of expelling the haunting memory of Christ, whose image is a tormenting presence in his life. Tormented by the idea of the "true Crystal Palace," the Underground Man reaches for the values of underground "freedom" and ressentiment "love" for the abstract *other*, only to realize that these are but shabby substitutes for that transcendent "something I long for but cannot find": without faith he can apprehend this majestic ideal only as a tangible absence. Like the "Pro and Contra" book of *The Brothers Karamazov*, *Notes from Underground* turns our attention to the "costs" of the Christian ideal: in a world exposed to the ultimate horizon of desire through Christ, those lacking the serenity of faith may be doomed to the torment of ressentiment.

Chapter Four

Dialogues on the Scaffold: *Notes from the House of the Dead* and *The Idiot*

> He [was] grateful for the world which purposefully puts divisions in place so that we can overcome them, feeling the joy of getting closer, even if deep down we can never forget the sadness of our insurmountable differences.
> —Nicole Krauss, *The History of Love*

"ANOTHER'S SOUL IS SHROUDED IN DARKNESS": OPTICAL ILLUSIONS IN *NOTES FROM THE HOUSE OF THE DEAD*

The "dialogical challenge" posed in *Notes from Underground*, whose hero makes an interlocutor indispensable to his very existence but denies him the status of ultimate, ontic reality, is answered by Dostoevsky's Christlike characters. They become practitioners of active empathy, whose communicative efforts do not threaten the subjects' sovereignty but result in spiritual growth and renewal. In *Notes from the House of the Dead* and *The Idiot*, temporary but significant victories of active empathy counterbalance the acts of underground aggression aimed at sabotaging any meaningful form of human togetherness. Here the process of spiritual self-refinement by means of a dialogical interaction with others, initiated by the self-searching convict Goryanchikov in *Notes from the House of the Dead* and by the Christlike Prince Myshkin in *The Idiot*, becomes an alternative to the monological closure of the self manifested in egoistic self-assertion, on the one hand, and masochistic self-abasement on the other. The intensification of vision brought about by this process and experienced as a revelation takes place in the eschatological world of last things and is conditioned by a special scaffold temporality in both novels.

An inmate in a Siberian prison, the hero of *Notes from the House of the Dead* (hereafter, *House of the Dead*) finds himself in a situation of extreme isolation—forced from his home and severed from his social ties. Indeed, the theme of estrangement receives religious overtones in the novel. The prison is portrayed as the mythical underworld, the domicile of the dead, whose ghostly inhabitants gaze at the realm of the living with insatiable longing:

> Beyond these gates lay the bright, free world, where people lived like everybody else. But on this side, that world seemed like an impossible fairy-tale. Here was our own peculiar world, unlike anything else at all; here were our own peculiar laws, our own dress, our own morals and customs, a house of the living dead, a life such as lived nowhere else, and people set apart. (*House of the Dead*, 7; *PSS*, 9)[1]

When Goryanchikov's fellow-convict, the erudite peasant Petrov, asks him: "Don't they say that people [in America] go about head downwards?" (*House of the Dead*, 122; *PSS*, 8:84), the reader is tempted to interpret the question metaphorically, for in relation to the chthonic anti-world of the prison, where all normal relationships are said to be reversed, everybody in the realm of the living would seem to walk "head downwards." Indeed, the prison is a special world located on the very edge of inhabited space and opposed to it, but Goryanchikov is "set apart" not only from the world beyond prison walls, but also from his fellow inmates, the forced inhabitants of the dead house. As a member of the nobility in a prison predominantly populated with peasant convicts, Goryanchikov is an exile among exiles, a constant target of abuse by the convicts of the lower class:[2]

> The prison in general regarded former members of the nobility with resentment and ill will. In spite of the fact that they had been deprived of all the rights of their position and reduced to complete equality with the others, the prisoners never recognized them as their fellows. This was not a result of conscious prejudice but happened quite simply, genuinely, and unaware. They sincerely acknowledged that we were gentlemen, even though they liked to taunt us with our fall. . . . They watched our sufferings, which we tried not to show them, with delight. (*House of the Dead*, 32; *PSS*, 26)

As a natural object of this impersonal, innate, and almost unconscious loathing, the erstwhile revolutionary and folk-lover Goryanchikov has no choice but to retreat into his protective silence, shunning any personal contact with peasant convicts and watching his tormenters with squeamish curiosity. In the beginning of the notes, the radical division between Goryanchikov and "them" is manifested in the narrator's selective use of personal pronouns. The peasant convicts are perceived as a powerful and awe-inspiring unity, as a "we" opposed to Goryanchikov's solitary "I": "'*We* are educated folks,' they often said, with a certain strange smugness" (*House of the Dead*, 11; *PSS*, 12); "'*We* are beaten folks,' they said; 'the insides have been beaten out of us; that is why we call out at night'" (*House of the Dead*, 18; *PSS*, 16); "'*We* are a lost people,' they said; 'we did not know how to live in freedom'; now it is: 'Break the green street and line up in the court yard!'" (*House of the Dead*, 13; *PSS*, 13). Goryanchikov can perceive this unity only from the outside; he cannot merge his voice with other voices in the choral "we" of the prisoners. In opposition to the collective "we" of the peasant convicts, the depersonalizing "we" is used to address Goryanchikov by his manservant. The ever-downtrodden Sushilov, Goryanchikov's voluntary lackey, consistently addresses him in the first-person plural: "He never said, for example, 'You have so many shirts; your jacket is torn,' and so on, but always: '*We* have so many shirts now; *our* jacket is torn' (*House of the Dead*, 83; *PSS*, 58). This condescendingly sympathetic "we," the only "we" uttered by a peasant convict in which Goryanchikov is included, mocks the very idea of unified plurality. It is a "we" that betrays involuntary and perhaps unconscious condescension of a servant to his helpless master, whose inferiority in matters of real importance, that is, in matters of survival, the servant realizes.

The mutually acknowledged equality of the participating parties, necessary for a true dialogue, is impossible between Goryanchikov and the peasant convict, who passionately hates and joyfully torments his erstwhile oppressor but nevertheless never ceases to regard him as a member of a higher class, as if the defiance of this largely nominal authority were the ultimate taboo that even the most fearless of the convicts dared not violate. ("They sincerely acknowledged that we were gentlemen, even though they liked to taunt us with our fall" [*House of the Dead*, 32; *PSS*, 26].) In relation to Goryanchikov, the peasant convict always appears in one of his two roles: as a persecutor of his class enemy, a vengeful master of his former master (Gazin), or as a voluntary servant (Sushilov, Petrov, Chekunov), both of which exclude any possibility of a close personal relationship. Thus the "we" of the convicts remains outside of Goryanchikov's field of communication; excluded from dialogical exchange, it becomes a monological "they." Indeed, surrounded by two hundred enemies, Goryanchikov could aptly describe his metaphysical situation using the Underground Man's statement of ultimate despair: "I am alone and *they are everyone*!"

But instead of scornfully ignoring the members of "the human herd," as the Underground Man does, Goryanchikov attempts to gain an understanding of the peasant convict, to penetrate his psyche in search of that innate source of spiritual health that enables him to bear his suffering with such admirable dignity. Throughout the memoirs, we often catch a glimpse of Goryanchikov the observer, eagerly absorbing the impressions of prison life, his scrutinizing gaze focused on the faces of the convicts around him, as if it could magically unlock their souls:

> "The House of the Dead!" I would say to myself sometimes as I watched, from the steps of our barrack, the prisoners, returned from work, lazily slouching about the prison yard in the dusk, from the barracks to the kitchen and back again. Watching them, I tried to discover from their faces and their movements what sort of people they were and what their characters were like. (*House of the Dead*, 99; *PSS*, 69)

Goryanchikov often sneaks a greedy peek at the unsuspecting convicts who escape to the stockade in search of privacy: "Here behind the buildings, some of the prisoners, the most unsociable and moody, liked to walk when they were not working, hidden from other eyes and thinking their own thoughts. . . . I liked to look at their sullen, branded faces and guess at their thoughts" (*House of the Dead*, 8; *PSS*, 9). At the prison hospital, Goryanchikov secretly watches a fellow patient battling insomnia, trying to imagine the workings of his mind: "Somebody, unable to sleep, would get up and sit for an hour and a half on his bed, with his night-capped head bent as if in thought. In an effort to kill time somehow, you would watch him for a whole hour, trying to guess what he was thinking of" (*House of the Dead*, 253; *PSS*, 165). Such intense, almost obsessive scrutiny of his fellow-sufferers, in an effort to uncover, at all costs, secret thoughts and smothered feelings that live a ghostly life behind the impenetrable exterior, could hardly be a mere exercise at "killing time somehow." Goryanchikov's desire to "peer into the souls" of his fellow inmates is a part of his search for truth, a search for a living soul in the house of the dead.[3]

When Goryanchikov suddenly wakes up in the middle of the night, reacting to the familiar sight of the prison barrack with the intensity of a first-time observer, he peers at his sleeping mates with doubled attention, trying to persuade himself of the reality of the nightmarish vision:

> I lifted my head in terror and looked round at my sleeping companions by the dim wavering light of the cheap prison candle. I looked at their pale faces, their wretched beds, at all that hopeless misery and beggary, *peering as closely as though I must make certain that all this was not the continuation of an ugly dream, but the real truth.* But it was the truth . . . . (*House of the Dead*, 198; *PSS*, 130)

According to Goryanchikov, only the real truth could withstand his ultimate stare-test, but he clearly overestimates the lucidity of his own vision. Goryanchikov is indeed awake, but what he sees around him is not "the truth" and certainly not "the real truth." The older, spiritually more mature narrator acknowledges the limitations of his vision during his first months in prison:

> Even though I looked at everything with such earnest and avid attention, yet, I could not distinctly see much of what lay under my very nose. Naturally, what struck me at first were the more sharply outstanding aspects, those on a large scale, but even these, perhaps, produced a mistaken impression on me, and they left behind in my soul only a feeling of oppression and hopeless melancholy. (*House of the Dead*, 89; *PSS*, 62)

Goryanchikov "did not penetrate to the inner depths of prison life" not only because his initial bitterness and melancholy considerably limited his perspective, as Jackson rightly points out,[4] but also because his understanding of the prisoners was strictly monological. Goryanchikov observes his fellow convicts secretly and silently—asleep or preoccupied with their daily troubles, they are unaware of his scrutinizing stare. His is a stolen look, a look that does not expect a look back and, perhaps, would not be able to withstand the challenge of such a contesting look. And the truth that is revealed as a result of such observation is a stolen truth; it is not enriched by the truth of the convict about himself, not contested dialogically; in a word, it is only half-truth.

To Goryanchikov's initial impulse "to peer into another's soul," the narrator of "The Peasant Marey," Dostoevsky's fable-like account of his conversion experience in prison published in *A Writer's Diary* for 1876, opposes the truth of the old Russian folk saying. "Chuzhaia dusha potemki" ("Another's soul is shrouded in darkness"). A childhood memory of a saintly peasant Marey who had once consoled him at a moment of distress with truly paternal compassion becomes a source of moral strength for the mature Dostoevsky, inspiring his belief in the peasant convict. "Through some sort of miracle," the narrator's former hatred and bitterness against his tormentors disappears, giving way to a feeling of hope, which stubbornly refuses to retreat before the terrifying reality of prison life. Another, timeless, truth now shimmers behind the empirical truth visible to the eyes. Looking at his newly resurrected fellow prisoners, the autobiographical narrator of "The Peasant Marey" no longer puts his faith in the lucidity of his vision: "I went off, *peeping intently into the faces of those I met.* This disgraced peasant, with shaven head and brands on his cheek, drunk and roaring out his hoarse, drunken song—why, he might also be that very same Marey; *I cannot peer into his heart, after all*" (*A Writer's Diary*, hereafter *WD*, 355; *PSS*, 22:49).[5]

The existence of Marey, however distant from reality this symbolic image may be, is the only proof Dostoevsky's autobiographical narrator needs to justify his hopeful vision of the peasant convict. He learns to believe in spite of the visible evidence of the contrary repeatedly presented to his eyes, to suspend judgment, and to avoid abstract psychologizing that gratifies the impulse to peer into another's soul. The narrator's newly found credo: "another's soul is shrouded in darkness" ("chuzhaia dusha potemki") does not mean that any revelation of another's soul is impossible; rather, it serves to protect the sovereignty of human consciousness from the monologically objectifying, finalizing glances from without. Indeed, for Dostoevsky, an authentic revelation of human personality is necessarily an active, dialogical one, as we shall be able to show later.

MYSHKIN'S CURSE OF LUCIDITY: *VZHIVANIE* IN *THE IDIOT*

A similar discussion of the sovereignty of another's soul (*chuzhoi dushi*) takes place in *The Idiot*. Replying to Rogozhin's question about his faith, Prince Myshkin tells him a number of rather puzzling parables demonstrating the problematic potential of the Russian people, which realizes itself now in saintly acts of compassion, now in unspeakable acts of cruelty. In Myshkin's tale, the images of human depravity—a peasant who murders his friend for a silver watch and a drunken soldier who sells his cross to Myshkin—are counterbalanced by the image of a young peasant woman whose profound understanding of Christian love makes a powerful impression on the Prince. Her iconized image illuminates Myshkin's vision of Russia much like the recollection of Marey illuminates the murky world of the Siberian prison in "The Peasant Marey." Humbled by that spontaneous expression of the people's religiosity, Myshkin suspends his judgment of the drunken soldier who has so easily parted with his cross: "I mustn't be too quick to condemn a man who has sold his Christ! *Only God knows what is locked away in these weak and drunken hearts* . . . . Who knows, perhaps she [the young peasant woman] was the wife of that soldier" (*Idiot*, 238; *PSS*, 8:183–84).[6] (Compare: "This . . . disgraced peasant . . . , why, he might also be that very same Marey, *I cannot peer into his heart, after all*" [*WD*, 355; *PSS*, 22:49].)[7]

Myshkin's resolution not to peer into the collective soul of the Russian people in search of the ultimately insufficient socio-psychological explanations of their often puzzling behavior but to believe in their spiritual potential by virtue of the absurd is consistent with his ethical stance in the novel. But such restraint from judgment, such deliberate restriction of vision can hardly be effortless for the man whose psychological insights astonish his interlocutors and whose extraordinary ability to predict future events borders on clairvoyance. When, in a conversation with Aglaya, Myshkin comments on Ippolit's attempted suicide, suggesting that Ippolit perhaps *did* have an unarticulated intention to elicit praise by his confession, Aglaya replies with indignation: "I think it's very wrong of you, for it's very callous to think like that and to judge a man's soul as you judge Ippolit. You have no tenderness: only truth and that's why you're unfair" (*Idiot*, 436; *PSS*, 354). Aglaya accuses Myshkin of the very thing he has promised himself *not* to do, namely of callously "peering" into another's soul. A secondhand discussion of Ippolit's inner personality is unfair, because it finalizes his consciousness, making it into a passive object of study. Ippolit cannot answer Myshkin's charges against him, however "true to life" and psychologically accurate they may be, for Myshkin's evaluation is divorced from dialogue, as Bakhtin notes in *PDP* (59–60).[8]

By nature of his outsideness in relation to Ippolit, Myshkin has what Bakhtin calls "another's surplus," that is, he may see things that are outside of Ippolit's limited field of vision. This visual advantage allows him to articulate his psychological insights illuminating Ippolit's behavior. But the limitation of vision obtains on both sides, for every consciousness also possesses intimate information about itself that cannot be gleaned from without but can only be revealed dialogically and even then only partially, for some of it will resist the process of communication, retreating from the field of contact into the inaccessible depths of the self. It is this "surplus of the self" that Ippolit is concerned about in his confession. Ippolit writes:

> In every idea of genius, in every new human idea, or, more simply still, in every serious human idea born in anyone's brain, there is something that cannot possibly be conveyed to others, though you wrote volumes about it and spent thirty-five years in explaining your idea; something will always be left that will obstinately refuse to emerge from your head and that will remain with you forever; and you will die without having conveyed to anyone what is perhaps the most vital point of your idea. (*Idiot*, 406; *PSS*, 328)

In Myshkin's evaluation of Ippolit's psyche in his conversation with Aglaya, Ippolit's surplus of the self, the "vital point" of his own truth about the world, is not taken into account. In Aglaya's opinion, Myshkin errs, because he mistakes actuality for truth; "only truth" is not the whole truth, for it concerns itself only with what Ippolit *is* (or appears to be from the point of view of another, consummating consciousness) and disregards the redeeming complexity of that stubborn residue of human personality which survives any attempt at empirical assessment. For Dostoevsky, "the whole truth" is a dialogical truth, which emerges as a result of the dynamic interaction of consciousnesses in the zone of contact, where several fields of vision intersect. Such truth is never final, for it is perceived synchronically, changing in the very process of revelation, and it concerns itself with both actuality and potentiality. Such truth may be revealed only to a consciousness that addresses another consciousness as a subject rather than regards it with an objectifying gaze, a consciousness that wants to be enriched with another's surplus of knowledge and willingly offers its own surplus to the other.

It is such truth that Myshkin seeks to reveal in his heart-to-heart talks with Rogozhin, Aglaya, and Nastasia Filippovna, although he finds it increasingly difficult to overcome the temptation of psychologizing. Ironically, it is the mocker Aglaya who accuses one of Dostoevsky's Christlike characters of lacking faith, faith in Ippolit's innermost "individual ineffable," in that inevitably obscure core of his *personal* being that lies much deeper than mere psychological motivation and may surprise us by manifesting itself in the most unexpected circumstances, no matter how unlikely this potential realization of ultimate spiritual freedom may seem from the standpoint of empirical probability or psychological intuition.

Indeed, Myshkin's faith in the potential goodness of his interlocutors is often troubled by his lucid insights into their psychology. The Prince is aware of Keller's intention to ask him for money at the very outset of his tearful confession (part 2, chapter 11). He foresees Ippolit's attack of vengeful rage, which "was bound" to follow the boy's public display of emotion in the Prince's drawing room in Pavlovsk, and his *post factum* admission of this foreboding throws the already inflamed Ippolit into a fury:

> He [the Prince] looked apprehensively at Ippolit, as though expecting something more from him.
>
> Suddenly Ippolit got up, dreadfully pale and with an expression of terrible, almost despairing shame on his distorted face. This was expressed chiefly in his eyes, which stared fearfully and hatefully at the company, and in the forlorn, twisted, and abject smile on his quivering lips. . . .
>
> "That's what I was afraid of!" cried the Prince. "That was bound to happen!" Ippolit turned round to him with a look of frenzied malice, and every feature of his face seemed to be quivering and speaking.
>
> "Oh, so you were afraid of that, were you? 'That was bound to happen,' in your opinion, was it? Well, let me tell you that if I hate anyone here—and I hate you all, all of you"—he spluttered in a shrill voice, wheezing and spitting involuntarily, "I hate you, you, sugary Jesuit soul, you idiot, you millionaire-philanthropist—more than anyone and more than anything in the world!" (*Idiot*, 314; *PSS*, 249)

Ippolit, who has, in his own opinion, just disgraced himself by baring his innermost feelings in front of a callous and undeserving audience, turns at his involuntary confessors in blind rage. His anger is a spontaneous reaction to the overwhelming feeling of shame, but his vicious attack on his audience is also an effort to reverse the effects of his humiliating self-exposure, to have the last word in a confessional dialogue gone wrong. Terrified by his own momentary sincerity, Ippolit immediately retreats into his protective shell; he wants to surprise his audience—who has recently been granted a peek into his soul of souls, and who, Ippolit believes, is now about to use its knowledge against him—with an unexpected gesture, a gesture of malice to be sure, which that audience, for all its presumed knowledge of his "type," did not anticipate. Thus Ippolit's fit of rage is at the same time a gesture of concealment, intended to block access to his inner personality, so indecently exposed a minute ago. By throwing himself at his confessors, Ippolit attempts to destroy what he believes to be a humiliating, unfairly finalizing image of himself created by his confession, and thus to wrest his private self, *cheloveka v cheloveke*, from the grip of public scrutiny. "So, you think you had me all figured out?!" Ippolit seems to be saying. "You think that I am a pathetic but essentially harmless fellow, whose actions are so utterly predictable. Well, here's what you get for peering into my soul—my everlasting hatred! Did you predict *this?!*" But, alas, Prince Myshkin did and, by uttering his embarrassed "it was bound to happen," insulted the humiliated Ippolit anew.

Myshkin is praised for his keen psychological intuition by Lebedev, but his behavior is hardly commendable from the point of view of Myshkin's own moral philosophy. The Myshkin we encounter in the Ippolit episode is different from the man who has solemnly proclaimed: "Another's soul is shrouded in darkness." The man who follows Ippolit with the look of doom on his face is a man of little faith. By predicting Ippolit's renunciation of his own confession Myshkin finalizes him, placing his living soul in a strait-jacket of psychological laws; by anticipating a certain reality, Myshkin helps to create it. Here the connection between potentiality and actuality, between thought and deed, which so fascinated Dostoevsky, comes to the fore. Myshkin's apprehensive look at Ippolit, full of almost mystical expectation, which could not have been anything but insulting to Ippolit, may well have pushed the desperate youth to the last limit. Thus Myshkin's faintheartedness has an effect on the empirical reality in the novel. The episode with Ippolit may be seen as one of Myshkin's "falls from faith," which resembles his earlier, more than passive anticipation of Rogozhin's attack.[9]

The same Ippolit, who so vocally protests the Prince's peering into his soul in part 2, later credits him with irrational faith, faith that suspends empirical evidence in search of a higher truth. "Yes, Prince, you have to touch it [the evidence of one's malicious intentions] with your finger in order not to believe it again," he pronounces mockingly, paying the Prince one of his characteristic back-handed compliments (*Idiot*, 526; *PSS*, 432). However, faith remains an object of intense and arduous striving for the man whose curse it is that he "[sees] through people," as Lebedev observes (*Idiot*, 326; *PSS*, 259), and for whom the achievement of grace seems to require deliberate self-blinding.

As was shown in chapters 1 and 2, an alternative to monological peering into another's soul is a process Bakhtin describes as "live-entering" (*vzhivanie*), an essentially dialogical relationship in which another's surplus of vision is used not as an ambush or a means of objectification but as a way of enriching another's consciousness, of inducing it to grow. Such an effect is secured precisely because no attempt is made to silence the suffering other or to make him a passive part of one's own, solely articulate, "I." "What would I have to gain, if another were to fuse with me?" Bakhtin asks in "Author and Hero," as if responding to Dostoevsky's ethical concerns. "If he did, he would see and know no more than what I already see and know, he would merely repeat in himself the inescapable closed circle of my own life; let him rather remain outside of me" (87). We shall recall that Bakhtin proposes an active approach to co-experiencing as an alternative to passive empathy:

> I actively enter as a living being [*vzhivaius'*] into an individuality and consequently I do not lose myself completely, nor lose my unique place outside that individuality. It is not the subject who unexpectedly takes possession of me as the passive one, but I who actively enter into him, *vzhivanie* is *my* act, and only that constitutes its productiveness and innovation. (*TPA*, 15, translation emended)

Indeed, *vzhivanie* may be seen as an ideal realization of the dialogical process, where neither party loses its active status as a speaking subject endowed with a unique voice, yet a maximum closeness and openness occurs. Each consciousness tries to reach an active understanding of the other, to enter another's world, but such live-entering is different from the monological peering into another's soul, because no consciousness is objectified in the process. The observer never ceases to regard the other as a subject; his glance is met by the other's contesting glance, it partially fuses with this glance or clashes with it, but never ignores it, never peers *through* another's face. Instead of merely regarding another from without (as a "him"), I attempt to imagine his consciousness from within (as another "I" facing me in the impending debate)—the two points of view intersect and result in the "you" of dialogue.

Clearly, a situation where both parties voluntarily open themselves to each other's scrutiny, withstand the temptation to silence another's living voice, and are willing to undergo the often painful exposure to their own externally perceived image revealed to them as a part of another's surplus—such a situation is an ideal one. In reality, pride, self-will, and shame may stand in the way of active empathy. Having opened up to a sincere exchange for a brief moment, one may retreat into monological self-contemplation, put on an impenetrable mask, or ignore the very presence of the erstwhile interlocutor, as it often happens with Dostoevsky's characters. On the other hand, as Ippolit notes, some ideas will never penetrate into the realm of another's consciousness and thus will always remain a part of the self's secret surplus. In fact, some knowledge is monological by nature. Thus *vzhivanie* should be recognized as an ideal concept that represents the unrealized and, perhaps, unrealizable potential of dialogue in Dostoevsky's world.

I argue that in *The Idiot* Myshkin strives toward achieving such an ideal understanding of his many interlocutors. His complex and often problematic relationship with Rogozhin illustrates both the accomplishments and failures of active empathy. The Prince's intriguing inner conflict in the episode preceding Rogozhin's attempt on his life may be seen as a struggle between the *passive* (monological) and the *active* (dialogical) approach to human personality, between the impulse to "peer into another's soul" and the desire to reach an active understanding of another's world by means of *live-entering*.

Having exchanged crosses in part 2, chapter 4, Rogozhin and Myshkin become brothers in Christ and part in the spirit of mutual forgiveness, but, immediately after the departure of his former rival, Myshkin begins doubting Rogozhin's sincerity in renouncing his claims to Nastasia Filippovna. His faintheartedness disguises itself as a revelation, a mystical foreboding of an inevitable catastrophe. Stirred up by his obtrusive visions of impending violence, Myshkin breaks his promise to Rogozhin and walks to Nastasia Filippovna's house, as if to test Rogozhin's capacity for transgression. Tempted by his demonic inner voice, Myshkin, in turn, tempts Rogozhin, whose attack he both anticipates and provokes. The characteristically Dostoevskian irony of the scene results from the discrepancy between thought and deed, between theory and practice, for it is on his way to Nastasia Filippovna's house, in the very process of betraying his brother in Christ, that Myshkin pronounces one of his most compelling sermons on faith and trust. He engages in an extensive imaginary dialogue with Rogozhin and reaches a profound understanding of his inner personality only to conclude the process of *vzhivanie* with a monological gesture.

Walking to Nastasia Filippovna's house, Myshkin is shamefully aware of his fall from grace. He tries to dispel his dark premonitions, to restore the integrity of Rogozhin's image by appealing to his newly elected motto: "He did . . . begin to believe passionately in the Russian soul. . . . But another's soul is shrouded in darkness, and a Russian soul is shrouded in darkness, shrouded in darkness for many. He had been friends with Rogozhin for a long time, they had been intimate friends, they had been 'like brothers'—but did he know Rogozhin?" (*Idiot*, 245–46; *PSS*, 190). For Myshkin, a soul shrouded in darkness is a soul that can be passionately believed in; it signifies an individuality that may enter into a relationship with him unaccompanied by the prejudice of secondhand information about it. The Prince desperately wants to believe that Rogozhin's soul, too, may emerge from darkness, revealing its inner truth in a meaningful dialogue. With the insistence that betrays a guilty conscience, Myshkin promises himself to discuss his misgivings with Rogozhin openly, face-to-face: "Yes, everything has to be made clear now, so that everybody can read the other's thoughts clearly . . . and let it all happen freely and . . . joyfully" (*Idiot*, 247; *PSS*, 191). In fact, he engages in such an imaginary dialogue with Rogozhin as he walks through the unfamiliar Petersburg streets on his way to Nastasia Filippovna. "Isn't Rogozhin capable of seeing the light?"—Myshkin asks.

> He says that he does not love her [Nastasia Filippovna] that way, that he has no compassion for her, "no such pity." It's true, he did add later that "your pity is probably even worse than my love," but he is being unfair to himself. Hmm, Rogozhin poring over a book—isn't this "pity," the beginning of "pity"? Doesn't the very presence of that book prove that he is fully conscious of his attitude toward *her*? [italics in text] Let alone what Rogozhin told him just now. No, this is deeper than sheer passion. And does this face inspire sheer passion? Can this face now inspire passion at all? It arouses suffering, it affects one's whole soul, it . . . and a poignant, agonizing memory suddenly pierced the prince's heart. (*PSS*, 191, my translation; see *Idiot*, 247)

Myshkin brings his surplus of vision to the dialogue, which he uses to enhance his interlocutor's understanding of himself: he intuits compassion underneath Rogozhin's passion for Nastasia Filippovna, the feeling Rogozhin himself is unaware of. The Prince suspects that someone who is capable of enduring such excruciating suffering for the sake of love may also be capable of self-sacrifice for the sake of the beloved and intends to share this insight with his imaginary interlocutor. He attempts to "live into" Rogozhin's soul, to look at the world through Rogozhin's eyes, without completely fusing with his interlocutor. As the Prince imagines Rogozhin's point of view of Nastasia Filippovna, his own memory of the familiar face imperceptibly intrudes into the imaginary realm of Rogozhin's consciousness. We feel Myshkin's compassionate gaze directed at Nastasia Filippovna, and the two glances intersect in the zone of contact: "Does this face inspire sheer passion?" (Rogozhin's imaginary point of view); "*Can* this face inspire passion at all?" (Myshkin's point of view, as it were, emerging within Rogozhin's); "It arouses suffering, it affects one's whole soul" (Myshkin's point of view).

Without silencing Rogozhin's voice, Myshkin gradually reveals his point of view to him, suggesting the existence of another truth, different from Rogozhin's, and trying to persuade his interlocutor to recognize that "other truth." In his turn, Rogozhin reveals his own surplus of vision to Myshkin, who is surprised and puzzled by his remark: "your pity is probably worse (*pushche,* literally, 'more so,' 'more intense') than my love." Like Rogozhin, who does not perceive the madness of his mistress, blinded by his own "insane" passion for her, Myshkin does not fully realize the devastating effect his love-pity has on Nastasia Filippovna. His location "inside" his equally intense feeling for Nastasia Filippovna often renders him blind to its tragic effects on the heroine. The Prince understands Rogozhin's observation merely as a suspicion of sexual involvement on his part and hurriedly vindicates himself, transforming his answer into a sermon on faith and compassion:

> And for the Prince it would be almost unthinkable to love this woman passionately; it would almost be cruel and inhuman. Yes, yes. No, Rogozhin is unfair to himself. He has a great heart that is capable of suffering and compassion. When he learns the whole truth, when he sees what a pitiful creature this hurt, this half-crazed woman is—won't he forgive her for all his suffering? Will he not become her servant, her brother, her friend, her Providence? Compassion will illuminate and teach even Rogozhin. Compassion is the chief and maybe the only law of all human existence. (*PSS*, 191–92, my translation; see *Idiot,* 247–48)

The Prince proceeds from another's point of view, within which he establishes his own strongholds, hoping that his consciousness will gradually influence the consciousness of his interlocutor, informing it of his truth. Rogozhin's passionate view of Nastasia Filippovna is evoked: "Rogozhin sees different reasons for everything, passionate reasons" (*Idiot*, 247; *PSS*, 191). Then Myshkin's point of view is introduced, but it is done in such a way that it does not exclude Rogozhin's perspective but, as it were, emerges from within it. The word "almost" is a loophole that permits the two points of view, Rogozhin's and Myshkin's, to coexist in the same utterance; it, so to speak, leaves the door to Rogozhin's world open:[10] "And for the Prince it would be *almost* unthinkable to love this woman passionately" (*Idiot*, 247; *PSS*, 191). For all the intensity of his passionate pity for Nastasia, Myshkin does not love her sexually, but, for a moment, he hesitates and imagines the possibility of sexual involvement in an effort to understand Rogozhin's love and his deep humanity, alien to the scarcely incarnated hero. Myshkin's sexual love for Nastasia Filippovna is almost unthinkable, but it is imaginable, for otherwise Rogozhin's world would be largely closed off to Myshkin—he would not be able to comprehend Rogozhin's reality, to engage in a true dialogue with him. Having considered Rogozhin's point of view, Myshkin now aspires to reveal his own understanding of Nastasia Filippovna to Rogozhin, in order to convert his "rival" to his faith. His words are dialogically addressed to Rogozhin: "When he learns the whole truth, when he sees what a pitiful creature this hurt, this half-crazed woman is—won't he forgive her for all his suffering?" (*Idiot*, 248; *PSS*, 191–92).

But if such a conversion, by means of dialogical exposure to another's (Myshkin's) truth, is possible, it requires a great deal of faith on Myshikin's part, faith which, the Prince realizes, he lacks. The more exalted and sermon-like Myshkin's discourse becomes, the more its agitated, prematurely triumphant tone betrays the speaker's uncertainty of the truth he preaches. Indeed, the final words of the passage: "Compassion will illuminate and teach even Rogozhin. Compassion is the chief and perhaps the only law of all human existence" seem to be intended for Myshkin's own ears. In Myshkin's consciousness, the mystical vision of Rogozhin the murderer, with its air of fated finality, imperceptibly replaces the unfinalized image of Rogozhin on the threshold of conversion that has emerged in the process of active empathy.

The spatial composition of the scene conveys the triumph of the monological perspective over the dialogical worldview: as Myshkin walks to Nastasia Filippovna's house, he is painfully aware of Rogozhin's presence behind his back, yet he never confronts Rogozhin, never openly addresses him. In fact, the roles become reversed, as Rogozhin openly acknowledges his presence, while Myshkin, overcome with shame, persistently avoids coming face-to-face with his stalker:

> It was he, the Prince, rather than Rogozhin, who had concealed himself. And now, at the house, he stood on the other side of the street, on the pavement opposite, about fifty paces away, with his arms folded—waiting. There he was completely in full view and, it seemed, purposely so. He stood there like an accuser and a judge and not as . . . And not as what? (*Idiot*, 249–50; *PSS*, 193)

When Myshkin the transgressor stares at the display window of the cutlery shop, as if possessed by the desire to kill, Rogozhin the judge observes him from behind his back. Thanks to this uncanny exchange of identities with his brother in Christ, Myshkin may experience the effects his fall from faith has on Rogozhin. For a moment, he may feel the burden of monological judgment and sense the destructive power of another's objectifying glance from behind one's back. But although this revelation makes Myshkin cower in shame, it does not induce him to turn around and face his silent accuser. The vicious process of monologization, which has the dynamism of a demonic force, cannot be easily reversed. Constantly aware of Rogozhin's presence, Myshkin persists in his silence. His sideward glance recognizes a familiar pair of eyes in the crowd fixed upon his face, but he does not look back, leaving Rogozhin's challenge unanswered. Myshkin's silent judgment of Rogozhin, his fainthearted capitulation before his inner demon signifies the ultimate failure of *vzhivanie* and the crisis of his faith in "the Russian soul shrouded in darkness."

As in the episode with Ippolit discussed earlier, Myshkin's intense anticipation of a certain reality, his belief in his "predestined" vision of the future, *creates* reality, as Edward Wasiolek rightly notes.[11] In this sense, Rogozhin's attempt on his life is as much provoked by Myshkin as it is predicted by him. Ironically, in Russian, Myshkin's final words before Rogozhin's attack: "Parfyon, I don't believe [it]" (*ne veriu*), that is, "I don't believe you are a murderer," his last desperate attempt to hold on to his diminishing faith, can also be interpreted as the self-deprecating "I don't believe" (I lack faith) (*Idiot*, 252; *PSS*, 195).

VZHIVANIE IN THE HOUSE OF THE DEAD

The hero of *The House of the Dead*, Goryanchikov, faces similar challenges of communication: like Myshkin, he has to learn to distrust his eyes and to suspend immediate judgment in order to attain morally and spiritually authentic understanding of his fellow convicts. When his neighbor's, Akim Akimovich's, knowledge about the convicts proves insufficient, Goryanchikov concludes: "No, evidently, I must test it out myself, not ask questions" (*House of the Dead*, 100; *PSS*, 69) and sets out in search of firsthand information about the strange new world around him. He spends hours scrutinizing his fellow convicts and analyzing their behavior but remains unsatisfied with his findings. "In the beginning of my stay in prison, I did not penetrate into the inner depths of this life, and indeed was incapable of doing so," the narrator confesses, "and therefore all its outward manifestations were then an unutterable torment and anguish to me" (*House of the Dead*, 306; *PSS*, 197). The knowledge Goryanchikov obtains as a result of silent observation proves to be just as insufficient as the information he has obtained from Akim Akimovich; it, too, is secondhand knowledge that does not take into account the convict's "surplus of the self." Goryanchikov speaks *about* the convict and not *with* the convict, he avoids the zone of contact, and his field of vision is inevitably limited to the realm of actuality, the "external manifestations" of the convict's personality, which often conceal his unrealized potential.

In his thoughtful study of Dostoevsky's early work, Tunimanov observes that in *The House of the Dead* "everything is tested and re-tested; nothing is taken for granted" (literally: "accepted on faith"—"nichego ne prinimaetsia na veru").[12] This is only partly true of Goryanchikov's method, for most important insights into prison life yield themselves to him precisely when he learns to *believe* in the peasant convict's vital potential ("prinimat' ego na veru"), suspending the all-too-obvious evidence of empirical observation. This belief comes as a result of a dialogical engagement with his fellow convicts.

It is when Goryanchikov half-consciously recognizes *himself* in his fellow convicts and discerns important points of identification between himself and his brothers in misfortune that his attitude begins to change. As a result, his strictly monological perspective gives way to a more interactive point of view; a look outward becomes a look inward. When, according to his habit, Goryanchikov silently observes the convicts after work lounging idly around the camp, one of them attracts his special attention:

> Here, behind the buildings, some of the prisoners, the most unsociable and moody, liked to walk when they were not working . . . thinking their own thoughts . . . I liked to look at their sullen, branded faces and guess at their thoughts. There was one convict whose favorite occupation, in his spare time, was to count the pales of the stockade. There were about fifteen hundred of them and he knew them all by their position and characteristics. For him, each one of them meant a day; each day he counted off one pale, and in this way, from the number remaining still uncounted, he could see at a glance how many days he must still spend in prison before the end of his term of servitude. (*House of the Dead*, 8; *PSS*, 9)

This fascinating image allows Goryanchikov to both display and defy the seminal chronotope of the convicts' life. In one imaginative move, the prisoner transcends both the temporal and the spatial limits of his confinement: he counts down the days separating him from freedom by mentally tearing down the prison's spatial boundary, the stockade, one pale at a time. Remarkably, in "The Peasant Marey," it is Dostoevsky *himself* who is described "wandering behind prison barracks, examining and counting off the pales in the sturdy prison stockade" (*WD*, 351; *PSS*, 22:46). Later in *The House of the Dead*, the narrator lets it slip that *his* "favorite occupation in a thousand different forms and applications" was "calculating when my term would come to an end" (*House of the Dead*, 114–15; *PSS*, 79). It seems that Goryanchikov, or perhaps Dostoevsky in the guise of Goryanchikov, momentarily steps outside himself to steal a sideward glance at himself as *other*, to imagine the way he himself must be regarded by his fellow inmates. In this context, it is remarkable that in "The Peasant Marey" it is by the stockade that Dostoevsky meets Miretsky, his symbolic double, whose words, "Je hais ces brigands," recognized as an expression of Dostoevsky's own resentment of his fellow sufferers, make him reevaluate his attitude toward the peasant convicts (*WD*, 351; *PSS*, 22:46). Located on the threshold of freedom, the stockade also becomes a threshold of dialogue in Dostoevsky's prison writings. Instinctively drawn to the place from which one could catch a glimpse of the "other" world, prisoners of all social backgrounds come to the stockade "to think their own thoughts" of freedom, and their paths cross. Their misery in the face of their common fate, their insatiable longing for the world beyond the stockade becomes a natural point of identification, and the rigid boundary between social classes temporarily vanishes. This enchanted place on the border between the world of the living and the realm of the dead is also a place where the boundary between the self and other may sometimes be transcended: here I may "live into" an other, and an other may catch a glimpse of my private self.[13] This emerging dialogical orientation "toward the other" in the face of the ultimate metaphysical limit, so tangibly represented by the prison wall, suggests a hopeful alternative to the Underground Man's tragic rejection of otherness in the presence of his own, philosophically insurmountable "last wall."

At first, Goryanchikov's recognition of himself in his fellow convicts only terrifies him, as when he contemplates a convict's release after many years of imprisonment, and the grim anticipation of his own future, the implied recognition of his own face in the sullen face of the aged prisoner makes his narrative especially poignant (*House of the Dead*, 8; *PSS*, 10). Mistakenly interpreting the prisoners' external calm as a sign of their reconciliation with life in captivity, he envisions with terror *his own* inevitable transformation into a complacent "creature of habit" who has forsaken the ideal of freedom: "The idea that *I* might in time come to regret this corner struck me with horror; even then I foresaw to what monstrous degree man is a creature of habit" (*House of the Dead*, 80; *PSS*, 56).

But it is precisely the prisoners' innate sense of freedom and their defiance of their captors that later serve as important points of identification between Goryanchikov and the peasant convicts. Oppressed by his captors and deprived of any other means of self-realization, Goryanchikov expresses his protest by taking persecution into his own hands, masochistically celebrating self-inflicted pain. "Here is the end of my pilgrimage: I am in prison," Goryanchikov repeats with bitterness:

> "Here is my anchorage for many long years, the corner to which I have come with such feeling of pain and misgiving . . . But who knows? Perhaps when, after many years, the time comes for me to leave it, I shall be sorry to go! . . ." I added, not without a tinge of that enjoyment of misfortune which is sometimes carried to the length of an irresistible desire to reopen one's wounds—as though one would be in love with one's own pain, as though one found true pleasure in the realization of the full extent of one's unhappiness. (*House of the Dead*, 80; *PSS*, 56)

The peasant convict, who passionately hates his persecutors, behaves in a very similar way. He does not consider himself guilty before his class enemy but understands that the point of view the authorities take on his crime is quite different from his own. Therefore he submits to his punishment with a sense of defiant resignation and derives a peculiar sense of pleasure from his suffering. As Jackson observes, "the hatred of the convict of his enemy—an enemy who is everywhere and is supreme—takes on a peculiarly passive, sublimated, and therefore disagreeable form: the deliberate acceptance of suffering or punishment. The psychologically underground character of the convict's struggle with his enemy is fully apparent."[14]

Goryanchikov, who is familiar with the desire to "reopen one's own wounds" (*House of the Dead*, 80; *PSS*, 56) and to "boast to [oneself] of one's own misery" (*House of the Dead*, 113; *PSS*, 77), may identify with such underground struggle for human dignity. His profound understanding of the convict's unconscious rebellion, evident in the following comments on prison violence, results from an inward look into *his own* psyche:

> Perhaps the whole cause of [a] violent outbreak in a man from whom it was not in the least to be expected, was a mournful desire for an abrupt display of personality, a longing to be his own self, a wish to declare himself and his own lowly personality, appearing suddenly and developing into a fury, insanity, the eclipse of reason, paroxysm, and convulsions. So, perhaps, one buried alive and awakening in his coffin, hammers on its lid and struggles to wrest it off, although, of course, reason might persuade him that all his efforts are vain. But that is just the point that it is not a question of reason but a question of nervous convulsions. (*House of the Dead*, 96; *PSS*, 67)

The convicts' essentially physiological will to freedom, which, as Jackson points out, "is stimulated not by faith in a God-given meaningful universe, but by despair,"[15] makes a profound impression on Goryanchikov, who is also buried alive in the house of the dead and whose frantic attempts to preserve human dignity in a dehumanized world are as much a matter of nervous convulsions as the peasant convict's violent fits of rage.

On the basis of this important affinity Goryanchikov attempts to establish a dialogical relationship with his fellow convicts. He develops a program of behavior intended to bring him closer to the other prisoners, which he resolves to follow with strict regularity:

> I was determined . . . to bear myself as simply and independently as possible, and by no means to display any particular striving after friendship with them, but also not to repulse them if they themselves wished to be friends. By no means to fear their menaces and hatred. . . . By no means to be reconciled to some specific points and to show no indulgence to some of their

habits and customs. . . . On the other hand, I had no desire to lock myself up in chilly and inaccessible courtesy, as the Poles did. (*House of the Dead*, 111; *PSS*, 76–77)

Goryanchikov's program contains several elements *of vzhivanie:* he remains open to a dialogical relationship with his fellow convicts ("[I resolved] not to repulse them if they themselves wished to be friends" / "I had no desire to lock myself up in chilly and inaccessible courtesy"), but he also has no intention of abandoning his own autonomous point of view or compromising his moral principles to win their favor ("I was determined . . . by no means to be reconciled to some specific points and to show indulgence to some of their habits and customs"). If Goryanchikov is to enter into a relationship with the peasant convicts, it will be on his own terms, as an active party who brings his own surplus of vision to the dialogue but is also willing to learn from his interlocutors.

Except for the cautious statement: "in the end, the majority of them [peasant convicts] liked me and recognized me as a 'decent person'" (*House of the Dead*, 32; *PSS*, 26), there are no indications in the text that such a close personal relationship was ever established between Goryanchikov and any of the peasant convicts at the time of his confinement. In fact, Goryanchikov's several attempts at rapprochement with his lower class peers end in crushing failure: he is rebuffed and ridiculed both after his attempt to join the others in menial labor and after offering to participate in their collective complaint about the poor quality of prison food. It is also telling that the only time in the novel that Goryanchikov claims to understand a peasant convict "completely" (*sovershenno*) is when, after the disastrous failure of the complaint, followed by the authorities' reprisals against the "inciters," his frequent companion, the erudite peasant Petrov, meets his question, whether the complainers are angry with the upper-class convicts for not supporting their cause, with utter incomprehension: "But . . . but how can you be our comrades?" Petrov asks, genuinely perplexed (*House of the Dead*, 322; *PSS*, 207). "But I *understood him completely* at that moment," the narrator states unequivocally, and it is significant that perhaps the only truth proclaimed about the peasant convict with absolute certainty in this novel of cautious speculations on what is hidden "behind these branded faces" is that of the radical socio-ontological gulf posed between him and the narrator by class: "I understood that I would never be accepted into their company, even though I was a convict, even if it were forever and a day,[16] even if I were in the special class" (*House of the Dead*, 322; *PSS*, 207).

Citing evidence from Dostoevsky's own letters written immediately after his discharge from prison and full of unconcealed hatred for the peasant convicts, Jackson convincingly argues that for Dostoevsky, as well as for

Goryanchikov, reconciliation with his fellow prisoners came long after his release from the Siberian camp.[17] From an embittered gentleman convict, blinded by his rage against his tormenters, who regarded his fellow inmates as "one hundred and fifty enemies [who] could not let up their persecution,"[18] the autobiographical narrator is transformed into a lucid "seer of the spirit," who recognizes in the depraved peasant convicts fellow human beings with a rich spiritual potential and glorifies them as "perhaps the most highly gifted and the strongest of our people" (*House of the Dead*, 360; *PSS*, 231). This pivotal transformation takes place through the process of writing, when the resources of artistic cognition are used to illuminate the subjective recollections of personal experiences.

According to Jackson, "the altruism of artistic vision," with its *post factum* lucidity, is necessarily a part of the diachronic perspective; it results from a reevaluative look back at the bygone years that transcends the bitterness and personal resentment obscuring the synchronic perspective. But in *The House of the Dead* the two perspectives coexist, as is apparent from Goryanchikov's comments on his own disappointing blindness in relation to the peasant convicts during the first years of prison life:

> The anguish of all that first year in prison was unendurable, and it made me irritable and bitter. Because of that anguish I did not notice many of the things around me. *I covered my eyes and refused to look*. Among my malicious and hostile prison comrades I did not see the good people, the people who were capable of both thinking and feeling, in spite of the repulsive crust that covered them on the surface. Among all the wounding words I never noticed the kind and affectionate word, which was all the dearer because it was spoken without any ulterior motive, and not infrequently from a heart that had borne and suffered more than mine. But why enlarge upon this? I was extremely glad if I found myself tired out as I returned home: perhaps I should sleep! For in summer sleeping was an agony, almost worse than in winter. (*House of the Dead*, 278; *PSS*, 178–79)

The voice of the older, philosophically detached Goryanchikov, channeled by the artistically distanced Dostoevsky, sternly judging his own past, is heard in the first part of the passage, while the irritable voice of the convict Goryanchikov, with his bitter irony, utters the concluding lines of the passage, as it were, impatiently interrupting the older narrator, whose calmness is incomprehensible to him. "But why enlarge upon this?" the convict Goryanchikov exclaims, "all this is a product of retrospective thought and can hardly concern me. All *I* am concerned with is my overwhelming suffering: my excruciating pain after a long day of labor, my insomnia, the torment I suffer at the hands of peasant convicts." The embittered voice that egoistically turns the reader's attention from the suffering of the peasant convicts to the all-important sensations of Goryanchikov's wounded self is a voice from the past. This voice is a carrier of the synchronic point of view that contests the truth of the diachronic perspective. As Robin Miller puts it, "*The House of the Dead* contains mutually coexisting messages of hope and despair, of irrevocable death and the possibility of renewal, of unresolved pain and delight achieved amid unspeakable squalor,"[19] and these messages are dialogically engaged with each other by the transgredient, aesthetically and ethically distanced author, who eludes identification with Goryanchikov, the frame narrator, or the historical Dostoevsky.

Jackson compares Dostoevsky's second visit to the House of the Dead at the time of creating his autobiographical novel to Dante's "educational" journey in *Divine Comedy*:

> The first, historical journey of Dostoevsky was an involuntary one, an excruciating experience that left deep psychological wounds and bitter feelings. The second, literary journey in *The House of the Dead*, like the journey of Dante the traveler, was an expedition to see and learn. The Dostoevsky who made the second journey in the figure of Goryanchikov was a person who had come to see himself and his subject in a new light. In this way *The House of the Dead* becomes vision and not autobiography, and the writing of that work becomes a process of self-overcoming.[20]

Indeed, by writing his memoirs, Dostoevsky-Goryanchikov embarks on a much more fruitful journey of discovery than the quest for knowledge the convict Goryanchikov initially undertook in *The House of the Dead* and the convict Dostoevsky embarked on in the Omsk prison. But the old self, overwhelmed with pain and suffering, is not dissolved in the new, artistically detached self. Rather, its distinct voice often contests the truth of the *post factum* vision, undermining the hegemony of the diachronic perspective. The process in question is then not "self-overcoming" but rather that of gradual dialogical self-refinement, where the empirical self, grounded in synchronic reality, is dialogically addressed by the older self, engaged in retrospective contemplation of the past. Each of these selves has a surplus of vision in respect to the other, and their interaction with each other in the process of writing results in continual refinement of the writing self. Dostoevsky alludes to such artistic "memory-correction" in "The Peasant Marey":

> All through my four years in prison I continually thought of all my past days, and I think I relived the whole of my former life in my memories. These memories arose in my mind of themselves; rarely did I summon them consciously. They would begin from a certain point; some little thing that was often barely

> perceptible, and then bit by bit they would grow into a finished picture, some strong and complete impression. I would analyze these impressions, adding new touches to things experienced long ago; and the main thing was that I would refine them, continually refine them. (*WD*, 352; *PSS*, 22:47)

Such analytical correction of a remembered event intensifies one's vision, unexpectedly bringing into focus things that were "barely perceptible" at the time of the event. This sudden illumination is caused by the surplus of vision that the reflecting self, diachronically removed from the analyzed event, has over the acting self, synchronically immersed in the event. The reflecting self views past events with the lucidity of a detached observer but lacks the immediacy of perception possessed by the acting self. It is this immediacy of perception, the special poignancy of its emotional outlook that constitutes the acting self's surplus. Both of these surpluses are used provocatively in a dialogue between the two narrators of Dostoevsky's semi-autobiographical vision in *The House of the Dead*. And it is this artistically rewarding, deliberately cultivated coexistence of disparate, at times competing perspectives that produces what Miller calls a fascinating "hybrid of intention and experience," on the pages of this semi-documentary novel, "of visionary desire in competition with horror amid loneliness and isolation, of events recollected after the fact . . . and thus artistically reshaped and transformed."[21]

One of the fundamental "corrections" or "refinements" that are made in the process of writing the memoirs is the profound change in the relationship between Goryanchikov and the peasant convicts, as Jackson points out.[22] The man who wrote "Scenes from the House of the Dead" has successfully implemented Goryanchikov's "plan of action." The desire of Goryanchikov the convict to enter into a closer relationship with the peasant convicts is gratified by Goryanchikov the memoirist, whose "Scenes from the House of the Dead" are not a discussion *about* his fellow inmates but *with* them. Here the correction of the past is made not on the level of events—no unrealistic gestures of camaraderie between Goryanchikov and the peasant convicts are invented by the converted memoirist—but on the level of interpretation: Goryanchikov's understanding of the peasant convicts is retrospectively enriched. The imaginary dialogue with the peasant prisoner that Goryanchikov the convict has barely initiated during the years of his confinement is developed and refined by Goryanchikov the memoirist.

Unlike the young Goryanchikov, who approaches the enigma of the peasant convict by carefully evaluating the empirical evidence "pro and contra," by testing out his ideas about him, Goryanchikov the memoirist finds courage to believe in the peasant convict in spite of the discouraging empirical evidence repeatedly presented to his eyes. Instead of condemning the peasant convict for his often unsavory behavior, the memoirist reflects earnestly on the perplexing moral dualities he exhibits and turns our attention to his rarely acknowledged spiritual potential, concealed behind the external layer of depravity. Instead of the monological peering into his soul, he challenges the peasant convict to articulate his own truth about himself, to reveal his "Russian soul," shrouded in darkness, dialogically.[23]

As a result, the memoirist's judgment of the prisoners is not divorced from self-judgment, and, for that reason, he usually avoides lapsing into abstract psychologizing. For example, Goryanchikov's own dissatisfaction with himself, the consciousness of his own unconquered resentment toward his fellow sufferers allows him to understand the bitterness and snobbery the peasant convicts display in their relations with each other:

> There is in the Russian character so much common sense and sobriety and so much inward mockery, of oneself first of all . . . Perhaps, it was this constant hidden dissatisfaction with self that caused all the impatience displayed in the everyday relations of these men with one another, and all their incompatibility and deriding of one another. And if once one of them, simpler or more impatient than the rest, came forward and expressed aloud what was in everybody's heart, giving reign to his dreams and hopes, he was at once roughly suppressed, snubbed, and ridiculed; but to my mind, his most zealous persecutors were precisely those whose dreams and hopes went even farther than his. (*House of the Dead*, 304–5; *PSS*, 196)

Goryanchikov, who laughs bitterly at his own impossible dreams, at his own convulsive attempts to regain personal dignity amidst unrelenting persecution and derives peculiar pleasure from such deliberate self-laceration, intuits an underground longing for self-realization in another soul. This essentially egoistic longing, Goryanchikov knows, manifests itself in deliberate infliction of suffering on self and others. Goryanchikov's understanding of the convicts' behavior, which is akin to Myshkin's intuition of Rogozhin's capacity for compassion, is inseparable from his insights into his own consciousness. His gaze constantly passes from his own carefully examined inner self to the self of the other; it gains access to another consciousness only after opening his own to another's scrutinizing glance, and this is the fundamental difference between Goryanchikov's dialogical soul-searching and his earlier monological peering into another's soul. Goryanchikov vindicates the convict's haughtiness in relation to his fellow inmates in hopes that he will respond to his gesture by forgiving Goryanchikov's own bitterness and resentment toward him.

The hero's dialogical engagement with his fellow convicts yields a sense of belonging, a feeling of solidarity with the prison community. When Goryanchikov undergoes preparation for Easter communion with his mates, he temporarily becomes a full-fledged member of the community that has hitherto ostracized and persecuted him. A childhood recollection of the peasants attending Easter services in his home town becomes a prologue to the communion scene:

> [When I was a child] I thought that those who stood near the door did not pray in the same way as we did, but meekly, fervently, with humility and a full consciousness of their lowly state.
>
> Now I myself had to stand in that place, and indeed, a worse one yet; we were fettered and stigmatized as criminals; everybody drew aside from us and even seemed afraid of us; we always had alms bestowed on us and I remember that this somehow even pleased me, and there was a peculiar subtlety in that strange feeling of satisfaction. "If it must be so, so be it!" I thought. (*House of the Dead*, 273; *PSS*, 176–77)

The transition from the state of restlessness and mental agitation to pious tranquility, from alienation to a sense of belonging, takes place imperceptibly and involuntarily on Goryanchikov's part (Compare: "I *had to* prepare for Communion" ["mne prishlos' govet'"] (*House of the Dead*, 272; *PSS*, 176); "If it *must be so*, so be it!" ["pust' zhe, koli tak"] [*House of the Dead*, 273; *PSS*, 177]). Goryanchikov simply follows prison regulations, he awaits the approaching holidays with indifference, accepting the necessity of communion as yet another inevitability of prison life. But, in the same spirit of passive resignation, he offers no resistance to the uninvited feeling of serene joy that suddenly descends upon him as he takes his place in God's temple among the lowest of the low, and his acceptance of grace results in a momentary communion with his fellow sufferers.

Similarly imperceptible is the transformation of disfiguring suffering into redemptive suffering that takes place in the communion scene. The "strange feeling of satisfaction" which accompanies Goryanchikov's realization of his humble social state, may be interpreted as masochistic enjoyment of one's fall, as the underground "pleasure in the realization of the full extent of one's unhappiness" (*House of the Dead*, 80; *PSS*, 56). Indeed, this subtle feeling has much in common with Goryanchikov's erstwhile desire "to reopen his wounds," but this time his admiration for and imitation of the peasant convicts' genuine piety saves him from masochistic self-laceration. For Goryanchikov, the peasant convicts' unfeigned gestures of religious devotion, however episodic and inconsistent this behavior may be, become an affirmation of their human dignity, a living proof of their alert conscience: "The prisoners were very zealous in their devotions," Goryanchikov reports, "and each of them always brought to the church his pitiful copeck for a candle or to put in the collection: perhaps as he gave it he thought or rather felt 'I too am a man, and in the sight of God all men are equal'" (*House of the Dead*, 273; *PSS*, 177).

As they shed their superficial arrogance and kneel before God and each other in a gesture of genuine humility, the convicts make a miraculous transition from disfiguring suffering that destroys "man in man" to purifying suffering that elevates the spirit. To use Jackson's terms, the essentially egoistic will to freedom, conditioned by despair, becomes transformed into altruistic free will, conditioned by a belief in a God-governed universe. Goryanchikov and the peasant convicts make this transition together. In fact, Goryanchikov receives grace only through his (respectful and partial) identification with and imitation of the peasant convicts. For a brief moment, the process of *vzhivanie* becomes real.

However, such instances of communion are extremely rare and short-lived in the character's prison experience. The largely monological reality of Goryanchikov the convict, the reality of deafening silence and devastating alienation, contrasts sharply with the simulated reality of dialogue, in which the *memoirist* dwells. Goryanchikov the convict states the impossibility of any close relationship between a peasant and a gentleman convict as an indisputable fact of life:

> However upright, good, and wise he [the nobleman] may be, they [the peasant convicts] will despise him as a group, they will not understand him and, most importantly, they will not trust him. He is not a friend, not a comrade, and although in the course of years he may finally come to the state of not being despised, nevertheless, he will not be one of them, and he will be eternally tormented by the consciousness of his alienation and solitude. Sometimes this alienation arises not from malice on the prisoners' part, but just so, unconsciously. He is not one of them and that is all. (*House of the Dead*, 308; *PSS*, 198)

This unquestionable verdict has the iron certainty of the "natural laws" that drive Dostoevsky's freedom-obsessed Underground Man into a mad rage. But, like the Underground Man, who realizes the inevitability of "two times two equals four," but refuses to live by that infuriating formula, reserving the right to declare: "two times two is five!," Goryanchikov does not capitulate before the "stone wall" of empirical reality. By writing his memoirs, he transgresses the "natural law" of silence between the Russian nobleman and the Russian peasant, creating an alternative reality, where a potential dialogue between them may begin.[24]

Toward the end of "Scenes from the House of the Dead," the stark empirical reality of Goryanchikov's prison life, with its vision of the peasant convict as his relentless persecutor, recedes into the background, and a new, redemptive image of the peasant convict comes to the fore, revealed from under the external layer of depravity that had long obscured it from view. In the chapter devoted to prison theatricals, the narrator's tribute to the peasant convict becomes a hopeful acknowledgment of his vibrant "individual ineffable":

> Peasant convicts] might laugh at me when they saw that I was useless to them as a helper at work . . . But now, in the theater, they made way for me. They recognized that in this matter I might be a better judge than they. Those among them who were least well disposed toward me now (as I know) desired my commendation of their theater and, without the least self-abasement, yielded me the best place. *This is my present judgment, based on my impressions at the time*. It seemed to me then, I remember, that their just estimate of themselves had nothing servile in it, but only a sense of personal dignity. The highest and most characteristic trait of our common people is their feeling for justice and their thirst for it. The cocky habit of putting oneself in front everywhere at whatever cost and whether one is worthy of the first place or not, is not found among the people. One need only remove the outer husk and scrutinize the grain within attentively, closely and without prejudice, to see things in the people of which one had never even dreamed. (*House of the Dead*, 184; *PSS*, 121–22)

By writing his memoirs, Goryanchikov indeed ventures to remove "the outer husk" surrounding the image of the Russian peasant. He endeavors to address him directly and thus to free himself from the prejudice of the secondhand information about him. Goryanchikov's narrative is a retrospective dialogue, "my *present* judgment, based on my impressions *at the time*," and it is his active dialogical stance in relation to the people that allows him to "scrutinize the grain" and to "see things in the people of which one never even dreamed."

Through the act of writing the memoirist is imperceptibly transported from the realm of mere actuality into an expanded space of dialogical creativity, open to spiritual potentiality, where empirical experiences are paradoxically enriched by faith. Jackson suggests that, in the process of retrospective memory correction, Goryanchikov resurrects the fallen image of the peasant convict and is himself resurrected through this act.[25] I would assess the hero's accomplishment more moderately, using Bakhtinian terms: in writing his memoirs, Goryanchikov ventures to consummate (but not finalize) his reluctant interlocutor and is himself fruitfully—if not conclusively—consummated in the process.

Chapter Four

BETWEEN REVELATION AND DIALOGUE: SCAFFOLD TEMPORALITY IN *THE HOUSE OF THE DEAD* AND *THE IDIOT*

It has been noted that, although the narrator of *The House of the Dead* shares many of his insights with the converted narrator of "The Peasant Marey," the conversion experience that is depicted in "The Peasant Marey" is not mentioned in *The House of the Dead*.[26] It seems that the reason for this omission is that, unlike the narrator of "The Peasant Marey," Goryanchikov the memoirist is not a converted man but a man presently in the process of conversion. The process of writing is itself a part of the conversion experience; the text itself constitutes a revelation, as Goryanchikov the memoirist persuades Goryanchikov the convict of his truth in the process of dialogical self-refinement. In this sense, the text is synchronic with the conversion process, which does not come to a close within its boundaries, but extends beyond the last page of the memoirs.

Some critics have recognized a similar synchronic temporality in *The Idiot*. For example, Romano Guardini observes that it is impossible for the reader to maintain an aesthetically objective perspective of *The Idiot*, for the ultimate meaning ("der letzte Gehalt") is not posited *in* the text but is realized outside of it. It is gleaned from the work only in the process of subjective appropriation; in other words, the idea does not signify until it is believed in, and, as with every religious choice, there always remains a risk that one may choose to believe in an absurdity.[27] Guardini argues that the peculiar ambivalence of Myshkin's image results from the special temporal perspective from which the reader inevitably approaches *The Idiot*:

> Sometime later the true meaning of Myshkin's image will be revealed; it will be decided whether Myshkin is indeed a symbolic incarnation of the divine being or simply a decadent man. . . . But the novel itself, from beginning to end, stands before that revelation. In it, one encounters Myshkin enveloped in mystery [*Nicht-gedeutet-sein*] and contradiction. The reader always stands in relation of simultaneity to the action.[28]

Guardini suggests that the perspective from which the reader regards Myshkin is similar to that from which Christ's contemporaries contemplated his deeds. Thus the reader who ponders over Myshkin's problematic behavior stands on the very threshold of revelation; like the witnesses of Christ's sacrifice, he lacks the wisdom of hindsight and finds himself in a world *before* resurrection, where nothing is a given and faith is a matter of tremendously difficult choices.

It may be argued that such a threshold perspective, common to both works, is conditioned by a special scaffold temporality. In *The Idiot*, the action takes place in the invisible presence of Myshkin's "condemned man" awaiting execution, the hero of his emotional narratives, whose image often fuses with that of the Prince. Myshkin's history of epilepsy allows him to imagine the condemned man's reality, for both men have lived through "last moments" preceding death or a death-like experience. The special threshold temporality associated with these experiences—also relevant for the similarly condemned tubercular Ippolit, the suicidal Nastasia Filippovna, and the apocalyptically minded Lebedev, who obsessively contemplates the last moments of the guillotined Madame du Barry—becomes characteristic of the whole novel, whose deeply ambiguous events, as Guardini insightfully pointed out, anticipate an impending, but ultimately extra-textual, revelation. In *The House of the Dead*, the characters' attention is similarly focused on one all-important threshold: the moment of freedom. Here, the marked instants are the seminal moments immediately preceding and following the prisoner's release, symbolically conceptualized as a "birth" or a resurrection from the house of the dead. In both novels, the sharp focus on the ultimate temporal limit (whether it is an opening or a closing one) profoundly affects the quality of the transitional moments. The temporal field becomes charged to the limit and the prisoner of the scaffold moment finds himself in the realm of concentrated time: at such moments temporality is transcended and the characters may experience earthly resurrection.

At first glance, scaffold temporality appears quite different from the temporality of prison life. The moment on the scaffold is a moment *lengthened* by an effort of the revolting consciousness that stubbornly refuses to resign itself to its fate. The precious time endowed with profound significance is the time "up to" the limit imposed by the executioner. Therefore, for Myshkin's condemned man, the last five minutes on the scaffold are "like . . . riches beyond the dreams of avarice; he felt that during these five minutes he would live through so many lives that it was quite unnecessary for him to think of the last moment" (*Idiot*, 83; *PSS*, 52). Here, by definition, the temporal limit that affects the transformation of transparent, prosaic time into concentrated time, marked by intense consciousness of its every instant, is the *closing* limit.

On the contrary, the mental efforts of a prisoner are directed toward *shortening* the time that separates him from freedom. The prisoner in *The House of the Dead* is said to squander money with astonishing ease, for, by dispensing of it at his own will, he obtains an illusion of freedom: "It was quite strange to see one of them keep his nose to the grindstone, sometimes several months on end, simply in order to squander all his earnings, down to the last copeck, in one day" (*House of the Dead*, 46; *PSS*, 34). The convict's squandering of money is also symbolic of his attitude toward his life in captivity, whose transitory, fleeting nature it was important to stress—the days in prison are also to be squandered away recklessly and with a certain bravado.[29] The time spent in prison appears unreal and ghostly, it is merely "time in between" that is not lived but passed or "killed":[30]

> The dreams of the man who is caged and deprived of freedom are quite different from those of the man who is alive in the real sense. The free man has his hopes, of course (for a change of lot, for instance, or the successful completion of an enterprise), but he lives and acts; real life with all its chances and changes wholly engrosses him. It is different for the prisoner. He also has, let us concede, a life—prison life, convict life; but whoever he is and for whatever term he has been confined, he is definitely and instinctively unable to accept his fate as something positive and final, as a part of real life. Every convict feels that he is not in *his own home*, but as it were on a visit. (*House of the Dead*, 115; *PSS*, 79, italics in text)

The time which every convict solemnly awaits and in which he passionately believes is the time immediately *after* the prisoner's release, when the "visit" ends and the prisoner may again feel at home in his life. Here the limit that endows the moment of cherished time with its special significance is the *opening* limit.

Yet, in spite of these differences, there is an important similarity between the two types of temporality: in both situations, the hero's gaze is directed at the border between life and death (or freedom, perceived as life, and captivity, perceived as death) and this vantage point yields an eschatological perspective of the world. In *The House of the Dead* and *The Idiot* Dostoevsky examines the time "around" *birth* (the convict on the threshold of resurrection from the House of the Dead) and *death* (the condemned man's moments before execution), and it is the apocalyptic frontier between time and timelessness that attracts his attention.

Whether the moment of revelation is located on the inner or the outer side of the limit, the apocalyptic consciousness constantly crosses the imposed boundary. The reader's knowledge of Dostoevsky's biography is here deliberately used to obscure the line between actual and potential reality: Dostoevsky the person, who has been both on the scaffold and in prison, and who has indeed lived through moments "before death" and "after resurrection," remains in the background of the narrative, lending credence to the extraordinary events of the novelist's fantastically expanded world. And if the "evidence" of Dostoevsky's well-publicized survival of his own death during mock execution, hinted on, if not explicitly mentioned in the text,[31] is meant to validate our imaginative leap in accepting the narrator's challenge to *live into* Goryanchikov's and Myshkin's incredible scaffold moments, this extra-textual witnessing also acknowledges the reality of another veiled but crucial referent of the quintessential condemned man in *The House of the Dead* and *The Idiot*—the condemned Christ on the brink of Crucifixion and Resurrection, whose *last moments* of earthly life and the *first moments* of a new, eternal life are symbolically evoked in the key chronotopes of these two mutually illuminating novels.

Both in *The House of the Dead* and in *The Idiot*, the hero's attention is focused on the impossible but by no means unimaginable future. "[Every convict] looks on twenty years as if it were two, and is quite confident that even at fifty-five, when he emerges from prison, he will still be the youth he is now, at thirty five," Goryanchikov reports. "'I can still live!' he thinks, and obstinately banishes all doubts and other tiresome thoughts" (*House of the Dead*, 115; *PSS*, 79). Myshkin's condemned man can't help but imagine the life after the day of his execution, the future that is not meant to be: "He said that the thing that was most unbearable to him at the time was the constant thought, 'What if I had not had to die! What if I could return to life—oh, what an eternity! And all that would be mine!'" (*Idiot*, 83; *PSS*, 52).[32]

Standing at the ultimate limit of earthly existence the Dostoevskian time-traveler begins to comprehend eternity. From this lofty observation point another, timeless reality becomes visible, so that the moment such revelation takes place can no longer be called "present," for, in the words of another Dostoevskian narrator, in it, "the whole essence of [one's] life is focused, the whole of the past, present, and, perhaps, future" (*PSS*, 10:145). For Myshkin, such are the moments preceding his epileptic fits, when the last "moment of sensation" is "harmony and beauty brought to their highest point of perfection and gives a feeling, undivined and undreamt of till then, of completeness, proportion, reconciliation, and an ecstatic and prayerful fusion in the highest synthesis of life" (*Idiot*, 243; *PSS*, 188). These moments are, indeed timeless: "'At that moment,' he once told Rogozhin in Moscow during their meetings there, 'at that moment, the extraordinary saying that *there shall be time no longer* becomes, somehow, comprehensible to me'" (*Idiot*, 244; *PSS*, 189, italics in text).

In this apocalyptic, timeless reality one may catch a glimpse of one's own, and the other's, timeless, unlimited potential. For that reason, in Dostoevsky, scaffold moments bring about a stern reevaluation of one's life with a sideward glance at such infinite potentiality:[33] "If I could return to life, . . . I should turn every minute into an age," the condemned man exclaims in *The Idiot*, "I should lose nothing, I should count every minute separately and waste none!" (*Idiot*, 83; *PSS*, 52). Goryanchikov's confinement in the House of the Dead also results in a self-evaluative look at his past:

> I reviewed all my former life, down to the last trifling detail, pondered over my past, judged myself sternly and inexorably, and at moments even blessed the fate that had sent me that solitude, without which there would have been neither the self-judgment nor the stern scrutiny of my earlier life. (*House of the Dead*, 343; *PSS*, 220)

Goryanchikov "blesses the fate" that had sent him a painful but enlightening apocalyptic moment, so that his temporal, and thus inevitably finalized self could encounter his timeless potential "I" and engage in a dialogue with it. This dialogue results in rigorous self-exploration and self-correction in the process of writing "Scenes from the House of the Dead," accomplished in "solitude," but through constant imaginative recourse to his equally potentiated *other*, the initially terrifying but ultimately redeemed and redeeming peasant convict, his compassionately acknowledged and retroactively appreciated fellow sufferer.

Concentrated time is so full, so dense with psychic and emotional energy that it inevitably explodes, rupturing from within. In a typical Dostoevskian plot line, these "atemporal" moments usually signal the beginning of a catastrophe or an impending scandal, as did that ominous minute when the past, present, and future coalesced for Stavrogin in *The Devils* (*PSS*, 10:145). Time stands still on the edge of the abyss, only to erupt as the characters plummet into the yawning depths. In *The Idiot*, Myshkin's moments of intensified consciousness precede his descent into darkness, leading to a complete loss of consciousness after an epileptic attack: "But those moments, those flashes of intuition, were merely the presentiment of the last second (never more than a second) which preceded the actual fit. This second was, of course, unendurable" (*Idiot*, 243; *PSS*, 188). By their very nature such experiences cannot last; they are of another, otherworldly reality and can be endured only for a brief instant. When Alexandra asks Myshkin about the fate of the pardoned convict sentenced to an execution, the Prince does not deny the empirical impossibility of prolonging the moment of concentrated time:

> "But tell me, what about that friend of yours who told you all those terrible things—his sentence was altered, wasn't it?—which means that he was granted that 'eternity of life.' Well, what did he do with that wealth afterwards? *Did he live counting every minute*?"
>
> "Oh no, he told me himself—I asked him about it—he didn't live like that at all, he wasted many, many minutes."
>
> "Well, let that be a lesson to you. It seems it's impossible actually to live 'counting every minute separately.' Whatever the reason, it's impossible."
>
> "Yes, whatever the reason, it's impossible," the Prince repeated. "I thought so myself . . . And yet I somehow can't believe it." (*Idiot*, 84; *PSS*, 53)

One cannot live one's life on the scaffold, but one can believe in the truth revealed on the scaffold. Myshkin, who "somehow doesn't believe" in the impossibility of realizing one's ideal during one's lifetime, would understand Goryanchikov's inexorable faith in a resurrection from the House of the Dead: "I thought, I determined, I swore to myself that the mistakes and lapses of the past should never occur again in the future. I drew up a program of my future and resolved to follow it strictly. A blind faith was born in me that I could and would fulfill it all" (*House of the Dead*, 343; *PSS*, 220). Goryanchikov writes his "Scenes from the House of the Dead" during a transcendent moment and the paradoxical optimism these lines exude is the optimism of a man standing on the very brink of revelation and experiencing "an ecstatic and prayerful fusion in the highest synthesis of life."

Jackson sees in *The House of the Dead* Dostoevsky's only portrayal of a successful conversion experience, Goryanchikov becoming the only character to "complete the spiritual journey Dostoevsky later charted for his 'great sinner.'"[34] Goryanchikov does undergo a conversion experience, but this conversion is not final, nor conclusive—nothing in Dostoevsky is. The character's portrayal in the introductory chapter preceding his memoirs as an embittered, spiritually crushed human being differs dramatically from the radiant image of a man resurrected from the dead, ennobled and strengthened by his suffering, that emerges from the final pages of "Scenes from the House of the Dead."[35] Like Myshkin's condemned man in *The Idiot*, Goryanchikov the man does not fulfill the resolutions made on the scaffold; he too is unable to prolong his epiphanic moment or make it relevant to his everyday struggles post-prison, outside of the narrative reality he creates as a writer. But life afterwards, with its disappointing failures and shortcomings in the face of the ideal, does not destroy the sanctity of the scaffold moment, as the historical impossibility of authentically dialogical contact between a nobleman and a peasant does not affect Goryanchikov's personalist faith in the spiritual necessity of such a class-transcending relationship. The spiritually productive dialogue that takes place on the pages of *The House of the Dead* is silenced outside the world of fictional reality, as Myshkin's efforts at *vzhivanie* largely fail outside the realm of the hero's dialogical imagination, but the belief in the ideal survives by virtue of the absurd, at least for the reader who is willing to take the risk of believing in an absurdity.

According to Gary Saul Morson, "two novels subsist within the . . . covers [of *The House of the Dead*], and the reader is given a choice, as are we all, between despair and hope, between the suffering that deforms and the suffering that ennobles."[36] In my opinion, the covers of *The House of the Dead* conceal only one novel, but a truly Dostoevskian one, marked by the characteristically Dostoevskian threshold temporality, where nothing is final and the most important choices are yet to be made. In this context, the conversion that takes place in *The House of the Dead* is not fundamentally different from other temporary conversions conditioned by a "scaffold" experience that take place in Dostoevsky's novels: Rogozhin's moments of saving grace, Dmitry's willingness to expiate his guilt by suffering, and Ippolit's gesture of deep respect paid to his ideological opponent, Prince Myshkin, when the dying youth declares his wish to "bid farewell to a Human Being" (*Idiot*, 429; *PSS*, 348).

Chapter Five

The Limit of Empathy: A Dostoevskian Saint on Trial

> What good is the bleeding heart? What's to be done with all this pitying?
> —Philip Roth, *Letting Go*

A VOCATION OF THE INDIVIDUAL INEFFABLE IN *THE IDIOT*: NASTASIA FILIPPOVNA

Dostoevsky's readers often find his positive heroes unconvincing, philosophically problematic, or ideologically immature. Others, moved by his art's Christian message, are troubled by their own emotional involvement with the "wrong" characters: they admit to reading *Crime and Punishment* for the sake of Raskolnikov, not Sonya, are ashamed of their guilty love affair with Stavrogin, or uneasy about their intellectual investment in Ivan Karamazov, at the expense of Alyosha. Fears over this kind of reception and a constant concern with the vitality, ideological sophistication, and fighting power of his ideal heroes never left the author, as he created a succession of saintly messengers poised to propagate a distinctly Dostoevskian version of the Gospel. Dostoevsky's worries that Myshkin may not have the winning balance of virtue and sympathy or that Zosima's existential answer to Ivan's philosophical challenge will be deemed inadequate may have been partly justified,[1] if only because the discussion over these issues is still under way. On the other hand, the lively interest generated by most of the Dostoevskian "saints" in critical literature testifies to their considerable vitality. If, as Arkady Dolinin notes, Dostoevsky's major novels are one cumulative attempt to locate and depict "a perfectly beautiful man,"[2] the most significant outcome of this lifelong effort is not the creation of one, most convincing, ideal type, but rather the generation of intense spiritual and intellectual interest in *the good* as such. For, perhaps more than any other nineteenth-century artist, Dostoevsky endeavored to make the good look not only attractive,[3] but also interesting and novel (*original'nym*), while consistently revealing evil's essential banality.

Nowhere is the question of a positive, Christlike hero posed more provocatively and at a greater risk to the author's cherished ideal than in *The Idiot*, where the test of "Prince Christ" in nineteenth-century Russia becomes a test of man's spiritual possibilities in the modern world. Here Myshkin's precarious *imitatio Christi*, that takes him to the very limit of ethical action, provokes the reader into a powerful emotional connection with the hero: the Prince puzzles and challenges, attracts and repels, but leaves no room for indifference, initiating an important dialogue about the fate of the good. The novel's catastrophic ending raises the question of the hero's responsibility, making us wonder whether the final tragedy symbolically commemorates the world's cruel antagonism to Christ's revolutionary mission or results from the actions of an imperfectly conceived or, perhaps, imperfectly incarnated Christ.[4]

I suggest that the spiritual trials faced by Myshkin indeed evoke those of Christ as defined in the Schelerian-Bakhtinian interpretation of Incarnation, and the hero's acceptance of these lofty challenges marks him as a Christ*like* hero, even as he fails to meet them. As a result, the perfection of the uniquely efficacious Christ is highlighted precisely through the hero's painfully obvious deviations from his model. By examining the Prince's empathetic efforts, I propose to redefine the hero's position in relation to the ultimate spiritual ideal posited in the novel, using the concept of *active empathy* as a measure of his successful incarnation. Drawing on the fruitful connection between the notion of *consummation*—an empathizer's active role in directing the other's "ineffable" inner person toward its ultimate realization in God—and that of Christian Incarnation, developed in the theoretical part of this book,[5] I will explore the hero's consummating activity as a challenging effort to make his empathetic knowledge of human *others* relevant to his special relationship with the *Divine Other*.

Myshkin's fundamental transformation throughout the novel may be seen as a passage from an *active* existential approach to the world, consistent with Dostoevsky's view of Christ's mission, to an increasingly *passive* attitude, which yields little in the way of spiritual renewal in those around the hero and embroils him in a spiral of tragic events leading to the final catastrophe. Joseph Frank explains this transformation by pointing to the change in Myshkin's response to another's suffering: throughout the novel, the Prince gradually moves from what Max Scheler calls a vicarious fellow feeling to the total coalescence with the object of empathy, Frank suggests, without explicating the relevance of the Christological aspect of active empathy in Scheler to Myshkin's Christlike mission.[6] In Bakhtin's terms, such a transition would signify a passage from *vzhivanie* to mere empathy, from creative to passive, duplicating understanding. Indeed, the Prince's anxious efforts to enter "another soul" ultimately result not in a hopeful meeting of two spiritually enriched personal beings, but in a reemergence of one *single*, hopelessly solipsistic consciousness that has, as it were, occupied the entire stage of dialogue, crowding out the other's hopeful presence. As we have seen in chapter 4, in his impatient, godlike empathy with Rogozhin, the Prince was often unable to sustain a truly responsible dialogical relationship, ultimately objectifying his partner in dialogue. But in his relationship with Nastasia Filippovna he faces, and ultimately succumbs to, another danger to the process of active empathy—that of the *self's* complete dissolution in the other. Let us examine the progress of Myshkin's mission in relation to the heroine.

In Nastasia Filippovna, the Prince immediately recognizes a kindred soul, kindred precisely in the monumental scope of its spiritual dimension, commensurable only with his own—a soul that is capable of fathoming his lofty purpose and of encompassing his messianic message in its depth. Hence the mutual "recollection" of the other's inwardly familiar image: Myshkin's "I seem to have seen your eyes somewhere . . . perhaps in a dream" (*Idiot*, 127; *PSS*, 90); Nastasia Filippovna's "But really it does seem as though I had seen him somewhere before" (*Idiot*, 127; *PSS*, 89; *Idiot*, 138; *PSS*, 99). Under the cynical exterior of Nastasia's public persona, that of a heartless courtesan, Myshkin detects the stifled movements of her *individual ineffable*, the high-minded and touchingly humble person within, whose considerable spiritual potential has been realized only in suffering. This is why the hero is immediately drawn to her pained face and to her peculiar beauty in suffering (*Idiot*, 103; *PSS*, 69). The Prince's persistent courtship of the heroine in part 1, his constant throwing himself between Nastasia Filippovna and her cynical retinue—foolish and tactless from the point of view of worldly decorum—is a pursuit of her *individual ineffable*. It is a staunch acknowledgment of her higher, ultimately real inner being in the face of those who have denied her any personal identity beyond the scandalous titles of "shameless creature" or "the fantastic woman."[7]

In Nastasia Filippovna, the entire spiritual dimension: the certainty of her value judgment, her lofty notion of love, her ferocious sense of justice—all these covert gifts of the spirit reveal themselves almost exclusively in her suffering. The heroine is brutally traumatized by the experience of childhood rape, yet her emotional response is not exhausted by grieving over her private misfortune, instead turning into a furious outrage over the denigration of goodness as such. Persecuted by Totsky and his shallow clique, she comprehends in full the moral horror of their activities—dismissed as entirely comme il faut by virtually every character but Myshkin—and suffers through spiritual torments unknown to her tormentors. Ultimately, Nastasia Filippovna blames herself for Totsky's sordid crimes. So much so, that suffering becomes the only "place" in her troubled soul where she is able to experience value, albeit in its negative realization—as indignation over the denial of agape, the corruption of justice, and the betrayal of the good. Thus, her entire spiritual drive is "used up" in the act of suffering, which is now valued as the only, if necessarily perverse, *activity* of the soul, the only part of her emotional faculty where she can still feel her moral self.

By confronting Nastasia with his own truth about her spiritual vocation, Myshkin wants to free her from her debilitating emotional pain, not only because his love demands the happiness of the beloved, but because, in liberating her spiritual essence from its entrapment in suffering, he must realize his higher, salvific mission in respect to her soul. He needs to awaken her *individual ineffable* and to lure it away from its confining domicile, so that her moral feeling can find another, hopeful, expression in her inner person, besides suffering. Only then could she discover the fullness of being and the richness of spiritual life: for the first time experiencing her act-center freely, she could love and answer love. In this context, Myshkin's initial consummating efforts in respect to Nastasia Filippovna do not exhaust or reify her potential, but, rather, give it a new, hopeful direction.[8] Thus, from the start, this process is motivated by deeply spiritual concerns: while his *compassion* moves Myshkin to relieve Nastasia's pain, his *love* is concerned with releasing her inner Person for a new spiritual existence. This is why any accusations of secular ministering to the weak or of a purely "hygienic" concern with Nastasia Filippovna's happiness as the end-value are unjust in regards to the Prince's motive.[9]

During the Prince's first encounter with Nastasia Filippovna and throughout part 1, he retains his unique surplus of vision in respect to the heroine and benefits from his external point of view in his understanding of the "fantastic woman." This privileged position allows him not only to glimpse the spiritual potential of her purely personal being, but also to notice those carefully constructed psychological barriers that trap it deep within her public self. The Prince comprehends the full extent of Nastasia Filippovna's suffering at the hands of her offenders, but he is also keenly aware of her active participation in her own persecution. He intuitively understands that a victim of abuse may respond to relentless harassment by taking persecution into her own hands, masochistically celebrating deliberate self-debasement. By vindicating Nastasia Filippovna from blame, he attempts to arrest the circular process of self-blaming and self-debasement, in which the heroine is helplessly trapped. "It's impossible that your life should be utterly ruined," the Prince asserts with conviction at Nastasia Filippovna's birthday party:

> What does it matter that Rogozhin came to you or that Gavrila Ardalionovich tried to deceive you? Why do you keep on harping on it? Few people are

> capable of doing what you've done. I don't mind saying it to you again. . . . You're proud, Nastasia Filippovna, but perhaps you're so awfully unhappy that you really think you are yourself to blame. (*Idiot*, 189; *PSS*, 142)

Although Myshkin vindicates Nastasia Filippovna from any blame for her involuntary involvement with Totsky, he reproaches her for her willful self-laceration, for endlessly "harping" on past injuries and gratifying the obsessive need to reopen old wounds. His extraordinary lucidity in respect to Nastasia Filippovna's inner personality results from his external point of view combined with a compassionate imagination, and the surplus of vision he dialogically reveals to his interlocutor makes her reevaluate her own image of herself. When Nastasia Filippovna marches into Ganya's apartment with the intent to avenge herself on her offender by scandalizing his whole family, Myshkin does not hesitate to stop her:

> "And aren't you ashamed of yourself?" cried the Prince suddenly with deep, hearfelt reproach. "*You are not the woman you pretend to be.* [*Razve vy takaia, kakoiu teper' predstavlialis'*.] Why, it isn't possible!"
>
> Nastasia Filippovna looked surprised. She smiled, but seemed to be concealing something behind her smile. She was a little embarrassed and, glancing at Ganya, went out of the room. But before she reached the entrance hall, she suddenly returned, went up to Mrs. Ivolgin, took her hand, and raised it to her lips.
>
> "He's right, I'm not really like that, he's guessed it" she whispered rapidly and fervidly, flushing all over, and, turning round again, walked out so quickly this time that no one had time to realize what she had come back for. (*Idiot*, 138–39; *PSS*, 99–100)

Unlike the Myshkin we encounter in the third and fourth parts of the novel, the Myshkin of the Ivolgin episode is still capable of passing judgment ("You should be ashamed of yourself!"), and it is precisely his independent, assertive, yet deeply compassionate tone that proves effective in a conversation with his emotionally fragile interlocutor. Exposed to another's truth about herself, Nastasia Filippovna suddenly becomes aware of a different—pure and high-minded—woman behind the image of a depraved courtesan: "'I'm not really like that, he's guessed it,' she whispered rapidly and fervidly" ("Ia ved' i v samom dele *ne takaia*") (*Idiot*, 139; *PSS*, 100).

The creative judgment we encounter here is akin to what Paul Tillich calls "the negation of the negation of love."[10] In its battle against the powers of hatred and ressentiment, "love must destroy what is against love, but not him who is the bearer of that which is against love," Tillich writes.[11] The creative "surplus" of love, its status as an *act*, and not merely an emotional state, consists not only in inducing love to grow but also in protecting its spontaneous movement. For that reason, "judgment is an act of love which surrenders [the forces that] resist love to self-destruction. When, out of love, God condemns this is not the negation of love, but the negation of the negation of love."[12] In Myshkin's soft-spoken reproach one discerns a powerful resistance to the forces of "not-love": the surplus of knowledge he reveals to Nastasia Filippovna is precisely a judgment against the lack of proper self-love and the powers of ressentiment that constantly stifle her ideal inner being, forcing her spiritual potential into the service of masochistic instincts. This is why Myshkin's judgment of Nastasia Filippovna is here different from his silent, finalizing judgment of Rogozhin during the "fall from faith" episode (see chapter 4). Myshkin's surplus of vision is dialogically revealed to Nastasia Filippovna and she is aware of his unwavering faith in her spiritual being. "And the Prince is the first man I've ever come across in my life in whom I can believe as a true and loyal person. He believed in me at first sight, and I believed in him," she confesses in a rare single-voiced passage (*Idiot*, 175; *PSS*, 131). Myshkin's active compassion for Nastasia Filippovna, his empathetic, but by no means duplicating understanding of her inner world affects a temporary change in the haughty heroine, making her renounce her meticulously planned insult to Mrs. Ivolgin and, in effect, ask for her forgiveness. *Vzhivanie* miraculously transforms the gesture of defiance into a gesture of reverence and respect. In the words of Varya Ivolgin, Myshkin of part 1 "has an influence over [Nastasia Filippovna]" (*Idiot*, 141; *PSS*, 101).

However, as in Myshkin's relationship with Rogozhin, the triumph of *vzhivanie* is temporary. In Nastasia Filippovna the Prince faces an interlocutor with an uncompromising, blindly aggressive position vis-à-vis the world and with a rigid, deliberately finalized image of herself, which resists his efforts to broaden and reshape it in the process of active empathy. In the abundant gallery of Dostoevsky's intensely self-conscious characters, Nastasia Filippovna's striking image is one of the most extreme examples of this characteristically underground pathology. Her vision of herself is immensely influenced by the perception of her public image through the eyes of the Petersburg aristocracy, whose opinion she cannot disregard, despite her public defiance of their judgment. When Nastasia Filippovna calls herself "a shameless slut" and "Totsky's concubine" (*Idiot*, 190; *PSS*, 143), she loudly and audaciously pronounces the words maliciously whispered behind her back. These words of another's discourse, appropriated by Nastasia Filippovna, belong to the monological realm: rumors and accusations abound behind her back and reach her ears via indirect channels. By repeating such judgments in public in the form of self-accusations, the heroine, as it were, challenges her silent accusers to an open confrontation. This perverse dialogical challenge is, of course, intended to scandalize her "decent," socially rewarded offenders. But the vector of her ressentiment aggression is directed against the self as much as against the others. Ultimately, the heroine's protest against such condescending monological judgment on the part of those she considers morally inferior takes a peculiar underground form of masochistic self-judgment.

Nastasia Filippovna answers the accusations of her silent judges by cultivating the objectified vision of herself they have created. She demonstratively forces her living self into the constricting matrix of her externally perceived public image, deliberately stifling her own potential. If the public perceives her as a shameless slut, she will become one, but, in exchange for the pain caused by this costly transformation, she will reserve the right to be her own sole judge and persecutor. According to Nastasia Filippovna's peculiar logic, "an honest woman" may have responded to Myshkin's proposal of marriage by returning his love, but "Rogozhin's slut" is capable only of ingratitude, deceit, and depravity. It is much more in keeping with her "nature" that she should prefer Rogozhin's gold-filled purse. "Is it possible?" the Prince exclaims in horror, having learned of Nastasia's decision to run off with Rogozhin:

> "Did you think it wasn't? Well, maybe I too am proud, shameless slut though I am! You called me perfection just now—some perfection to go into the slums just to be able to boast of having trampled on a million and a title! What sort of wife should I make you after that?" (*Idiot*, 190; *PSS*, 143)

Nastasia Filippovna's circular reasoning, which always remains in the service of her masochistic instincts, is fully apparent in this deliberately public self-analysis: she is running off with Rogozhin because she is unworthy of marrying the Prince, and she is unworthy of marrying the Prince because she is running off with Rogozhin. Nastasia Filippovna's self-judgment for the past "crimes" (her victimization at the hands of Totsky) is psychologically justified by carefully staged scandalous acts in the present: "Look, Prince, your fiancée has taken the money because she is a slut [*rasputnaia*], and you wanted to marry her!" Nastasia exclaims even before her acceptance of Rogozhin's indecent proposal (*Idiot*, 191; *PSS*, 144). These newly committed transgressions constitute yet another source of guilt, and the process of masochistic self-blaming continues ad infinitum.

Admittedly, there is much irony and theatrical exaggeration in her public self-judgment, which, as in the case of the Underground Man, can be suspended or reversed as soon as other judges dare to repeat it as their own. But, unlike the Underground Man, Nastasia Filippovna cannot easily "shrug off" her ressentiment-inspired self-accusations, because, in her masochistic zeal, she has herself closed most of the characteristic loopholes usually pervading a double-voiced discourse of this sort, leaving few paths to self-justification. Eventually, these bitter condemnations seep down into the very core of her personality. Initially produced for external use, the vulgar labels gradually become identical with her private self-definition.[13]

By trying to live up, or rather "live down," to the finalized, utterly objectified image of a depraved whore, Nastasia Filippovna deliberately renounces her own potential, destroying the last remnants of faith in herself. Here we witness a paradoxical denial of what Bakhtin calls the I' s "absolute future," the completely open, unfinalizable space of becoming, in which the "I-for-myself" always locates its most essential part. In the heroine's ressentiment revolt, the "I" renounces its sacred inner territory. Thus the self begins to experience itself not in the open *act* of becoming and consummation but precisely in the reified *product* of its violent self-objectification: the "I-for-myself" must become identical with the perversely finalized "I-for-another."[14]

Myshkin, who understands Nastasia Filippovna's emotional struggle better than anybody else in the novel, shares his insights into the underground psychology with Aglaya:

> Oh, she keeps crying every minute in her frenzy that she refuses to admit she has done wrong, that she is the victim of other people, the victim of a libertine and a villain. But whatever she may say to you, I want you to know that she is the first not to believe it and that she believes with all her heart that, on the contrary, she is herself to . . . to blame. When I tried to dispel that dark obsession of hers she suffered such agonies that my heart will never heal as long as I remember that dreadful time. I feel as though my heart had been pierced through once and forever. She ran away from me—do you know why? Simply to prove to me alone that she was a depraved creature. *But the most dreadful thing is that perhaps she did not realize herself that she wanted to prove it to me alone, but ran away because inwardly she felt that she had to do something disgraceful so as to be able to say to herself at once: "There, you've done something disgraceful again, so you must be a depraved creature!"* Oh, perhaps you won't understand this, Aglaya! Do you know that she seems to derive some dreadful, unnatural pleasure from this continual consciousness of shame, a sort of revenge on someone. (*Idiot*, 443–44; *PSS*, 361)

Myshkin's sensitive diagnosis brings to the fore both the unconscious character of Nastasia Filippovna's psychological motivation and the profound confusion between her external and internal self-definitions, culminating in a coalescence of the "I-for-another" and the "I-for-myself" ("she wanted to prove it to *me alone* [that she is depraved]"; "she . . . wanted to tell it to *herself* at once: . . . 'you are base'"). Nastasia Filippovna, who is not fully conscious of her active role in her own persecution, desperately needs to be exposed to this truth about herself, the truth that can be revealed only to a consciousness located firmly *outside* of her anguished psyche, with its apparent blind spot.

What is needed is precisely the judgment against the lack of love, an acknowledgment of Nastasia's cruel aggression against self-love, which renders her tragically unresponsive and "unreachable" to the love of others. She needs to know that, although she is not to blame for being "the victim of a libertine and a villain," she is guilty of inflicting suffering on herself and others in an effort to justify her self-finalized image. And she needs to hear this truth not from the spiteful lips of her rival Aglaya, as she eventually does, but from the lips of a compassionate, although not passively empathetic interlocutor. In Schelerian terms, this is the Prince's chance to love Nastasia Filippovna in a way that is spiritually more authentic than her own love for herself, thus unobtrusively reshaping her perverted *ordo amoris* and teaching her authentic self-love in the process (see Scheler, *GW*, 2:483). But Myshkin, who does not hesitate to reproach Nastasia Filippovna in the beginning of the novel, becomes ever more passive and non-judgmental as time goes by.[15] He seems unable to reveal to Nastasia Filippovna his most essential surplus of vision in respect to her inner being. Instead, he offers her unconditional forgiveness, complete and permanent absolution of all sins, past and future, and such undiscriminating acceptance eventually drives the justice-seeking heroine to despair.

Like Rogozhin, who is devastated by Nastasia Filippovna's lack of offense at his beating, because he realizes that "she thinks so little of me that she can't even feel much resentment against me" (*Idiot*, 229; *PSS*, 176), in her most hopeless moments, Nastasia Filippovna interprets Myshkin's lack of judgment as an expression of moral superiority, the sign of ultimate pride, which is so supreme, so unconcerned with gratifying the impulses of vanity, that it is easily confused with authentic humility. "[She] . . . told me straight out that she did not ask anyone for condescending pity, nor for help or for 'raising her up to one's level,'" the Prince confesses to Aglaya (*Idiot*, 444; *PSS*, 361–62). Myshkin's goal is, of course, far from "raising Nastasia Filippovna to his level." Rather, his lack of judgment results from the complete dissolution of his self in the self of his fellow-sufferer, but, in Dostoevsky's world the characters' supreme pride and supreme humility may have identical effects on those around them.[16] Both may provoke the characters to assert their personality in a Promethean rebellion of self against God and ultimately cause them to lose their faith both in their mortal ego and in their immortal Creator. As Romano Guardini notes,

> [Myshkin's selfless compassion] could be interpreted as passivity, as the loss of individual character in the other's suffering, or even as a mystical self-surrender to the forces of primordial chaos, and the drowning of the "I" in the "Thou," behind which there emerges a universal, all-encompassing "Thou." . . . In actuality, Myshkin's compassion often drives a character to the limit, where he threatens to turn away from God.[17]

THE "DUEL" SCENE AND THE ROLE OF JUDGMENT

Myshkin's gradual loss of a firm "footing" outside of Nastasia Filippovna's anguished soul, his growing powerlessness in the face of her emotional deterioration and the inability to stand up to her relentless aggression against her own *individual ineffable* become fully apparent after his choice of Nastasia Filippovna in the famous "duel" scene between the female rivals. During Aglaya's Schillerian confrontation with Nastasia Filippovna, the latter becomes exposed to the very *surplus of vision* that was withheld from her by Myshkin. In Aglaya's psychological assessment of Nastasia Filippovna, blurted out as part of her accusatory speech, we recognize several familiar insights the Prince had earlier shared with Aglaya during their intimate conversation on the green bench. But the tones of love and mercy give way to those of cruel contempt, as Myshkin's compassionate discourse becomes reaccentuated in Aglaya's merciless revelation. Compare:

> MYSHKIN TO AGLAYA
> "Do you know that *she* [*Nastasia Filippovna*] *seems to derive some dreadful, unnatural pleasure from this continual consciousness of shame* [*pozora*], a sort of revenge on someone." (*Idiot*, 444; *PSS*, 361)
>
> AGLAYA TO NASTASIA FILIPPOVNA
> ". . . *All you are able to love is your sense of shame* [*svoi pozor*] *and the constant thought that you have been dishonored* [*opozoreny*] *and offended*. If your dishonor were less, or if it had not existed at all, you'd be more unhappy than you are." (*Idiot*, 572; *PSS*, 471)

In the "duel" scene, Myshkin's crucial surplus of vision is used as an ambush against Aglaya's vulnerable rival, who is caught off guard by the pitiless, cruel nakedness of Aglaya's truth.[18] Here Aglaya shows no scruples about using "only truth" without "tenderness," the kind of judgment of which she has once accused Myshkin in her own tender, altruistic moments (*Idiot*, 436; *PSS*, 354).[19] This cruel truth, stripped of Myshkin's characteristic tenderness, is especially painful for Nastasia Filippovna, because in its stinging tones she dimly recognizes the content of a different, severe, but ultimately hopeful *judgment* that Myshkin had attempted to reveal but was unable to "carry across" to her wounded psyche, blinded by pain. Ultimately unutilized by the hero, this active surplus of love is "picked up" by Aglaya and, in her hands, finds its way back into action, now as an exquisite *weapon* against Nastasia Filippovna.

No longer a "judgment against the lack of love," Aglaya's judgment does not spare "the bearer of that which is not love," blaming Nastasia Filippovna even for her mistreatment at the hands of Totsky—in Myshkin's words, precisely "for being the victim of a villain and a libertine" (*Idiot*, 443; *PSS*, 361). In her fury, Aglaya resorts to the same heartless and unjust labels that have become so familiar to Nastasia Filippovna, and the fact that Aglaya's wording in addressing her rival evokes the most characteristic euphemism used to describe "the kept woman" is hardly accidental. "He [the Prince] is such a simple-minded man and, in his simplicity, he believed that he could be happy . . . with a woman . . . of *that sort of character* [*s zhenshchinoi . . . takogo kharaktera*]," Aglaya blurts out, evoking the earlier references to "that sort of woman" in the novel (*Idiot*, 571; *PSS*, 471). (Compare Myshkin's: "Are you *that sort of woman*?" ["Razve vy *takaia*"] [*Idiot*, 138; *PSS*, 99] and Nastasia Filippovna's own: "Everyone knows . . . *what sort of woman* I am" ["Ia . . . izvestno *kakaia*"] [*Idiot*, 233; *PSS*, 179].) Imperceptibly, judgment against the lack of love turns into judgment against love.

It is when Aglaya enlists Myshkin as her ally in condemning Nastasia Filippovna, as it were, putting his signature under Aglaya's cruel verdict, that Nastasia Filippovna loses all constraint and reverts to the sheer use of power: "'He [the Prince] has told me already that he hates you,' Aglaya could just bring herself to murmur" (*Idiot*, 575; *PSS*, 474). Faced with yet another condemnation, which ultimately amounts to the familiar "You *are* that sort of woman!" Nastasia Filippovna retaliates in her usual fashion. With a mixture of grief and indignation, she embraces her newly confirmed public image and furnishes the final "proof" of her ruthlessness and depravity. "Well, take your treasure . . . ," she shouts to Aglaya with a growing challenge, "there he is, he's looking at you, he's too stunned to talk, take him, take him, but on one condition: get out of here at once! This minute!" (*Idiot*, 575; *PSS*, 474). This deeply ambivalent exclamation is a cry of despair on the verge of lapsing into rage. It is Nastasia's last attempt to hold on to her spiritually redeeming self-definition by releasing the "perfectly beautiful man" for a life of happiness. But, as Rogozhin's "Take her . . . She's yours! I give her to you!" (*Idiot*, 240; *PSS*, 186), addressed to Myshkin on the eve of his attempted murder, this promise of sacrifice is revoked the moment it is uttered:

> She [Nastasia Filippovna] sank into an arm-chair and burst into tears. But suddenly something new blazed up in her eyes; she looked steadily and intently at Aglaya and got up from her seat.
>
> "But if you like I shall order him—or-der him at once—do you hear?—I have only to order him and he'll leave you—leave you at once and stay with me for good and marry me, and you'll run back home alone. Do you want me to? Do you want me to?" (*Idiot*, 575; *PSS*, 474)

Shrugging off the sting of Alaya's brutal insult, Nastasia bites back, showing her erstwhile idol just "what kind of woman" she can be. She reverts to the tried technique of giving her audience a taste of just what they've ordered, while playing the game on her own terms. But here it is the Prince, her cherished hero, who becomes the pawn of her manipulation:

> "Damn you [Prince], then, damn you for being the only one I believed in. Get out, Rogozhin, you're not wanted here!" she cried, almost unconscious of what she was saying, forcing the words out with difficulty, with a distorted face and parched lips, evidently not believing a single word of her boastful speech, but at the same time wishing to prolong the scene, if only for a second, and so deceive herself. The impulse was so violent that perhaps she could have died—at least the Prince thought so. "There he is—look!" she cried at last to Aglaya, pointing to the Prince. "If he won't come up to me now, if he won't take me and give you up, then you can have him. I'll let you have him. I don't need him!" (*Idiot*, 575–76; *PSS*, 474)

Nastasia Filippovna shouts her half-hearted threats in utter desperation, but, in her grief, she gambles with her most prized possession. By testing Myshkin's loyalty, Nastasia tempts her would-be savior and exploits his Christlike compassion. This negative evocation of the Temptation of the Abyss reveals the seriousness of the heroine's transgression against Myshkin's saving mission. "Save me now," she, in effect, proclaims, "or you are not the savior I believed in!" ("Damn you then for being the only one I *believed* in"). It is a provocation of agape, a capricious demand to be saved this very minute, not because she has now freed herself for a spiritual renewal through the Prince, but because her salvation becomes a means to spite her haughty rival. Here the dual nature of Nastasia Filippovna's aggression—directed at both *self* and *other*—becomes fully apparent, as her crimes against self-love lead to transgressions against the other's—Myshkin's—sacrificial love.

The heroine's fall from grace during the "duel" scene also becomes a tragic acknowledgment of the ultimate failure of her self-sacrifice, thwarted by the dark forces of ressentiment. (This point marks her final spiritual demise, the suicide of her *individual ineffable*.) Without this sacrifice, the only active expression of her love for Myshkin, she seems no longer capable of bearing her suffering or of endowing it with meaning.

During the heroines' violent standoff, the inwardly torn Myshkin takes his eyes off Aglaya, jolted by the spectacle of Nastasia's ultimate despair, her "agony unto death": "The impulse was so violent that perhaps she would have died, at least the Prince thought so" (*Idiot*, 576; *PSS*, 474). Here the Prince is faced, painfully, with the question of the limits of suffering and of co-suffering. How long can one endure excruciating pain without giving up on hope? And how can one's co-suffering in the face of the other's unbearable torments transcend its "rootedness" in her grief and gain the creative, hopeful energy of compassion? "Pierced through the heart" by Nastasia Filippovna's pain, the Prince will go on suffering *with* his fateful beloved to the end, but will no longer be capable of true, active compassion. He, too, will perhaps die, unable to bear his burden: "I . . . I shall soon die in my sleep," he tells Evgeny Pavlovich after his break with Aglaya (*Idiot*, 587; *PSS*, 484). And while loving compassion, with its "surplus of vision," is capable of transcending the apparent limit of the sufferer's pain, of carrying the empathizer beyond the dead end of the other's hopelessness, mere co-suffering knows its rigid limitations. It can add nothing to one's debilitating pain, nor take away from it.

How does Myshkin's passionate empathy degenerate into tragically helpless co-suffering? This development seems to follow from that troubling inability to retain a unique place in Being that had so concerned Scheler and the early Bakhtin.[20] Terrified and overwhelmed by Nastasia Filippovna's torments, Prince Myshkin feels violently drawn into the very center of her battered self. And, with each new blow to her personal dignity, he finds it more difficult to reemerge from his dark dwelling, as it were, back into the light of day, as his initially *active love* becomes increasingly paralyzed by his *reactive empathy*.[21] This process of losing himself in the other culminates in the uncanny, largely pantomimic scene immediately following "the duel," in which the Prince comforts Nastasia Filippovna, so unexpectedly "chosen" by him after her emotional collapse: the Prince half-consciously mimics Nastasia's movement, he laughs when she laughs and cries when she cries. Enveloped in one unitary feeling of quiet desperation, the couple gradually become silent and comfortably numb (*Idiot*, 576–77; *PSS*, 475).

Now entirely *within* Nastasia Filippovna's consciousness, Myshkin cannot support or affirm her personal being. He can offer her no hope, for, within her self, there is only hopelessness and self-condemnation. Here we are reminded of Bakhtin's description of the solipsistic (unincarnated) spirit as both helpless and hopeless in its pure inwardness, without the enabling energy of the flesh or the saving recourse to the other.[22] Myshkin's spiritual mission in respect to Nastasia Filippovna—the vocation of her *individual ineffable* and its realization outside of suffering—fails, because the "summoner" now finds himself "inside" Nastasia's all-encompassing pain. In fact, he can no longer offer her any consummation. Nor can he forgive or absolve the mortally anguished heroine, because, as Bakhtin notes, the act of absolution necessarily issues *from outside* of the repenting consciousness: like other fundamentally social acts, it presupposes an ontological distance between subjects.[23]

After the confrontation between the heroines and Nastasia Filippovna's collapse, the Prince courageously attempts to stay the course of agape, but without its active, hopeful surplus, his love loses its power and creative potential. With tragic resignation, he surrenders himself to the course of the unfolding events, having accepted his troubling knowledge about Nastasia Filippovna:

> His opinion of Nastasia Filippovna was firmly fixed, otherwise, of course, everything about her would have appeared enigmatic and incomprehensible to him now. But he genuinely believed that she could still be restored to life [literally: "resurrected"]. He had quite truthfully told Radomsky that he loved her truly and sincerely, and in his love for her there really was a sort of attraction to some sick pathetic child whom it was difficult and even impossible to leave to its own devices. . . .
>
> But it was this opinion of Nastasia Filippovna's mental condition that saved him to some extent from all sorts of other perplexities. Now she was quite different from the woman he had known three months before. Now, for instance, he no longer wondered why she had run away from marrying him then, with tears, with curses and reproaches, and was now insisting herself on marrying him as quickly as possible. "So it seems," thought the Prince, "that she is no longer afraid as she used to be then, that her marriage to me would be my ruin." Such rapidly restored confidence in herself could not, in his opinion, be natural to her. . . .
>
> In short, . . . [various] reasons . . . might have contributed to it; *but what was most evident to him was what he had been suspecting for a long time, that the poor infirm soul could no longer bear the strain*. Though all this did, in a way, save him from misunderstandings, it could not give him any rest nor any peace of mind all that time. *Sometimes he, as it were, tried not to think of any of this*. (*Idiot*, 593–94; *PSS*, 489–90)

The Prince may have responded to Nastasia Filippovna's misguided call for salvation in the duel scene but he can hardly bring about her resurrection. In this context, the narrator's "he sincerely believed that she could still be resurrected" sounds especially flat and unconvincing within the general context of the passage. If anything, this is merely belief by inertia.

Rather, the hero believes, hopelessly, and has believed "for a long time," that "the poor soul has given up." In effect, he gives up *with* her, choosing to share her somber journey to the limit of suffering (*khozhdenie po mukam*), even if his empathy can no longer lessen the shared load.

The Prince's knowledge about Nastasia Filippovna, no matter how intimate, is now too immediate to be of use to the Prince, because he has no hopeful "place" outside her purview, where he could take it to gain perspective, and no sovereign self where he could personalize it or make it relevant to his future. This is why there is a troubling sense of detachment from any "information" about the heroine expressed in the passage. His knowledge about Nastasia Filippovna now exists only in the form of his "established opinion," the pragmatic minimum of information about her immediate needs that shields the Prince from the tragic truth. His established opinion is to delay an opinion—not to think of anything ("ni o chem ne dumat'") and so, march on bravely to the bitter end.

Thus, having exhausted his creative surplus of vision, the Prince finds himself at the tragic limit of passive empathy. Unable to consummate Nastasia Filippovna, the hero, in effect, forces her to consummate herself.[24] His failure to provide creative judgment the heroine so desperately needs drives her to seek ultimate judgment and absolution under Rogozhin's sacrificial knife.

FROM POTENTIALITY TO ACTUALITY: TWO VISIONS OF A CATASTROPHE

The novel's irresistible movement toward a catastrophe, the powerful gravitation of its plot to the end, which could be explained by the text's eschatological temporality,[25] can thus also be seen as the tragically doomed movement of agape that has lost its active, empowering surplus. Having lost his creative influence on Nastasia Filippovna, the hero can do nothing but passively follow her to the final limit of her suffering. As we have seen, the question of Nastasia Filippovna's resurrection, so important in Dostoevsky's notebooks for *The Idiot*[26] and central in the novel, is answered in the negative long before the tragic finale, predetermining the development of the novel's external events.

A number of distinct structural similarities between two major catastrophe scenes—Myshkin's discovery of Nastasia Filippovna's artfully concealed corpse in part 4 and his earlier discovery of Rogozhin hiding at the hotel before his murderous attack in part 2—point to an important relationship between the two key moments in the life of the Christlike hero, one engendering and predetermining the other. The eerie similarities of Myshkin and Rogozhin's two journeys through the city, the symmetry of their highly symbolic itineraries and the significant pattern of looks exchanged by the two heroes in both scenes—all these affinities suggest a system of symbolic equivalencies between the two episodes that illuminate the central relationship between Myshkin, Rogozhin, and Nastasia Filippovna. They also shed light on the issue of the hero's responsibility, suggesting that the first, ultimately thwarted, catastrophe, the "fall from faith" episode, analyzed in chapter 4, is an ominous rehearsal of the novel's finale.

The novel's final chapter (part 4, chapter 11), featuring Myshkin's discovery of the heroine's murder, is structured in such a way as to constantly send the reader back in time, to the various points in the narrated past that contain the "seeds" of the unfolding catastrophe. With its distinctly choreographed ritualistic walk to Rogozhin's house and a ceremonial presentation of Nastasia Filippovna's corpse, this chapter is especially closely linked with the equally ritualistic scene of Rogozhin's attack on Myshkin and the adjacent scenes of his mysterious chase after the Prince in part 2 (chapter 5 and the ending of chapter 6). Throughout chapter 11, the characters' memory of their previous, ominous encounters in Petersburg ("that [last] time"; "then" / "tot raz"; "togda")—in Rogozhin's house, on Petersburg streets and at the hotel "The Scale"—is constantly alive, providing an important reference system to the reader. Trying to track down Rogozhin to get word about his runaway bride, the alarmed Prince stops to recuperate at "The Scale" and relives his previous experience at the fateful hotel. He ventures to predict Rogozhin's next move by recollecting their last encounter at "The Scale":

> He recalled Rogozhin himself, as he had seen him recently at the funeral service, then in the park, then—suddenly *here in the corridor* as he had *then* hidden in the corner and had been waiting for him with a knife. He could now remember his eyes—the eyes that glared at him *then* in the darkness. (*Idiot*, 606; *PSS*, 499)

The Prince realizes that, "like the last time," Rogozhin will not be eluded—his urgent mission will once again bring him to the appointed place: "If Rogozhin is in Petersburg, then, even if he is hiding for the time being, he will certainly end up coming to see him, the Prince [to the hotel], with good or with evil intentions, quite likely *as he had done the last time*" (literally: *then*, "pozhalui *khot' kak togda*") (*Idiot*, 606; *PSS*, 499–500). Rogozhin, too, seems to correlate their final "coming together" with the previous, equally catastrophic meeting at "The Scale." The Prince's tremors upon seeing Nastasia Filippovna's lifeless body are surely a sign of epilepsy, Rogozhin predicts warily, just as the previous times he saw Myshkin before a seizure, "[just the way] it was before your fit" ("[kak] kak raz bylo pered pripadkom")

(*Idiot*, 611; *PSS*, 503). The previous time Rogozhin saw Myshkin in Petersburg "before a fit" was, of course, during his attempt on the Prince's life, thwarted by the miraculous onset of the illness.

The characters' peculiar, dance-like processions through Petersburg streets, distinctly symmetrical in the two scenes, also bind the episodes together, pointing to their shared symbolic content. In the "fall from faith" episode (episode 1) Myshkin *begins* his journey, accompanied by Rogozhin stalking him at a distance, from Rogozhin's house and *ends* it at the hotel, while in the novel's finale (episode 2), the direction is reversed: the characters' procession *begins* at the hotel, *ending* at Rogozhin's house. In both cases, Nastasia Filippovna is the shared thought guiding the characters and bonding them together. She is the ultimate destination of their walks: in part 2, Myshkin half-consciously leads the spellbound Rogozhin, lurking close behind, to Nastasia Filippovna's house, while in part 4, Rogozhin becomes the guide, solemnly instructing Myshkin to walk after him for a final visit to Nastasia Filippovna.[27] In both cases, the heroine is tellingly absent: away in Pavlovsk in episode 1; dead in Rogozhin's study in episode 2.

In both episodes the two walk on different sides of the street. Episode 1: "And now, at the house, he [Rogozhin] stood *on the other side of the street, on the pavement opposite*, [*po drugoi storone ulitsy . . . na protivopolozhnom trotuare*] barely fifty paces away, with his arms folded—waiting" (*Idiot*, 249; *PSS*, 193); episode 2: "Look here, Lev Nikolaevich, you go on straight there, to the house, you know, don't you? And I'll walk *on the other side* [*po toi storone*]. And see that we keep together" (*Idiot*, 607; *PSS*, 500). They come together, bridging their ritualistic distance, at the end of their journeys: for a dramatic clash at the hotel (episode 1); for a final sojourn at Nastasia Filippovna's somber wake at Rogozhin's house (episode 2).[28]

The same alternating pattern of detachment and approach evident in the distinct choreography of their ballet-like movement through Petersburg is mirrored in the pattern of looks, both exchanged and averted, during the two fateful meetings between the heroes.[29] Upon his return from Moscow, Myshkin soon becomes aware of Rogozhin's flashing eyes following his every move through the city. Visiting Rogozhin at home, the Prince counters Rogozhin's menacing gaze from behind his back with a direct look into his eyes:

> While he [Rogozhin] led the Prince to an arm-chair to make him sit down at the table, the latter *happened to turn round to him* [*sluchaino obernulsia k nemu*] and was startled by his strange, somber stare. Something seemed to transfix the Prince and at the same time he remembered something somber and painful that had happened not so long before. Without sitting down and standing motionless for some time, *he looked Rogozhin straight in the eyes*

> [on nekotoroe vremia *smotrel Rogozhinu priamo v glaza*], which at the first moment seemed to flash even more distinctly. (*Idiot*, 223; *PSS*, 171)

But Myshkin's consistent pressure for a directly dialogical, face-to-face and eye-to-eye contact with his unlikely soul mate meets with Rogozhin's sullen suspiciousness. Even after exchanging crosses with the Prince at a moment of sudden spiritual intimacy, Rogozhin shrinks back from Myshkin's touch, refusing to seal his new brotherhood in Christ with an embrace:

> "But, good Lord, let me at least embrace you before we part, you funny fellow!" cried the Prince, looking at him with tender reproach as he was going to embrace him. But no sooner did Rogozhin raise his arms than he let them fall again. He could not bring himself to do it; *he turned away so as not to look at the Prince* [*on otvertyvalsia, chtoby ne gliadet' na kniazia*]. He did not want to embrace him. (*Idiot*, 240; *PSS*, 185)

In a momentary outburst of magnanimity, Rogozhin eventually grants Myshkin's wish and even "throws in" Nastasia Filippovna as a generous bonus for his new brother in Christ, but the forced nature of this impatient sacrifice is too apparent to reassure the reader, or the anxious Prince:

> "Never you fear! I may have taken your cross, but I won't cut your throat for your watch!" he [Rogozhin] muttered thickly and suddenly broke into a sort of strange laugh. A moment later his face became completely transformed: he grew terribly pale, his lips trembled, his eyes blazed. He raised his arms, embraced the Prince tightly and said breathlessly: "Well, take her, if that's how it is to be! She's yours! I give her to you! . . . Remember Rogozhin!" And, leaving the Prince, he went hurriedly in *without looking at him* [*ne gliadia na nego*] and slammed the door behind him. (*Idiot*, 240; *PSS*, 185–86)

Love so immoderately expressed immediately turns into hatred. Resenting both the strained intimacy of their protracted good-byes and his impossible promise to the Prince, Rogozhin again averts his eyes in defiance of the hero's dialogical challenge. Here the gesture of the character's furious retreat, leaving Myshkin on the threshold of his anthropomorphic, "Rogozhin-like" home, is especially emphatic. Slamming the door on the Prince, Rogozhin, as it were, retreats from the threshold of dialogue into the gloomy privacy of his distrustful self, away from Myshkin's probing gaze and his calls for brotherly love. In the context of the passage, the twice-repeated gesture of raising his hands in an aborted embrace ("No sooner *did* Parfen *raise his arms / hands* than he let them fall again"; "Parfen . . . tol'ko *podnial svoi ruki*, kak totchas zhe opustil ikh") calls to mind the idiomatic "to raise a hand against somebody" ("*podniat' ruku* na kogo-to") and anticipates Rogozhin's emblematic movements during his murderous attack on Myshkin: "His [Rogozhin's] right hand *rose* and something flashed in it; the Prince didn't try to stop it" ("Pravaia ruka ego [Rogozhina] *podnialas'*, i chto-to blesnulo v nei; kniaz' ne dumal ee ostanavlivat'" (*Idiot*, 252; *PSS*, 195).[30]

As Myshkin walks away from Rogozhin's house to Nastasia Filippovna's, incited by his inner demon to test Rogozhin's promise, it is now the Prince who avoids direct looks at his omnipresent stalker, eluding Rogozhin's defiant stare.[31] Ashamed of his suspicions, Myshkin turns away from Rogozhin as soon as their eyes meet, unable to endure his silent judgment: "And why had he, the Prince, not gone up to him now himself, but *turned away from him*, as though he had not noticed anything, though *their eyes had met*" (*Idiot*, 250; *PSS*, 193). Exhausted by the battle with his inner demon, who has led him away from an "open and clear" face-to-face dialogue with his brother in Christ,[32] Myshkin seems almost relieved by the sight of Rogozhin rising in front of him on the staircase of the hotel, poised for a murderous attack: "For a second *they stood face to face* and almost touching each other. Suddenly the Prince *seized him by the shoulders and turned him round toward the staircase*, closer to the light: he wanted to see his face more clearly" (*Idiot*, 251; *PSS*, 195).

The Prince's bizarre gesture immediately preceding his cry: "Parfyon, I don't believe it!" is his last attempt to appeal to Rogozhin directly and openly, in the spirit of that surprisingly productive compassionate dialogue with Rogozhin that the Prince had enacted in his mind during his fateful walk to Nastasia Filippovna's house. Conscious of his own fall, Myshkin reasserts the ideal of agapeistic dialogue, insisting on confronting his assassin *face-to-face* and summoning all his faith in Rogozhin. His turning Rogozhin toward the light may be another call "to read each other clearly," to reestablish that long-cherished dialogical addressivity that was lost during the rival-brothers' mutual fall from faith. (Compare: "[It was necessary to] be able to read each other's thoughts clearly . . . and let it all happen freely and . . . joyfully" [*Idiot*, 247; *PSS*, 191].)[33]

If, *on the plane of mythical action*, the heroes' two silent, spellbound walks ending in an encounter with death are evocative of a chthonic journey to the land of the dead conducted by a psychopomp guide—with its characteristic notion of keeping sacred distance and ritualistic prohibitions on looking—*on the spiritual level*, the complex pattern of the heroes' movements toward and away from each other signifies their difficult path to communion. Here their spatial relationship, expressed through walking, touching, and gazing, is as much a part of their intense emotional communication as any discursive expressions of dialogue. Consider, for example, the importance of Myshkin's walking with and behind Rogozhin as a peculiar means of living into Rogozhin's soul, of "walking in his shoes," discussed in the previous chapter.

The contrast between face-to-face and secondhand communication, between looking into someone's eyes and stealing a sideward glance at them in passing, evident in the analyzed passages, acquires spiritual and ethical significance in the context of Myshkin's resolution to approach "the Russian soul shrouded in darkness" directly and openly, unprejudiced by the secondhand "truths" about it. Myshkin's inability to sustain the absolute spiritual chastity required for such ideal communication reflects his arduous struggle with the demands of active love and agapeistic dialogue. And although Rogozhin's relationship to the dialogical ideal is less obvious, the questions of sustaining dialogical addressivity and enduring dialogical distance are relevant to Rogozhin's inner struggle as well. "When you are not *before my eyes*, Lev Nikolaevich [kak tebia net *predo mnoiu*], I begin to hate you at once," Rogozhin confesses to Myshkin during the Prince's first visit in his Petersburg home. "Now you haven't been with me a quarter of an hour and all my hatred is disappearing and you are as dear to me as before" (*Idiot*, 226; *PSS*, 174). For the emotionally immediate Rogozhin, an agapeistic feeling for Myshkin is possible only in Myshkin's presence, as it were, under the direct gaze of Myshkin's own agape that melts away hatred and resentment.

Rogozhin's unexpected affection for the Prince, that goes against the logic of rivalry ingrained in Rogozhin's competitive and vengeful character, is a spontaneous response to the irresistible call of Myshkin's love, surprising even to Rogozhin himself. This is why he often resents this inexplicable affection, as it were, "forced" from him. The peculiarly reactive nature of Rogozhin's feeling makes it extremely volatile and fragile: it is so immediate that it cannot separate itself from its source in Myshkin's love. It is, as it were, contained *within* Myshkin's loving gestures—his unaffected smile, his reassuring voice addressed to Rogozhin—and cannot be experienced outside of them. This is an extreme case of "out of sight, out of mind" or rather "out of heart," as the Russian version of the proverb has it ("S glaz doloi—iz serdtsa von"). For that reason, for Rogozhin, avoiding Myshkin's gaze may be a way of eluding the inexplicable power of the Prince's demanding, dialogue-seeking love.

The distinct pattern of "dialogical" and "monological" gestures (*vzgliad v glaza / vzgliad v storonu; poiavlenie drug pered drugom / otvertyvanie, povorot v storonu*; a look into one's eyes / a look away, facing each other / turning away or to the side) is completed in the concluding sections of both episodes, where the estranged heroes decisively come together. After following each other through Petersburg on the opposite sides of the street and consistently avoiding direct contact in a kind of solemn initiation, the two knights come face-to-face in the name of their lady, look into each other's eyes and together discover the terrible truth of their common mission. In the novel's finale (episode 2), Rogozhin seems to answer Myshkin's gesture of turning him to the light in episode 1 by bending him down to a chair, so he could face him:

> EPISODE 2
>
> "Why don't you light a candle?" asked the Prince.
>
> "No, let's not," replied Rogozhin and, *taking hold of the Prince's hand, bent him down, forcing him into a chair*; he *sat down opposite,* pulling up his chair, so that their knees were almost touching. (Rogozhin [. . .] *vziav kniazia za ruku, nagnul ego k stulu*; sam *sel naprotiv*, pridvinuv stul tak, chto pochti soprikasalsia s kniazem koleniami.) (609; *PSS*, 502)

> EPISODE 1
>
> He [the Prince] had already taken a step but could not restrain himself and turned around. Those two eyes—*the same two eyes*—suddenly met his own (italics in text). The man who was hiding in the niche had also taken a step forward. For a second they stood face to face and almost touching each other. *Suddenly the Prince seized him by the shoulders, turned him round toward the staircase, closer to the light: he wanted to see his face more clearly*. (Odnu sekundu oba stoiali drug pered drugom pochti vplot'. *Vdrug kniaz' skhvatil ego za plechi i povernul nazad, k lestnitse, blizhe k svetu: on iasnee khotel videt' litso.*) (251; *PSS*, 195)

A strange intimacy is born, as the heroes conclude their intricate dance by approaching the partner closely ("[Rogozhin] pochti soprikasalsia s kniazem koleniami"; "oba stoiali pochti vplot'"), assuming the directly dialogical position of standing or sitting *opposite each other* ("[Rogozhin] sel *naprotiv*" / "oba stoiali *drug pered drugom*"). In part 2, it is the terrible intimacy of a murderer and his victim, the last flare of Rogozhin's impatient love-hatred about to consume its object. In part 4, it is a somber union between a sinner and his confessor, Rogozhin's timid agape returning into its "domicile" in Myshkin's. In both cases, the heroes are on the threshold of a new, if terrifying, communion with each other. Whether the intense closeness of "almost pressing against the other" promises a deadly clash or an embrace, this emphatic stance signifies a return to togetherness, if not dialogue.

Table 3 demonstrates the abundant symmetries between the core episodes of the two symbolically linked chapters.

What is shown or "presented" to Myshkin in these two spellbinding scenes that read as one? After an initiation of sorts, conducted by the sinister master of ceremonies, Rogozhin, a concealed object is ostentatiously, even

Table 3: Semantic Correspondences between Catastrophe Scenes in *The Idiot*[34]

Episode 1 (Part II, chapter V)	**Episode 2** (Part IV, chapter IX)
1) Lestnitsa, na kotoruiu kniaz' vzbezhal iz-pod vorot, vela v koridory pervogo i vtorogo etazhei, po kotorym i byli raspolozheny nomera gostinitsy. Eta lestnitsa, kak vo vsekh davno stroennykh domakh, byla kamennaia, temnaia, uzkaia i vilas' okolo tolstogo kamennogo stolba. Na pervoi zabezhnoi ploshchadke v etom stolbe okazalos' ***uglublenie, vrode nishi***,[A] ne bolee odnogo shaga shiriny i polshaga glubiny. Chelovek, odnako zhe, mog by tut pomestit'sia. Kak ni bylo temno, no, vzbezhav na ploshchadku, *kniaz' totchas zhe razlichil, chto tut,* ***v etoi nishe***, *priachetsia zachem-to* **chelovek**.[B] Kniaziu vdrug zakhotelos' proiti mimo i ne gliadet' naproavo. *On stupil uzhe odin shag, no ne vyderzhal i obernulsia.*[C] *Dva daveshnie glaza, te zhe samye, vdrug vstretilis' s ego vzgliadom.*[D] Chelovek, taivshiisia v nishe, tozhe uspel uzhe stupit' iz nee odin shag. Odnu sekundu oba *stoiali drug pered drugom pochti vplot'*.[E] *Vdrug kniaz' skhvatil ego za plechi i povernul nazad, k lestnitse,*[F] *blizhe k svetu: on iasnee khotel videt' litso.* (*PSS*, 194–195)	**2)** **A**) Voshli v kabinet. V etoi komnate, s tekh por kak byl v nei kniaz', proizoshla nekotoraia peremena: cherez vsiu komnatu protianuta byla zelenaia, shtofnaia, shelkovaia zanaveska, s dvumia vkhodami po oboim kontsam, i otdeliala ot kabineta ***al'kov***,[A] v kotorom ustroena byla postel' Rogozhina. Tiazhelaia zanaveska byla spushchena i vkhody zakryty. No v komnate bylo ochen' temno; letnie "belye" peterburgskie nochi nachinali temnet', i esli by ne polnaia luna, to v temnykh komnatakh Rogozhina, s opushchennymi storami, trudno bylo by chto-nibud' razgliadet'. Pravda, *mozhno bylo eshche razlichat' litsa*, khotia ochen' neotchetlivo. Litso Rogozhina bylo bledno, po obyknoveniiu; glaza smotreli na kniazia pristal'no, s sil'nym bleskom, no kak-to nepodvizhno. —Ty by svechku zazheg?—skazal kniaz'. Net, ne nado, otvetil Rogozhin i, *vziav kniazia za ruku, nagnul ego k stulu*[F]**;** sam sel naprotiv, pridvinuv stul tak, chto *pochti soprikasalsia s kniazem koleniami*.[E] (*PSS*, 502) **B**) *Kniaz' shagnul eshche blizhe, shag, drugoi, i ostanovilsia.*[C] On stoial i vsmatrivalsia minutu ili dve; oba, vo vse vremia, u krovati nichego ne vygovorili; u kniazia bilos' serdtse tak, chto, kazalos', slyshno bylo v komnate, pri mertvom molchanii komnaty. No on uzhe prigliadelsia, tak chto *mog razlichat' vsiu postel'*; na nei kto-to spal sovershenno nepodvizhnym snom; ne slyshno bylo ni maleishego shelesta, ni maleishego dykhaniia. Spavshii byl zakryt s golovoi beloi prostynei, no chleny kak-to neiasno oboznachalis'; vidno tol'ko bylo,

Table 3: continued

Episode 1 (Part II, chapter V)	**Episode 2** (Part IV, chapter IX)
	po vozvysheniiu, chto lezhit protianuvshis' **chelovek**.[B] (*PSS*, 503) Kniaz' gliadel i chuvstvoval, chto chem bol'she on gliadit, tem eshche mertvee i tishe stanovitsia v komnate. Vdrug zazhuzhzhala prosnuvshaiasia mukha, proneslas' nad krovat'iu i zatikhla u izgolov'ia. Kniaz' vzdrognul. —Vyidem,—tronul ego za ruku Rogozhin. Oni vyshli, uselis' opiat' v tekh zhe stul'iakh, *opiat' odin protiv drugogo*. Kniaz' drozhal vse sil'nee i sil'nee *i ne spuskal svoego voprositel'nogo vzgliada s litsa Rogozhina*.[D] (*PSS*, 503)

artfully, revealed to the Prince. In a dark, narrow enclosure ("uglublenie," "nisha" / "al'kov," "postel'"; "cavity," "niche" / "alcove," "bed") a buried prize, a "person" awaits discovery: "Dark as it was, on reaching the landing, the Prince immediately *made out* that *there, hiding in the niche, was* ***a person***" (*Idiot*, 251; *PSS*, 195); "But his [the Prince's] eyes had already got used to the dark, and *he could make out* the whole bed . . . ; all one could see by the raised outlines was that *there, stretched out full length, was a* ***person***" (*Idiot*, 611; *PSS*, 503). The notion of being hidden or buried (*chelovek spriatavshiisia v nishe; chelovek spriatannyi v al'kove*; a person hiding in the niche; a person hidden in the alcove) is reinforced by carefully chosen vocabulary: "*priachetsia* zachem-to chelovek"; "chelovek *taivshiisia* v nishe" (literally: "for some reason, a person is *hiding*"; "a person *concealing himself* in the niche"). "There [at the teacher's wife's] he [the Prince] will find me first thing in the morning, but you will *conceal* me [a ty menia *skroesh'*]," Nastasia Filippovna will also tell Rogozhin on the eve of the murder (*Idiot*, 611; *PSS*, 504). Hours before Myshkin's final visit to Rogozhin the latter is said to be "hiding (lit. *concealing* himself) for the time being," "*skryvalsia* na vremia" (*PSS*, 499).

There seems to be a deliberate superimposition of images here—one ominous vision of a hidden person (*chelovek*) summons another, establishing a visual paradigm reminiscent of cinematic montage. Rogozhin's artfully revealed figure, a macabre jack in the box springing at Myshkin, already promises another, exquisitely wrapped "surprise" awaiting the Prince at the

Table 4: Translation of Table 3

Episode 1 (Part II, chapter V)	**Episode 2** (Part IV, chapter IX)
1) The stairs, which the Prince ran up from under the gateway, led to the corridors of the ground and first floors, along which were the rooms of the hotel. This staircase, as in all old houses, was of stone. Dark and narrow, it twisted round a thick, stone column. On the first half landing there was ***a cavity*** in the column**, *something like a niche*,**[A] not more than a yard wide and about eighteen inches deep. But there was enough room for a person to stand there. Dark as it was, on reaching the landing, the Prince immediately noticed (lit.: made out) that there, hiding in the niche, was ***a person***.[B] The Prince suddenly wanted to pass by without looking to the right. *He had already taken one step, but could not restrain himself, and turned around.*[C] *Those two eyes—the same two eyes—suddenly met his own.*[D] The person who was hiding in the niche, had also taken a step forward. For a second *they stood face to face and almost touching each other.*[E] *Suddenly the Prince seized him by the shoulders and turned him around toward the staircase, closer to the light*[F]*: he wanted to see his face more clearly.* (*Idiot*, 251)	**2)** **A)** They went into the study. Since the Prince had been there, there had been a certain change in the room: a green damask curtain was stretched right across the whole length of the room; it could be drawn aside at either end, dividing the study from the ***alcove*****,**[A] where Rogozhin had placed his bed. The heavy curtain was drawn at both ends. But it was very dark in the room; the summer "white" Petersburg nights were beginning to get darker, and if it were not for the full moon, it would have been difficult to make out anything in Rogozhin's dark rooms with the drawn curtains. It is true, they could still see each other's faces, though very dimly. Rogozhin's face was pale, as usual; his lusterous eyes stared at the Prince intently but somewhow motionless. "Why don't you light a candle?" asked the Prince. "No, let's not," replied Rogozhin and, taking hold of the Prince's hand, *he bent him down forcing him into a chair;*[F] he *sat down opposite* pulling up his chair, *so that their knees were almost touching.*[E] (*Idiot*, 609) **B)** *The Prince took one step closer, then another, and stopped.*[C] He stood still, staring for a minute or two; neither of them uttered a word while standing by the bed; the Prince's heart beat so violently that it seemed it could be heard in the room, in the dead silence of the room. But his eyes had already got used to the dark, and he could make out the whole bed; someone lay asleep on it in an absolutely motionless sleep; not the

Table 4: continued

Episode 1 (Part II, chapter V)	**Episode 2** (Part IV, chapter IX)
	faintest movement could be heard, not the faintest breath. The sleeping person was covered, from head to foot, with a white sheet, but the limbs were, somehow, faintly visible; all one could see by the raised outlines was that there, under the covers, stretched out full length, lay **a person**.[B] (*Idiot*, 610) The Prince looked and he felt that the longer he looked the more still and death-like the room became. Suddenly a fly, awakened from its sleep, started buzzing, flew over the room and settled at the head of the bed. The Prince gave a start. "Let's go back," Rogozhin touched his arm. They went back and sat down in the same chairs, *again facing each other*. The Prince was trembling more and more violently and *he did not take his questioning eyes off Rogozhin's face*.[D] (*Idiot*, 610–11)

end of the novel. It is as if, in the momentarily arrested image of Rogozhin poised for a murderous attack, there flashes another motionless image, that revealing the *completion* of his somber labor. Within a dark, tomb-like enclosure lurks death itself—Myshkin's, Nastasia Filippovna's, and ultimately Rogozhin's as well.

The dark, confining space sheltering the hidden "person" in the novel's finale is evocative of the stifling, hopeless love offered to the heroine that has imprisoned her spirit and sealed her doom: there is no room for *another* in Rogozhin's possessive love; no room for *himself* in Myshkin's increasingly passive empathy. Neither relationship can support Nastasia Filippovna's quest for personhood, but in her death she attains the proud title of *person* denied to her in life. The use of "chelovek" in the finale is especially significant because it is the word that is consistently used in relation to Myshkin and evokes Christ, the biblical "Son of Man" in the novel. We shall recall that Ippolit uses this unassuming title in relation to the Prince as a sign of deep respect: "Let me bid farewell to *a Human Being*" ("Ia s *Chelovekom* proshchus'") (*Idiot*, 429; *PSS*, 348) and Nastasia Filippovna herself exclaims: "Farewell, Prince, you are the first *human being* I've seen" ("v pervyi raz *cheloveka* videla") (*Idiot*, 195; *PSS*, 148).[35] She who recognized and honored the Son of Man in Myshkin now finds a personal, Christian identity in death. This meaningful word also identifies Rogozhin, uniting the murderer and his victim in the loving consciousness of the Christlike hero. Both are equally precious addressees of his agape, seen from the eschatological, timeless perspective of these "last moments" as simply human beings, liberated from the objectifying labels that had accompanied them in life.

It is merely as "sons of man," and no longer as enemies, rivals, or even friends, that Myshkin and Rogozhin encounter each other in the novel's finale, where Myshkin's love gathers its flagging strength and once again becomes active for one last radiant moment of grace. In Myshkin's merciful ministering to Rogozhin after Nastasia Filippovna's murder Romano Guardini sees the image of the Savior before His death, praying for those who had crucified Him: "Father, forgive them, for they know not what they do" (Luke 24:34).[36] In a similar vein, Russian critics have recognized a visual detail of a Russian icon, "Christ leading Adam out of Hell," in the gesture of Myshkin holding Rogozhin's hand after the ceremonial "unveiling" of Nastasia Filippovna's body.[37] But this remarkable gesture can also be interpreted using internal textual reference, namely, by a reference to the structurally and symbolically symmetrical chapter 5, part 2. It is a somber fulfillment of Myshkin's erstwhile call for an all-revealing and open encounter with Rogozhin, the kind of communion that knows no shame, no forced promises or self-conscious renunciations: "Now the darkness is dispersed, the demon banished, there are no more doubts, his heart is full of joy! . . . Yes, he would have liked to meet Rogozhin now, he *would have taken him by the hand* and they would have gone together," the Prince exclaims as he battles his shameful suspicions about Rogozhin in part 2 (*Idiot*, 247; *PSS*, 191).

There are indeed no doubts, suspicions, or gestures of concealment during the heroes' final sojourn, when things hidden ("spriatannye," "skrytye," "taivshiesia") are revealed, once and for all, in a moment of sobering, almost unendurable clarity. A crucial change occurs in Rogozhin: he now experiences his strange affection for Myshkin without shame or secret resentment. For the first time, he stands *before* the Prince ("pred toboi"), trustingly and unself-consciously open to his agape. And in Myshkin's last offering to Rogozhin—in the fact that he mourns where Rogozhin is unable to mourn, cries when Rogozhin cannot cry and repents *for* the unrepenting hero—one may recognize a sacrificial substitution, a kind of completion of Rogozhin's spiritual image before God's eyes, amounting to a somber *consummation* of his brother in Christ. But this momentary union, based on the mystical transparency of souls on the verge of non-being that makes dialogue unnecessary is hardly the kind of deeply personal, active togetherness Myshkin had called for on the eve of Rogozhin's first murderous attack. In keeping with the novel's notion of realism, it takes place beyond the boundary of this life, as an ironic afterthought to Myshkin's messianic ideal.

THE CHALLENGES OF A DOSTOEVSKIAN CHRIST

What is the essential metaphysical meaning of the meticulous symmetry between the two visions of a catastrophe, so methodically foregrounded in the text, and how does it illuminate the fate of the hero's Christlike mission?[38] Symbolically, the two episodes may be seen as one and the same event, "unfolded" in time, but viewable from the eschatological perspective as one concentrated "moment" of being. Ultimately, Rogozhin's knife was always intended for Nastasia Filippovna, and, from the point of view of purely spiritual, non-pragmatic, and non-psychological motivation, Myshkin's obstinate pursuit of Rogozhin on the eve of his assassination attempt may be seen as a self-sacrificial gesture (though inconsistently realized as such), ultimately "addressed" to Nastasia Filippovna and analogous to his shielding of her from the officer's slap and of Varya from Ganya's (*PSS*, 291, 99). From this perspective, the two episodes may be described as two stages or moments of one and the same crime: episode 1 reveals its inception, while episode 2—its sinister fruition. If, in episode 1, with its deliberately unfinalized narrative discourse, pervaded by loopholes, and its interruption of the crime, Rogozhin's defining act is shown largely in its *potentiality*, in episode 2, the same act is depicted in the mode of *actuality*, as a potential fulfilled and an intention realized. In this context, it is especially significant that we see only the aftermath of the murder—presented not as an *act* but as the final and irrevocable *product* of Rogozhin's activity.

In an especially poignant form, this episodic sequence dramatizes a theme central for the entire novel—the "beautiful man's" confrontation with the reality of evil. In his struggle to remain true to his Christlike mission, the hero must face a fundamental question: *how does one responsibly acknowledge the reality of evil and take an active stance toward it?* Can one lucidly recognize an act of evil without condemning the evildoer and brutally finalizing his spiritual self in the process? (Here we are again reminded about the challenges of that infinitely subtle yet powerful "judgment of love," aimed to destroy that which is against love but not the bearer of that which is against love.) And how can one preserve the crucial faith in the sinner's better self, capable of spiritual renewal, without averting one's gaze or running away from the disheartening evidence of evildoing?

Both of these tasks become highly problematic for the Prince, whose love is tested for its potency in counteracting evil while saving the evildoer in the crucial period *between the two episodes*, before Rogozhin's, still largely potential, proclivity for transgression comes to its realization in the novel's finale. As I have shown in chapter 4, in episode 1, Myshkin both averts his eyes from the deeply troubling signs of evil and loses faith in the evildoer. By instigating Rogozhin's attack, he also becomes complicit in an act of evil, provoking its actualization. The Prince's refusal to see the signs of the brewing violence, expressed in the literal gesture of looking away, is initially a means of preserving his faith in Rogozhin, of resisting the temptation to proclaim him a murderer. But, imperceptibly, this motivation changes: as Myshkin's premonition strengthens into a prophecy and Rogozhin's murderous image becomes completely objectified, the Prince is no longer running away from his shameful suspicions about Rogozhin, but from Rogozhin himself.

Instead of denying the discomforting truth of Rogozhin's pernicious aggression, the Prince needs to find another, hopeful truth in Rogozhin's inner being, in the words of Myshkin's own earlier sermon on compassion—the truth capable of turning Rogozhin to the light. But, simply averting his eyes from the troubling actuality, the Prince gradually loses faith in Rogozhin's spiritual potential as well. Reifying Rogozhin's image and confirming his gruesome intention ("Was it certain that Ragozhin woud kill?!" [*Idiot*, 246; *PSS*, 190]), Myshkin silences the hero's living voice, denying Rogozhin his vital "surplus of the self." As we have shown in chapter 4, the profoundly dialogical act of *consummation* ultimately turns into that of cruel, entirely monological *finalization* of the hero's inner person.

Guardini compares Myshkin's ordeal in part 2 chapter 5 to Christ's temptation of the abyss: "If Thou be the Son of God, cast thyself down" (Matthew 4:6).[39] It seems that the hero's spiritual test is also evocative of Christ's temptation at the cross by the mocking crowd: "If Thou be the Son of God, come down from the cross" (Matthew 27:40). Losing his faith in Rogozhin, Myshkin tempts him by walking to Nastasia Filippovna's house, knowing full well that he had promised Rogozhin not to interfere, and testing Rogozhin's own immediately regretted promise to "cede" Nastasia Filippovna to the Prince. Christ's "Thou shalt not tempt the Lord" becomes "Thou shalt not tempt thy brother in the Lord" for Myshkin, while his faint-hearted denial of Rogozhin's challenge also tempts him to run away from it and from his own personal mission of the cross in respect to both Nastasia Filippovna and Rogozhin.

But, as the Prince succumbs to the first temptation, to a large degree provoking Rogozhin's attack, his transgression immediately becomes his punishment. Consumed by guilt, he acknowledges his share of responsibility for Rogozhin's fall, opening up a path to redemption: Myshkin's uncanny empathy with the character, bordering on "becoming Rogozhin," which accelerates Rogozhin's slide into violence, will later become a means of taking Rogozhin's sins upon himself, a spiritual undertaking that comes to fruition in episode 2. Ultimately, the Prince also withstands the latter test: overcoming the temptation to look away ("The Prince suddenly wanted to pass by *without looking to the right*" [*Idiot*, 251; *PSS*, 195]), he courageously faces his assassin and proclaims his faith in him. However, the fact that after Rogozhin's aborted attack the Prince virtually abandons his saving mission in respect to Nastasia Filippovna reveals the lingering spiritual effects of the Prince's momentary weakness.

When Myshkin resumes his mission of the cross after the "duel" scene, once again making himself responsible for Nastasia Filippovna, it is as a Christ who is faithful to his sacrificial task but who can no longer resurrect. Losing his struggle to pronounce a judgment against the denigration of love without condemning those who transgress against love, the Prince also loses the hopeful, creative power of his sacrificial love. Unable to keep the crucial balance between his own and the other's personal "surplus," Myshkin either abuses his surplus of vision in respect to others, as in the case with Rogozhin during the fall from faith episode, or is unable to use it at all, as in his relationship with Nastasia Filippovna. In terms of the theory of active empathy, we may say that his relationship with the suffering others becomes increasingly passive, lapsing into duplicating understanding, as the productive ontological distance between dialogical partners disappears.[40]

Because no surplus of vision is utilized to fuel the movement of spiritual creativity, the hero's engagement with Rogozhin and Nastasia Filippovna can no longer effect a meaningful spiritual change. Myshkin's courageous but utterly hopeless (and helpless) ministering to Rogozhin in the closing scene of the final chapter illustrates the tragic desperation of his spiritual quest and recalls a similar, earlier, example of "hospice care" offered to Nastasia Filippovna in chapter 8:

> The Prince was sitting beside Nastasia Filippovna, gazing at her steadily and stroking her head and face with both hands, as though she were a little child. He laughed when she laughed and was ready to cry when she cried. He never said a word, but *listened intently to her abrupt, rapturous, and incoherent babble; he hardly understood anything*, but smiled gently; and the moment he thought that she was again beginning to fret or weep, to reproach or to complain, he immediately began stroking her head again and passing his hands tenderly over her cheeks, comforting and soothing her like a child. (*Idiot*, 576–77; *PSS*, 475)

Compare:

> Now and again Rogozhin *began to mutter suddenly, loudly, harshly and incoherently;* he began uttering little screams and laughing; then the Prince stretched out his trembling hand and gently touched his head and his hair, stroking them and stroking his cheeks—*he could do nothing more*! He began trembling again himself, and again his legs suddenly seemed to give way under him. . . . at last, he lay down on the cushion, as though in utter exhaustion and despair, and pressed his face against Rogozhin's pale and motionless face; tears flowed from his eyes on Rogozhin's cheeks, *but perhaps he no longer noticed his own tears and knew nothing about them.* (*Idiot*, 615; *PSS*, 506–7)

With the disappearance of the surplus of vision, no exchange of information, no true communication may take place. Two people are in the room, but there is only one consciousness, only one integral point of view, shared by both. Myshkin mechanically imitates Nastasia Filippovna's movements, he laughs when she laughs and cries when she cries. His tears flow on Rogozhin's face and moisten his dry, unrepenting eyes, but the Prince no longer notices the boundary between himself and other. A new, almost unbearable closeness is born, but this unmediated intimacy does not yield an understanding of another's soul: "[The Prince] hardly understood anything, but smiled gently" (*PSS*, 475). In both scenes, a single, agitated voice is heard, the carrier of monological discourse that soon degenerates into muffled and incoherent noises which no longer signify: Myshkin hears Nastasia Filippovna's "abrupt, rapturous and incoherent babble"; Rogozhin begins to "mutter suddenly, loudly, harshly and incoherently." The dissolution of one consciousness in another is soon followed by the eclipse of the remaining consciousness; the death of dialogue becomes the precursor of physical death.

The emphatically parallel scenes give final expression to a theme that has appeared as a gnawing leitmotif throughout the novel—that of the tragic limit of empathy. For this despairing Christ, empathy is no less than a courageous participation in the sufferer's excruciating agony, but it is also no more than that. The narrator's matter-of-fact "he could do no more" brings to mind Lev Shestov's discomforting definition of pity as simply an "[admission] that one can no longer be helped by other means."[41]

AN IDEAL OR AN IMPOSTOR?

Thus, in *The Idiot*, the process of active, "dialogical" empathy is constantly frustrated. Myshkin, who serves as a dialogical partner to all major characters in the novel, repeatedly fails in his role as communicator, unable to gain or retain an active understanding of another consciousness, to "live into" another soul without losing his own unique individuality. As a keen psychologist who "sees through people" on the one hand, and a passionate believer in "the Russian soul" by virtue of the absurd, the Prince succumbs to both dangers of monologization delineated by Bakhtin and Scheler. His premature judgment of Ippolit and Rogozhin antagonizes both characters, who resent Myshkin's tendency to replace a living voice with a ready-made, finalized image of the speaking person. On the other hand, his passive empathy and lack of positive judgment in relation to Nastasia Filippovna drive her to ultimate self-destruction. In the first case, *another's* (Rogozhin's) consciousness is finalized and objectified, becoming merely a function of Myshkin's master consciousness ("Thou" is dissolved in the global "I"); in the second case, Myshkin's *own* distinctive voice is silenced, merging with the voice of Nastasia Filippovna ("I" becomes dissolved in the global "Thou").[42] Both situations entail the loss of one surplus of vision—as a result, only one consciousness performs the role of a thinking, emotionally active subject (*the self* in the case of monological peering into another soul; *the other* in the case of complete fusion with one's dialogical partner). In either case, dialogue, which requires an active interaction of two points of view, ceases, lapsing into monological discourse, and the process of understanding loses its productivity.

The application of the Bakhtinian-Schelerian theory of intersubjectivity to Myshkin's empathetic experience is especially productive, because, in the wider context of the philosophers' theologically founded notion of empathy, the twofold failures of the hero's communicative efforts reflect the challenges of Christ. In chapters 1 and 2 we have shown the basis of Bakhtin's and Scheler's notion of an active existential approach in Incarnation: through Christ, God actively lives into a human being without ever relinquishing His otherworldly divinity. In the context of Bakhtin's later terminology, Christ, so to speak, withstands both temptations of "monologization," retaining both surpluses of vision: the divine and the human points of view. (Hence the profoundly *creative* essence of Incarnation as a model act for both philosophers and its message of hope for the life of the spirit, energized and empowered by its "dialogical" other.) In this context, the long-debated question of the fullness or deficiency of Myshkin's *incarnation* as an intended Christ figure can be approached from the point of view of his (active) empathy with others.

Many prominent readers have suggested that Dostoevsky's "Prince-Christ" (*Kniaz' Khristos*) is not sufficiently incarnated (and Incarnated). According to Vyacheslav Ivanov, in Myshkin "we have a soul that has plunged from that 'place beyond the skies' . . . described by Plato where with the gods men unborn contemplate the forms of eternal beauty," and "all the secret suffering of this soul, which does not achieve incarnation, arises from the incompleteness of this incarnation."[43] In a similar vein, for Bakhtin of *PDP*, the Prince also "lacks the necessary *flesh of life,*" which would grant him a definite position in being (173, italics in text). For that reason, he forever remains "on a tangent to life" (*PDP*, 173). Sergei Bocharov links a certain ghostliness of Dostoevsky's character with Goethe's scarcely incarnated Homunculus and Baratynsky's "nedonosok" ("a miscarried child"), noting the hero's lack of a specific place not only in space, but also in time,[44] while P. Bitsilli most likely refers mainly to the failure of Dostoevsky's "perfectly beautiful man" in his comment on Dostoevsky's typical "everyman," an "individuality potentiated to the utmost degree" at the expense of its personal vitality.[45] Romano Guardini brings the issue more directly into the context of Christian Incarnation when he examines the challenges of Myshkin's Christian mission. "His 'God problem' is not how he can come to God or how he can dwell in Him," Guardini suggests, "but rather how he can bear and accomplish his journey *from* God *into the world* that is so different from God, dark and hardened against Him."[46]

This kind of uncanny proximity to God, the hero's rootedness in the realm of the Absolute, that distant "place beyond the skies," may explain his Godlike perspective in respect to Rogozhin and Ippolit and the enormity of his surplus of vision that completely overpowers and consumes theirs. But in Myshkin's relationship with Nastasia Filippovna we encounter the opposite loss of balance: the hero becomes completely "drowned" in her self, as it were, too fully incarnated in the other. This crucial imbalance has important implications for the success of Myshkin's spiritual mission, that arduous task of carrying the message of divine agape from God into the world that Guardini sees as his defining purpose. In both relationships, the divine and the human partners are, so to speak, not available to each other. In the first case, *man* is excluded, since he is entirely "crowded out" by the hero's godlike consciousness. (In this context, we may mention Myshkin's curious refusal to give a direct answer to Rogozhin's question whether he believes in God in part 2, chapter 4, which, as Guardini suggests, seems to highlight the absurdity of the inquiry in respect to someone so immediately "*with* and *in* God"—to use Walker Percy's playful aphorism, "God is not religious." This absence of a mediated *relationship* with God makes it difficult for Myshkin to make His truth palatable or realistically "available" to his human others.)

In the second case, there seems to be no room for *God* in this crowded union. Entirely steeped in Nastasia Filippovna's consciousness, Myshkin can no longer invite the divine Other. He cannot channel divine mercy or absolution for the heroine, for these gifts issue *from without*. Myshkin's helplessness after the collapse of dialogue illustrates Bakhtin's observation that solipsistic spirit (in this case, both human and divine, or at least, godlike) is essentially weak and ineffective: it needs the empowering and transfiguring energy of its "other."[47] This is why Guardini's conclusion about Myshkin's entirely *human* weakness at the end of the novel does not contradict his earlier statement about the hero's exceptional proximity to God.[48] Incarnation is a matter of precarious (miraculous?) balance and a deficiency of one "surplus" impacts the effectiveness of the other.

In a letter to his wife Dostoevsky once wrote that he lacked the appropriate "form and gestures" to express himself to others ("Formy, zhesta ne imeiu" [*PSS*, 28.2:189]) and later voiced the same concern through the lips of one of his most beloved characters: "I don't have the right gestures [to express myself]," Myshkin confesses with some embarrassment to General Epanchin's guests. "My gestures are always contrary [to what I want to express]" (*Idiot*, 556) ("Ia ne imeiu zhesta. Ia imeiu zhest vsegda protivopolozhnyi" [*PSS*, 458]). This characteristic phrase gains special significance in the novel, where the question of *form* is of paramount importance. I believe that the fundamental problem faced by the tragically failing hero is not that of love in the sense of affection, but of empathy as love's practical realization, as a challenge of giving love a *form* personally adequate to its object.[49] The carrier of the most pristine, agapeistic feeling in the novel, Myshkin is unable to give it adequate form. Having exhausted empathy's active "surplus," he is ultimately unable to consummate his neighbors, to complete the other's spiritual image by summoning the realization of his *individual ineffable*. As a result, the answering gesture is equally inadequate,[50] and the hero is not fruitfully consummated by others, lacking their reciprocal incarnating touch.

In some ways, *The Idiot* and its protagonist illustrate the existentialist thesis George Steiner saw expressed through Dostoevsky's darker heroes, namely, that Dostoevsky's God is indeed in need of man.[51] In Myshkin's otherworldly messenger we encounter a divinely inspired being in need of a human consummating touch. In this sense, the novel highlights the fundamentally social nature of Incarnation in Dostoevsky's world: as humans, we are indeed consummated and incarnated by others through love and active empathy. In the form of human dilemmas, Myshkin's arduous mediating efforts reveal the tremendous challenges of Christ's spiritual undertaking. To extend Guardini's conclusions, *The Idiot* does not only foreground the difficulty of *choosing* Christ but also that of *being* Christ—a life journey fraught with temptations of active love, whose hopeful surplus should not be lost either "from above" or "from below."

This difficulty also translates into the challenge of interpretation: "reading" the Prince's actions, one must always balance the human logic of pragmatic or purely psychological motivation with the often astonishing logic of his divine calling. In this context, it is important to defend the hero from unjust accusations launched in a recent wave of literary criticism focused on

The Idiot. This trend of scholarship tends to conclude that Myshkin's failure demonstrates that he is not meant as a Christlike hero from the start, but rather as a familiar Dostoevskian impostor who "blocks" the real Christ from the rest of the characters, so direly in need of Christian redemption.

While Christ's uniqueness is a given for Dostoevsky, the author's journalism and notebooks give abundant examples of searching for the active ways of *imitatio Christi*. For example, Dostoevsky's repeated proposition "imagine that everyone is like Christ" (literally: "imagine that all people are Christs" / "Voobrazite, chto vse Khristy") from the notebooks for *The Devils* (*PSS*, 11:192–93) is not a denial of Christ's uniqueness but an expression of the author's staunch belief in the *reality* of Christ, whose descent into the world reveals man's spiritual possibilities. Dostoevsky's eccentric prince is certainly not "*the* Christ" but rather a practitioner of Christlike agape (a singular of Dostoevsky's "Khristy"), whose reverence for the ideal of neighborly love symbolically alludes to his glorious predecessor. Moreover, by taking the course of Christian love and empathy, the hero does not re-create Christ's image "typologically" or merely "ideologically," as some critics suggest,[52] but follows him in the most personal way, the only kind of imitation Dostoevsky deemed adequate to an authentic understanding of Christ.[53] By striving to *live into* his neighbors through active, Christian compassion, Myshkin also *lives into* Christ. For that reason the Prince does not usurp Christ's place, as some interpreters claim,[54] but always makes a gesture toward him, even in his failure. As Guardini puts it:

> The "place" where human impossibility and weakness makes its appearance [in the novel] is precisely that moment that completes the transfer of the symbolic sign to Christ. That which for Christ is the incomprehensible, worship-inspiring transcendence of the human limit is here translated into human impossibility, but so that it becomes an eloquent impossibility.[55]

In his spiritual undertakings, the hero always makes an appeal to agape, even when his empathy can no longer be an adequate carrier of this profoundly active love. The joyful "helpfulness" of the Christlike Prince, his fruitful activity and effectiveness (*pol'za*) in aiding all the central characters, which is the hero's prominent characteristic in a section of the notebooks for *The Idiot*,[56] may not have been realized in the novel, but the hero never loses *faith* in the reality and necessity of love. Having lost his capacity to help, the hero never abandons his belief in the crucial importance of another's (and the Absolute Other's) help. And therein lies his fundamental metaphysical opposition to Dostoevsky's quintessential "impostor," Stavrogin, a spiritual traitor, who does not believe in the efficacy of the others' help, rejecting the ontological necessity of Otherness as such (in the notebooks for *The Devils*,

Dostoevsky defines Stavrogin's essence in one telling sentence, inapplicable to Myshkin: "he does not believe in another person's help and regards it with scorn" ("prezira[et] i ne veru[et] v pomoshch' drugogo cheloveka") [*PSS*, 11:208]).

Scheler once observed: "The only thing that makes pity bearable is love that it betrays" (*GW*, 7:143). Prince Myshkin's courageous pity may fall short from the ideal of active, Christian empathy, but it never becomes utterly passive, because, even in its most hopeless moments, it always betrays love. Through the "eloquent" failure of its imperfectly incarnated Prince-Christ, the novel commemorates the spiritual achievement of his divine predecessor, issuing a call for powerful, profoundly creative Otherness. This call remains unanswered in *The Idiot*, but it extends a challenge to the author's later novels, eventually inspiring yet another attempt at incarnating Christ's otherworldly love in the image of Alyosha Karamazov.

Chapter Six

From *The Idiot* to *The Brothers Karamazov*: The Progress of Dostoevsky's Ideal Hero

> You were given a sharp, acute, uncomfortable grain—the actual meeting; horribly painful as often as not; yet in absence, in the most unlikely places, it would flower out, shed its scent, let you touch, taste, look about you, get the whole feel of it and understanding, after years of lying lost.
> —Virginia Woolf, *Mrs. Dalloway*

A NEW SAINT EMERGES

Dostoevsky's last novel, *The Brothers Karamazov*, reexamines the question of man's spiritual possibilities and offers a new, strikingly original answer to the problem of *imitatio Christi* in the modern world. In Alyosha Karamazov we encounter a very different ideal *other* than the courageous but spiritually fragile Prince Myshkin. Rosy-cheeked and complete with an erotic drive, Alyosha is an expression of that rare Schelerian *Durchdringung*, a dynamic unity of life and spirit that frees agape from the realm of empty potentiality and releases it for ethical action. The least "natural" of Dostoevskian saints, Alyosha freely chooses his demanding vocation and carries its burdens with unprecedented grace. Arguably the most effective and universally appreciated *neighbor* in Dostoevsky's world, Alyosha proves consistently, and often surprisingly, adequate both to his God-given task and to his human environment. As a result, this unlikely saint solicits the greatest response to a divinely inspired gesture of neighborly love in Dostoevsky's novels.[1] What explains the unprecedented success of Alyosha's ministry?

This chapter will discuss Alyosha's unique position vis-à-vis his neighbors (*blizkie* and *blizhnie*) as an alternative to Myshkin's existential stance. I will argue that at the end of his literary career Dostoevsky did create a more effective Christlike hero, whose empathy toward others closely resembles *vzhivanie*. The secret of Alyosha's success is the rare balance he shows as both an exemplary *giver* and an exemplary *recipient* of love. I will demonstrate that in *The Brothers Karamazov* the process of active empathy is not one-sided, as in *The Idiot,* because, unlike Myshkin, Alyosha benefits from being spiritually completed or, in Bakhtin's terms, lovingly consummated by others. This happens, I argue, not because Alyosha is born into a less hostile, more perfect world than Myshkin. Rather, this more convincingly incarnated divine agent lends himself better to the others' consummating and individualizing touch, affirming the dialogical, profoundly interactive nature of enfleshment in Dostoevsky.

These conclusions will be reached by comparing Alyosha's and Myshkin's analogous, highly symbolic, temptations to abandon the mission of agape (the second section of this chapter), by locating parallel textual passages that document the psychological manifestations of Christlike empathy in the two novels, and by classifying them as a special type of discourse with consistent features (*vzhivanie* discourse) (the third section). It will be argued that the *vzhivanie* discourse signals key places in the novels where the protagonist's agape is tested in fundamentally similar ways. Finally, the last six sections of the chapter will highlight Alyosha's special skill of balancing the active and receptive functions of agape, demonstrating the importance of Alyosha's status as an exemplary *beloved* in Dostoevsky's renegotiated vision of a Christian community (sections four through nine).

THE BURDEN OF INCARNATION

Marked for their exceptional spiritual depth and inimitable sense of justice, Prince Myshkin and Alyosha Karamazov occupy a special place in the symbolic cosmos of their respective novels: both are conceptualized as Christlike emissaries, sent into a fallen, deeply troubled world with a message of neighborly love. Virtually "uninsultable," the two heroes are among the precious few in the Dostoevskian universe who refuse to pay back for the hurt visited on them by others and thus disrupt the vicious circle of hurting-and-being-hurt perpetuated by the numerous power-driven characters around them. Whatever their differences and shortcomings, these two are perhaps the most prominent representatives of *a loving human being* in Dostoevsky, the characteristically Dostoevskian *homo amans*, and it is in this particular function that they will be compared in this chapter.

The two heroes face similar challenges in their Christian mission: they witness impending violence and attempt to prevent murder; they must confront and condemn evil, without condemning the evildoers. Both are thrust between opposing, uncompromising passions and then pressured to choose between their loyalties to rival characters, a decision that threatens to compromise their agape, enlisting it in a pernicious battle of wills (Myshkin's problematic commitment to both Nastasia Filippovna and Aglaya; Alyosha's challenging mediation between the conflicting interests of his father and brothers). Deeply concerned with the plight of their neighbors, the two heroes counsel those in need of a healing word. They deal with injured pride, try to convince others to accept sympathy and charity (Myshkin and Ippolit; Alyosha and Captain Snegiryov) and minister to a dying youth (Ippolit; Ilyusha). In every comparable situation, be it mediation between rival heroines (the "duel" scenes between Nastasia Filippovna and Aglaya and between Grushenka and Katerina Ivanovna), or the heroes' analogous efforts to ensure that the help they extend to others is offered in an ethically acceptable way (Myshkin and Ippolit; Alyosha and Captain Snegiryov), Alyosha's behavior generally resembles Myshkin's. However, Alyosha introduces small but crucial changes, as it were, editing Myshkin's actions and words, to emerge far more successful in his ministry. To understand this subtle but seminal revision of Dostoevsky's saintly hero, let us turn our attention to the parallel series of trials to which the protagonists are subjected in the two novels to test their capacity for active, Christlike love: the way each hero reacts to these temptations of agape determines the success and longevity of his mission.

Both Prince Myshkin and Alyosha Karamazov are aware of their special calling and acknowledge the enormous emotional and spiritual demands of their missions at several key points in the novels; both experience Gethsemane-like moments of hesitation and consider abandoning their responsibilities to others. This realization of the burden of Incarnation is especially acute in Myshkin's internal monologue following two consecutive scandalous events in Pavlovsk, the Prince's confrontation with Burdovsky and his retinue and Nastasia Filippovna's first attempt to scandalize Evgenii Pavlovich and the Epanchin family (part 2, chapter 11).

After witnessing Nastasia Filippovna's impudent attack on one of his guests, carried out outside of his dacha, in front of the petrified Epanchins, the Prince is demonstratively shunned by Elizaveta Prokofievna and spends the following day at home, coming to grips with his responsibility for the events of the "monstrous" evening (*PSS*, 8:252).[2] Although, in the current chapter, only enigmatic hints are given to the reader in lieu of an explanation, we can deduce that the Prince has become aware of two dangerous developments, or "intrigues," that concern him: Nastasia Filippovna is deliberately, and ruthlessly, scandalizing Aglaya's suitor, while the daredevil Aglaya, outraged by Nastasia's unsolicited interference, is seeking a meeting with her, despite the immense social stigma associated with such a step. Soon Myshkin will also learn that Lebedev has been aiding Nastasia Filippovna and using his friendship with the Prince to scandalize him and his friends.

Alarmed by these troubling developments, the Prince decides to gather his thoughts by taking a walk in one of Pavlovsk's parks. At this point in the novel, the hero's anxiety is twofold: on the one hand, he dares himself to embrace his growing love for Aglaya and to act on this reciprocated feeling; on the other hand, he continues to feel responsible for Nastasia Filippovna and begins to realize his dangerous role as a catalyst for the heroine's aggression against Petersburg high society. Overwhelmed by his conflicting responsibilities to so many seeking, and exploiting, his compassionate love, the Prince contemplates an escape from the world he had entered six months earlier:

> *He suddenly felt a terrible urge to leave all of it here and to go back where he had come from*, some place far away, in the wilderness, to go away at once, without even saying goodbye to anyone. He had a premonition that if he stayed here, even just for a couple more days, he would certainly be pulled into this world irretrievably, and this world would become his life and his fate from then on. But he did not consider it even for ten minutes and immediately decided that it was "impossible" to run away, that it would almost be cowardice, that he was facing such crucial tasks [*takie zadachi*], that he had no right whatsoever not to complete them or, at least, not to make every effort to complete them [ne *razreshit'* ili po krainei mere ne upotrebit' vsekh sil k razresheniiu ikh]. In this state of mind he returned home, having walked less than a quarter of an hour. *He was perfectly miserable at that moment*. (*PSS*, 8:256, italics, here and throughout, are added, unless otherwise indicated)

In the context of the Prince's Christlike image, symbolically reinforced throughout the novel, and his saving mission "to rehabilitate and resurrect [one] person" (*PSS*, 9:264),[3] the spiritually anguished and socially humiliated Nastasia Filippovna, this momentary despair is evocative of Christ's prayer to take this cup away from him (Matthew 26:39; Mark 14:36; Luke 22:42). It is thus significant that the hero's escape is judged unthinkable precisely in view of his special assignment, the fundamental "tasks" he is uniquely equipped to fulfill.

Myshkin's "cowardly" wish to retreat from his mission to the Edenic place "where he had come from" calls to mind Alyosha's emotional state upon learning of the Elder's decision to send him "into the world," to practice and teach Christian love outside the monastery (*PSS*, 14:71). Having witnessed his father's deliberately scandalous outburst at the monastery, in some ways reminiscent of the scandalous encounters that bring about Myshkin's Gethsemane-like moment, the reluctant Alyosha is instructed to leave Zosima's cell to accompany his troubled family to dinner. On his way there, he is consumed by worries about the growing strife between his father and brothers and about his own uncertain future in the secular world after Zosima's death. "But how will he remain without him [Zosima], how can he bear not to see him, not to hear him?" the narrator asks, gradually merging with Alyosha's inner voice:

> *And where will he go*? He is telling me not to cry and to leave the monastery, O Lord! *Alyosha had not felt such anguish in a long time.* He hurried though the woods that separated the Elder's cell from the monastery and, unable to bear his thoughts that weighed so heavily on him, stared at the century-old pines on both sides of the wood path. (*PSS*, 14:72)

As Diane Thompson rightly points out, this passage foregrounds an important Christological motif in *The Brothers Karamazov*, situating Alyosha within the novel's elaborate system of biblical references as "the one who is sent [by the Heavenly Father]" (compare John 8:18; 12:45).[4] Indeed, only moments earlier, the Elder has blessed him for a life of Christian service outside the church with the words "I don't doubt you, that is why *I am sending you* [into the world]. Christ be with you!" ("S toboi Khristos!") (*PSS*, 14:71–72), which symbolically equates the small forest trail on which Alyosha feels so much anguish with the proverbial path of following Christ, *Via Crucis*. The notion of "being sent" into the world with a particular mission (*zadacha*), in Alyosha's case that of "appeasing and uniting" his warring community (*PSS*, 14:178), as Zosima puts it,[5] likens the hero to his predecessor in *The Idiot*. Like the Prince, who feels responsible for both Aglaya and Nastasia Filippovna during his Gethsemane moment, Alyosha is concerned about his conflicting responsibilities to his divided family: the Elder has just instructed him to attend to his brothers, and "*not* [*to*] *just one of them, but both*" (*PSS*, 14:72).

The intense suffering associated with the burden of their mission is also shared by the two Christlike characters (compare: "He [the Prince] was perfectly miserable at that moment" [*PSS*, 8:256]); "Alyosha had not felt such anguish in a long time" [*PSS*, 14:72]). In Alyosha's case, this proverbial "burden of the cross" is also made palpable through the use of symbolically marked vocabulary: the hero's oppressive premonitions of his future responsibilities "weigh heavily" on his shoulders. (Literally: "[Alyosha] couldn't even bear his thoughts [(byl) ne v silakh dazhe *vynosit'* svoi mysli], so heavily they weighed on him" (do togo oni *davili* ego") [*PSS*, 14:72]). Like Myshkin, Alyosha laments the violent discord and moral uncertainty of "this world," the world that will become *his* life and *his* fate, if he fulfills Zosima's wishes. "*Why, why had* [*I*] *left* [the monastery]," Alyosha exclaims later in the novel, when he returns to the monastery to see the dying Zosima one last time, after attending to the needs of friends and family in town—mediating between Grushenka and Katerina Ivanovna and receiving yet another of Mitya's ominous confessions—"*why did he* [the Elder] *send him 'into the world'? There is peace, there is holiness here, and there—only confusion and darkness, in which one will at once get lost and go astray*" (*PSS*, 14:144).

Both Alyosha and the Prince are uneasy about answering a call from above; both hesitate to embark on a spiritual career so exacting that it will tolerate no partial commitment, consuming every aspect of their lives and demanding such radical and risky choices that the spiritual good may be opposed to the ethical. The two heroes yearn for the sheltered life they had led before stepping into the world of earthly passions and realize that exchanging the facile sanctity of their cloistered past for the responsibility of action may be a frightening and irretrievable step. In the case of "Prince-Christ," this yearning to return to the primordial world prior to Incarnation, serene and, as it were, morally neutral, is especially evident. His wish to step back into the chthonic wilderness whence he came, first voiced in the passage quoted above, is reiterated even more emphatically in the scene directly preceding Nastasia Filippovna's second scandalous assault on Evgeny Pavlovich.

As he accompanies the Epanchins to the outdoor concert in the Pavlovsk pleasure gardens, the Prince is emotionally conflicted: he is both savoring Aglaya's recent gesture of affection (the preceding "non-proposal" scene) and fearfully awaiting Nastasia Filippovna's arrival, an event, I believe, he anticipates before anyone else does, with his characteristic, psychic-like clairvoyance.

> The Prince wasn't even noticing that others were talking and paying compliments to Aglaya, there were moments when he almost forgot that he himself was sitting next to her. *Sometimes he wanted to go away, to disappear from here altogether. He would even prefer a somber, desolate place, so long as he could be alone with his thoughts and no one knew where he was. . . .*
>
> There were moments when he daydreamed of mountains and, in particular, of one familiar place in the mountains that he always liked to recollect and where he liked to go when he still lived there, to look at the village below, at the white, dimly glistening thread of the waterfall, at the white clouds and the ruins of an old, abandoned castle. Oh, how he wanted to be transported there now and to think of one thing only—one thing only all his life—and it would be enough for a thousand years! And let them forget about him here, let them forget about him altogether. *Oh, it is even necessary, it would even be better if they hadn't known him at all and this whole vision would have been only a dream. And after all, what difference does it make whether it's a dream or reality*! (*PSS*, 8:286–87)

As in his previous Gethsemane-like episode, the omissions in Myshkin's selectively revealed stream of consciousness are remarkable. What single thought does he intend to contemplate eternally in the timeless limbo of his Swiss hideaway? Is it his "impossible" wish for happiness with Aglaya? Or the fate of his saving mission in respect to Nastasia Filippovna, which, in moments of weakness, he wishes to postpone indefinitely? The former is more likely, but the ambiguity of Myshkin's private confessions, registered by the ostensibly omniscient narrator, signals the character's persistent difficulty in articulating his intentions in an ethically acceptable manner. The responsibilities to both of his loves weigh heavily on the Prince's shoulders in the concert episode, and the nagging necessity to reconcile these two conflicting commitments with each other occasions a momentary escape from the realm of ethical decisions.

It is likely that the scene depicts a silent epileptic seizure, capturing a characteristically epileptic experience of time, where the anticipated future may be superimposed on the present.[6] Although the narrator is strategically silent about the reasons for the Prince's embarrassing distractedness, the passage is charged with intense anticipation of Nastasia Filippovna's arrival, and it is Rogozhin's face in the crowd, the ominous harbinger of that arrival, that exacerbates the hero's semi-conscious anxiety only several paragraphs later.[7] Oscillating between the immediate present (with Aglaya) and the anticipated future (Nastasia Filippovna's arrival), the hero mediates, half-consciously, between the two women who share his heart. Sensing Nastasia's imminent approach in a trance-like, almost extrasensory manner, Myshkin comes to realize that he himself is, in fact, the most powerful trigger attracting her scandalous assaults on the Epanchins and their courtly satellites. And while the ostensible goal of Nastasia Filippovna's impending attack is, of course, to discredit Evgeny Pavlovich, Aglaya's seemingly respectable, comme il faut suitor, and thus pave the way for the Prince's proposal, the aggressive nature of her sacrifice makes one question the purity of her motive.

The expressive choreography of this Hoffmannesque scene also foregrounds the Prince's intensely provoking position between his two irreconcilable loves. In the open, theatrical space of the Pavlovsk pleasure gardens, the Prince's entrance with Aglaya on his arm stirs the crowd and immediately triggers the appearance of another polarizing couple, Nastasia and Rogozhin. Through this revealing tableau, the reader is shown, though never explicitly told, how the Prince's public courtship of Aglaya attracts Nastasia Filippovna and intensifies her rage against the Petersburg high society. And, inside the novel's frame, the Prince becomes palpably, indeed viscerally, aware of his "magnetic" effect on Nastasia Filippovna and Rogozhin, whom he seems to attract by means of a mysterious psychic force. Thus, in the concert scene, as in the episodes leading to Rogozhin's attack in part 2, Myshkin both *anticipates* Nastasia Filippovna's violent outburst and *provokes* it. And, in a moment of weakness, the Prince wishes to abstract himself from the scene of impending turmoil, simply letting "them forget about him here, . . . forget about him altogether" (*PSS*, 8:287).

But such an escape would signify a self-effacement that has nothing in common with the humility of Christian self-sacrifice. Like his Gospel predecessor, a modern-day Christ may not sabotage the mission of Incarnation by retreating back into the realm of pure spirit, symbolized by the celestial dreamscape of the Swiss Alps in the novel. The Prince may claim that it makes no difference whether his experience is "a dream or reality," but, if he is to follow in Christ's path, his involvement in the life of his neighbors has to be real and immediate, and not imaginary or merely symbolic.

Thus, several important similarities emerge between Myshkin's and Alyosha's moments of hesitation, when the characters are tempted to walk away from the mission of Christian love. Both feel drawn back to the sheltered domicile "whence [they] came" and where they had, as it were, dwelt directly in God before stepping into the human world (Myshkin's heavenly homeland in the Alps; Alyosha's monastery), and are overwhelmed by the challenge of applying their divinely inspired agape to concretely embodied, tragically imperfect human beings, their sub-celestial neighbors. Their moments of doubt are located between scandalous, explosive scenes, in which deadly passions are unleashed in a powerful clash that forebodes even greater, catastrophic violence: Alyosha hesitates about his calling after the notorious showdown between his father and brother Dmitry at the monastery, and then again after witnessing the brutal confrontation between romantic rivals, Grushenka and Katerina; Myshkin momentarily reconsiders his involvement following, and anticipating, Nastasia Filippovna's kamikaze missions against the Petersburg elite. In each novel, the hero is called upon to prevent impending violence by mediating between warring souls; he must put the message of agape into practice without taking sides or becoming embroiled in a power struggle. The special challenge associated with this task is evident to both men: unlike their erotic passions, their Christlike love must be responsible *to all.* For Myshkin, it must be equally attentive to Nastasia and Aglaya; for Alyosha, it must embrace Dmitry and Feodor Pavlovich, even as the two relentlessly battle with each other, threatening to involve Alyosha in their dangerous tug-of-war.

THE CHRISTLIKE HERO LIVES INTO THE WORLD: *VZHIVANIE* AS AN ACT AND AS A DISCOURSE

In the episodes analyzed above, the temptation of love is suggestively linked with Christ's spiritual trial at Gethsemane (Matthew 26:36–46; Mark 14:32–42) and the temptation at the cross (Matthew 27:40), signaling the danger of simply aborting the heroes' Christian missions. Although the characters do not walk away from their "crosses," working through their doubts and fears in each of the episodes, the temptation of agape becomes a continuous, novel-long, process[8] that poses the same seminal questions in *The Idiot* and

The Brothers Karamazov: how can agape simultaneously help those in opposing (ideological or metaphysical) camps, without becoming dangerously partisan? And how can it ensure its fruitful reception, especially by those who reject Christian love on ideological grounds? Or, to put it in the context of Bakhtin's and Scheler's problematics: how can agape remain *active* in the face of tremendous obstacles and how can it ensure the beloved's equally active response?

As Myshkin and Alyosha compassionately mediate between their warring neighbors, they face these questions time and again. And if we are to trace the trials of love in the two novels, we must ask: where is the internal struggle of Dostoevsky's *homo amans* most fully revealed in the text? In chapters 4 and 5 we have already come across some important passages that document the difficult work of love and empathy in *The Idiot*. There are indeed locatable "places" in the two texts where the Christlike heroes work through their temptations, with varying degrees of success. In Dostoevsky, the Christlike hero is tested when his love for the Absolute Other seeks (and, optimally, finds) incarnation in the deeply personal love for a concrete human other, a uniquely cherished *neighbor* (*blizhnii*). This process takes the form of "living into" another soul and is often stylistically foregrounded by Dostoevsky. Indeed, in both novels, there are some revealing displays of the heroes' consciousness in the process of loving empathy with others. These intimately narrated passages, some of which were analyzed in chapters 4 and 5, usually employ free indirect discourse to access, albeit selectively, Alyosha's and Myshkin's dialogized inner speech, just as the heroes themselves imaginatively access the minds of those around them.

This interesting psycho-narrative zone is where the Dostoevskian *homo amans* tests out his hypotheses about others, works out potential strategies for helping them, and sometimes addresses obstacles to his actions. In a word, this is where he *practices* his agape, and we, as readers, are allowed more or less sustained glimpses into this internal psycho-spiritual process. (Characteristic examples include Prince Myshkin's investigation of Rogozhin's soul, "shrouded in darkness," on the day of Rogozhin's attack [part 2, chapter 5], analyzed in chapter 4, and the Prince's later attempt to determine "what was hidden in [Aglaya's] soul" in part 4, chapter 8 [*PSS* 8: 467], as well as Alyosha's mental deliberations en route to see Katerina Ivanovna, before two seminal confrontations, between Grushenka and Katerina Ivanovna [book 3, chapter 10] and between Ivan and Katerina Ivanovna [book 4, chapter 5], where the youngest Karamazov attempts to imagine the world from the point of view of each of his brothers.) I would like to define this psycho-narrative space as *the internal discourse of vzhivanie*.

As the hero imaginatively enters the minds of his peers, he may rehearse his future conversations or deepen the past ones (the latter is characteristic of Myshkin's imaginary exchange with Rogozhin before the attack; the former—of Alyosha's attempt to live into the minds of Ivan and Katerina Ivanovna in "Laceration in the Living Room," examined in detail in subchapter 6.5). In its totality, the process of active empathy must encompass both, these *imaginary* or mental dialogues, and the *real* ones, conducted by the ideal hero face-to-face with his addressees, and it is the hero's ability to effectively balance these two components of *vzhivanie*, so that the rehearsed or retroactively "corrected" dialogues do not eclipse, but facilitate and enrich the real ones, I argue, that predicts the success of his mission.

Common features of *vzhivanie* as a discourse in *The Idiot* and *The Brothers Karamazov* include the following:

(1) *Vzhivanie* is often associated with spatial movement: the hero typically enters the other's inner world as he *walks* to an actual meeting with him or her;
(2) *Vzhivanie* usually unfolds in proximity to the ultimate temporal limit, intensified by the threat of a central character's death, and
(3) is perceived as a means of resolving a crucial moral-spiritual *task* (*razreshenie zadachi*), where the lexeme *razreshit'* (to solve / to resolve) is consistently used in reference to the desired completion of the hero's mission;
(4) This resolution is to be achieved through a process similar to Bakhtinian *consummation*, a loving completion of another's spiritual image by helping her discover her better, ideal self; resolving the other's *personal* essence here becomes synonymous with resolving her fate and works against the terminal, *impersonal* finalization prepared for the characters by the plot of criminal intrigue in each novel.

Because these features are fairly consistent in the two novels, by identifying them, one may trace the way Dostoevsky sets up the original "assignment" for the agents of agape in *The Idiot* and *The Brothers Karamazov* as, essentially, one and the same archetypal task. Let us examine each of these features in detail.

(1) Both Alyosha and Myshkin tend to practice their empathy "on the go": they often traverse the minds of others as they *walk* from one key location in the novel to another. Thus, the heroes' tumultuous internal dialogues are typically framed by laconic descriptions of their itineraries. This way, the unfolding movement of the heroes' thought is "mapped" by the narrator, by noting the points of *departure* and *destination* in their physical journeys. Typical examples are Myshkin arriving at Nastasia Filippovna's door, en route to her birthday party, lost in thought over Nastasia's future (*The Idiot*, part 1, chapter 13), and the equally contemplative Alyosha on the threshold

of Mrs. Khokhlakov's house, about to mediate in the confrontation between Katerina Ivanovna and Grushenka (*The Brothers Karamazov*, book 3, chapter 10). Here, as the heroes prepare to *enter* the dwellings of the distressed heroines awaiting their help, they also mentally prepare themselves to enter their minds and souls. The physical distance between Dostoevsky's principal dialogists and their addressees is thus provocatively conceptualized as emotional and metaphysical distance.

We must note that, in a larger typology of Dostoevsky's prosaic discourses, the *vzhivanie* discourse is a variety of the urban hero's internal discourse "on the go," which is characteristic of most of Dostoevsky's intellectually inclined city dwellers, who think through their problems and dilemmas as they wander through city streets. Bakhtin connects this perennial restlessness of the Dostoevskian hero with the general Menippean "threshold" chronotope of the author's novelistic universe, always on the brink of a transition (see, for example, *PDP*, 170, 176, 61, 73), whereas Nikolai Antsiferov links it to the western European tradition of urban prose, with its tendency to structure a novelistic plot around the constantly moving flaneur. Antsiferov notes the characteristic narrative multitasking of Dostoevsky's "Petersburg wanderer" (peterburgskii skitalets), whose walks through Russia's most cerebral city produce fascinating *soli loquia* documenting the hero's inner struggles, as it were, superimposed on a cityscape.[9] Raskolnikov, the Adolescent, Ordynov, and Goliadkin are mentioned in the category of the "Petersburg wanderer" or "flaneur," whose internal speech is habitually overheard by Dostoevsky's narrators. What distinguishes these characters' internal monologues from the *vzhivanie* discourse of Prince Myshkin or Alyosha is that the latter are occupied with thoughts and concerns about *others* and are engaged in an imaginary, loving dialogue with these others. If Dostoevsky's flaneur typically discovers "the truth about his own soul" during his urban excursions, as Antsiferov concludes,[10] the novelist's *homo amans* seeks to discover the truth about *others*' souls, as he imaginatively enters them during his pensive walks.

The transitional state of the empathizer's consciousness, suspended between several contemplated decisions, is thus often conveyed through movement in Dostoevsky: the hero *leaves* one dwelling and *arrives* at another in each novel, where he meets his addressee(s) in person, and the inner discourse of *vzhivanie* (the hero's mental preparation for a face-to-face encounter with these addressees) is typically placed *between* these two geographical limits in the text. This threshold time-space is often delimited by the verbs *vyshel* (walked out) / *voshel* (walked in / entered) or their variants, a fairly stable minimal pair that frames the heroes' most intense imaginary dialogues. Thus, metaphorically, the hero "walks out" of his own consciousness (*vykhodit*) and "enters" another (*vkhodit*), as it were, giving new meaning to Morson and Emerson's rendition of *vzhivanie* as "live *entering*."[11] It is on his way to Nastasia Filippovna's birthday party that Prince Myshkin considers "the most crucial questions" and the hero's emotional turmoil reaches its peak as he *steps over* her threshold:

> The Prince was very worried as he ***went up*** the stairs [***vskhodia***] and tried to encourage himself, as best he could. . . .
>
> [A condensed version of the ***vzhivanie*** **discourse is placed here**]
>
> But in the end, in spite of all of these anxieties and doubts, he nevertheless ***entered*** [***voshel***] and asked for Nastasia Filippovna. (*PSS*, 8:114)
>
> (**framing verbs**: ***vskhodia / voshel***)

It is evident from the rest of the novel that the Prince's "anxieties and doubts" are related to his plans to rescue Nastasia Filippovna, and this, mostly concealed, inner dialogue becomes part of his compassionate investigation of her troubled soul.

As we have seen in chapter 4, Myshkin's fascinating imaginary dialogue with Rogozhin in part 2, chapter 5 is also performed "on the go," as the Prince walks from Rogozhin's house to the hotel "The Scale" and then from "The Scale" to Nastasia Filippovna's flat, followed by his macabre addressee. Part of this extensive internal dialogue is also framed by verbs signifying departure and entry: "The Prince *walked out* [*vyshel*] [of the hotel] and mechanically walked ahead where his eyes took him" (*PSS*, 8:186). We may recall from our close readings in chapter 4 that in the next eight pages the narrator painstakingly records Myshkin's turbulent stream of consciousness: here the hero mentally revisits his previous encounters with Rogozhin, tries to imagine the world and Nastasia Filippovna from Rogozhin's perspective and attempts to persuade his brother in Christ to be compassionate. In a word, here the Christlike hero attempts to "*live into*" Rogozhin's mind. As both Myshkin's disoriented walk and his difficult inner dialogue with Rogozhin near conclusion, the Prince finally *enters* the zone of contact, about to meet his interlocutor face-to-face: "The staircase, which the Prince *ran up from under the gateway* [*vzbezhal* iz-pod vorot], led to the corridors of the first and second floors, along which the hotel rooms were located" (*PSS*, 8:194), the narrator reports before describing Rogozhin's attack on Myshkin. Once again, the discourse of *vzhivanie* is placed between the actions of exiting and entering (framing verbs: *vyshel / vzbezhal*).

Alyosha Karamazov also attempts to "live into" the minds and souls of those in need of his help, as he *walks* across town from one of his charges to another. The young novice considers the most effective ways of mediating between the many warring parties around him, while walking to meet Katerina Ivanovna, first to arbitrate in the verbal duel between her and

Grushenka, and later to intervene in a heated confrontation between Ivan and Katerina Ivanovna. He attempts to imagine the world from the perspective of each rival (initially Dmitry and Ivan; later—Katerina and Grushenka), "living into" each personality. Framing the mental process of *vzhivanie* are again the familiar verbs of motion, *vyshel* and *voshel*:

> Alyosha ***walked out*** of his father's house [***vyshel***] in an even more battered and depressed state of mind than when he had entered it [kogda ***vkhodil*** k ottsu].
>
> [***Vzhivanie* discourse is placed here**]
>
> When Alyosha ***entered*** the waiting room [***voshel***] and asked the maid who had let him in to announce him, those in the living room evidently already knew about his arrival. (*PSS*, 14:132–33)
>
> (**framing verbs: *vyshel / voshel***)

When Alyosha walks into Mrs. Khokhlakov's house in the chapter entitled "Laceration in the Drawing Room" (book 4, chapter 5), the narrator emphasizes that Alyosha's mental preparation for a dialogue with Ivan and Katerina immediately precedes his face-to-face encounter with these characters:

> The moment Alyosha and Mrs. Khokhlakov ***entered* [*voshli*]**, Ivan was getting up to leave.
>
> [***Vzhivanie* discourse is placed here**]
>
> And so, all of these hesitations and speculations flashed through his [Alyosha's] mind at the very moment when he was ***stepping into*** the living room [v tot mig kogda on ***vstupal*** teper' v gostinuiu]. (*PSS*, 14:169–70)
>
> (**verbs signaling the closing of the frame: voshli; vstupal**)

It is important that in both episodes above Alyosha works to reconcile the conflicting interests of his variously related neighbors. If during the first episode Alyosha intervenes in the triangular relationship between Katerina Ivanovna, Grushenka, and Dmitry, during the second one, he intends to untangle another contentious triangle, that between Katerina Ivanovna, Dmitry, and Ivan.

Thus, as the hero "walks out" of his own consciousness to enter another, a mental transition often coinciding, and thus metaphorically equated with, entering a house or a room in Dostoevsky, the question arises: will the host let the visitor in? (We realize the possibility of a negative answer when Nastasia Filippovna's apartment proves incredibly difficult to locate upon Myshkin's first, unannounced visit; when, in part 2, Rogozhin grudgingly invites Myshkin into his gloomy, inhospitable, Rogozhin-like house, whose expressive "physiognomy" resembles its host's face, or, post-murder, peeks at the Prince stealthily from behind a curtain, but does not open the door;

or when Dmitry is said to be hiding from his youngest brother on the day before the murder.) As we pause on the threshold with Alyosha or Prince Myshkin, about to enter another character's soul, we ask: *will the hosts allow the Christlike hero to enter their inner dwelling and share their emotional experience? And will the latter be a gracious guest, not overstaying his welcome* (like Myshkin did on his protracted visit to Rogozhin's house before the attack in part 2)? *Finally, will the hero emerge emotionally and spiritually enriched after his visit, free to help others, or be detained against his will by his host* (as Myshkin is by Nastasia Filippovna after the "duel" scene between the two heroines, when, prevented from following Aglaya, he finds himself "stuck" in Nastasia's house in Pavlovsk and, metaphorically, in her hopeless, tormented soul till the end of the novel)?

(2) In addition to spatial boundaries, proximity to a closing *temporal* limit is also characteristic of *vzhivanie* in Dostoevsky's novels: Myshkin gains extraordinary insight into Rogozhin's "Russian soul" as he faces the threat of Nastasia Filippovna's murder and his own approaching epileptic attack; the anticipation of Feodor Pavlovich's murder and of Zosima's expected death makes Alyosha's investigation of Mitya's and Ivan's inner worlds especially urgent. And, in the face of these impending tragedies, both protagonists envision a finalizing denouement, an ultimate *resolution* of deep emotional and ideological conflicts ("*razreshenie* voprosov / konfliktov") [see (3) and (4)].

On the one hand, a "fateful," tragic resolution of deep-seated conflicts through murder or suicide is feared and urges the Christlike hero to engage in a dialogue with the warring parties. (Such is Alyosha's fearful foreboding of a deadly "resolution" on the eve of his father's murder. "Above everything else there towered, like a mountain, the main, fateful and *irresolvable question* [*nerazreshimyi vopros*]: *how will it end* between his father and brother Dmitry with this terrible woman?" the narrator reports, merging with Alyosha's anguished inner voice, as the latter attempts to enter the minds of his brothers after the violent showdown between Dmitry and Feodor Pavlovich [*PSS*, 14:132].) On the other hand, in the process of *vzhivanie*, the hero usually proposes his own, *active* resolution of major existential questions that challenge the anticipated denouement. It is in search of such a hopeful resolution that Myshkin grapples with an "*unresolved* question" (*nerazreshennyi* vopros) on his way to Nastasia Filippovna's party, a question "of such capital significance that the Prince was afraid even to think of it" (*PSS*, 8:114). This question is never explicitly spelled out, but it is most certainly related to Myshkin's role in saving the suffering heroine and, more specifically, to his courageous proposal of marriage. Indeed, for the Prince, to *resolve* the question of Nastasia Filippovna's moral-spiritual essence is also to (positively) resolve the question of her fate, by actively intervening in her suicidal plan of action.

In search of an acceptable "solution," Alyosha, too, tests out his theories about his troubled neighbors as well as possible strategies of helping them. On his way to Mrs. Khokhlakov's house, about to witness the revelation of Katerina Ivanovna's masochistic passion for Ivan, Alyosha intends "*to resolve*" a painful suspicion about her relationship with his two brothers: "It so happens, that *one of Alyosha's doubts, one troubling riddle that had plagued him for some time was being resolved* at that moment" ("dlia Aleshi *razreshalos' teper' odno iz somnenii, odna bespokoinaia zagadka ego muchivshaia*") (*PSS*, 14:169). During his earlier, equally contemplative walk to Katerina Ivanovna's house, Alyosha prepares for a heart-to-heart talk with Katerina Ivanovna about Dmitry by, once again, "*resolving*" a difficult problem: "Alyosha set out [for Katerina Ivanovna's house] hoping that on his way to town he would somehow have time to *(re)solve a problem that had tormented him*" ("upovaia, chto po doroge k gorodu uspeet kak-nibud' *razreshit' tomivshuiu ego zadachu*") (*PSS*, 14:93). It is likely that the unresolved (or unsolved) riddle mentioned here is the immensely complicated relationship between Dmitry, Katerina Ivanovna, and Grushenka, gradually illuminated throughout the text. But, in the context of the entire novel and its moral problematics, "tomivshaia ego *zadacha*" is also an *assignment*, an actively posited *task* of helping all parties involved in the two deeply entangled love triangles: Katerina Ivanovna, Dmitry, Grushenka, Ivan and Feodor Pavlovich.

Thus, for both, Alyosha and Myshkin, such a hopeful, *internal* resolution of seminal existential questions (*"razreshenie voprosov / zadach"*), achieved by the Christlike hero through the work of love and empathy, becomes an alternative to the much feared *external* resolution, through a series of anticipated, tragic events (*"rokovoe razreshenie / okonchanie konflikta"*). If he is to avoid the terminal consummation prepared for the key characters by the initial plot of criminal intrigue present in each novel (the anticipated murders of Nastasia Filippovna and Feodor Pavlovich and the resulting moral or spiritual suicides of Dmitry and Ivan), Dostoevsky's *homo amans* has to propose his own, positive, psychologically and metaphysically sustainable "resolution" for each character. In this way, he may intervene in the predetermined plot of criminal intrigue already set in motion in each novel.[12] Here we may say that the Bakhtinian interpersonal *consummation* (the non-terminal, hopeful *zavershenie / "razreshenie" lichnosti*) works against the formal, "generic" consummation (*"rokovoe razreshenie" sud'by*), associated with both, the expected plot mechanisms of a crime novel on the narrative level, and the anti-personal, permanently objectifying finalization of one's uniquely individual "I" on the metaphysical level. Thus, the Christlike hero's struggle to understand and spiritually resurrect his charges before they irrevocably succumb to the inertia of their plot-driven "fate" (that of a permanently victimized camellia; that of a murderous slave of passion etc.) becomes a race against time.[13]

ALYOSHA'S NOVEL APPROACH TO EMPATHY

Both Alyosha and Prince Myshkin struggle to respond to this immense challenge efficiently, but Alyosha achieves greater success in the mission of *vzhivanie* from the start. While both heroes are able to gain considerable insight into the minds of their neighbors, Alyosha finds it easier to connect and cooperate with others, and so ultimately *uses* his knowledge more productively. How does Alyosha's "empathy on the go" differ from Prince Myshkin's analogous undertakings?

Some important symbolic differences are immediately apparent in the itineraries of these two compassionate mediators, who connect the inhabitants of Dostoevsky's fictional world by walking from one character to another to offer help. The epileptic Myshkin's absent-minded meandering through Petersburg streets contrasts with Alyosha's practical, goal-oriented itineraries in *The Brothers Karamazov*. Myshkin's path to Nastasia Filippovna's birthday party is a confused loop through Petersburg, as the Prince is led astray by his carnivalesque guide, General Ivolgin. And later, when Myshkin leaves "The Scale," ultimately to walk to Nastasia Filippovna's house, he, once again, wanders erratically through the unfamiliar, phantasmagorically hostile city, now half-consciously following the direction of his stalker Rogozhin: "The Prince walked out [of the hotel] and *walked ahead mechanically wherever his eyes took him* [*kuda glaza gliadiat*] . . . ; *for some time he wandered about aimlessly; he didn't know the city well*" (*PSS*, 8:186); "*he was again walking almost without noticing the way*" (*PSS*, 8:189). These passages contrast sharply with the description of Alyosha on his many errands in Skotoprigonievsk: "he *knew every path and every back way in town like the back of his hand*" ("*a vse eti khody on znal v gorodke kak piat' pal'tsev*"), the narrator notes, as he traces both Alyosha's efficient trajectory and his similarly goal-oriented thoughts on the way to Katerina Ivanovna (*PSS*, 14:94). In a very important sense, Alyosha knows where he is going.[14]

While Myshkin's labyrinthine journey through the impersonal, spectral Petersburg in part 2 of *The Idiot* is emphatically anonymous, Alyosha acknowledges everyone on his path and is recognized by his neighbors: "every single person knew him and everyone greeted him," the narrator observes with approval (*PSS*, 14:95).[15] If Alyosha reciprocates his neighbors' addressivity by seeking direct encounters with others and insisting on coming face-to-face with his interlocutors, Myshkin at times shrinks from direct contact, refusing to recognize Rogozhin in his persistent stalker in part 2, chapter 5, and admitting to himself that he is walking to Nastasia Filippovna's house for reasons other than seeing her: "he knew almost for sure that he would not find her at home . . . , *and so if he was going there now, it was certainly not to see her*" ("itak, *esli on shel teper', to, uzh konechno, ne za tem, chtob ee videt'"*) (*PSS*, 8:189). Ironically, as we have seen in chapter 4, Myshkin's extensive *imaginary* dialogue with Rogozhin and Nastasia Filippovna took place precisely during that spellbound walk, when opportunities for a *direct dialogue* with his two addressees were rejected by the Prince.[16]

While Alyosha also occasionally shuns direct contact with others, it is clear that these rare instances are exceptions rather than the rule, as his several refusals to look at his interlocutors and his costly failure to see his brother on the day of the murder are all consequences of one single, short-lived fall from faith occasioned by Zosima's death, from which Alyosha promptly and fully recovers. Unlike Myshkin's, Alyosha's imaginary negotiations with others are never divorced from face-to-face dialogue and serve as preparation for such personal encounters. It is important that each time Alyosha receives secondhand information about Dmitry and begins to analyze it, he feels an urgent need to see his brother and to discuss his concerns with him personally. "[Although he feared that he would not find his brother at home], Alyosha very much wanted to *see* [*povidat'*] . . . Dmitry before that fateful conversation [with Katerina Ivanovna] and to stop by at his place," the narrator reports (*PSS*, 14: 94). And the hero's wish is granted, when an opportune shortcut to Katerina Ivanovna's house leads Alyosha to his brother before his visit with Dmitry's long-suffering fiancée.[17] Alyosha's knowledge of the most direct route to everyone's home, his ability to leap over fences in one jump and to find advantageous shortcuts is deeply symbolic: bridging ontological distances between people, Alyosha easily finds his way to another's heart. Paraphrasing Max Scheler, we may say that Alyosha knows everyone's address in Being and uses this knowledge effectively.

According to Scheler, failure to face another person directly and earnestly, a refusal to *see* the other's real, and not imaginary or wishfully "retouched" countenance, leads to an inability to apprehend his individual value. In fact, it may lead to an atrophy of one's sense of value altogether, eroding the distinction between good and evil. Therefore, it is not accidental that the problem of maintaining addressivity mentioned above is related to the challenge of confronting evil in the two novels. In this context, we must note another significant contrast between Myshkin and Alyosha, namely, their differing reactions to the impending threat of murder. Indeed, recognizing and confronting evil intentions and taking an active stance against evil, without condemning the evildoers, is another arduous task faced by the Christlike hero in both *The Idiot* and *The Brothers Karamazov*. This aspect of acknowledging the ontic reality of another's existence is perhaps the most challenging part of *vzhivanie* for the two protagonists, and, once again, Alyosha handles this challenge better than his predecessor.

Both heroes are shocked by signs of emerging murder plots and initially refuse to believe the facts, taking time to "think through" their terrifying discoveries. We may recall that Prince Myshkin becomes convinced that Rogozhin will strike against him quite early in the chase sequence (part 2, chapter 5), but is notoriously hesitant to acknowledge Rogozhin's increasingly more ostentatious threats, or even to admit that he is being followed by his rival-turned-brother-in-Christ:

> Having made sure that he wasn't mistaken (of which he had actually been perfectly certain even before the test), he left the cutlery shop and hurried away from it. *He needed to think all of this over right away* [vse eto *nado skoree obdumat'*], most definitely; now it was clear that he hadn't just imagined it [Rogozhin stalking him] at the train station either, that something real certainly happened to him and it was definitely connected to that earlier worry of his. But some overpowering inner feeling of repulsion got the better of him again: *he did not want to think it over, he decided not to think it over; he started to think about something entirely different"* [*on ne zakhotel obdumyvat', on ne stal obdumyvat'; on zadumalsia sovsem o drugom*]. (*PSS*, 8:187)

The Prince consistently averts his eyes from the spectacle of impending violence. He refuses to give serious consideration to his ominous "thought," the realization that Rogozhin is contemplating murder, partly because he is shamefully aware that he himself has provoked the attack: "He immediately felt that *it was terribly disgusting and almost impossible to continue thinking about 'his idea'"* (*"Obdumyvat' dal'she 'svoiu ideiu' emu totchas zhe stalo uzhasno protivno i pochti nevozmozhno"*) (*PSS*, 8:189).[18] As was shown in chapter 5, failure to responsibly acknowledge Rogozhin's violent intentions ultimately leads to the Prince's refusal to acknowledge Rogozhin's very presence, as Myshkin repeatedly fails to recognize him or to meet his gaze.[19]

Alyosha feels the burden of his forebodings as acutely as Myshkin, but acts differently. Afraid of losing both of his "fathers," the terminally ill Father Zosima and Feodor Pavlovich, threatened by Mitya's patricidal rage, the boy feels "*incapable of bearing his thoughts*" ("*ne v silakh vynosit' svoi mysli*") (*PSS*, 14:72). Like Myshkin, Alyosha is initially tempted to ignore the threat of an impending catastrophe, as the similarity in wording suggests. After witnessing Mitya's violent clash with their father and Ivan's admission that he shares Mitya's murderous wishes, Alyosha is afraid to synthesize his scattered thoughts, trying to delay the obvious conclusions:

> Alyosha walked out of his father's house in an even more battered and depressed state of mind than when he had entered it. *It seemed that his mind was also fragmented and scattered, while at the same time he felt that he was afraid to connect the scattered parts and to perceive a general idea in all the*

> *painful and contradictory experiences of that day.* [*Um ego byl tozhe kak by razdroblen i razbrosan, togda kak sam on vmeste s tem chuvstvoval, chto boitsia soedinit' razbrosannoe i sniat' obshchuiu ideiu so vsekh muchitel'nykh protivorechii perezhitykh im v etot den'.*] Something was almost bordering on despair in his heart, which never happened to Alyosha. Above everything else there towered, like a mountain, the main, fateful and irresolvable question: how will it end between his father and brother Dmitry with this terrible woman? (*PSS*, 14:132)

But, unlike Prince Myshkin, Alyosha overcomes this initial impulse "*not to think*" about the likelihood of a deadly denouement in his family. He finds the courage to recognize the validity of his "general idea," without making it into the pernicious idée fixe that paralyzed Myshkin precisely because the Prince refused to acknowledge his suspicion about Rogozhin on the conscious level. The realist Alyosha knows that he may not run away from the reality of brewing violence. Instead, he needs to make every effort to understand the logic and origin of the warring passions that threaten to destroy his family. And that means "thinking through" the somber questions that so terrified Myshkin. "Meanwhile, *it wasn't an option not to think about it*" ("A mezhdu tem *nel'zia bylo ne dumat'*") (*PSS*, 14:170),[20] Alyosha says to himself later, referring to the dangerous rivalry between Dmitry, Ivan, and Feodor Pavlovich, and this pithy sentence becomes an answer to Myshkin's escapism.

VZHIVANIE AT WORK: A SAMPLE CLOSE READING

The following passage, an example of *vzhivanie* discourse, demonstrates just such a courageous attempt on Alyosha's part to untangle a complex web of conflicting relationships, *thinking through* Ivan's, Dmitry's, and Katerina's possible thoughts and intentions, in order to *act* in the most responsible way toward each of them. The excerpt opens the chapter "Laceration in the Drawing Room," the first in a series of three "lacerations" (*nadryvy*) in book 4 ("in the drawing room," "in the cottage," and "in the fresh air"), featuring Alyosha's dealings with several uncooperative, self-lacerating interlocutors: Katerina, Ivan, and Captain Snegiryov. Serving as a prelude to his intervention in a contentious quarrel between Ivan and his self-deluding inamorata, the passage reveals Alyosha's anguished reflections about the future of his divided family. In a characteristic Dostoevskian fashion, the process of *live-entering* documented here takes place on a literal threshold, just as Alyosha is about to *enter* Mrs. Khokhlakov's drawing room and meet Ivan and Katerina face-to-face:

The conversation was already drawing to a close in the living room; Katerina Ivanovna was in a state of great excitement, although she also looked very determined. At the moment when Alyosha and Mrs. Khokhlakov ***entered*** [***voshli***], Ivan Feodorovich was getting up to leave. His face was rather pale and Alyosha looked at him with concern. *It so happens that one of Alyosha's doubts, one troubling riddle that had plagued him for some time* ***was being resolved*** [***razreshalas'***] *at that moment*. Already about a month ago he was told repeatedly and by different people that brother Ivan loved Katerina Ivanovna, and, what was most important, that he was really intent on "stealing her away" from Mitya. Until very recently this had seemed monstrous to Alyosha, although it did worry him a great deal. *He loved both of his brothers and feared that kind of rivalry between them.* Meanwhile, all of a sudden, Dmitry Feodorovich himself openly announced to him yesterday that he was even happy about that rivalry with Ivan, and that it would help him, Dmitry, in a number of ways. What, in the world, would it help him with? To marry Grushenka? But Alyosha considered that a desperate business and the worst possible outcome. Besides all of that, Alyosha had believed without a doubt until last night that Katerina Ivanovna herself loved brother Dmitry passionately and stubbornly—but he had believed that only until last night. Besides, for some reason, it seemed to him that she couldn't love someone like Ivan, but loved his brother Dmitry instead, and precisely the way he was, in spite of all the monstrosity of such love. But yesterday, during the scene with Grushenka, he suddenly, as it were, had an inkling of something else. The word "self-laceration" [*nadryv*], pronounced by Mrs. Khokhlakov just now, made him almost startle, because that very night, half-awake at dawn, he suddenly pronounced, perhaps answering his own dream: "Laceration, laceration [*Nadryv, nadryv*]!" He was dreaming of yesterday's scene at Katerina Ivanovna's [the brutal facedown between Katerina and Grushenka that ended in her cunning insult of Katerina] all night long. And now Mrs. Khokhlakov's straightforward and insistent assertion that Katerina Ivanovna loves brother Ivan and is deliberately playing some kind of game, out of "self-laceration" [*nadryv*], is lying to herself and tormenting herself with a pretend love for Dmitry, as if out of some kind of gratitude—this assertion struck Alyosha: "Well, maybe, in actuality, the whole truth is precisely in these words!" But, if that's the case, Ivan's lot is not enviable. Alyosha felt by some kind of instinct that a personality like Katerina Ivanovna's had to reign over others, and she could only reign over someone like Dmitry, and not at all over someone like Ivan. Because only Dmitry could (granted, after a long time) submit to her, "for his own good" (which Alyosha would even wish for him), but not Ivan, Ivan wouldn't be able to yield to her, and this submission wouldn't bring him happiness. This somehow was the opinion Alyosha for some reason inadvertently formed of Ivan. *And so, all of these hesitations and speculations flashed*

> *through his mind at the very moment when he* ***was stepping*** **[*vstupal*]** *into the drawing room.* Another thought flashed by—suddenly and irresistibly: "And what if she doesn't love anyone, neither one, nor the other?" I must note that Alyosha was, as it were, ashamed of these thoughts and always reproached himself for them, when they sometimes occurred to him during the past month. "What do I even understand in love and in women, and how can I make such decisions?" he thought with self-reproach each time he had this kind of thought or suspicion. *Meanwhile, it wasn't an option not to think about it.* For example, he understood instinctively that now this rivalry was too important an issue in the life of his two brothers, too much depended on its outcome. "One viper will eat another," brother Ivan said yesterday with irritation about father and brother Dmitry. So, brother Dmitry is a viper in his eyes, and maybe has been a viper for some time? Perhaps since the time Ivan met Katerina Ivanovna? These words, of course, slipped out inadvertently, but they are the more important for being inadvertent. And if it's so, this does not speak well for peace [between the brothers], does it? Aren't these, on the contrary, new reasons for hatred and animosity in their family? *And, most importantly, whom should he, Alyosha, pity? And what should he wish for each brother? [kogo emu, Aleshe, zhalet'? I chto kazhdomu pozhelat'?] He loves both of them, but what should he wish for each of them amidst such terrible contradictions? In this chaos one could get utterly lost, and Alyosha's heart couldn't bear uncertainty because his love was always active. He couldn't love passively; once he loved someone, he would immediately start helping them. And to do so he needed to set a goal, he needed to know what was good and necessary for each person, and, once he became convinced of the correctness of the goal, naturally, to help each one.* (*PSS*, 14:169–71)

Here Alyosha's investigation of his brothers' state of mind resembles the Schelerian *Soseins-Setzung*,[21] a phenomenological assessment of someone's fundamental *personal* core that involves setting up a "hypothesis" about her and continuously refining it to gradually reveal her "individual ineffable." Intuited insights about the others' personal essence are checked against empirical observations; past conversations are reexamined and imaginatively expanded; questions unasked during actual encounters with Ivan and Dmitry are boldly posed and considered in earnest in this remarkable passage. In his imaginary projection into their minds, Alyosha focuses on the way Katerina Ivanovna, Ivan, and Dmitry experience love and hatred. Thus, using Scheler's terminology, we may say that Alyosha aims to ascertain their *ordo amoris*, to define their personal essence by revealing what and whom they hold dear. However, the task of determining who loves whom and in what way is so complicated by open and covert rivalries that even the seer of the heart, Alyosha, feels out of his depth.

Either lexically or grammatically, the underlined sections convey some degree of uncertainty and signal moments of hesitation in Alyosha's thought process, documented by an equally hesitant narrator. The abundance of indefinite pronouns ("*some kind* of game," "*some sort of* gratitude," "with *some kind of* instinct," "for *some* reason," "*as it were* [*kak-by*], ashamed") and modal introductory words ("perhaps," "maybe," "probably"), plentiful interrogatory constructions, and the use of the subjunctive mood create consistent loopholes in this volatile discourse, as it were, leaving room for further corrections and specifications. Alyosha might have believed in Katerina Ivanovna's passionate love for Dmitry "undoubtedly," but only "till last night." His vague suspicion of Katerina's power-driven attraction to Dmitry is followed by an equally tentative acknowledgment of her probable erotic interest in Ivan, but this later revelation does not negate or supersede the earlier one. In a similar fashion, the sentence "Well, *may be / in actuality / the whole truth /* is precisely in these words [that Katerina 'loves' Dmitry only out of gratitude]" expresses three varying degrees of certainty and leaves the reader unsure as to which part of the utterance should be accentuated.

What is immediately evident in Alyosha's *vzhivanie* discourse, in comparison to Myshkin's, analyzed in the two preceding chapters,[22] is the highly tentative quality of Alyosha's assessments, underscored by the narrator's vigilance against finalizing the character's opinions prematurely. Alyosha's genuine uncertainty about Katerina's, Dmitry's, and Ivan's motivation contrasts with the exaggerated confidence of Myshkin's words about the allegedly converted, compassionate Rogozhin in part 2, chapter 5, with their prematurely triumphant tone and rhetorical flourish. In fact, Alyosha's inability to reach a definite conclusion about the others' motives ("how can I make such decisions?") becomes *an asset* in his practical interactions with these others, because it leaves room for their own crucial self-definition. Alyosha's investigation results in insightful, but imperfect, provisional definitions that are meant to be revised and corrected with the help of Ivan, Dmitry, and Katerina Ivanovna themselves. And this is exactly what happens as the novel progresses: *direct* interactions with Ivan and Katerina Ivanovna in the subsequent scenes refine Alyosha's understanding of these characters, making the process of *vzhivanie* truly dialogical.

Indeed, the three distinct possibilities delineated during his preliminary reflections: (1) Katerina Ivanovna loves Dmitry; (2) Katerina Ivanovna loves Ivan; (3) Katerina Ivanovna loves neither man—will be synthesized and refined by Alyosha during his face-to-face encounter with Katerina, when he will reveal his (revised) opinion directly, as his unique *surplus of vision*. "You torture Ivan only because you love him . . . , and you torture him because you love Dmitry out of pride and a need for self-punishment [*nadryvom liubite*] . . . you love him falsely . . . because you've assured yourself of it," Alyosha says to Katerina Ivanovna, after hearing of her decision to follow Dmitry forever, although Dmitry has broken off their engagement (*PSS*, 14:175). This plainspoken assessment of Katerina Ivanovna's perverted *ordo amoris* sends the haughty heroine into a fit of wrathful hysterics and certainly does not secure the joining of hands between her and Ivan, so ingenuously demanded by Alyosha earlier in the chapter. However, it serves as an important eye-opener for both Ivan and Katerina, by revealing the artful mendacity of their ressentiment-driven relationship. Here Alyosha demonstrates his consistent stance in regard to love: he affirms genuine, unacquisitive, and disinterested love by exposing its corrupted impostor that only masquerades as love hurting its unfortunate objects.[23]

As the *vzhivanie* passage demonstrates, Alyosha's inner word about the other lacks finalizing certainty precisely because it is not self-important or self-sufficient, but subordinate to the practical *work* of love. From the beginning of the novel, Alyosha's word urgently seeks incarnation in morally productive, helpful action: "Whom should [I] pity?" Alyosha asks lucidly and adds, pragmatically: "And what should [I] wish for each brother?" ("Kogo emu, Aleshe, *zhalet'*? I chto kazhdomu *pozhelat'*?") (*PSS*, 14:170). Thus, the question, "How can agape help those in opposing 'camps,' without taking sides and becoming embroiled in existing power struggles?," crucial for both Myshkin and Alyosha, is consciously posed only by the latter, who fully recognizes this dangerous threat to his mission. To stay the course of agape, Alyosha has to devise a concrete program of action that would respond to each brother's individual needs. Here it is extremely important that, for Alyosha, to sympathize with one of his brothers (*pozhalet'* brata) means to make a wish or a plan for him (*pozhelat'* emu chego-to). As this near homophone verbal pair suggests, active empathy entails not only understanding the other, but also *helping* him. Or, to put it differently, for Alyosha, to truly know another means to know how to help him.

The yet undetermined "wish," contemplated here as an optimal program of action for each brother, would provide the much desired *resolution* (*razreshenie*) of their inner conflicts, suggested by the beneficent other (Alyosha) and synonymous with the function of Bakhtinian *consummation*.[24] In this sense, for Alyosha, the "*solution* of the riddle" of each brother's personality, mentioned as a task in the beginning of the passage ("one troubling riddle was being solved [*razreshalas'*] for Alyosha at that moment"), would also become an active *re-solution* of their fate. In the context of the novel's prominent theme of universal human brotherhood, Alyosha's self-imposed task formulated in this passage can also be understood more broadly: as someone who "cannot love passively," Alyosha is called upon to actively empathize with each of his Christian brothers (and sisters) in the novel and to use his empathetic knowledge productively in order to help them.

Because for Alyosha emotional cognition is thus inseparable from action, he avoids the danger of abstract psychologizing, to which Prince Myshkin is prone in *The Idiot*. If Myshkin repeatedly closes his eyes to the deadly power struggles around him, Alyosha faces intense conflicts head-on and is not easily discouraged by his own failures as mediator. He is saddened by the fact that Katerina Ivanovna receives his ingenuous advice as an insult, as yet another painful, unforgivable blow that will fuel her relentless ressentiment aggression against herself and others. "But she cried, insulted anew," he tells Mrs. Khokhlakov and shamefully covers his face (*PSS*, 14:177). Yet, as he surveys the damage caused by his courageous but clumsy intervention between Ivan and Katerina, his decision "*not to 'think'* about the mess he has created . . . , but *to do* what needs to be done [to improve things]" instead ("*ne 'dumat'* o seichas nadelannoi im 'bede' . . . , *a delat' delo*" (*PSS*, 14:179)) could not be more different from Myshkin's repeated resolutions "*not to think*" about the dangerous repercussions of his similarly well-intentioned actions (*PSS*, 8:189). The unsentimental, matter-of-fact commitment to the most prosaic work of love expressed in Alyosha's words is an alternative to Myshkin's spiritual fatigue.

ALYOSHA CONSUMMATES OTHERS: THREE CASE STUDIES

Indeed, with the exception of his costly but short-lived rebellion that made him neglect his family on the day of the murder, the youngest Karamazov remains *active* in his neighborly love throughout the novel. This activity is sustained by retaining his surplus of vision, communicating it to others in a gentler, less overwhelming manner than Prince Myshkin, and by keeping the others equally engaged in the process of loving dialogue. Whether in his ability to "tell the truth" to Katerina Ivanovna, that compares favorably with Myshkin's failure to be honest with Nastasia Filippovna, or in his ultimate success at persuading Captain Snegiryov to accept charity and love, that contrasts with Myshkin's analogous, largely thwarted efforts in relation to Ippolit, Alyosha is more effective at carrying his helpful word across the ontological gulf. The hero's greater success at helping others is due to the fact that he does not do their work *for them*, but rather helps them find their own path to spiritual growth. Without issuing a judgment of his own, Alyosha makes others conscious of their transgressions against love (both self-love and love of others) and then, following the others' gesture of repentance, supports their moral renewal from the outside, precisely as an *other*.

Alyosha's famous conversation with Ivan in book 11, chapter 5, exemplifies this active approach to empathy. The oft-quoted dialogue takes place on one of the novel's crucial thresholds: on the eve of Dmitry's trial, as Ivan struggles to assess his own legal and moral responsibility for the death of his father, before testifying in the case against his older brother. Quite in keeping with this threshold chronotope, Alyosha runs into Ivan on the staircase leading to Katerina Ivanovna's apartment, as Ivan hastens to leave after a heated dispute on the subject of Dmitry's guilt. Obeying Katerina's command not to leave Ivan alone, Alyosha follows his distraught brother into the street and firmly declares Dmitry's innocence to him:

> Ivan Feodorovich suddenly stopped.
>
> "So who is the murderer then, in your opinion?" he asked with apparent coldness, and there was even a condescending note in the tone of his question.
>
> **"You yourself know who," Alyosha said in a quiet, penetrating voice.**
>
> "Who? That fairy tale about that crazy idiot and epileptic? About Smerdyakov?"
>
> Alyosha suddenly felt that he was trembling all over.
>
> **"You know yourself who," he let it slip powerlessly. He was gasping for breath.**
>
> **"So who then, who?" Ivan shouted almost fiercely. All his restraint suddenly vanished.**
>
> **"I only know one thing," Alyosha continued in the same tone of voice, almost in a whisper. "*It wasn't you* who killed father."** [italics in text]
>
> "'It wasn't you'! What does it mean, 'it wasn't you'!" Ivan was thunderstruck.
>
> **"It wasn't you who killed father, it wasn't you!" Alyosha repeated firmly.**
>
> For about half a minute there was silence between them.
>
> "Of course, I know myself it wasn't me, are you out of your mind?" Ivan pronounced with a faint, crooked smile. His eyes were riveted on Alyosha. Both were once again standing by the street light.
>
> "No, Ivan, you said it to yourself several times that you are the murderer."
>
> "When did I say that? . . . I was in Moscow . . . When did I say that?" Ivan mumbled, utterly at a loss.
>
> "You said it to yourself many times when you were alone these two dreadful months," Alyosha continued in the same quiet and articulate voice. But now it was as if he was beside himself, speaking not of his own will, but obeying some irresistible command. "You blamed yourself and confessed to yourself that the murderer was no one else but you. **But it wasn't you who killed him, you are mistaken, you are not the murderer, do you hear me, it wasn't you! God has sent me to tell you this."**

Both fell silent. The silence lasted one whole, long minute. . . .

"Brother," Alyosha began again in a trembling voice, "I told you that because you will believe my word, I know you will. I have told it to you for your whole life: *it wasn't you*! [italics in text] **Do you hear, for your whole life. And it was God who put it into my heart to tell you that, even if you will hate me forever from now on."** (*PSS*, 15:39–40)

This important conversation is an example of Alyosha's *consummating* efforts: it is an attempt to find a morally affirmative, hopeful resolution (*razreshenie*) of Ivan's inner conflict. In *Problems of Dostoevsky's Poetics*, Bakhtin suggests that, by preventing Ivan from permanently defining himself as a murderer, Alyosha wants to acknowledge, and make primary, that inner voice in Ivan's divided self that had protested and condemned his wish for his father's murder (see, for example, *PDP*, 255–56, 259).[25] This positive definition of Ivan's inner being would release him from terminal self-finalization that threatens to block his path to redemption and, outside of the novel's narrative frame, from the equally depersonalizing finalization prepared by the plot of criminal intrigue—as a villainous accessory to murder, whose function in the novel has already been exhausted.[26] Thus, Alyosha's goal is presumably to persuade Ivan that he is *not* the murderer of their father, but he chooses a peculiar strategy to achieve this objective.

Alyosha's initial utterances are emphatically and unnervingly ambiguous. Why does he pause in his response to Ivan's "who is the murderer then?," avoiding a direct answer not once, but twice? Why does Alyosha let Ivan get progressively more agitated, finally making his brother lose his temper, before he offers his redeeming: "I only know one thing, it wasn't you who killed father"? By delaying his own response and repeating "You yourself know who" instead, Alyosha compels Ivan to supply the answer himself, and the anguish manifested in Ivan's reaction confirms that, for Ivan, this answer is indeed, "*I am* the murderer." Even the provocative phrasing of Alyosha's rejoinder: "*ty sam* / znaesh' kto" ("*you yourself* / know who") suggests the possibility of reading the first two words on their own, as "*ty sam*," "*you yourself are*," as in: "you yourself are the murderer," the way Alyosha's guilt-ridden addressee had most likely interpreted them initially, before the rest of the sentence was uttered to reveal a very different message. No doubt, Alyosha's suggestive pause is deliberate and morally significant.

Forced to reflect on his own role in the murder by Alyosha's unceremonious prodding, Ivan reveals a profound confusion about his past intentions and desires, and the readers' persistent difficulty with ascertaining the exact share of his responsibility underscores the troubling disconnect between words and deeds in Ivan's world.[27] The irreverent creator of "The Geological Cataclysm" and the poem "The Grand Inquisitor," Ivan has established himself as an experimental author with a preference for oral genres and a flair for shocking his listeners. It is in this spirit of venturous artistic experimentation that he shares his provocatively unfinalized musings about the impossibility of love and the legitimacy of murderous wishes with various audiences, without any concern about the practical impact of his words. But when his lackey half-brother Smerdyakov enthusiastically joins his fan club, Ivan's rhetorical experiment goes terribly awry: when Ivan's freely circulating, menacing, but playfully uncommitted words enter Smerdyakov's embittered, narrowly pragmatic consciousness, they become ordered into a coherent and conclusive *plot*—that of their father's murder, and, after its brilliant execution, Ivan finds himself challenged to confirm or deny his problematic "authorship." Alyosha understands that Ivan needs to define his relationship to what Alyosha immediately recognizes as *Smerdyakov's* deed: after the murder, Ivan's moral-spiritual task is, indeed, first and foremost, "to vindicate himself before himself" in respect to the family tragedy, as Ivan formulates it (*PSS*, 15:70).

But if this process is to have any moral value, it cannot take the form of smug self-justification in the manner of the Underground Man, where Ivan's considerable responsibility for the murder would be ultimately dismissed. Rather, Ivan needs to be entirely honest with himself: he must recognize as *his own* the murder-sanctioning words heard by Smerdyakov and enacted by the latter as an unambiguously evil deed. Only then can Ivan separate this guilty voice from the opposing, moral, voice within his divided psyche and affirm this latter voice as the guiding principle of his reevaluated acting self.[28] By redirecting the question of responsibility back to Ivan ("You *yourself* know who"), Alyosha emphasizes the urgent necessity of Ivan's own carefully searched out answer and acknowledges his brother's emerging repentance, of which the latter himself is not yet fully conscious.

Only *after* Ivan, no doubt, accuses himself during Alyosha's stubborn waiting game, does Alyosha tell him: "It is not you," precisely as an *other*, adding that he is doing so at the behest of the *Absolute Other*, God. Only after Ivan's inner voice condemns him *from within*, will Alyosha's absolution come down *from the outside*, as grace. Because Alyosha thus makes room for Ivan's self-judgment, absolution does not supersede repentance, as it happens with Myshkin's instant absolution of the blatantly unrepentant Rogozhin.[29]

On the other hand, Alyosha also wants to prevent Ivan's *excessive* self-judgment (à la Nastasia Filippovna), that would deny his brother any moral residue: if Ivan condemns himself wholly and irredeemably, such complete loss of self-value would eventually cause him to rebel against the world in ultimate despair. To prevent such brutal self-consummation, Alyosha needs to use his productive *outsideness* in relation to Ivan. If, *from the inside* of Ivan's guilt-ridden consciousness, his desires appear indistinguishable from his intentions, *from the outside*, where Alyosha firmly locates himself, the boundaries between desiring and enacting murder are clear. It is this crucial distinction that Alyosha is able to demonstrate to Ivan as part of his unique *surplus of vision*: while Ivan may have desired his father's murder, he did not intend it, nor carried it out, Alyosha concludes confidently. While hardly a triumphant exoneration from blame, this distinction certainly provides an important "mitigating circumstance" in defense of Ivan's compromised, but viable, moral core and a source of hope for his future.[30]

In this context, it is significant that, during his third and final meeting with Ivan, which directly follows the "not you" conversation with Alyosha in the novel's chronology, Smerdyakov structures his similarly worded rejoinders in exactly the opposite way, as he issues his own, *terminal*, consummation of Ivan's image. As a direct inversion of Alyosha's strategy, Smerdyakov's negative consummation effectively highlights the affirmative nature of Alyosha's efforts:

> Ivan looked at him [Smerdyakov] silently. Even that unexpected, so utterly and surprisingly condescending tone in which this former lackey of his addressed him was unusual. Even last time [during their previous, second, meeting] he hadn't used such a condescending tone.
>
> **"I told you, you have nothing to worry about. I won't testify against you, there's no evidence. Look at those hands shake! What's with those fingers jittering? Go home, *you're not the killer*** [***ne vy ubili,*** italics in text]."
>
> **Ivan gave a start, he remembered Alyosha.**
>
> ***"I know it wasn't me," he began to mumble.***
>
> "Oh, you kno-o-ow, do you?" Smerdyakov resumed once again.
>
> Ivan jumped up and grabbed him by the shoulder:
>
> "Go on, tell me everything, you viper! Tell me everything!"
>
> Smerdyakov wasn't at all frightened. He only riveted his eyes on Ivan with utmost hatred:
>
> **"Well, you've asked for it—*it's exactly you who is the killer*" [*vy-to i ubili*]," he whispered to him furiously. . . .**
>
> ***"It was you who killed* [Feodor Pavlovich], *you are the main murderer, and I was only your helper, your faithful servant Licharda, and I did the deed following your word*" [*i po slovu vashemu delo eto i sovershil*].** (*PSS*, 15:59)

If Alyosha initially honors Ivan's emerging self-condemnation, to eventually exonerate him *from the outside*, as a loving other, Smerdyakov *begins* by mockingly proclaiming Ivan's innocence: "Go home, *you are not the killer* [*ne vy ubili*]," leading Ivan to complacently justify himself *from within* ("I *know it wasn't me*"), only to issue a merciless and irrevocable condemnation *from without*, as an ambush, a moment later: "*it's exactly you who is the killer*!"; "*You are the main murderer*!" Unlike Alyosha, who wants to free Ivan's inner self (his essential "man in man") from the terminally objectifying label of patricide, Smerdyakov proclaims Ivan's essential identity with his *function* in the intricately executed plot of Feodor Pavlovich's murder. And, in Smerdyakov's assessment, this defining "plot function" is not merely an accessory to murder, as Ivan had feared, but its mastermind, which casts Smerdyakov in the secondary role of a hired henchman (the "servant Licharda"). While Smerdyakov holds Ivan ultimately responsible for creating the master script of the crime, which he claims to have merely executed ("I did the deed following your word"), he skillfully uses this adopted "script" to execute his ressentiment revenge against the family that never acknowledged him as their own. Ultimately, he takes the authorship away from Ivan, as he bullies him into keeping his silence with the police, making Ivan an obedient character in what is now clearly the plot of Smerdyakov's own design.

If Alyosha's definition opens Ivan's existential horizon as the potential hero of an entirely new, hopeful tale—perhaps that "other story" depicting Ivan's and Alyosha's future fates that Dostoevsky contemplates in the margins of *The Brothers Karamazov*'s main intrigue (*PSS*, 15:48)[31]—Smerdyakov identifies Ivan as the permanently compromised hero of the present tale, which has essentially ended. Also concerned with the moral and legal conclusion of "the present tale," Alyosha has to help Ivan close one boundary before he can open another. Ivan has to come clean to himself about his half-conscious participation in Feodor Pavlovich's murder and furnish a worthy denouement to the present tale by doing his best to exonerate Dmitry, before he can become a spiritually renewed hero of a new story. By contrast, Smerdyakov expects nothing new from Ivan. He is convinced that at the next day's court proceedings Ivan will be entirely "in character": too vain and cowardly to oppose Smerdyakov's word in public and thus change the pre-scripted sequence of events, of which Smerdyakov now alone claims control. Unlike Alyosha's, Smerdyakov's ultimate assessment of Ivan has no future dimension: his definition closes Ivan's inner self to any development and is perceived as exhaustive and final. Consequently, each "consummator" acts according to his psychological goals. Alyosha alerts Ivan's conscience and then meets his emerging (*inner*) self-condemnation with a gesture of affirmation *from the outside*, while Smerdyakov does the opposite: he cunningly lulls Ivan's conscience to sleep, encouraging his *inner* complacency, only to "slap" him with a crushing, punishing accusation *from without*.[32]

It is important that these two acts of consummation are issued as the two heroes' very different "last words" to Ivan: Alyosha offers his hopeful word "for [Ivan's] whole life," while Smerdyakov's somber testament is uttered during his last meeting with Ivan, shortly before Smerdyakov's suicide, his ultimate, consistently nihilistic *act*.[33] The confidence of Alyosha's deeply affirmative last word to Ivan contrasts sharply with Myshkin's fundamental fear of saying the last word, noted by Bakhtin (*PDP*, 242),[34] which renders the Prince less potent in affirming Nastasia Filippovna or Rogozhin. Though not immediately effective (Alyosha understands that demonstrating his awareness of Ivan's most shameful self-accusations will initially make his brother "hate him"), this authoritative word is intended as a long-acting spiritual remedy that will support Ivan's gradual self-renewal and counteract Smerdyakov's hopeless last word to him.[35] As for immediate consequences, Alyosha's conversations with Ivan prompt both his second and third visits to Smerdyakov, initiating a painful but necessary investigation of both the practical circumstances of the murder and Ivan's (ideological) part in it.

Alyosha uses a similar strategy with his eldest brother, as they discuss Mitya's tentative plans to escape from impending Siberian punishment. Alyosha allows Mitya a moment of self-condemnation for rejecting what the latter sees as redemptive, Christlike suffering and only then voices his support for Mitya's decision to flee from prison. When, on the eve of the trial, Mitya first mentions Ivan's secret preparations for his escape, fearfully awaiting the judgment of the only person who "would stand before me like my own conscience" (*PSS*, 15:35), Alyosha characteristically refrains from comment, entrusting the final decision to Mitya: "You are right," he says matter-of-factly, "it is impossible to decide before the court verdict. After the trial you will decide yourself; *you will find a new person in you by then, he will decide*" (*PSS*, 15:35). It is indeed only after the trial, when Dmitry has become well aware of "the new," repentant and spiritually alert person within him and has despaired over not being able to fulfill this new person's strict moral dictates, that Alyosha unambiguously voices his approval of Ivan's plan.

> "Listen, brother, once and for all," he [Alyosha] said, "these are my thoughts on the matter. And you know I won't lie to you. So, listen: you are not ready, and this kind of cross is not for you. Moreover, you don't need such a martyr's cross when you are not ready for it. If you had murdered our father, it would sadden me to see you reject your cross. But you are innocent and that kind of cross would be too much for you. You wanted to resurrect the other person in you [*drugogo* cheloveka] through suffering; in my opinion, you just need to remember about this other person in you all your life, wherever you escape to, and that will be enough for you. The fact that you did not accept the great suffering of the cross will only make you feel a stronger sense of duty your whole life, and this unceasing awareness will perhaps further your renewal more than if you had gone *there*. Because there you won't be able to bear it

> and will rebel and in the end perhaps will indeed say, "I have paid my dues [ia skvitalsia]." The lawyer spoke the truth in this case. Heavy burdens are not for everyone, for some they are impossible." (*PSS*, 15:185, italics in text)

As in his conversation with Ivan, analyzed above, Alyosha first gives his interlocutor, Dmitry, the opportunity to judge himself. As with Ivan, he then counters his interlocutor's dangerously severe, excessive self-judgment with a positive gesture of affirmation from without. And, as with his deeply confident "last word" to Ivan, pronounced "for [Ivan's] whole life" ("na vsiu zhizn'"), his thoughts regarding Mitya's future are uttered "once and for all" ("raz navsegda") (*PSS*, 15:185). Although Mitya is not guilty of his father's murder, he had nearly killed the servant Grigory, his childhood protector and caretaker; he scandalized his fiancée and publicly humiliated the downtrodden Captain Snegiryov and his son Ilyusha, Mitya's most cruel escapade that ultimately leads to the boy's death. Finally, like Ivan's seemingly abstract patricidal fantasies, Mitya's violent outbursts and repeated threats against his father enable Smerdyakov to carry out his murderous plan. Morally awakened by the dual effects of Grushenka's compassionate love and the trauma of wrongful conviction, Mitya must be gradually becoming aware of these, and other, transgressions committed against his neighbors, but fears that his decision to "run away from suffering" (*PSS*, 15:34) will compromise his spiritual transformation. Alyosha's goal is to support the voice of Mitya's newly alerted conscience, to nurture the morally superior "other person" in him, but to do so in a practical, psychologically sustainable way.

Alyosha understands that if Mitya rushes into martyrdom, submitting himself to twenty years of hard labor mandated by his sentence, he would soon come to resent this undeserved punishment, effectively silencing the newly awakened voice of conscience in a proud rebellion against the world, as somebody who has already paid his dues ("skvitalsia"). Such rash self-sacrifice would be an example of what Dostoevsky calls *skoryi podvig* ("hasty heroism") elsewhere in the novel (*PSS*, 14:25, 54),[36] a tendency to immediately gratify one's spiritual impulses without considering the long-term consequences and spiritual benefits of one's actions. Although escaping to America may seem like a lesser "cross" to Mitya, Alyosha realizes that this path of patient, gradual self-renewal would actually require a greater spiritual effort from his notoriously impulsive brother, if Mitya wants his conversion to have a lasting effect. Ever the pragmatist, Alyosha supports the unheroic and even ethically questionable escape plan over the hastily chosen martyrdom as both psychologically sustainable and more morally productive for Dmitry in the long run.

By making an emphasis on protecting "the new person" within Mitya (and that means foregoing the severe trials of the Russian *katorga* that would most likely kill it), Alyosha underscores Mitya's responsibility for keeping this ideal inner "I" alive. And his strategy is at least initially effective, as his abstention from judgment immediately activates the stern voice of Mitya's own conscience: "But know that I will never judge you. And it would be strange, how could I be your judge in this matter?" Alyosha concludes (*PSS*, 15:185–86). "'*But I will judge myself* !,' Mitya exclaimed. 'I will run away, it has already been decided without you: could Mit'ka Karamazov do anything but run away? But I will judge myself and will pray for my sin there [in America] till the end of time!'" (*PSS*, 15:186).

Another encounter that showcases the importance of keeping one's partner *active* during compassion-guided dialogue, albeit by revealing Alyosha's initial failure to do so, is his first, failed attempt to persuade Captain Snegiryov to accept Katerina Ivanovna's charitable donation. Once Alyosha realizes his mistakes and makes adjustments in his approach to this painfully sensitive interlocutor, he succeeds at fulfilling Katerina Ivanovna's request. The episode demonstrates the hero's growing competence in dealing with ontological divisions between individuals, and the general structure of his difficult but ultimately productive negotiation with Snegiryov "across the ontological gulf" is essentially analogous to that of his conversations with Mitya and Ivan analyzed above.

In book 4 Alyosha is sent to Snegiryov with explicit instructions to talk this recent victim of Mitya's violence into accepting 200 rubles from Katerina Ivanovna, "tactfully and carefully, as only [Alyosha] can" (*PSS*, 14:177), not as Mitya's payment for Snegiryov's silence about his unsavory behavior, but rather as charitable aid from Mitya's long-suffering fiancée. Realizing the potential offensiveness of Katerina Ivanovna's message and of his own visit as the offender's brother, Alyosha proceeds with caution: he surveys the shabby quarters occupied by the Captain's family, meets its variously ailing members, and lets Snegiryov relate the heartbreaking tale of father and son's humiliation by Dmitry, before announcing the main purpose of his visit. Patiently bearing his interlocutor's many barbs directed at him as a Karamazov, Alyosha remains unprovoked by Snegiryov's passive-aggressive antics, and the genuine interest he takes in Ilyusha gradually earns him the Captain's trust. He hands Snegiryov the money when the Captain's anguished tale of Ilyusha's suffering reaches crescendo, as a magical solution that would deliver the family from desperate circumstances, and cheers on as the dumbfounded paterfamilias fantasizes about spending the miraculous sum, only to see him proudly reject the gift minutes later. Recollecting the episode during a soul-searching conversation with Lise in the following chapter, Alyosha admits his mistakes, but stands by his decision not to renew his efforts to persuade Snegiryov immediately after the outburst. After all, "the mistake turned out to be for the best," he concludes (*PSS*, 14:195). What has caused the Captain's sudden change of heart, and how did Alyosha's behavior contribute to this unforeseen, if ultimately fortunate, outcome?

Like Ippolit after his indecent self-exposure in front of the Epanchins in part 2, chapter 10 of *The Idiot*, Snegiryov immediately regrets his emotional nakedness before an undeserving audience, the brother of his tormenter, ashamed of sharing his joy at the unexpected gift with such artless sincerity. Like Ippolit, who angrily retracted his confession, negating the preceding moments of emotional closeness with Lizaveta Prokofievna, Snegiryov resents his unwarranted intimacy with Dmitry's brother and wants to reclaim his dignity by refusing the charity and sympathy received so ecstatically minutes earlier.[37] On the other hand, Alyosha's own lack of emotional restraint contributes to Snegiryov's humiliation when he offers the Captain his own money: "Katerina Ivanovna will send you more," he exclaims expansively when the Captain considers whether the newly acquired funds would be enough to relocate the family to another town, "as much as you want, and, you know, I also have money, take as much as you need, as from a brother, from a friend, you'll pay me back later" (*PSS*, 14:192). This impulsive generosity must be especially objectionable to Snegiryov, because, at the outset of the conversation, Alyosha took pains to assure him that the gift issues from Katerina Ivanovna alone: "*not from Dmitry, who abandoned her too, not at all from him, and not from me, his brother, and not from anyone else, but from her, only from her*!" (*PSS*, 14:190). Katerina Ivanovna has a moral right to offer Snegiryov financial support, Alyosha is careful to note, because she and the Captain "were both hurt by the same person" (*PSS*, 14:190). In fact, according to Alyosha, "she only remembered about you when she suffered the same kind of insult (an insult of the same magnitude) that you did from him [Dmitry]! This means a sister comes to a brother offering help" (*PSS*, 14:190).

Alyosha is initially careful to distance himself from Katerina's helping gesture because, as another victim of Dmitry's cruelty, she is able to identify and sympathize with Snegiryov in ways that he himself cannot, especially as Dmitry's brother. Although in reality Katerina Ivanovna's motivation may well be damage control, and not neighborly or "sisterly" love, as she claims, Alyosha tactfully describes her as Snegiryov's fellow sufferer. Thus, he is initially respectful of the ethical divide between the offender and the offended that the freshly wounded Snegiryov insists on observing. It is when he hastily dismisses that sensitive boundary, offering Snegiryov "as much as he needs" from his own pocket and calling himself Snegiryov's "brother and friend," that the Captain becomes indignant and furiously stomps on the money. Indeed, once Alyosha makes himself one of the Captain's financial benefactors, the gift ceases to be a sympathetic gesture of support from another of Dmitry's victims, but may now be interpreted as a way of making amends for

Dmitry's transgressions on behalf of the Karamazov clan. In this case, its acceptance may carry a contractual expectation of pardoning Dmitry's violent outburst, something the Captain is certainly not ready to do, especially since Dmitry himself has made no effort to apologize, as Snegiryov noted wryly earlier in the chapter (*PSS*, 14:186).

There is another ethically significant ontological distinction that Snegiryov brings to the fore in his refusal to accept the money. The Captain may be acutely sensitive about his own humiliation by Dmitry, but what makes his emotional recovery especially difficult is *Ilyusha's* share in their mutual hurt (*obida*). Snegiryov repeatedly reminds Alyosha about Ilyusha's pain, whose depth and intensity cannot be fathomed by anyone but himself and the all-knowing God: "For what he suffered through when he kissed your brother's hands and cried 'Forgive my daddy! Forgive my daddy!'—this only God Himself knows and I" (*PSS*, 14:187); "Nobody saw us then [when, after days of enduring his classmates' ridicule, Ilyusha wept about his father's humiliation in his arms]. Only God saw us, maybe he'll put it in my file" (*PSS*, 14:190). Careful to discourage his interlocutor from any identification with himself or *his* child, Snegiryov draws an emphatic distinction between Ilyusha's harrowing ordeal and anything Alyosha may have experienced in his own, presumably carefree, sheltered life. "And this is how our children—that is, *not your children, but our children*, the children of despised but noble paupers, learn the truth on this earth at the ripe age of nine" (*PSS*, 14:187), he bitterly tells Alyosha, making sure he does not have to share any possessive pronouns with his interlocutor, who is both relatively wealthy and a Karamazov.

Humiliated and hurt by the same offender, father and son suffer together and may initially be experiencing what Scheler classifies as a "joint feeling" (*das unmittelbare Mitfühlen*), a shared pain that presupposes immediate access to the other's emotional state (see, for example, Scheler, *GW*, 7:23).[38] Nevertheless, no matter how close their emotional experiences, the son's torment may not be regarded by others simply as a subcategory of the father's pain, and that is an underlying theme in the Captain's narrative. The son's pain has an independent ontological significance and, like the pain of the child killed by the general's hounds in Ivan's famous parable in "Pro and Contra," cannot be forgiven by proxy, by the child's parent on the child's behalf, even if the parent himself is ready to forgive his own, *parental* pain at the child's torment. This ethical point about observing another crucial aspect of the ontological gulf is so important that the Captain insists on making it even at the expense of his family's financial well-being. Just like Ilyusha, who sacrificed his own pride as he kissed Dmitry's hands, begging him to release his father, but remained deeply pained by *his father's* unavenged humiliation, the Captain may forgive his offenders for his own terrible ordeal, but refuses to forgive them for his son's torments. "And what would I say to my boy if I took money from you for *our* shame?" he cries out tearfully to Alyosha before making his final retreat from the scene (*PSS*, 14:193).

Alyosha realizes that the Captain now regards the gift as a form of blood money, or "shame money," to be precise, and it is to Alyosha's credit that he does not run after Snegiryov, as Lise suggests *post factum*, but allows him to exit on his own terms. Just as, in the previously analyzed episode, Mitya's hasty acceptance of martyrdom would likely result in a spiritual rebellion, so would Snegiryov's hasty acceptance of charity make him eventually rebel against his benefactors and could result in his permanent rejection of the others' aid. Instead, Snegiryov is allowed to provide his own, conclusive, response to Alyosha's offer and leaves thinking that he has not only rejected, but likely destroyed the insulting "shame money." We then learn that, after Snegiryov is safely out of sight, Alyosha picks up the crumpled bills, that have miraculously remained "completely intact" (*sovershenno tsely*) (*PSS*, 14:193), and decides not to renew the offer until the next day, respecting the Captain's answer and allowing him a sense of closure after his proud exit. As Alyosha tells Lise in the following chapter:

> "Now he [Captain Snegiryov] left terribly proud and triumphant, although he knows that he has 'doomed himself' [*pogubil sebia*]. Therefore, there is nothing easier now than to make him take these two hundred rubles no later than tomorrow, because he has proven his sense of honor, he threw away the money and stomped on it . . . For he certainly couldn't have known when he stomped on the money that I would bring it to him again tomorrow." (*PSS*, 14:196–97)

What results is then a kind of Kierkegaardian leap of faith: a complete, ethically justified rejection of what is seen as an unacceptable contractual gift is followed by a miraculous, non-contractual discharge of benefit that comes down vertically, like grace, only when all hope for it has been renounced. *From the inside* of Snegiryov's consciousness, locked as it is within the punishing limits of strict ethical conduct, there is an uncompromising, and "dooming," refusal of a conditional reward. *From the outside* (from above) there unexpectedly descends unconditional benefit. Instead of selling his honor, the Captain has defended it, and his *post factum* reward becomes effectively dissociated from his, and Ilyusha's, shame at the hands of Dmitry.

Snegiryov's ultimate acceptance of the 200 rubles is not shown in the novel, but we are told that, although the delivery was delayed by Zosima's posthumous scandal, the Captain eventually received the money "exactly as Alyosha had predicted it" (*PSS*, 14:486). It is also clear from the subsequent developments that, in time, the Snegiryovs come to accept Alyosha's help as acts of love, rather than an expression of condescending pity or a way of preventing legal repercussions for Dmitry's hurtful behavior. And so, Alyosha was right to conclude that his initial failure to convey Katerina's aid to Snegiryov was "for the best": it prevented a facile, premature communion that could not last, but would only embitter an unjustly punished man and isolate his struggling family. This fortunate mistake teaches the youngest Karamazov a lesson in social diplomacy: instead of demanding instant emotional intimacy from his interlocutors in the manner of Prince Myshkin, Alyosha will learn to tread slowly, gradually acquainting himself with Snegiryov and developing a friendship on the terms the latter can accept. In time, when Alyosha becomes an intimate in the Snegiryov household, as an indispensable liaison between the family and the growing circle of Ilyusha's well-wishers in town, he will indeed become "a friend and brother" to the Captain, earning the right to a spiritual kinship he had claimed too hastily during their first encounter.

It is important that, in his later efforts to counteract the pernicious effects of Dmitry's violence, Alyosha will make amends specifically to Ilyusha, skillfully uniting him with his former bullies to create a loving circle of friends around him. He thus honors Ilyusha's suffering, acknowledging precisely that share of the Snegiryovs' pain that the Captain did not want to be overlooked by the Karamazovs. No longer represented by proxy, Ilyusha is now himself able to grant forgiveness, if not to his original offender (Dmitry), then to his later victimizers in the same chain of reciprocal violence originated by Dmitry (the schoolboys), and the boys' mutual forgiveness becomes a compelling model of Christian brotherhood in the novel. Enveloped by that irresistible spirit of reciprocal forgiveness permeating Ilyusha's mini-community, Alyosha and the Captain will enter it without the baggage of their affiliations with victims or victimizers—simply as two people equal in their Christian personhood, two human beings united by their love for a dying boy. When this, qualitatively different, level of togetherness is reached, the ethically significant distinctions between Alyosha and the Captain, upon which the latter had insisted during their first meeting, become transcended by brotherly love. Here, ethical relations ultimately give way to a spiritual union that suspends them, but, as Alyosha comes to learn, such a life-altering transition must be embraced by all of the parties and cannot be rushed or simply willed unilaterally.

Thus, some important patterns emerge in all three episodes analyzed in this section. For the characters' self-renunciation to have a moral and spiritual value, it cannot be contingent upon an external reward: Ivan and Mitya cannot judge themselves with the purpose of securing Alyosha's (or God's) exoneration; Snegiryov's rejection of the money cannot be merely a pose, a clever ploy to trick Alyosha into offering it again. Paradoxically, only when such a reward is completely and unequivocally renounced, will it be secured. Alyosha, who understands the asymmetrical logic of these exchanges very well, learns to be a tactful intermediary between his despairing interlocutors and their ultimate addressees—those who had sent him to Snegiryov, Ivan and Mitya with a valuable "commission" (Katerina Ivanovna; God). And, as an ever more competent mediator, he is wise to remain within the bounds of his important but auxiliary role, recognizing the necessity of Mitya's, Ivan's and Snegiryov's own, *internal*, entirely disinterested, and perhaps punishing, self-definition, before he can usher hope and affirmation *from without* (as a non-contractual monetary reward in the case of Captain Snegiryov; as an exonerating word of God that will crown, but not supersede, Ivan's repentance, in Ivan's case).

Hence, in all three episodes, Alyosha keeps the others (Ivan; Dmitry; Snegiryov) *active* in the process of compassionate communication. Instead of making crucial decisions for them, he encourages and supports their spiritual search, looking for a solution that would be effective over the long term. He respects Ivan's, Dmitry's, and Snegiryov's self-assessments and responds to them with his own, positively consummating definitions, enriched by a surplus of vision issuing from the outside of their anguished psyches. Unlike Myshkin, Alyosha always leaves room for the other's response and takes that response seriously. He does not repent in Ivan's place, does not judge Dmitry in Dmitry's place, and does not push Snegiryov into a friendship the latter is not ready to accept.[39] Instead, he encourages each of them to take responsibility for their self-renewal, to confidently sign their names under their own acts, as Bakhtin may have put it. As a result, Ivan's repentance, Dmitry's spiritual regeneration, or Snegiryov's acceptance of sympathy and charity are not imposed from the outside or "ready-made," to borrow Dostoevsky's own apt expression (*PSS*, 5:133).[40] Although Alyosha is there to help each of the characters, he realizes that these moral-spiritual developments can be attained only by Ivan, Dmitry, and the Captain *themselves*, through earnest inner work.

Finally, in all three episodes, Alyosha learns that it is crucial to acknowledge the ontological gulf between persons before searching for productive ways of bridging it. This, learned, as much as instinctual, sensitivity to differences on Alyosha's part helps him mediate skillfully between his variously divided neighbors. Indeed, for Dostoevsky's last Christlike hero, a keen awareness of ontological boundaries means that he will not be paralyzed by them.

FRUITFUL EXCHANGES: ALYOSHA IS CONSUMMATED BY OTHERS

Alyosha becomes especially competent as a compassionate mediator, capable of "appeasing and uniting" his divided community, after a religious conversion that ends his metaphysical rebellion and transforms him from a pure-hearted but essentially naive believer into a mature *homo religiosus*. Some readers credit Alyosha's spiritual healing to his direct communion with Christ, the incarnated Word of God, in the Cana of Galilee chapter.[41] However, the process of Alyosha's spiritual recovery begins in the chapter immediately preceding the conversion proper, prosaically entitled "An Onion." In true Dostoevskian fashion, a communion with Christ ("Cana of Galilee") is preceded and enabled by a human communion with the least likely Christ-bearer, a ruthless businesswoman and the cause of Mitya's bitter rivalry with his father, Grushenka Svetlov ("An Onion").

What begins as Grushenka's attempt to seduce and compromise the unnervingly virtuous Alyosha, on the one hand, and Alyosha's desperate self-corruption in response to Zosima's posthumous disgrace, on the other,[42] unexpectedly turns into a deeply personal communion between two equally flawed human beings, each offering the other hope for redemption by performing a small act of kindness. Grushenka's act of kindness is simply her refusal to go through with her malicious plan, and her unexpectedly pious respect for Alyosha's grief restores the hero's faith both in his human and in his divine *other*. Instead of being part of the temptation, Grushenka miraculously becomes part of Alyosha's spiritual healing; instead of feeding his metaphysical rebellion, she provides a spiritual solution by offering a living proof of Christlike compassion. And making her helpful, indeed, saving, role known to Grushenka becomes Alyosha's act of kindness in respect to her. Unlike the ungrateful sinners in Grushenka's humorous legend, whose ruthless struggle to wrest the salvific onion from each other lands them back in the fiery lake of hell, he is able to receive his "onion"[43] with gratitude and dignity and to hold on to it: preserving the delicate equilibrium of helping and being helped, he does his part to secure redemption for both, the giver and the recipient of charity.

This critical interdependence of *offering* and *receiving* love becomes the most important lesson of the "Onion" chapter. As Gary Saul Morson eloquently puts it,

> Grushenka's unwitting kindness, performed as carelessly as the woman in the folktale gave the onion, turns out to make a significant difference. She hardly knows what has happened but feels their roles unexpectedly reversed. Allowing her to think of herself as the one who is superior, the one who has helped *him*, constitutes Alyosha's unexpected gift to her. She gives him an onion, and allowing her to do so is the onion that he gives her.[44]

The hopeful *consummation* the two offer each other is thus grounded in mutuality. By renouncing her erstwhile plans, Grushenka defines herself as something more than a cunning seductress in Rakitin's plot; by accepting and fully appreciating her saving gesture, Alyosha refuses the role of a spiritually defeated victim, a betrayer of Father Zosima, prepared for him by Rakitin. By *giving* an onion, Grushenka proves that she is not "that sort of woman," as some have labeled her in Skotoprigonievsk,[45] but "a sister" and a friend to Alyosha (*PSS*, 14:318). By *receiving* his onion graciously, Alyosha demonstrates that he is not "with those of little faith," as Father Paisy had feared several hours earlier (*PSS*, 14:305), but someone who has not despaired of God and His people and thus remained faithful to Zosima's ideals.

But Grushenka's absolved status as "*not* that sort of woman" cannot be secured without Alyosha's whole-hearted belief in her Christlike potential, which is simultaneously the guarantee of his own reconfirmed status as a man of faith. In this context, it is extremely important that the restoration of Alyosha's faith is at least partly dependent on Grushenka's honoring of his redeeming vision of herself, while the validity of her hopeful, "clean slate" image, in turn, depends on Alyosha's spiritual potency, on his having enough strength to believe in and support her moral renewal. In other words, for this mutual redemption to be truly productive, each character has to take the other's positive consummating word about him- or herself seriously, because failure to value *oneself* properly will immediately affect *the other's* spiritual well-being. As in the legend of the onion, a properly executed *giving* gesture also grants salvation to the one who *receives* it, but the reception must equal the giving gesture in sincerity and moral purity.

Thus, the crucial significance of the "Onion" chapter for Alyosha's development is that these two characters are redeemed together, each affirming the other's ideal self and becoming responsible for the other's renewal. It is important that Alyosha's moral recovery begins by *receiving* another's (Grushenka's) love and culminates in achieving a perfect balance of giving and receiving charity, rare in Dostoevsky's world. This experience becomes a model for the post-conversion Alyosha, who will make every effort to ensure that his active love secures the other's equally active response. When Alyosha's encounter with Christlike love in "An Onion" is decoded scripturally in the following chapter, it is appropriate that the biblical passage mystically enacted in his dream beside Zosima's bier tells of Christ's joyful *reception* of a poor family's hospitality at a wedding in Cana, which elicits his reciprocal miraculous gift. Importantly, this constitutes Christ's first miracle, after which his disciples begin to believe in him (John 2:11),[46] that is, they, in their turn, actively *reciprocate* his love. Post-conversion, a similar response may be expected from Alyosha's multiple disciples in the novel.

Finally, Grushenka's affirmation of Alyosha during a "Gethsemane moment" of spiritual uncertainty leads to his final exit from the monastery, to defend agape in the unsheltered realm of earthly passions, in full compliance with Zosima's wishes for *his* disciple. The incarnating significance of this transition is underscored by Alyosha's iconic gesture of kissing and embracing the earth in the conclusion of "Cana of Galilee." Thus, in an important way, Grushenka's consummating touch anoints Alyosha for a life of service *in the world*, a path that will commemorate Christ's descent to Earth. The consummating effect of another's (Grushenka's) compassion, that "grounds" Alyosha spiritually and emotionally, also symbolically completes his incarnation in the novel.

Having recognized Grushenka's crucial contribution to Alyosha's spiritual coming of age,[47] it is important to note that Alyosha is positioned as a gracious *recipient* of gifts from the beginning of the novel. With a hagiographer's pride, the narrator tells us that, as a child, Alyosha was not at all ashamed of being raised through the charity of virtual strangers and, unlike his brother Ivan, received shelter and care from distant relatives without discomfort, entirely at peace with living at someone else's expense. According to Miusov's entirely plausible prediction, if left without any means in an unfamiliar city, Alyosha would be immediately taken care of and given all things necessary, not only without the slightest imposition for his benefactors, but to their greatest pleasure (*PSS*, 14:20). What's more, the youngest Karamazov is an expert *recipient of love* in the novel.

In a remarkable display of affection, unprecedented in Dostoevsky's works, almost all major characters perceive Alyosha as the most desired addressee, a uniquely authoritative interlocutor, with whom they share their most intimate secrets and discuss most urgent questions.[48] When Alyosha joins another character for a conversation, small talk gives way to questions of ultimate importance, a tavern room or a garden gazebo cinematically expand, and the world sheds its distracting particulars to reveal the essential reality of dialogue: Alyosha and his interlocutor, alone in the infinite universe—two dialogically contraposed *beings* in the silent vastness of *Being*. It is in keeping with this tendency that Mitya speaks of himself as "a being" (*sushchestvo*) about to let loose of "everything earthly and [to] fly into the otherworldly" in "The Confession of an Ardent Heart, in Verse" (*PSS*, 14:97), claiming that the requests and confessions he is about to make to Alyosha are of such dire importance that they could only be made "at death's door" (*PSS*, 14:97). Ivan sojourns with Alyosha in the town tavern "to solve the age-old questions," boasts of having "the whole eternity of time" at his disposal (*PSS*, 14:212), and, after sharing his poem "The Grand Inquisitor," feels disappointed "that he wasn't able to express himself well . . . to a *being* like Alyosha [s takim *sushchestvom*, kak Alesha], in regard to whom he, in his heart, undoubtedly had great expectations" (*PSS*, 14:242).[49]

Alyosha's singularity (*edinstvennost'*) as each major character's "one and only," uniquely competent friend, confessor, or advisor is consistently emphasized in the novel. When Feodor Pavlovich exclaims tearfully: "well, I do feel, don't I, that *you* [Alyosha] *are the only person in the world* who has not judged me [chto *ty edinstvennyi chelovek na zemle*, kotoryi menia ne osudil], my dear boy" (*PSS*, 14:24), we have reason to believe that this feeling is something more than an expression of facile sentimentality or an act of habitual play-acting on the part of the old scaramouche. The haughty Kolya Krasotkin designates Alyosha as the only being in the world whose command he would obey: "*there is only one being in the whole world* [*est' tol'ko odno sushchestvo v tselom mire*] that can order Nikolai Krasotkin to do something, here is this person," he declares to a visiting doctor and points at Alyosha (*PSS*, 14:506). Alyosha is also the only person in the world Lise Khokhlakov has elected to receive her most intimate, and shameful, confessions: "How could I possibly tell *anyone else in the whole world* what I have told you?" ("Razve ia *komu-nibud' v mire skazhu*, chto vam govorila?")—she says to Alyosha in a moment of despair (*PSS*, 15:25).[50]

Two main attributes evident in these definitions of Alyosha—(1) Alyosha's "*thou-ness*" (his consistent identification as other characters' "one and only" interlocutor, addressed in an ongoing dialogue) and (2) his frequent characterization as "*a being*" (*sushchestvo*), which highlights the ontological aspect of his activity, the relevance of his mission to the fundamental questions of existence—testify to the fact that Alyosha is recognized not as a particular social type or character, but rather as *a person*, so to speak, in the pure essence of his personhood. Put together, these two key attributes spell out the affirming "*Thou art*!" addressed to Alyosha by each major character in the novel.[51]

THE SAINTLY BELOVED

Alyosha's emergence as nearly everyone's preferred addressee, a universally identified beloved *other* in the novel, is the culmination of one of the book's major themes, the theme of "another person" or neighbor. Endlessly varied in *The Brothers Karamazov*, this poignant theme is apparent in Ivan's agonized questioning of our ability to love and pity another human being, our neighbor—after all, he is another and not I, and cannot be fully understood. It is heard in the discomforting question raised, more or less explicitly, by both the prosecutor and Dmitry's defense attorney at the trial: what if Dmitry had a different father, kind and caring, a real *blizhnii*, and not the debauched and ever absent Feodor Pavlovich? Could Dmitry have been spared from his spiritual turmoil, and the world—from the consequences of his violent rage? This theme is revealed in its religious dimension in the musings of a Russian peasant, who wonders if "somewhere out there," perhaps at the end of this world, there is "someone holy and higher [than us]," a redeeming alternative to his own sinful soul (*PSS*, 14:29), and in Feodor Pavlovich's curious craving "for someone faithful and close to him," an imaginary other, entirely different from Feodor, not debauched, but good, and therefore comforting in his alterity:

> There were also exceptional occasions of the higher order, very subtle and complicated ones, when Feodor Pavlovich himself couldn't have explained *the extraordinary craving for someone faithful and close to him*, which sometimes suddenly and unaccountably seized him all in a moment [*tu noobychainuiu potrebnost' v vernom i blizkom cheloveke*, kotoruiu on nepostizhimo vdrug inogda nachinal oshchushchat' v sebe]. . . . Utterly depraved and often cruel in his lust, like some vicious insect, Feodor Pavlovich was sometimes, in moments of drunkenness, seized by spiritual terror and moral convulsions . . . At such moments *he liked to feel that there was next to him, near at hand*, if not in the same room, then in the lodge, a loyal, strong-willed person, *completely unlike himself* [on liubil, *chtoby podle, poblizosti . . . byl takoi chelovek*, predannyi, tverdyi, *sovsem ne takoi, kak on*], not depraved, who had seen all his debauchery and knew all his secrets, but would be ready in his loyalty to overlook all that, not to object, above all, not to reproach him or threaten him with anything, neither in this life, nor in the next, and, if need be, to defend him—from whom? From somebody unknown, but terrible and dangerous.
>
> The point was precisely that it should be *another* person [nepremenno *drugoi* chelovek] [italics in text], an old, familiar friend, so that he might summon him at a painful moment just to look at his face, or, perhaps, exchange some insignificant words with him. And if the other were all right with it, not angry, his heart felt lighter, and if he were angry, well, then he felt more despondent. (*PSS*, 14:86–87)

In Feodor Pavlovich's spiritually superior *other* who knows all secrets and forgives our transgressions, we may recognize an oblique reference to the all-knowing but merciful God, the Other above us. But the wishfully imagined "other person" *beside* Feodor Pavlovich ("*podle* [Fedora Pavlovicha]") is also his neighbor (a "*blizkii* chelovek" is also a "*blizhnii*"), with all the implications of the word's Christian semantics. If we recall that, in his last conversation with Ivan, Smerdyakov tellingly refers to God as a certain other, "a third . . . *next to us*" ("*podle* nas-s") (*PSS*, 15:60),[52] it becomes apparent that "drugoi" (other) in *The Brothers Karamazov* is at once our divine and our human other, and the crucial link that connects these two consistently related signifiers is Incarnation.

In the narrowest sense, the referent of "another person" in the passage above is the servant Grigory, who lives close by in the lodge, nurses Feodor Pavlovich after his drunken fights, defends him from Mitya's violent outbursts, and is occasionally asked in for no apparent reason, simply to allay his master's existential malaise. But we sense that the spiritual function assigned to the intensely desired "other person" is not carried out in full by Grigory, Marfa, or Smerdyakov, that is, by any of Feodor Pavlovich's actual neighbors at the time of this private confession. The "nepremenno drugoi chelovek," who so unexpectedly takes up residence in Feodor Pavlovich's morally atrophied psyche is deliberately designated as a *potential* other, an intentionally vague label with yet unspecified content, as the passage's emphatically tentative phrasing demonstrates. The extreme intensity of Feodor Pavlovich's need for a redeeming other, accompanied by "spiritual dread" and "moral convulsions," tells us that in the other's beneficent presence the old Karamazov seeks something more than a cynical alibi for his own moral inertia. The character's "extraordinary" craving is so strong because it remains mostly unsatisfied: what Feodor Pavlovich secretly craves is, of course, love, which remains outside of his emotional capabilities, much like it does for his ideological kinsman, the Underground Man, who can define love and faith only as "something I long for but cannot find" (*Notes*, 26; *PSS*, 5:121). For that reason, the role of Feodor Pavlovich's optimal other, who could fully satisfy his surprisingly vital spiritual drive, is not assigned to anyone at this point in the novel; it is only contemplated, wistfully and secretly.

In this sense, the most loyal servant Grigory, who has indisputable influence over Feodor Pavlovich, or Smerdyakov, whose unprecedented honesty in financial dealings makes Feodor Pavlovich trust him more than anyone else in his household, may be "auditioning" for the part, but no single actor has secured the role. Reflecting on the significance of the passage retrospectively, from the vantage point of the novel's conclusion, *we* may ironize that, later in the novel, Ivan will fall disappointingly short of fulfilling the requirements for the "job" of Feodor Pavlovich's neighbor, specified in his wish list, as evidenced in Ivan's ambivalent vigil on the staircase of his father's house the night before the murder. Only a few steps away from his father's bedroom (*poblizosti* ot Fedora Pavlovicha), Ivan will listen, curiously, for the signs of potential violence, but will ultimately choose not to "defend him . . . from someone terrible and dangerous"—the lackey-turned-murderer Smerdyakov, another presumably failed contender for the role of Feodor's beneficent neighbor. But these assessments could only be made from the privileged position outside of the novel's frame. From the point of view of Feodor Pavlovich, at the time of this private confession, "the close and loyal other person" has no concrete referent among the novel's characters. It belongs to the realm of wishes, and there is characteristically Dostoevskian irony in the fact that it is left to a misanthropic buffoon to contemplate, yearningly, the full potential of what one human being can be to another emotionally and spiritually. We may say that all of these "job applications" are still under consideration: at this point in the novel, the intensely desired *other person*, a full-value neighbor, exists for Feodor Pavlovich solely as a vacancy.

And here comes a Dostoevskian miracle, hidden, provocatively, in plain view. Feodor Pavlovich's abstractly envisioned *other* materializes as a concretely embodied, individually cherished *neighbor* right before our eyes. In a passage that concludes the paragraph containing the excerpt quoted above, the narrator tells us that Feodor Pavlovich "also felt something of the sort" in respect to Alyosha, "*after* his arrival" (*PSS*, 14:87), which dates the period of Feodor's intense spiritual longing for a better other as the time *before* Alyosha's return to his native town. From the narrator's account we learn that, like Feodor Pavlovich's wishfully imagined neighbor, Alyosha "lived [with him], saw everything and did not condemn anything" (*PSS*, 14:87), responding to his father's cruel buffoonery with unconditional love. But Feodor Pavlovich's direct words to Alyosha, uttered in an earlier chapter, reveal that this acknowledgment of his youngest son's remarkable capacity for agape secures him an exclusive status in Feodor's eyes: Alyosha is not simply *a* person who "did not condemn" Feodor Pavlovich, but "*the only person in the whole world* who did not condemn [him]" (*PSS*, 14:24). With this recognition of his unique qualifications to be Feodor Pavlovich's redeeming other, Alyosha effectively wins the "audition" for the role of beloved neighbor, implicitly held in the novel.

In the context of the entire novel, it becomes clear that, for Feodor Pavlovich, Alyosha is indeed *the only* person with whom he can experience, however minimally, the spiritual aspect of human togetherness. Unlike Grigory's or Marfa's professionally motivated tolerance for their depraved master, Alyosha's non-judgmental affection for Feodor Pavlovich at his cynical worst has no ulterior motive and is so undeserved, so astonishingly devoid of practical logic, that it shocks the old buffoon into taking love seriously. Because Alyosha accepts Feodor Pavlovich just as he is, without any reservations or wishful "corrections," he is able to acknowledge his father's ultimate, ontic reality the way no one else can, and the latter spontaneously reciprocates this gesture by, in turn, recognizing the reality of Alyosha's neighborly love. Feodor Pavlovich feels embraced by a spiritual force he cannot deny; he cannot but share in Alyosha's affirmative love and eventually comes to experience his son's comforting proximity as deep emotional closeness. And that, indeed, makes Alyosha the only full-fledged, spiritually meaningful *neighbor* in Feodor Pavlovich's life.

Thus, we are witnessing a critical transformation of a *theoretically posited other* (Feodor Pavlovich's imaginary "other person"), experienced only as a palpable void, into a real, emotionally and spiritually available neighbor, cherished in his concrete individuality (Alyosha). The Schelerian "sphere of the Thou," the original sphere of Being that is always present, a priori, in our consciousness, even if it is not "filled" with any concrete content (as in the case of Scheler's imagined "absolute Robinson Crusoe," who has an intuitive idea of communality even in the absence of concretely embodied others [Scheler, *GW*, 8:57; 7:77]),[53] is illustrated, most intriguingly, by Feodor Pavlovich and his emphatically theoretical addressee, the "nepremenno *drugoi* chelovek" ("a person necessarily other than me"). This inevitably posited region of the other, that could have remained forever vacant for the misanthropic, emotionally handicapped Feodor Pavlovich, as it does for the Underground Man or for Stavrogin, who, as Romano Guardini correctly notes, has no neighbors in the spiritual sense,[54] is here filled with concrete content. An ephemeral, abstractly present other, who for Dostoevsky, as for Scheler, can become fully real and spiritually available only through love, gains flesh and blood, and rosy cheeks to boot, before our very eyes.

We are privy to a crucial movement of Incarnation that symbolically commemorates Christ's enfleshment in the novel. Importantly, just as the sphere of the Thou is "filled" through Alyosha, another a priori sphere of consciousness in Scheler's system that may remain forever vacant—that of the Absolute (the Divine Thou)—becomes filled with spiritually "available," personally meaningful content for several characters through their contact with Alyosha (Mitya's and Grushenka's renewed commitment to a deeply personal God, supported by the youngest Karamazov, and Alyosha's successful spiritual education of the boys, especially the precocious atheist Kolya Krasotkin, are only a few examples of this seminal transformation). This dual achievement effectively demonstrates how both man's human other and his Absolute Other (God) are saved from the fate of empty potentiality through Incarnation in Dostoevsky's world.

Estimating the evolution of Dostoevsky's spiritual ideal from the early works to his final novel, Dmitry Chizhevsky insightfully observes that, in the later works, Dostoevsky's positive hero becomes a better "saint" inasmuch as he becomes a better neighbor: "the unification and integration of the saintly image in Dostoevsky's work is based on the concept of 'neighbor,'" Chizhevsky notes.[55] If we use this criterion for measuring the characters' spiritual achievement, Alyosha's progress in respect to his predecessor Prince Myshkin becomes evident. The call for an optimal, loving and lovable, neighbor, issued by Feodor Pavlovich is echoed by many other characters in the novel, and Dostoevsky's last saint is always able to meet their similarly intense need for a spiritually satisfying "other person." In fact, he becomes the one person whose presence is sufficient to satisfy their communal instinct—as it were, an instant one-man-community that saves them from the fate of Scheler's absolute Robinson Crusoe. Epitomized most poignantly by Ivan's: "It's enough for me to know *that you* [Alyosha] *are somewhere here* [in this world] [chto *ty tut gde-to est'*] and I won't lose the will to live" (*PSS*,

14:240), this aspect of Alyosha's uniqueness is revealed in the confessions of several major characters. Alyosha is perceived as the one person capable of saving them from the despair of absolute solipsism; one person whose presence would make life worthwhile, even if all others were to forsake them. Ivan may have been silent "with the whole world" about what's most important to him, but feels compelled to reveal his metaphysical dilemmas to "a being like Alyosha" (*PSS*, 14:242). Mitya, who contemplates suicide but is delivered from desperate thoughts upon seeing Alyosha in "One More Lost Reputation" (*PSS*, 14:142), is reconciled to everyone's ridicule of his "silly" confessions, as long as his youngest brother takes him seriously (*PSS*, 14:99), while the troubled Lise Khokhlakov challenges the whole world, "not excluding *anyone*," to persecute and torment her (italics in text), but asks Alyosha to weep for her in her spiritual rebellion, because "it is *your* tears *alone* that I need" ("mne *tol'ko vashikh* slez nado") (*PSS*, 15:25).

These examples demonstrate that Alyosha is sought by others in his function of *homo amans*, as someone who would *love them* in a spiritually satisfying way. The necessity and urgency of this search "for someone who would love me" becomes clear in light of Dostoevsky's cherished motto, given to the hapless Captain Snegiryov in *The Brothers Karamazov*—that every human being, no matter how sinful, deserves to be loved. Expressing gratitude for his family's affection in the face of his many shortcomings as husband and father, the drunkard Snegiryov utters one of the novel's most significant passages: "This is a great thing the Lord has arranged for every person like me [dlia kazhdogo cheloveka v moem rode-s]. *For it is necessary that even a person like me have a chance to be loved by someone*, sir" ("*Ibo nadobno, chtob i cheloveka v moem rode mog khot' kto-nibud' vozliubit'- s*") (*PSS*, 14:183). The universal nature of this necessity to be loved in Dostoevsky's world comes to the fore when it is expressed by a less deserving paterfamilias, Feodor Pavlovich Karamazov. "I keep thinking about it: who will ever say a prayer for me? *Is there such a person in the whole world*?" ("*Est' li v svete takoi chelovek*?") (*PSS*, 14:23), the old Karamazov asks half-jokingly, realizing, with surprise, that in Alyosha he has secured just "such a person," indeed, perhaps *the only* person "in the whole world" who will evoke him lovingly, in thought and in prayer. Similarly surprising is the fact that Alyosha can love "someone like" Ivan: "You seem to *love me* for some reason, Alyosha, don't you?" ("Ty, kazhetsia, pochemu-to *liubish' menia,* Alesha?"), Ivan exclaims joyfully (*PSS*, 14:209).[56]

But what is more surprising and, arguably, exceptional, in Dostoevsky's world is that someone like Ivan can love Alyosha: "I eventually *came to love* your expectant gaze," Ivan confesses with uncharacteristic tenderness in the tavern scene (*PSS*, 14:209). Mitya is also surprised that he, too, can love in an authentic, unacquisitive way, and this spiritual capacity seems to be awakened by Alyosha: "So then there indeed exists a person that *even I love* [i.e.: *even someone like me can love*], because here is that little guy, my sweet little brother, *whom I love* more than anyone in the world, *the only person I love*!," Mitya declares passionately in the last chapter of part 1 ("Da ved' est' zhe, stalo byt', chelovek, *kotorogo i ia liubliu*, ved' vot on, vot tot chelevechek, bratishka moi milyi, *kogo ia vsekh bol'she na svete liubliu i kogo ia edinstvenno liubliu*!" [*PSS*, 14:142]). Finally, what is most astounding—"someone like" Feodor Pavlovich becomes capable of love when Alyosha offers himself as its object: "Feodor Pavlovich [*came to love*] *him* sincerely and deeply *and in such a way as someone like him surely had not been able to love anyone*" ("Fedor Pavlovich *poliubi*[*l*] *ego* iskrenne i gluboko i *tak, kak nikogda, konechno, ne udavalos' takomu, kak on, nikogo liubit*'") (*PSS*, 14:19).[57]

By thus transforming someone whose very nature seems incompatible with love Alyosha sets a new record among Dostoevsky's saintly protagonists and turns our attention to the importance of inspiring and properly receiving love in Dostoevsky's world. Because of Alyosha, Feodor Pavlovich could now say, emending the words of Captain Snegiryov: "It is a great thing the good Lord has arranged for anyone like me. For *it is necessary that even someone like me love somebody*." Alyosha's remarkable gift to Feodor Pavlovich reveals that he is not only a consistent *homo amans*, a character type already well represented in Dostoevsky's novels, but a generally acknowledged *homo amatus*, an exemplary beloved, capable of inspiring love in the most unlikely places, and this is a fundamentally new spiritual trait for a Dostoevskian protagonist. This extraordinary talent is confirmed by Grushenka's repeated words of affection for Alyosha, by Kolya Krasotkin's "declaration of love" for the youngest Karamazov, and by Father Paisy's "surprising" realization, upon Zosima's death, that "this young soul has come to mean so much in my heart" (*PSS*, 14:304). But perhaps the most remarkable aspect of Alyosha's gift is captured in Zosima's prophecy for his disciple: "even your very enemies will love you," the Elder tells Alyosha (*PSS*, 14:259). Not only Alyosha's practical enemies, but his ideological opponents in Dostoevsky's metaphysical cosmos—that is, those who oppose agape on ideological grounds, such as Ivan Karamazov—will love him, in spite of themselves, and thus will come to apprehend, emotionally, the spiritual value they had rejected rationally.

In his religious-philosophical study of Dostoevsky's major novels, Romano Guardini perceptively notes that there is always "room for a Thou" in Alyosha,[58] which makes him the quintessential communal man in *The Brothers Karamazov*. I would like to underscore that it is equally important, and fundamentally novel, in Dostoevsky's world that Alyosha creates room for a Thou (himself) in others, enabling *them* to love (or, in the context of Scheler's theory of intersubjectivity, Alyosha *activates* and inhabits the sphere of the Thou already present in everyone a priori). By graciously submitting himself to the others' consummation, Alyosha becomes a better consummator himself. By keeping the other active in the process of loving dialogue, he, too, remains active in his love. In fact, in the thoroughly interconnected world of *The Brothers Karamazov*, productive spiritual activity is possible only as interactivity. To succeed spiritually, the characters need to consummate each other, to accept and share divine love with their human neighbors, for, as David Cunningham notes, no one can bear God's image alone in Dostoevsky's last novel.[59] And, following the characters' lead, the reader is also encouraged to consummate or "finish" Alyosha's image beyond the novel, as Robert Bird suggests,[60] which is one of the main reasons Alyosha comes across as the character "invested with the greatest future dimension" in *The Brothers Karamazov*.[61]

By creating a spiritually balanced Christlike hero in his last novel, Dostoevsky demonstrates the equal importance and interdependence of two major functions performed by an effective Christian neighbor—those of giving and receiving love—but the ability to properly receive and inspire love is certainly emphasized in Alyosha as an essentially new element, largely lacking in the hero's predecessors, especially in Prince Myshkin. Alyosha is so firm in his commitment to the other and so certain in his faith in the other's highest potential that the answering gesture paradoxically precedes his own act of love: "You know, this whole past month I have been telling myself: 'we'll either become friends forever or will immediately part as enemies till the grave,'" Kolya Krasotkin tells Alyosha during their first meeting, "And saying so you certainly already loved me," Alyosha responds with joyful confidence (*PSS*, 14:504).

According to the narrator, Alyosha "contained the gift to inspire special love for himself, so to speak, in his very nature, artlessly and spontaneously" (*PSS*, 14:19), and this effortlessly elicited love for himself, indeed, becomes the most precious *gift* he offers to his many neighbors in *The Brothers Karamazov*. To extend Gary Saul Morson's definition of Alyosha's spiritual accomplishment in the "Onion" chapter to the entire novel, each major character offers Alyosha love—they give him "an onion," and allowing, or rather, enabling them to do so is the onion he gives *them*. And that is no small onion, especially in the context of Prince Myshkin's essential failure to secure a fruitful reception for his otherworldly love that remains suspect to most of his neighbors till the end of the novel. Recollecting Zosima's definition of hell as the inability to answer love,[62] we could say that in *The Idiot* Nastasia Filippovna's personal hell was precisely her tragic inability to respond to Myshkin's agape. In *The Brothers Karamazov*, Dostoevsky's last Christlike hero grants his neighbors the gift Myshkin was unable to bestow on his—not the gift of being loved, but that of actively experiencing love for others. This remarkable ability to enable others to love is the most apparent

Christlike feature in Alyosha's character, which evokes that living miracle of Christ's *personality* that Dostoevsky consistently privileged over the doctrinal aspects of Christianity.

Although Alyosha becomes nearly everyone's best loved neighbor, he does not allow them to exhaust their love on him alone. We sense that he will not remain "the one and only" beloved, a one-man-community to others for long. On the contrary, through this quintessential neighbor, other neighbors become real and accessible to the novel's characters in a deeply personal way: Alyosha brings Kolya and the boys to Ilyusha, he supports and deepens the growing spiritual bond between Dmitry and Grushenka, and gradually makes Ivan conscious of his grave failures as neighbor (*blizhnii*) to their father and brother Dmitry. Indeed, something in Alyosha's very nature prevents those who love him from idolizing him at the expense of other spiritual-emotional ties: unlike the Underground Man's abstract love for others, "inapplicable to anything human" (*PSS*, 5:133),[63] that dissipates at the sight of a concrete object, their love grows and opens up to new recipients at this optimal point of application.

The fact that loving Alyosha opens the characters to other objects of love means that he is also a potential conduit of Holy Otherness, or God, for his neighbors. Whether carrying out Mitya's or Katerina Ivanovna's errands, quoting Father Zosima's words in his conversations with Kolya, Lise, or the boys,[64] or Christ's answer to the Grand Inquisitor in his response to Ivan's poem, Alyosha routinely acts and speaks on behalf of others, and when he tells the despairing Dmitry that "God will arrange it as best as He knows, so as to prevent the horror" (*PSS*, 14:112) and confidently conveys God's word of love to Ivan before the trial, he is able to speak to his human *others* on behalf of the Absolute *Other*. In this context, the fact that Alyosha's very being—his countenance (*lik*), a direct manifestation of personhood (*lichnost'*)—alludes to the absent, once forgotten others (Alyosha bears an extraordinary likeness to his mother, evocatively named Sophia, and to Zosima's beloved, saintly brother Markel),[65] is imbued with religious significance, conjuring symbolic associations with the monastic term "Pre*podobnyi*" ("exceedingly like [Christ]"). Someone who reminds us of the suffering, unjustly forgotten others is, by extension, a reminder of the suffering Christ. In this subtly suggested function of a living icon, Alyosha points to human images (Markel, manifested by Alyosha to Zosima; Sophia, manifested to Feodor Pavlovich and her other son, Ivan) that, in turn, point to Christ (Markel's passionate embracing of Christianity before his death; Sophia's characteristic gesture, remembered by Alyosha, of pointing to the icon of the Mother of God, or, more precisely, using the toddler Alyosha, whom she ecstatically lifts up in the air and holds toward the icon, as a living pointer to the divine image [*PSS*, 14:18]). "Someone like" our beloved others (*pokhozhii; podobnyi*) is potentially "someone like Christ" (*Prepodobnyi*) and may manifest his spiritual countenance.

Thus, Alyosha's social-ontological connectedness in the world and openness to the Absolute guard against solipsism: this one-man-community has a built-in community of neighbors that will become available to those who love him. As a result, he does not usurp or monopolize the others' love, preventing them from spending all of their spiritual capital on him only. And, in his turn, at least after Zosima's death,[66] Alyosha also does not exhaust the rich surplus of his love in one place. He is equally attentive to Dmitry and Ivan, Grushenka and Katerina Ivanovna, Ilyusha and Kolya Krasotkin and, unlike Myshkin's, his love manages to resist enlistment in deadly power struggles between its many recipients, as his father testifies with surprise: "You love him [Mitya] and I am not afraid that you love him. And if it had been Ivan who loved him, I would have been afraid for myself that he loves him," Feodor Pavlovich tells Alyosha (*PSS*, 14:159).

CONCLUSIONS: A NEW VISION OF HUMAN TOGETHERNESS

This chapter's comparative analysis of *The Brothers Karamazov* and *The Idiot* has revealed two Christlike heroes facing analogous tasks: both Alyosha and Prince Myshkin are called upon to leave their sheltered domiciles (Myshkin's idyllic Swiss Alps / Alyosha's monastery) and to *act out* their divinely inspired love for the concrete, tragically imperfect neighbors in a world consumed by warring passions and alienated from the ideals of agape. Both heroes overcome their initial temptations to retreat from their mission, but the strength and effectiveness of their love for the world and its people continue to be tested throughout each novel. *Vzhivanie,* the process of "living into" the world and the minds and souls of its inhabitants, documented by means of a special discourse in *The Idiot* and *The Brothers Karamazov*, becomes a primary example of such rigorous spiritual testing in Dostoevsky's world, and an evocation of Incarnation. Will the Christlike hero be able to enter the inner world of his suffering neighbor, to understand the essence of his or her spiritual struggle and to suggest a spiritually productive, socially sustainable *solution* before the tragic *re-solution* of conflicts through murder thwarts his efforts?—Dostoevsky asks in each novel. While Dostoevsky's uncompromisingly realist answer to this question is "no" in both texts (both protagonists fail to prevent murder and experience a crisis of faith at a critical point in each novel's plot), there is a telling difference in the way the two heroes deal with their failures. Unlike Myshkin, Alyosha is able to recover from his fall from grace and to achieve small but significant victories through compassionate mediation primarily after the novel's main catastrophe. (The creation of a brotherhood of boys around the dying Ilyusha and Alyosha's success at helping Ilyusha's father receive charity and love graciously; gaining the friendship of the teenage nihilist Kolya Krasotkin, securing his reunion with Ilyusha and making him a potential disciple, that is, a practitioner of active love; keeping Dmitry from ultimate despair during and after the trial, and bringing him and Katerina together to grant each other forgiveness—are just some of Alyosha's achievements, which, indeed, testify to his ability to "appease and unite" ["primirit' i soedinit'"] many members of his community, just as Zosima had wished him to do [*PSS*, 14:178]).

The considerable spiritual stamina evident in Alyosha's tenacious activity is due to the subtle but crucial changes Dostoevsky's last ideal hero demonstrates in his approach to others in respect to his predecessor in *The Idiot*. Unlike Myshkin, whose wishful, prematurely finalized vision of a compassionate, reformed Rogozhin right before his attempt on the Prince's life is so strikingly at odds with reality, Alyosha is always able to see the real person beside him, without wishfully "retouching" her image. Be it Mitya's capacity for violence or Katerina Ivanovna's need for dominance, Alyosha recognizes these negative traits lucidly, without, however, letting them obscure the person's hopeful potential. He learns to face his interlocutors directly and does not run away from painful confrontations, nor does he turn away from the reality of evil. Unlike the Prince, Alyosha withstands the temptation "not to think" about the threat of impending violence, but carefully thinks through the existing conflicts in search of viable solutions, before deciding that he will no longer *think* but *act*.

Indeed, unlike Myshkin's, Alyosha's word is always subordinated to goal-oriented action. For that reason, his reflections on the others' inner life are never divorced from direct interactions with these others. Because his knowledge of others is thus enhanced through direct dialogical contact, he avoids secondhand definitions, to which Myshkin is sometimes prone. As a result, while Myshkin's imaginary exchanges with Rogozhin on the day of the attack have no positive impact on the Prince's *actual* conversations with his brother in Christ,[67] Alyosha's *vzhivanie* moments have the function of preliminary or preparatory negotiations with Dmitry, Ivan, and Katerina Ivanovna. The degree of closure or "finalization" is smaller in Alyosha's mental dialogues with others than in Myshkin's analogous imaginary exchanges, because the former leaves room for corrections and refinements of the other's image during future *face-to-face* encounters with him or her. This cheerful openness to life's unforeseen and often unforeseeable surprises makes it easier for Alyosha to recover after failed attempts to commune or even simply to communicate with others, for example, as he does when he rethinks his actions after the first, unsuccessful attempt to forward Katerina Ivanovna's monetary gift to Snegiryov. Simply put, Alyosha's practice of agape is generally more effective precisely because he indeed *practices* his empathetic techniques, finding an individual approach to each neighbor through trial and error and learning to get back on his feet after painful falls.

As we have seen, Alyosha uses his surplus of vision gently during his preliminary investigations of another's mind and consistently retains it in his face-to-face conversations, always succeeding at communicating something his interlocutors are unable to see or reluctant to acknowledge, be it Katerina Ivanovna's repressed attraction to Ivan and ressentiment-driven obsession with Dmitry, or Ivan's initially unacknowledged role in Smerdyakov's murderous plan. If Myshkin's self becomes virtually dissolved in Nastasia Filippovna's, as it were, drowned in her immense suffering, which renders him incapable of helping the despairing heroine, Alyosha remains firmly *outside* of those he counsels and helps, and this productive exteriority is the source of his spiritual effectiveness. Instead of doing their moral-spiritual work for them, Alyosha supports their inner renewal from the outside, precisely as an *other*. Such is his support of Ivan's emerging repentance and of Mitya's spiritual awakening in the aftermath of the murder, and his tactful approach to uniting the dying Ilyusha with his erstwhile bullies, whom he brings together ("svodit") without forced sentiment or moralistic preaching, stepping aside to let each boy reconcile with Ilyusha on his own terms.[68]

Because Alyosha thus preserves both his own sovereignty and that of his interlocutors, his love also remains staunchly independent, effectively resisting temptation: it is not easily manipulated or used as a weapon in the power struggles between its recipients, as it happens to Myshkin's love for Nastasia Filippovna in the notorious confrontation scene between Aglaya and Nastasia, analyzed in chapter 5.

Preserving the surplus of vision secures Alyosha's *active* position in relation to Dmitry, Ivan, the Snegiryovs and other suffering neighbors, allowing him to offer hope and help as a gift issuing *from the outside* of their despairing selves, the way Myshkin was unable to. Indeed, this productive outsideness, coupled with Alyosha's emotional and practical proximity to others (with the exception of one fateful day, he is usually on hand to lend a helping hand), ensures his ability to give of himself in a responsible way. By contrast, Myshkin's deficient sense of self-worth ultimately precludes him from making an acceptable gift of himself to others—to apply Romano Guardini's fitting expression, he, like Stavrogin, is virtually "unschenkbar," that is, he cannot be "*given*" or "*gifted*" to others,[69] hence the ultimate rejection of his sacrifice by Nastasia Filippovna. Importantly, Alyosha's proper self-love ensures his profound confidence in offering his support, compassion, and advice to those who need it. In Schelerian terms, Alyosha is certain of his irreducible value "qua person," as a being deeply cherished by his divine creator, and this quiet self-assurance, which is entirely compatible with Christian humility, is one of the reasons he is perceived as life's treasured gift by so many characters in the novel. Unlike Myshkin, he is immanently "givable" (*schenkbar*) and for that reason can also *receive* gifts of love with grace and confidence.

I have argued that it is precisely in this role as a gracious recipient of the others' love that Alyosha secures his greatest spiritual achievement in the novel: he becomes the quintessential *beloved other* ("drugoi chelovek") for nearly all major characters, enabling even those who are temperamentally or philosophically hostile to love (notably Ivan and Feodor Pavlovich) to experience love practically and thus to apprehend its value in the spontaneous act of loving Alyosha. Because of Alyosha, these characters are able to fulfill, albeit sometimes in a minimal way, the ultimate spiritual task of earthly existence defined by Zosima in his "On Hell and Hellfire: A Mystical Reflection." According to Zosima, God's sole purpose in granting us a temporal, bodily existence in "the infinite expanse of Being, not measurable by the categories of time or space," was to give each human self one, and only one, chance to say: "I am and I love" (*PSS*, 14:292), that is, to attain incarnated personhood in a concrete, distinctly temporal moment of "living, active love" (*PSS*, 14:292). We can say that, in their nearly unanimous declaration of love for Alyosha, the principle characters are each able to proclaim their redeeming "*I am and I love*," directing this dual affirmation to the novel's most beloved addressee.[70] And although Ivan's and Feodor's unexpected, spontaneously felt affection for Alyosha may not rise to the level of morally productive, *active* love endorsed by Zosima, as it has little effect on their self-serving actions, the mere fact of awakening the capacity for love in such characters already amounts to a seminal spiritual achievement in Dostoevsky's world. This undeniable accomplishment should remain on Alyosha's "resume," irrespective of the fate prepared for him in Dostoevsky's projected sequel for *The Brothers Karamazov*.

Because Alyosha *receives* compassion and forgiveness from others, he is productively consummated (both humbled and affirmed) by their acceptance, which completes the process of his symbolic Incarnation in the novel, enabling him, in turn, to support others from what Bakhtin would call a concrete place in Being. In Bakhtinian terms, Alyosha becomes a better *consummator* because he is himself fruitfully *consummated* by others. The fact that Alyosha's neighbors (Grushenka, the schoolboys, Kolya Krasotkin) play an important role in their shared spiritual victories also ensures Alyosha's own sustained *activity* in agapeistic dialogue. We can now answer the key question raised in the beginning of this chapter: how does Alyosha remain active in his neighborly love? Simply put, Alyosha stays active by keeping the others active, and this crucial interdependence of giving and receiving love is one of Dostoevsky's major spiritual discoveries in *The Brothers Karamazov*.

In his final masterpiece Dostoevsky revisits the problem of *imitatio Christi* in the modern world, most poignantly posed in *The Idiot* in his previous writings, offering a significant revision of the contemporary Christlike hero in Alyosha Karamazov, a character who embodies new, thoroughly edited concepts of Christian love and empathy in the author's evolving value system. In Alyosha's vision of "practical Christianity"—affirmed, if still only minimally *realized* in *The Brothers Karamazov*—eros opens up to agape, proper self-love meets the love of others, and human communion yields encounters with the Divine. As a result, no quintessential *other* is crowded out or excluded from the process of active dialogical negotiation that is shown to be the basis of all spiritually productive human relationships in the novel. Rephrasing Bakhtin, we may say that, in his final reflections on the ideal of human togetherness, Dostoevsky endorses the kind of love that respects and preserves the manifoldness of Being, an important value judgment that likely reveals one of the philosophical bases for the novelist's literary polyphony. This deeply affirmative, lofty, yet practical, vision of neighborly love may account for the staunch optimism exuded by Dostoevsky's last novel, one of his gloomiest plot-wise.

Conclusion

FUNDAMENTAL AFFINITIES: THE WHY AND HOW OF EMPATHY

Bakhtin believed that to mature to their full potential, ideas need time and a stimulating reception outside of their birthplace in intellectual history. Viewed from a productive distance, they enter into a global dialogue with other similarly liberated ideas in what Bakhtin called "great time" to reveal surprising new facets and unexpectedly fruitful applications. This project has been an attempt at such a dialogue in *great time*—a simulated discussion between three kindred thinkers separated in time and cultural space—on a topic of seminal importance to each, that of the human capacity and need for empathy.

For Bakhtin and Scheler the concept of loving empathy is fundamental in both their respective models of Being and in the particular structure of their philosophical careers. For Scheler, loving empathy unifies the world: as the last original function of the spirit, it constitutes a link in Being (*Seinsverkettung*) between human individualities (see, for example, *GW*, 7:137). Similarly, in Bakhtin's view, answerable empathy is "a way into the unity of Being," while the affirmation of the parties' irreducible individuality through love ensures the diversity and uniqueness of Being (*TPA*, 17–18, 15, 64). Because of the major ontological significance imparted to empathy in both theories, the investigation of this fundamental emotional phenomenon remains relevant to the thinkers' inquiries throughout their philosophical careers. Indeed, delving into the essence of fellow-feeling may provide an answer to the question that occupied Scheler his whole life: ultimately, *what can one human being be to another* (see, for example, *GW*, 7:211)? For Bakhtin and Scheler, love and empathy are those relationships that allow one human being to be *the most* to another, and, as a measure of productive togetherness, they relate to all other social relationships. For that reason, Scheler's study of empathy may be seen as an essential link between the philosopher's various investigations of what is now known as intersubjectivity. In this lifelong study he establishes the existence of an individual hierarchical core of values, the "order of the heart," that enables love and empathy, touching on the subject of "Ordo Amoris" in *On the Nature of Sympathy* and in posthumously published essays, suggests the possibility of its perversion in *Ressentiment*, and sketches a model of a spiritually productive relationship with the Absolute Other in *On the Eternal in Man*. In Bakhtin's oeuvre, the concept of active empathy also provides a foundation for many of the thinker's later inquiries. After all, his studies of dialogue, the novel, and the chronotope all demonstrate the creative mechanics of "living into" the artist's variously defined *others*: literary characters, readers, the represented time and space.

Bakhtin and Scheler also pose the essential question of empathetic understanding in similar terms: to what extent can I become part of the other's inner life, and how can I make this inevitably limited emotional immersion spiritually enriching for both parties? Both thinkers find the answer in the paradoxical act of live-entering performed by the model empathizer, the incarnated God-Man Christ. Because through Incarnation our Divine Other abandons the indefinite, as it were, anonymous, position in Being, in favor of an individual, personal stance in relation to humanity, Incarnation is seen as a model of an active approach to one's neighbor or dialogical partner. For Scheler and Bakhtin, after Incarnation there is no longer any abstractly conceived value nor any impersonal, standardized goodness, but only the value of an *act* of love performed by the *person* of Christ. It is important that addressing others through an act of loving empathy is thus seen as a means of embodying the spiritual movement of love, of giving it a concrete personal form, which brings us to one of the central questions raised in Dostoevsky's novels.

Perhaps best expressed in Shatov's characteristic remark to Stavrogin in *The Devils*: "We are two beings and have come together in infinity,"[1] one of the most crucial questions that occupies a Dostoevskian hero is indeed: What can one human being ultimately be to another? It is followed by the equally urgent: How can love be effectively realized or "applied" to those concrete human others, our neighbors?, to paraphrase the befuddled Underground Man.[2] Because the foundation of human togetherness, namely, the concept of active empathy, is linked to embodying or "applying" love in both Scheler's and Bakhtin's Christological theories, it is deeply relevant to Dostoevsky's Incarnation-centered universe.

I demonstrate that, with some (Schelerian) revision, the concepts of *consummation* and *surplus of vision*, largely abandoned by the later Bakhtin, are excellent tools for tackling the problem of just *how* love is realized or applied in Dostoevsky's world. For the early Bakhtin, one's external position in relation to another's inner being (surplus of vision) enables one to complete or "consummate" her spiritual image, calling the ideal person within to actualize itself. Symbolically alluding to Incarnation and Resurrection in early Bakhtin, consummation must respect both the inner and the outer boundaries of the consummated self. By affirming another's palpable spiritual achievements, I save him from the fate of empty potentiality; by resisting a finalizing definition, I ensure that this acknowledged realization does not exhaust his vital potential, rendering the act of consummation terminal. Employing Bakhtin's implicit theological metaphors, one could say that consummation is merely an incarnating moment in the self's journey toward a spiritual rebirth.

Defined as such, the concept of consummation becomes a useful measure of the characters' empathetic achievements in Dostoevsky's works. In *Notes from Underground*, the hero resists consummation by others and is himself incapable of consummating those around him or even of apprehending any uniquely personal aspects of their being. In this sense, the Underground Man resembles the Schelerian Robinson Crusoe, a hypothetical character to whom the other is given only as an abstract sphere of consciousness but not as a concretely embodied person. In Schelerian terms, the underground hero suffers from a metaphysical delusion: his ephemeral, invariably objectified others are completely dependent on his own being and sphere of interests. Because he refuses to grant others the status of ontological reality, which he wishes to reserve only for himself, he, in turn, proves incapable of sustaining a sovereign place in Being. Predictably, this hubristic attempt to monopolize the sphere of ultimate reality proves an impossible feat and the "I" eventually suffers the fate of the depersonalized, utterly abstract others. In fact, viewed from the underground, Being as a whole acquires a ghostly, eerily hypothetical quality in the novel. Unwilling to claim a responsible ontological position, resisting the incarnating touch of love, the Underground Man is equally incapable of resurrecting Liza.

If in *Notes from Underground* the ideal of compassion is defined negatively, in *The Idiot* and *Notes from the House of the Dead* we witness real, if short-lived, triumphs of active empathy and consummation. In both novels, life-changing insights into the others' and one's own inner being are revealed to the heroes during special transitional or "scaffold" moments preceding real or symbolic death or birth. In Dostoevsky's semi-autobiographical novel the hero's investigation of the enigmatic Russian soul takes place in the half-mythical netherworld, a Siberian prison whose inhabitants resemble chthonic beings barred from the realm of the living. Goryanchikov's entry into the soul of his fellow convict is inspired by the thoughts of their impending resurrection from the house of the dead. In *The Idiot*, Prince Myshkin's understanding of another's soul, "shrouded in darkness," is enhanced by his efforts to "live into" the last moments of a man awaiting execution and by his own "scaffold" experiences before the momentary death of epilepsy.

Myshkin's empathetic focus oscillates between two essential "moments" dominating a scaffold experience: the instant of "gathering" oneself in the face of death and the intense anticipation of a radically new beginning, the impossible wish for resurrection that seems to be granted to the condemned man largely through Myshkin's compassionate narrating. In a process resembling the Schelerian "Sammlung," Myshkin's condemned man concentrates all of his conscious life in one profoundly dense instant, out of which an entirely new spiritual existence could spring. This "original" act of living into a consciousness on the threshold of the ultimate deadline is paralleled by Myshkin's mental immersion into Rogozhin's troubled psyche on the eve of his own brush with death (part 2, chapter 5). If in the scaffold episode Myshkin makes a spiritually meaningful connection between the two "moments" that remain hopelessly separate within the condemned man's own experience, in his projection into Rogozhin's world, he seeks to reveal a path to Rogozhin's redemption, invisible from Rogozhin's own place in being. My Bakhtinian analysis of Myshkin's problematic but Christologically inspired "soul-entering" experience reveals a constant relation between the images of Rogozhin's *actual* and his *potential* person, as Myshkin struggles to reconcile the "old" with the "new," dialogically reformed Rogozhin. During his simulated dialogue with his rival and brother in Christ, Myshkin gathers all of his knowledge about Rogozhin "up to this point," not merely to understand but also to *transform* and radically *renew* Rogozhin's consciousness. The insights gleaned from Myshkin's peculiar empathetic encounter with the condemned man also inform his faith in a positively *new* beginning for Nastasia Filippovna, whose resurrection becomes a test of his Christlike potential in the novel.

If Myshkin's compassionate imagination dwells on the last moments *before* death, transgressing the final boundary in hopes of a new beginning for the many "condemned men" in the novel, the hero of *The House of the Dead*, so to speak, finds himself on the other side of the border. Symbolically speaking, he is already dead, anxiously awaiting the resurrecting moment of freedom. Goryanchikov begins to gain morally and spiritually relevant knowledge about the peasant convict only when he learns to see him in the category of becoming, already on his way toward emotional and spiritual rebirth.

In this context, my side-by-side analysis of the two novels brings to the fore the two symbolic referents of consummation delineated in the theoretical chapters, *Incarnation* and *Resurrection*. Dostoevsky's Christlike heroes complete the image of their human other with reference to the framing limits of Christ's earthly life, in which the end is simultaneously a new beginning. In both novels, the heroes' efforts to "live into" their neighbors entail a constant movement between the *last* and the *first* moments of the other's spiritual life. This dynamic perspective links realization with potential and deprives a consummating definition of finalizing power, by connecting a closing limit of one's spiritual search to an opening one. Here we are reminded of Bakhtin's definition of fruitful consummation: "The demand is: live in such a way that every given moment of your life would be both the consummating final moment and, at the same time, the initial moment of a new life" ("AH," 122).

To fulfill this task one needs another's consummating, but not finalizing, touch, a gesture that is sometimes easier to master in a retrospective or imaginary dialogue than in a face-to-face encounter, as Goryanchikov's and Myshkin's experiences demonstrate. Because *the other's* role of calling forth one's ideal self "from the outside" is crucial in this process, the loss of the ontological distance between persons arrests and ultimately thwarts the process of consummation, as my analysis of Myshkin's empathetic failures illustrates in chapter 5. Alyosha, who consistently acknowledges the ontological gulf between individuals, proves to be more effective at "applying" agape to his variously afflicted neighbors precisely because he observes a productive distance to their pain, never losing a hopeful surplus of vision that enables him to remain *active* in his empathetic efforts. Demonstrating an admirable balance as both a *consummating* and a *consummated* self, the two equally important functions of a Christlike empathizer, Alyosha is especially successful at *offering* love to others because he is able to *receive* their love in a gracious, ethically acceptable manner, as chapter 6 shows.

INDIVIDUAL VIEWS OF THE PROBLEM

In the course of our discussion, three kindred personalist thinkers have answered a seminal question: What makes emotional co-experiencing ethically, spiritually, and aesthetically productive? What unique "surplus" of information has each brought to the table?

With his vast corpus of work covering diverse philosophical topics, Max Scheler helps us locate the concepts of *active love* and *empathy* in the wide context of related philosophical issues. Scheler brings home the major *ontological significance* of active empathy and shows us its relation to love, hatred, and ressentiment. He, so to speak, gives us its "address" in Being, pointing out its location vis-à-vis the "ontological gulf," the "Individual Ineffable" and the "Absolute Other." Scheler's "ontological map" then helps us find the related concepts in Bakhtin's less obviously demarcated model of the world and to open the concept of *vzhivanie* to wider philosophical meanings. Scheler's expertise in philosophical psychology and his concept of ressentiment as a peculiar inversion of active love and empathy help us reveal the crucial link between the *psychological* and the *spiritual* levels of the hero's protest in Dostoevsky's *Notes from Underground*. Hence, in my Schelerian interpretation, the Underground Man's psychological and emotional inertia is an expression of his torturous spiritual search for the absent ideal. Unable to attain the value of absolute affirmation symbolized by "the true Crystal Palace" of faith and love, the Underground Man embraces absolute negation of the Underground (chapter 3).

Scheler's solid background in the phenomenology of religious experience facilitates our understanding of active love as a constant relation between the *human* and the *divine other*, an important but somewhat sketchily developed connection in Bakhtin's system. Finally, Scheler provides a truly *dynamic* model of interaction between self and other and between the self and the Absolute Other ("das ganz Andere"), where each party remains active. Against this well-balanced concept, a certain sluggishness of Bakhtin's early model of communication comes to the fore, as chapter 2 demonstrates. In my view, Scheler's existentialist vision of God's and Man's mutual becoming *in* and *through* each other has special relevance for Dostoevsky's world, which, as Romano Guardini notes, always emerges before our eyes in the very process of becoming, fluid and unfinished, as if still "lying in the hand of God with a sense of immediacy."[3]

Bakhtin's unique contribution to the concept of active empathy is his imaginative description of the peculiar mental acrobatics of "entering" and "exiting" another consciousness. His concept of *consummation*, in some ways similar to Scheler's "vocation of the Individual Ineffable," is original in its attention to the formal structure[4] inherent in love and empathy. With greater detail than Scheler, Bakhtin attempts to answer the question of exactly "*how*" one may gain an active understanding of another consciousness. Like Scheler, Bakhtin sees the model of active empathy in Christ's Incarnation, a creative "entry" into the world without losing his otherworldly divinity. But the paradoxical notion of Christian Incarnation is predicated on such precarious balance between the human and the divine points of view that Bakhtin proves incapable of sustaining this miraculous equilibrium within his own ideal concept of empathy.

I have argued that Bakhtin's live-*entering* becomes ultimately unnecessary in both his early and middle period ("Toward a Philosophy of the Act"/ "Author and Hero" and *Problems of Dostoevsky's Art* respectively). In the early works, the self's surplus of vision in relation to the consummated other is so enormous that the process of "entering" is simply superfluous, for no new information about the other could be gained from this empathetic endeavor. In the Dostoevsky study, dialogical contact is equally superfluous, since there it is the *other* who already possesses all the knowledge that could possibly be gained about the world. In an ironic twist, Bakhtin's imbalances echo similar "lapses" in empathy characteristic of Dostoevsky's heroes, as my analysis of Myshkin's spiritual challenges demonstrates (chapter 5). In this context, Scheler's balanced vision of the divine-to-human communication provides a fruitful model for revising Bakhtin's theory.

With his unique ability to dramatize complex philosophical positions, Dostoevsky provides invaluable case studies to illustrate and test the theories at hand. In Dostoevsky's world, the identification of Christ with the *redeeming other*, or the innermost other in me ("chelovek v cheloveke"), results in a special appreciation of *otherness* as an ontological category. For a Dostoevskian person the *other* is a source of grace and hope: in the words of Stepan Trofimovich from a preliminary version of *The Devils*: "I am worse than you, I have disgraced this earth, *but you are better than me, and I rejoice*" ("Notebooks for *The Devils*," *PSS*, 11:176). While many characters are painfully aware of the inevitable ontological distance between persons, the centrality of Christ as the ultimate *other* posits a hopeful model of partially bridging this natural existential divide. Because entering other souls is symbolically linked with the process of *imitatio Christi* in Dostoevsky's ethics, an ideal, agapeistic approach to another consciousness is never based on merely duplicating understanding. Rather, such an entry into another soul presupposes a creative, imaginative participation in another's emotional life that respects the unapproachable core of her personality, her unique "surplus of the self."

Understanding the underlying religious significance of *otherness* in Dostoevsky, which Scheler and early Bakhtin help illuminate, reveals religious meanings in the most secular contexts in Dostoevsky's works. My analyses of the Underground Man's ideologically based rejection of the other's help, and of Feodor Karamazov's paradoxical yearning for a better *other* ("*drugoi* chelovek"), provide examples of such important religious subtexts. But although the privileged ontological status of the other is recognized by saints and villains alike in Dostoevsky, very few are willing or able to accept and follow the ideal of Incarnation through faith and active love. Although not without challenges, an "entry" into another consciousness is an achievable accomplishment for Dostoevsky's heroes, but that of "exiting" and effectively consummating the attained knowledge presents a problem for most. Puzzled by "what to do" with their critical knowledge, the characters are unwilling or unable to make a transition from mere co-experiencing to an ethically and spiritually productive *act*. In this respect, Scheler's and Bakhtin's insights about the significance of this transition as the essence of *active* love and empathy are extremely useful in analyzing the empathetic efforts of Goryanchikov and Prince Myshkin (chapter 4). The characters' important, if short-lived, successes at practicing dialogical empathy are due to their direct and *active* approach to their interlocutors. At their empathetic best, Myshkin's and Goryanchikov's knowledge of the other's inner world is constantly mediated and enriched, but not eclipsed, by self-knowledge: a look outward is followed by a look inward.

Scheler's implicit observations about the dual effects of Incarnation resulting in both man's and God's *personal* becoming—a kind of mutual "consummation," are especially productive in demonstrating the twofold challenges of a Dostoevskian Christ in *The Idiot* (chapter 5). I conclude that in the final analysis Dostoevsky's "Prince-Christ," Myshkin, is unable to withstand the temptations of active love, losing the hopeful surplus of Christian agape either "from above" or "from below." Myshkin's empathetic endeavor ultimately ends in the frustration of dialogue: (a) another consciousness is objectified, becoming a function of Myshkin's or (b) Myshkin's own distinct point of view becomes lost, merging with the other's. These two dangers to *active* communication symbolically allude to the challenges of Christ, who manages to retain the advantages of both the divine and the human points of view. As a result, this insufficiently incarnated Dostoevskian hero proves tragically ineffective in propagating the Christian ideal and in ministering to his suffering others.

Fully actualized only by the Supreme Dialogist, who had "actively lived into" humanity without losing his divine surplus of vision, *creative empathy* acquires the status of a spiritual ideal in Dostoevsky's work. It becomes a desired goal, whose realization on earth is imminent for a believer and dubious for a skeptic. My readings of the characters' communicative efforts in Dostoevsky's world thus suggest an elaboration on Bakhtin's thesis in *Problems of Dostoevsky's Poetics*: Dostoevsky's heroes find themselves not only on the threshold of revelation and rebirth but also on the threshold of truly active, agapeistic dialogue.

In the 1920s, Scheler and Bakhtin felt compelled to defend empathy from Nietzsche's attacks by demonstrating that it is not a re-active phenomenon. After World War II ethically minded thinkers as different as Hannah Arendt and Varlam Shalamov have launched a renewed critique of empathy as a value, recognizing its failure to respond to unprecedented acts of genocide that became the hallmark of the twentieth century.[5] These critics condemn empathy as a spiritual tranquilizer, a passive, merely sentimental identification with suffering that somehow eliminates our responsibility to aid the sufferer. Perhaps the view of empathy espoused by Scheler and Bakhtin holds an important lesson for the world of modernity: if empathy is not simply a merging with the other but a responsible, deeply creative act, it cannot become an alibi for inaction. As if anticipating this wave of criticism, the thinkers discussed in this study demonstrate the active, non-duplicating nature of fellow-feeling, unrecognized by some to this day. Authentic empathy is not duplicative. It is not a morally validated acknowledgment of the status quo, but an arduous striving to effect positive change by making use of one's external "surplus" of knowledge, love, and hope.

Recent advances in social psychology and neuroscience also validate the general definitions of morally potent empathy presented here, revealing the precociousness of Scheler's and Bakhtin's major insights. The recently established connection between infant motor imitation and human empathetic reactions supports the existence of a deep psychological foundation for empathy prior to the development of complex thought and language,[6] a view also held by Scheler. The discovery of mirror-neurons,[7] which has demonstrated that patterns of neural activation in an individual lead to corresponding patterns of activation in the observer via manifested behavior or facial expressions, points to the fundamental significance of *embodiment* in the process of relating, a central thesis in both Scheler's and Bakhtin's theories. In the context of these neurological discoveries, an unequivocal distinction is now being made by psychologists and philosophers alike between empathy and emotional contagion, a seminal difference emphasized by Scheler nearly a century earlier. It is hypothesized that neuro-mirroring processes underlie the (largely unconscious) experiences of emotional contagion, while more complex, cognitive empathy, accessible to introspective awareness, often dubbed "mind reading," may be subserved by a different brain system and a different, less immediate, psycho-neurological mechanism that involves re-construction or mental "enactment" of another's emotional state.[8] While it is still unclear whether these two "routes to empathy" overlap with each other or whether sophisticated mirroring processes ultimately underpin the so-called re-constructive route as well,[9] there is a growing consensus among scholars that *morally relevant* empathy involves some amount of "mind reading" and demands clear differentiation between self and other, usually absent in emotional contagion.

As twenty-first-century science becomes increasingly more focused on what *follows* our empathetic entry into another's emotional world, in a move that echoes the key question of Bakhtin's early writings, namely, what must one *do* with the successfully gleaned knowledge of another's inner life?, the importance of the self-other distinction, tirelessly underscored by both Scheler and Bakhtin, comes to the fore as a major predictor of the empathizer's capacity for effective help in many psychological and neuroscientific studies. Self-other differentiation is essential for empathy because it allows for an optimal distance from the sufferer, where "we are neither fused nor detached" and can best aid him, most contemporary theoreticians agree.[10] Recent pioneering studies examining the excesses of empathy (Oakley et al., *Pathological Altruism* [2012]; see also Oakley, *Cold-Blooded Kindness* [2011])[11] highlight the long-overlooked dangers of over-identification, which entails the loss of this crucial distinction, against which Scheler had warned a century ago, to often disastrous effects. By focusing psychological attention on co-dependent victims of serial violence, compulsive animal hoarders, empathically over-aroused caretakers, so overcome by their patients' pain that they can no longer tend to them, and other cases of empathy-gone-mad, the authors of this provocative collection remind us that mere identification with others is not a good in itself. Rather, empathetic affect can wreak havoc on both the hyper-empathizer and the unfortunate objects of her unbridled empathy, if it is not restrained and guided by a coolly pragmatic regard for the parties' long-term well-being—or it can even be used maliciously as a kind of psychic "reconnaissance" to expertly inflict pain on an emotionally transparent and thus more vulnerable victim.

As Scheler, Bakhtin, and, perhaps most eloquently, Dostoevsky show us, it is love that can save empathy from lapsing into passive identification, by guiding it toward productive ethical action, just as love is itself nurtured and sustained by its continuous practical "actualization" through empathy. In this context, it is meaningful that the first fMRI (functional magnetic resonance imaging) studies of the neurobiology of romantic and maternal love have shown that love can keep one's potentially volatile empathetic instinct in check, guarding against empathetic over-arousal and helping us maintain a positive, actively compassionate attitude even in the face of highly distressing stimuli.[12] In other words, just as Scheler has predicted, love is precisely that invaluable spiritual "surplus" that can regulate empathy, making it not only bearable but helpful and morally efficacious. Newly available scientific methods of registering the neurobiological manifestations of love will no doubt give rise to more studies detailing the symbiotic relationship between love and empathy, an investigation that would likely be welcomed by Scheler, Bakhtin and Dostoevsky as a means of validating and enriching their own, differently gleaned "laboratory" data on the subject, although all three would note that the essence of loving empathy cannot be reduced to pure biology.

Thus, for all three forward-looking, surprisingly modern thinkers discussed in this book, active empathy is a cherished ideal deeply relevant to the ethical dilemmas of our at once emotionally overloaded and compassion-deficient age. It provides a specific, personal *form* in which love may realize itself in the challenging, often depersonalizing world of modernity. Unlike passive emotional identification, active understanding can never be complete or exhaustive. It does not aspire to eliminate the ontological distance between selves, but precisely therein lies its creative potential. In this sense, it is not a "given" (das *Gegebene* / *dannoe*) but a "posited" (das *Aufgegebene* / *zadannoe*)—an ever-urgent quest or a work in progress, rather than a fully achievable spiritual undertaking. For that reason, one is always faced with a daunting but deeply rewarding *task* in regard to one's suffering other—the task of active empathy.

Notes

INTRODUCTION

1. Compare, for example, Ken Hirschkop's largely justified concern with a kind of "pan-dialogism" that often emerges from modern interpretations of Bakhtin's middle period. Hirschkop is correct in pointing out the overextension of the term, noticeable already in the Dostoevsky book and even more pronounced in *Discourse in the Novel*, where dialogue is seen as "built into" language itself, while linguistic units become endowed with attributes of personhood (Ken Hirschkop, "Is Dialogism for Real?," in *The Contexts of Bakhtin: Philosophy, Authorship, Aesthetics*, ed. David Shepherd [Amsterdam: Harwood Academic Publishers, 2008], 185–86). Mikhail Gasparov, who remained famously antagonistic to Bakhtin's analytical method throughout his life, voices the somewhat differently motivated skepticism, shared by many Russian philologists raised in the tradition of Formalist criticism, when he berates "the post-Bakhtinian meditations about the dialogism of everything in the world" (Nataliia Avtonomova, *Otkrytaia struktura: Iakobson—Bakhtin—Lotman—Gasparov* [Moscow: ROSSPEN, 2009], 137; see also M. L. Gasparov, "Istoriia literatury kak tvorchestvo i issledovanie: Sluchai Bakhtina," in *Russkaia literatura XX–XXI vekov: Problemy teorii i metodologii izucheniia. Materialy mezhdunarodnoi nauchnoi konferentsii 10–11 noiabria 2004 goda* [Moscow: 2004], 8–10). A more detailed discussion of the problems inherent in the Dostoevsky study, as they relate to Bakhtin's early concept of consummation, is contained in chapter 2.

2. G. S. Batishchev, "Dialogizm ili polifonizm? (Antitetika v ideinom nasledii M. M. Bakhtina)," in *M.M. Bakhtin kak filosof*, ed. L. A. Gogotishvili and P. S. Gurevich (Moscow: Nauka, 1992), 123, 139.

3. Ruth Coates, *Christianity in Bakhtin: God and the Exiled Author* (Cambridge: Cambridge University Press, 1998), 92; see also Coates, "The First and the Second Adam in Bakhtin's Early Thought," in *Bakhtin and Religion: A Feeling for Faith*, ed. M. Felch and Paul Contino (Evanston, Ill.: Northwestern University Press, 2001), 75.

4. See, for example, Robert Louis Jackson, *Dialogues with Dostoevsky: The*

Overwhelming Questions (Stanford, Calif.: Stanford University Press, 1993); Michael André Bernstein, "The Poetics of Ressentiment," in *Rethinking Bakhtin: Extensions and Challenges*, ed. Gary Morson and Caryl Emerson (Evanston, Ill.: Northwestern University Press), 197–224; Caryl Emerson, *The First Hundred Years of Mikhail Bakhtin* (Princeton, N.J.: Princeton University Press, 1997); Rachel Pollard, *Dialogue and Desire. Mikhail Bakhtin and the Linguistic Turn in Psychotherapy* (London, Eng.: Karnac Books, 2008), 75–76; Avtonomova, *Otkrytaia struktura*, 118.

5. Nina Perlina, "Mikhail Bakhtin and Martin Buber: Problems of Dialogic Imagination," *Studies in 20th Century Literature* 9, no. 1 (1984): 23–25; see also Gary Saul Morson and Caryl Emerson, *Mikhail Bakhtin: Creation of a Prosaics* (Stanford, Calif.: Stanford University Press, 1990), 220. On the "left" side of the ideologically divided Bakhtinian scholarship, we should note Anthony Wall's criticism of Morson and Emerson's interpretation of Bakhtin's middle period for incorrectly portraying Bakhtin as "a philosopher of the ideal speech situation" (Wall, "Chatter, Babble, and Dialogue," in *The Contexts of Bakhtin: Philosophy, Authorship, Aesthetics*, ed. David Shepherd [Amsterdam: Harwood Academic Publishers, 1998], 205). Although this criticism of Morson and Emerson's lucid interpretation is, in my view, unjustified, Wall is correct in demonstrating how little attention Bakhtin himself gives to the notion of ideal, spiritually productive dialogue during his middle period. Caryl Emerson acknowledges Bakhtin's reluctance to address the depictions of the ideal in Dostoevsky: "Bakhtin is not especially good at accounting for epiphanies, spiritualized wholes or Great Time in the novelistic masterpieces," Emerson remarks (*The First Hundred Years of Mikhail Bakhtin*, 42).

6. See, for example, Mikhail Bakhtin, *Sobranie sochinenii v semi tomakh*, ed. S. G. Bocharov et al., 7 vols. (Moscow: Russkie Slovari, 1996–), 6:33, 34, 36; Bakhtin, *Problems of Dostoevsky's Poetics* (hereafter, *PDP*), ed. and trans. Caryl Emerson, intro. Wayne C. Booth (Minneapolis: University of Minnesota Press, 1984), 26, 28.

7. Bakhtin, *Sobranie sochinenii*, 6:33, my translation; *PDP*, 26.

8. Natalia Reed, "The Philosophical Roots of Polyphony: A Dostoevskian Reading," in *Critical Essays on Mikhail Bakhtin*, ed. Caryl Emerson (New York: G.K. Hall, 1999), 138–39.

9. This objection to what is seen as a significant lacuna in *PDP* is also widespread among Bakhtin's critics. Expanding Robert Louis Jackson's argument (*Dialogues with Dostoevsky*), Rachel Pollard suggests that "Bakhtin ignores the prevalence of suicides, murders and cruelty in Dostoevsky's fiction, as if the deeds of his characters had no significance" (*Dialogue and Desire*, 73). Similar objections are also raised by Bernstein ("The Poetics of Ressentiment"), Emerson (*The First Hundred Years of Mikhail Bakhtin*), and Reed ("The Philosophical Roots of Polyphony").

10. *Vzhivanie* is defined as a "new concept" of Bakhtin's early period and insightfully, if briefly, described in relation to his later theories in Gary Saul Morson's and Caryl Emerson's *Mikhail Bakhtin: Creation of a Prosaics* (53–54, 66). Craig Brandist, who also discusses the notion of interpersonal co-experiencing in "Author and Hero in Aesthetic Activity," sees it as a theme of peripheral significance in *The Bakhtin Circle: Philosophy, Culture and Politics* (London: Pluto, 2002). While T. Shchittsova indirectly deals with the problems of communication in early Bakhtin in her *Sobytie v filosofii Bakhtina* (Minsk: I.P. Logvinov, 2002), she concentrates on another key concept, that of "event," whose centrality in Bakhtin's philosophy becomes the book's thesis. In this context, Bakhtin's various concepts of communication are classified as subspecies of the *event*, for example, as "a dialogical event." In a similar fashion, in A. Kalygin's study of Bakhtin's early aesthetic theories, the "[moment] of *vzhivanie*" or the "near-coalescence between the author and hero," examined by Bakhtin in "Author and Hero" is discussed only in its function in a work of art and not in its extraliterary interpersonal dimension (Kalygin, *Rannii Bakhtin: Estetika kak preodolenie etiki. Ego-personalism, liricheskii geroi i edinstvo esteticheskikh teorii* [Moscow: RGO, 2007], 25, see also 26–31). It is not singled out as a separate concept and is seen only as one of the means of authorial objectification in respect to the lyrical hero. As such, it is part of what Kalygin calls Bakhtin's theory of "historical ego-personalism," a phenomenology of the author's consciousness in the process of complete, aesthetically motivated identification with that of the hero (67, 120).

11. Both works were first published after Bakhtin's death, and the exact time of their composition is unknown. According to the editors of Bakhtin's collected works, "Author and Hero" was most likely written between 1923 and 1924 and "Toward a Philosophy of the Act" between 1918 and 1922 (*Sobranie sochinenii*, 1:496–99, 352, 414–17). However, some have argued convincingly for a later composition date of "Author and Hero," placing it between 1924 and 1927, a view I also endorse (see Brian Poole, "From Phenomenology to Dialogue: Max Scheler's Phenomenological Tradition and Mikhail Bakhtin's Development from 'Toward a Philosophy of the Act' to his Study of Dostoevsky," in *Bakhtin and Cultural Theory*, ed. Ken Hirschkop and David Shepherd, 2nd ed. [Manchester, Eng.: Manchester University Press, 2001], 109–35). For the Russian text, see *Sobranie sochinenii*, vol. 1. The English translations are published in the following editions: Mikhail Bakhtin, *Art and Answerability: Early Philosophical Essays by M.M. Bakhtin*, ed. Michael Holquist and Vadim Liapunov, trans. and notes Vadim Liapunov (Austin, Texas: University of Texas Press, 1990), 4–256; and Bakhtin, *Toward a Philosophy of the Act*, trans. and notes Vadim Liapunov, ed. Vadim Liapunov and Michael Holquist (Austin: University of Texas Press, 1993).

12. The theories in question, generally known as theories of "projection empathy," share a common understanding of the phenomenon as a case of emotional identification, a passive merging with the other's inner world. For example,

according to Theodor Lipps, a major proponent of this approach, the act of empathizing consists in the reproduction of the other's feeling, or rather in the evocation of a similar feeling within the empathizer's emotional realm, followed by a mental projection of this artificially manufactured feeling into the other's psyche (see, for example, Lipps, *Die ethischen Grundfragen: zehn Vorträge* [Hamburg: Voss, 1899]; *Ästhetik: Psychologie des Schönen und der Kunst*, 2 vols. [Hamburg: Voss, 1903–6]; and Gustav Störring, *Psychologie des menschlichen Gefühlslebens* [Bonn: Friedrich Cohen, 1916]). Bakhtin's and Scheler's relationship with the theories of passive or projective empathy is addressed in chapter 1.

13. Natalia Bonetskaia, "Primechaniia k 'Avtoru i Geroiu': Prodolzhenie (k izdaniiu 'Estetika Slovesnogo Tvorchestva')," in A. P. Valitskaia et al., *Bakhtinologiia: Issledovaniia, perevody, publikatsii* (St. Petersburg: Aleteia, 1995), 85–86, 243.

14. O. B. Breikin, "Filosofia postupka M. Bakhtina i problema absoluta," in *Bakhtinologiia: Issledovaniia, perevody, publikatsii*, ed. Valitskaia et al., 217.

15. Giovanni Palmieri, "'The Author' according to Bakhtin . . . and Bakhtin the Author," in *The Contexts of Bakhtin: Philosophy, Authorship, Aesthetics*, ed. David Shepherd (Amsterdam: Harwood Academic Publishers, 1998), 52–53.

16. Michael André Bernstein, *Bitter Carnival: Ressentiment and the Abject Hero* (Princeton, N.J.: Princeton University Press, 1992).

17. Hilary B. P. Bagshaw, *Religion in the Thought of Mikhail Bakhtin: Reason and Faith* (Surrey, Eng.: Ashgate, 2013), esp. 18–42.

18. Ibid., 132.

19. Other scholars who share my non-sectarian definition of Bakhtin's "sense of faith" are Gary Saul Morson and Caryl Emerson, Ruth Coates, and George Pattison, to name just a few (see, for example, Morson and Emerson, *Mikhail Bakhtin: Creation of a Prosaics*; Emerson, "Russian Orthodoxy and the Early Bakhtin," *Religion and Literature* 22, no. 2–3 [1990]: 109–30; Coates, *Christianity in Bakhtin*; and Pattison, "Freedom's Dangerous Dialogue: Reading Dostoevsky and Kierkegaard Together," in *Dostoevsky and the Christian Tradition*, ed. George Pattison and Diane Oenning Thompson [Cambridge: Cambridge University Press, 2001], 237–56). Supporting this view are such facts as Bakhtin's lifelong admiration for the Protestant Kierkegaard and the Catholic Scheler, the two thinkers whose philosophy is thoroughly permeated by theological motifs—and for the broadly erudite Vladimir Soloviev, whose mission was to philosophically renew Russian Orthodoxy, opening it up to other Christian traditions and making it relevant to the problems of modernity (see, for example, Bakhtin, *Besedy s V.D. Duvakinym*, ed. S. G. Bocharov et al. [Moscow: Soglasie, 2002], 42–43). For Bakhtin's use of Soloviev see, for example, Caryl Emerson, "Soloviev, the Late Tolstoy and the Early Bakhtin on the Problem of Shame and Love," *Slavic Review* 50 (1991): 663–71. For a discussion of Bakhtin's indebtedness to Kierkegaard, see Alexander Haardt, "Ethische und ästhetische Persön-

lichkeit: Zum Verhältnis des Ethischen und Ästhetischen bei Sören Kierkegaard und Michail Bachtin," *Studies in East European Thought* 61 (2009): 165–79; and T. Shchyttsova, "Die Idee der 'antwortenden Subjektivität' im Werk von Søren Kierkegaard und Michail Bachtin," in *Diskurse der Personalität*, ed. A. Haardt and N. Plotnikov (Paderborn: Fink, 2008), 241–50. In his pre-dialogical works, Bakhtin tellingly references Saint Francis of Assisi, Dante, and Giotto, rather than any Orthodox figures, as he discusses the essence of a Christian worldview (see, for example, Bakhtin, *Art and Answerability*, 57, 243–44).

20. Brandist, *The Bakhtin Circle*, 39.

21. Ibid., 50, 95.

22. Vladimir Nikiforov, "First Philosophy as Philosophy of Individual *Postupok*," *Symposion* 4–6 (1999–2001): 61–105.

23. Brian Poole, "From Phenomenology to Dialogue," esp. 128 and 118.

24. Max Scheler, *Gesammelte Werke*, ed. Maria Scheler and Manfred Frings, 15 vols. (Bern: Francke Verlag, 1954–97), 3:73.

CHAPTER ONE

1. A version of this chapter was published as "Bakhtin and Scheler: Toward a Theory of Active Understanding" in *Slavonic and East European Review* 86, no. 1 (2008): 58–89.

2. Hereafter "Author and Hero in Aesthetic Activity" will be cited in the text as "AH," with page numbers referring to Bakhtin, *Art and Answerability* (1990). *Toward a Philosophy of the Act* is abbreviated as *TPA* and also cited in the text, with page numbers referring to *Toward a Philosophy of the Act* (1993).

3. It has been established that Bakhtin was acquainted with several of Scheler's major works. In his article "From Phenomenology to Dialogue: Max Scheler's Phenomenological Tradition and Mikhail Bakhtin's Development from 'Toward a Philosophy of the Act' to his Study of Dostoevsky," Brian Poole explores the most explicit correspondences between Bakhtin's work and Scheler's study of sympathy in its 1926 edition (*Wesen und Formen der Sympathie*), citing archival materials to document Bakhtin's familiarity with his source. Bakhtin's acquaintance with *The Nature of Sympathy* and *Formalism in Ethics and Non-Formal Ethics of Values* is also acknowledged in *Problems of Dostoevsky's Art* (1929), where Scheler is named as "the most noteworthy contributor to the critique of monologism as a specific Kantian form of idealism" (Bakhtin, *Sobranie sochinenii*, 2:60–61). Bakhtin's alleged knowledge of *On the Eternal in Man* is documented in the interrogation records of his arrest in 1928 (see I. A. Savkin, "Delo o Voskresenii," in *M.M. Bakhtin i filosofskaia kul'tura XX veka: Problemy Bakhtinologii*, vol. 2, ed. K. G. Isupov et al. [St Petersburg: Obrazovanie, 1991], 111). Among them is a description of Bakhtin's two lectures on Scheler delivered at the meetings of the religious society "Resurrection" and containing a

rather idiosyncratic account of Scheler's religious thought, distantly corresponding to "Repentance and Rebirth" ("Reue und Wiedergeburt"), a section of *On the Eternal in Man* (see Scheler, *GW*, 5:27–59; for a discussion of Scheler's idiosyncratic account of this work, see Bagshaw, *Religion in the Thought of Mikhail Bakhtin*, 35–41). It is also significant that Bakhtin's close friend and a member of his philosophical circle, Matvei Kagan, studied phenomenology with Scheler's follower and interpreter, Nikolai Hartmann, who further developed Scheler's ethics of interpersonal relationships in *Grundzüge einer Metaphysik der Erkenntnis* (1921) and *Ethik* (1926), the works with which Bakhtin was probably familiar (see B. Poole, "From Phenomenology to Dialogue," 123). Besides the archival evidence of the availability of *The Nature of Sympathy* in the original, we know that numerous reviews of Scheler's works were available to Bakhtin in Russian, as Vladimir Nikiforov demonstrates ("First Philosophy as Philosophy of Individual *Postupok*," 66). For a discussion of Scheler's influence on Bakhtin, see also the commentary to *Toward a Philosophy of the Act* and "Author and Hero" in Bakhtin's *Collected Works* (*Sobranie sochinenii*, 1:351–492, 492–706) and the excerpts from *Sympathy* recorded by Bakhtin's wife, published in the same edition (*Sobranie sochinenii*, 2:657–93).

4. See also Friedrich Nietzsche, *Nietzsche Werke: Kritische Gesamtaufgabe*, 9 vols., ed. G. Colli and M. Montinari (Berlin: W. de Gruyter, 1967–2005), 6.3:171. Hereafter references to Scheler's works will be provided in the text. Unless otherwise indicated, the references are to the collected edition, *Gesammelte Werke* (*GW*) (1954–97) and are accompanied by the volume and page numbers. Translation is my own, unless otherwise indicated. Before the reference to the volume and page in *GW*, I have also provided the titles of individual works by Scheler (books or articles)—in English, where a well-known translation exists (for example: *On the Eternal in Man*, *GW*, 5:23), or in the original German, for untranslated or lesser known works (e.g. "Manuskripte zur Lehre vom Grunde aller Dinge," *GW*, 11:209).

5. Bakhtin's indebtedness to Scheler in reiterating this particular point of Scheler's phenomenological theory is documented in Bakhtin's notebook containing a synopsis of *The Nature of Sympathy*, made by his wife, as Brian Poole demonstrates ("From Phenomenology to Dialogue," 116).

6. See Theodor Lipps, *Die ethischen Grundfragen: Zehn Vorträge* and *Ästhetik: Psychologie des Schönen und der Kunst*; see also Störring, *Psychologie des menschlichen Gefühlslebens,* and Benno Erdmann, *Grundzüge der Reproduktionspsychologie* (Berlin: W. de Gruyter, 1920). For a more charitable, recent interpretation of Lipps and related theories exploring the uses of reproductive empathy, see Gregory Currie, "Empathy for Objects," in *Empathy: Philosophical and Psychological Perspectives*, ed. Amy Coplan and Peter Goldie (Oxford: Oxford University Press, 2011), 82–95.

7. One of the sources of this enduring connection between life and art in

Bakhtin's thought can be found in the writings of Vladimir Soloviev. In "The General Meaning of Art," Soloviev states that, in order to become fully realized, "goodness and truth must become a *creative* power in man," aesthetically transforming and reshaping reality (*Sobranie sochinenii Vladimira Sergeevicha Solov'eva*, 9 vols. [St. Petersburg: Obshchestvennaia Pol'za, 1901–7], 6:73). For Soloviev, a human being may participate in the life of the divine both by being creative in his relationships with others and through properly aesthetic activities (poetry, music, painting). For example, in his interpretation of Fet's poem "You no longer suffer" ("Ty otstradala, ia eshche stradaiu"), Soloviev makes a persuasive case for the active interpenetration of life and art: Fet's artistic activity imparts new life to his deceased beloved, Soloviev claims, aesthetically realizing the poet's creative, and, indeed, life-giving love for her. Thus aesthetic creativity becomes a major force in both life and art (Soloviev, "On Lyric Poetry," *Sobranie sochinenii Vladimira Sergeevicha Solov'eva*, 6:229–33).

8. Although not specifically addressed in Bakhtin's early works, Tolstoy's concept of "infectious art" formulated in his 1897–98 article "What Is Art?" should also be included in the theoretical context of Bakhtin's writings on aesthetic empathy. Tolstoy's definition of art as "a human activity in which one human being deliberately, with the help of certain signs, transmits to others the feelings he has experienced, while other people are infected by these feelings and experience them" places the same emphasis on the role of contagion in the aesthetic process as do the Western theories of passive empathy (Lev Tolstoy, *Sobranie sochinenii v dvadtsati dvukh tomakh*, ed. M. B. Khrapchenko, 22 vols. [Moscow: Khudozhestvennaia literatura, 1982], 15:80). Tolstoy also depicts aesthetic activity as the product of one solitary consciousness, that of the artist or empathizer, taking for granted the artist's precise expression of his (human) object and describing the merging between the artist and his audience as complete—a rather simplified portrayal of the artistic process from Bakhtin's point of view.

9. If Bakhtin is concerned with preserving the uniqueness of both the *creative act* and all of its participants, Scheler accuses an entire philosophical tradition of failing to acknowledge the individual character of either the *love act* itself or of its performers. He sees the so-called reproductive theories as part of a larger, erring philosophical trend that grossly misinterprets the meaning of empathy and love. According to Scheler, sovereignty and primacy characterize *love* both as the highest spiritual act and the highest expression of spiritual content, the *loving person, homo amans*. Thus the *naturalistic theories* of love and empathy, which include the phylogenetic and the ontogenic varieties, with Feuerbach and Freud as their respective representatives, err because they derive love, in Scheler's view, the original spiritual act, from natural factors (see *Sympathy*, *GW*, 7:175). On the other hand, the proponents of *metaphysical theories* tend to treat the loving self, "the concrete spiritual act-center," as merely a function of all-spirit (be it the transcendental absolute consciousness [Husserl] or the

absolute unconscious spirit [E. von Hartmann]), or derive man's love entirely from God's love of Himself, denying it any independent metaphysical meaning (Hegel, von Hartmann, Spinoza). Schopenhauer, who is also classified as a metaphysical theorist, is first credited by Scheler with recognizing that one participates in another's suffering immediately and not by means of "transfers" of emotional experiences, and is then criticized for assigning positive value not to compassion, as ethically valid, active co-suffering, but to suffering itself as a means of redemption (Scheler, *Sympathy*, *GW*, 7:62). The proponents of what Scheler terms "monistic metaphysics," which include theorists ranging from Schelling, Hegel, and Wundt to Bergson and Volkelt, can be congratulated for endowing love and empathy with metaphysical significance as original phenomena but fail to recognize the lover and the beloved as sovereign spiritual entities, Scheler argues (*Sympathy*, *GW*, 7:66–67). In *Toward a Philosophy of the Act* and "Author and Hero in Aesthetic Activity," Bakhtin reacts to many of the same texts that had evoked Scheler's passionate criticism (see, for example, "Author and Hero," 62–67). Both thinkers are responding to the works of Theodor Lipps, Henri Bergson, Johannes Volkelt, Eduard von Hartmann, and Wilhelm Wundt, to name a few shared sources (see Volkelt, *Das aesthetische Bewußtsein*; Bergson, *L'Evolution Créatrice*; *Essai sur les données immédiates de la conscience* and *Matiere et Memoire*; E. von Hartmann, *Philosophie des Schönen*).

10. Hermann Cohen's concept of aesthetic love and love-like sympathy is another source here, as Bakhtin himself notes parenthetically ("AH," 81, 82). See Cohen's *Ästhetik des reinen Gefühls* (1912). For a detailed discussion of the relationship between Bakhtin's early aesthetic theories and Cohen's *Ästhetik des reinen Gefühls* as well as his earlier work, *Ethik des reinen Willens* (1904), see Liisa Steinby, "Hermann Cohen and Bakhtin's Early Aesthetics," *Studies in East European Thought* 63 (2011): 227–49. Although Cohen is undoubtedly one of Bakhtin's sources here, the two philosophers' concepts of love do not coincide, Steinby cautions (241). "The consummation of a person in aesthetic creation . . . means for Bakhtin the generation of the aesthetic shape of a person *in his* individuality, rather than, as in Cohen, elevating him into the unity of soul and body of the human being *despite* his individuality," Steinby explains (241, italics in text).

11. Such contents are described by Scheler as the specific "whatness" of conscious existence: "what" one thinks, wills, or feels within the given "here and now" (*Sympathy*, *GW*, 7:45).

12. This translation of the Schelerian term ("intentionale Daseinsdistanz") belongs to Manfred Frings (see his *The Mind of Max Scheler* [Milwaukee: Marquette University Press, 1997]).

13. Karl Barth expresses a similar point of view in *Evangelical Theology*, stressing the ultimate sovereignty of the believer and his deity even in the course of the most intimate contact: "Christian faith occurs in the *encounter* of the be-

liever with him in whom he believes. It consists in communion, not in identification with him," Barth explains (*Evangelical Theology: An Introduction*, trans. Grover Foley [New York: Holt, Rinehart and Winston, 1963], 99).

14. Scheler describes God as an "infinite loving Person," or a "Person of all Persons," who is absolutely free and perfect (see, for instance, "Absolutsphäre und Realsetzung der Gottesidee," *GW*, 10:187 and *Sympathy*, *GW*, 7:86).

15. B. Poole, "From Phenomenology to Dialogue," 118.

16. Ibid., 117.

17. In my opinion, this "chronological" representation of active co-experiencing should be understood as a formal device, a means of clarifying Scheler's complex argument by providing a palatable exposition of his fundamental concepts rather than an attempt at creating a diachronic "documentary" of emotional processes. As we shall see later, just as the individual "steps" in the event of active empathizing ("live-entering") in Bakhtin's system should not be seen as diachronic stages of the process, the components of active understanding in Scheler's theory should not be interpreted as separate, chronologically ordered stages of love.

18. This notion of loving empathy as the discoverer of the other's ontic existence is consonant with Kierkegaard's depiction of Christian love. According to Kierkegaard, only love that acknowledges the other's undeniable, concrete reality as my neighbor makes me truly conscious of his presence in being: "it is only this kind of love [Christian love understood as duty] that finds out that the neighbor exists [*er til*] and—it is one and the same—that everyone is that," Kierkegaard writes in one of his journals (*Works of Love*, ed. and trans. Howard V. Hong and Edna H. Hong [Princeton, N.J.: Princeton University Press, 1995], 430).

19. According to Scheler's rather detailed classification of sympathetic feelings, which divides sympathy into four major categories: joint feeling ("das unmittelbare Mitfühlen"), fellow feeling ("Mitgefühl"), emotive contagion ("Gefühlsansteckung"), and emotive identification ("die echte Einsfühlung"), only the two highest modes of sympathy, joint feeling and fellow feeling, are associated with granting the object of sympathy equal reality status (*Sympathy*, *GW*, 7:23–32, 70–71). In most cases, when speaking of empathy steeped in love, Scheler has in mind fellow-feeling (*Mitgefühl*), arguably the highest and most ethically productive form of sympathetic understanding in his system. This reference system also obtains for our discussion.

20. Continuing his polemics with contemporary projection theories, Scheler joins Edith Stein's critique of Theodor Lipps's concept of aesthetic empathy. According to Scheler, Lipps is wrong to interpret aesthetic empathy as emotional identification (*Einsfühlung*) between the artist and his audience, for example, ascribing our aesthetic enjoyment of an acrobatic performance to a psychic merging with the acrobat. Turning for support to Stein's *On the Problem of Empathy*, Scheler quotes her more appropriate assessment of the phenomenon: "We

are not one with the acrobat; we are by his side," Stein explains (*The Collected Works of Edith Stein, Sister Teresa Benedicta of the Cross, Discalced Carmelite*, trans. Waltraut Stein, vol. 3 [Washington D.C.: ICS Publications, 1989], 16, translation emended, quoted by Scheler in *GW*, 7:29).

21. A similar multi-stage program, already implicitly contained in Scheler's study, is proposed by Scheler's follower and interpreter, Nicolai Hartmann, who names "Einfühlung" (co-experiencing with another person, literally: "feeling into" another self) and "Rückeinfühlung" (return into the self) as the two principal components of sympathetic understanding (N. Hartmann, *Ethik* [Berlin: W. de Gruyter, 1926], 70; see B. Poole, "From Phenomenology to Dialogue," 123).

22. Peter Heath's translation is used to render this passage (Scheler, *The Nature of Sympathy*, trans. Peter Heath, intro. W. Stark [New Haven, Conn.: Yale University Press, 1954], 153–54). The corresponding passage in Scheler's original is in *GW*, 7:156.

23. In his 1998 article "'The Author according to Bakhtin' . . . and Bakhtin the Author," Giovanni Palmieri briefly notes that in both "Author and Hero" and in Scheler's work love is presented as a revealer of value, without elaborating on this important insight (52–53).

24. This act of bestowing form on the valued subject constitutes the moment of properly aesthetic activity for Bakhtin, who, as Craig Brandist rightly points out, adds to Scheler's concept of sympathy by discovering the aesthetic component of personal interaction. According to Brandist, Bakhtin depicts aesthetic seeing (*videnie*) as something akin to the Husserlian intuition of essences but, under the influence of Scheler, applies this intuition to values (*The Bakhtin Circle*, 31). This observation illuminates the inextricable connection between the ethical and the aesthetic in Bakhtin, for the revelation of value, which lies at the core of *ethical* action in Scheler, becomes a decisively *aesthetic* event in Bakhtin's architectonic.

25. Natalia Bonetskaia points out that in his depiction of value-creation in the process of *vzhivanie*, Bakhtin may have been influenced by yet another source available to him at the time of creating "Author and Hero," namely, the work of Heinrich Rickert. Rickert's concept of "Voll-endung" (compare Bakhtin's *zavershenie* / *svershenie*—consummation) denotes the activity of the subject who actualizes a value (Bonetskaia, "Primechaniia k fragmentu 'Avtora i geroia,'" 250). Translations of Rickert's works appeard in *Logos*, a philosophical publication in Moscow, in 1912–14 ("Primechaniia k fragmentu 'Avtora i geroia,'" 250).

26. It is important to understand that in Scheler individuals are as unique and different in value as they are in their spiritual makeup (they are "soseinsverschieden"), but they are all equal in value "qua person," as equally loved children of God.

27. In *Christianity in Bakhtin*, Ruth Coates rightly observes that "for Bakhtin, self-rejection is a phenomenological fact of one's self-experience" (44).

28. Here we find Bakhtin in implicit polemics with Nietzsche, whose views on value apprehension have influenced Scheler. In *Toward a Genealogy of Morals* and *Beyond Good and Evil*, Nietzsche defines the difference between master and slave morality in terms of value attribution: while the masters actively ascribe value to themselves, a slavish personality receives value from others, submitting to their judgment "quite apart from any consideration of its utility and also apart from truth and falsehood" (*The Complete Works of Friedrich Nietzsche*, ed. Oscar Levy, trans. Horace B. Samuel, 18 vols. [Edinburgh: T. N. Foulis, 1909–13], 12:233). Ultimately, this assessment leads Nietzsche to conclude that Christian empathy, as essentially a product of ressentiment and slave morality, is a fundamentally passive, reactive emotion. Without launching an ethical critique of Nietzsche's system, Bakhtin could reject such a binary opposition on purely phenomenological grounds, for, according to Bakhtin, a self-assigned value is a phenomenological impossibility.

29. For a very insightful recent discussion of self-value and self-love in Scheler, see Wei Zhang, "Person und Selbstgefühl im phänomenologischen Personalismus Max Schelers," *Studia Phaenomenologica* 11 (2011): 265–84.

30. Kierkegaard, *Works of Love*, 429; see also 18, 22–23.

31. Ibid., 100.

32. In *Christianity in Bakhtin: God and the Exiled Author* Ruth Coates devotes a number of passages to the "Incarnation motif" in Bakhtin's oeuvre, using separate biblical images to reconstruct what she sees as a profoundly religious, largely consistent philosophical worldview (21, 33–34, 49–50). Gary Saul Morson and Caryl Emerson also acknowledge the significance of this central biblical event for Bakhtin's thought by stating that "Bakhtin's theology, to the extent he had one, is . . . [that] of incarnation" (*Mikhail Bakhtin: Creation of a Prosaics*, 61).

33. In his later years, Bakhtin reportedly stated that the kingdom of God is *between* persons, "between us, between me and you, between me and God, between me and nature" (see V. V. Kozhinov, "Kak pishut trudy, ili proiskhozhdenie nosozdannogo avantiurnogo romana," *Dialog, Karnaval, Khronotop* no. 1 [1992]: 114–15).

34. As Xiaofeng Liu rightly observes, there is a strong connection between Scheler's entire metaphysics and the Christian teachings on incarnation (Liu, *Personwerdung: Eine theologische Untersuchung zu Max Schelers Phänomenologie der "Person-Gefühle" mit besonderer Berücksichtigung seiner Kritik der Moderne* [Bern: Peter Lang, 1996], 89).

35. Heinz Leonardy, *Liebe und Person: Max Schelers Versuch eines "phänomenologischen" Personalismus* (The Hague: Martinus Nijhoff, 1976), 194–95, my translation.

36. Despite his emphasis on the active relationship between the spiritual and the vital forces, Scheler has been criticized for not creating an effective

model of their fruitful interaction. In his 2001 article, "First Philosophy as Philosophy of Individual 'Postupok,'" Vladimir Nikiforov, who conducts an intriguing analysis of Bakhtin's early work in the context of contemporary German philosophy, claims, together with D. Frisby, that Scheler's philosophy fails to provide adequate mediation between spirit and life (David Frisby, *The Alienated Mind: The Sociology of Knowledge in Germany, 1918–1933*, 2nd ed. [New York: Routledge, 1992], 33, quoted in Nikiforov, "First Philosophy," 68). According to Nikiforov, Bakhtin must have sensed this particular impotence not only in the works of Scheler and related moral philosophies employing what is seen as an elitist, hierarchical concept of an individual, but also in the lamentable failure of the Russian intelligentsia to "bring to life" the high-minded, idealistic concept of a *person* in the crisis-ridden, militantly anti-personal post-revolutionary Russia. Bakhtin thus rejected the Schelerian "person" as the basis for his philosophy in favor of "the act" (*postupok*) as a non-hierarchical, ultimately real concept, Nikiforov claims ("First Philosophy," 65–69). While it is not the goal of this study to assess Scheler's success at "vitalizing" his concept of a spiritual being or to examine the role of "postupok" in Bakhtin's philosophy, it needs to be said that the extreme importance of "the act" for the concept of the person in Scheler's phenomenology (defined as an "act-substance" and the living unity of acts) points to Scheler's continued influence on Bakhtin and not to a fundamental rejection of the Schelerian model. Although Nikiforov is right in classifying the Bakhtinian "postupok" as more closely related to Scheler's "Handeln" (practical, externalized action) than to the "Akt" (an inner process, liberated from time and space), many of the attributes ascribed to "postupok," as a concrete, dynamic, yet structurally unified fragment of life and not a lifeless *product* of human activity, can also be found in the Schelerian "Akt." Consider, for example, the act's unique nature, its inextricable connection with the act-subject and, regardless of the employed terminology, its profoundly personal nature in both philosophical systems.

37. Here Scheler seems to present the opposition between agape and eros mainly as that between the spiritual and the vital. In contrast to the more contemplative agape, the dynamic, sensual eros, strongly connected with primal drives, is capable of energizing agape, as it were, setting it in motion, while agape, in its turn, "spiritualizes" eros. This implied relationship between the two interpenetrating emotional currents already anticipates Scheler's later belief that purely spiritual love is essentially powerless, needing a vital impulse to become truly active. However, in his earlier writings, Scheler clearly privileges agape, describing the opposition between the two loves in somewhat different terms: while eros is depicted as acquisitive love for the sake of gaining the superior virtues of the beloved, agape is defined as a gesture of absolute affirmation, utterly independent of the beloved's values yet capable of revealing and enriching these

values (*Ressentiment*, *GW*, 3:70–95). For an excellent general philosophical definition of the concept of agape and a discussion of its effective guidance of compassion, see Steven Tudor, *Compassion and Remorse: Acknowledging the Suffering Other* (Leuven: Peeters, 2001), 109–18.

38. Note Bakhtin's reference to Saint Francis's "brotherly" relationship with the entire nature and his loving acceptance of the body as an example of celebrating that which is "the other for God," as it were, a new means of practicing incarnation. Together with Dante and Giotto, Saint Francis is named as a representative of what Bakhtin sees as the "second trend" in the evolution of Christianity, the properly Christian (i.e., post-incarnation) worldview, that, in contrast to the earlier Neoplatonic tendencies, partially absorbed by Christianity, affirmed the equal importance of one's relationship to oneself and one's relationship to the other ("AH," 57, 243–44).

39. In his 1995 article "Filosofiia postupka M. Bakhtina i problema absoluta" (in Valitskaia et al., *Bakhtinologiia: Issledovaniia, perevody, publikatsii*, 217–24), O. Breikin observes that both Bakhtin and Scheler draw a dividing line between the sphere of abstract values and the sphere of actuality; he points to Bakhtin's placement of the ultimate moral authority in the subject of a responsible act rather than in any historical system of moral values as a debt to Scheler's personalism (217).

40. As Rodolphe Gasché explains, "in Scheler, this 'good-in-itself' is a 'good-in-itself-for me' in the sense that there is an experienced reference to me . . . which is contained (descriptively put) in the special non-formal content of this good-in-itself, something that comes from this content . . . and points to 'me,' something that whispers, 'For you.' The value-essence of my person is a good-in-itself that, rather than being universal, general and abstract, is singular. Content-wise, this good-in-itself contains a pointer, an indexical mark directed at me alone. It is a good-in-itself for *me*, not because *I* would experience it as such, but because it is given to me by an Other, and is that which the loving Other—God—holds out for me" (Gasché, "A Material *A Priori*? On Max Scheler's Critique of Kant's Formal Ethics," *Philosophical Forum* [2010]: 123, italics in text; the excerpts Gasché quotes here are from Scheler, *Formalism in Ethics and Non-Formal Ethics of Values*, trans. Manfred S. Frings and Roger L. Funk [Evanston, Ill.: Northwestern University Press, 1973], 490). Because of this indissoluble connection between personhood and value-actualization, for Scheler "the question 'what is the good?' [*Was is das Gute?*] does not mean 'what is a good action?,' but rather 'what is a good *person*?,' as Wei Zhang aptly puts it ("Person und Selbstgefühl," 279).

41. It is important to note that for Bakhtin spatial and temporal specificity contributes to the individualization of value, while for Scheler value, as well as the Act and the Person, are located outside of time and space.

CHAPTER TWO

1. Some of the preparatory material for this chapter was published as 'Revisiting Early Bakhtin: Problematic Aspects of *Vzhivanie*,' in *Proceedings of the XII International Bakhtin Conference, Jyväskylä, Finland 18–22 July, 2005*, ed. Mika Lähteenmäki, Hannele Dufva, Sirpa Leppnen, and Piia Varis (Jyväskylä, 2006), 414–23.

2. Eugene Kelly, "Zu Schelers Begriff der Philosophie," in *Vernunft und Gefühl: Schelers Phänomenologie des emotionalen Lebens*, ed. Christian Bermes, Wolfhart Henckmann, and Heinz Leonardy (Wurzburg: Königshausen & Neumann, 2003), 129. "The theory of an acting human being as a morally responsible agent remains unclear and uncertain in Scheler," Kelly writes (129). Similar criticisms have been voiced against Bakhtin's early discussions of intersubjectivity, pointing to his reluctance to address the *practical* aspects of ethically responsible relationships with others in *TPA* and "Author and Hero." For example, Leslie Baxter, who has used Bakhtin's theories to study familial, social, and personal relationships, notes that in the early period of Bakhtin's career it remains unclear "how it is that persons concretely accomplish creation, authoring, and answerability"(Baxter, *Voicing Relationships: A Dialogic Perspective* [Los Angeles: Sage, 2011], 26).

3. Kelly, "Zu Schelers Begriff der Philosophie," 126.

4. As we shall see, this question is eventually addressed, although in a rather cursory manner, in chapter C: "Vom Fremden Ich" ("Other Minds"), which appears at the end of the text and was expanded in the book's second edition.

5. Heinz Leonardy, for instance, notes that in Scheler's work the *immediacy* of phenomenological contemplation is much more apparent than in Husserl's system, with its preferred method of phenomenological bracketing (*Liebe und Person*, 60).

6. For an in-depth discussion of the "natural delusion" in Scheler, see chapter 1 of this study.

7. Bakhtin uses this particular expression to describe the author's deliberate and responsible "exit" from the realm of the hero's life ("AH," 14–15).

8. As we have seen, for Scheler, this humble love includes authentic self-love, which results in the revelation of one's own personal essence (see chapter 1).

9. Kelly, "Zu Schelers Begriff der Philosophie," 131.

10. Here we are not concerned with the complex relationship between the terms "philosophy" and "phenomenology" in Scheler's oeuvre, using them as nearly synonymous concepts. It is helpful to remember that for Scheler phenomenological exhibition of essences is the founding act of philosophical cognition.

11. In his seminal study of Scheler's philosophy, Heinz Leonardy notes the strong connection between the concept of "phenomenon" and that of Augustinian revelation in Scheler's understanding of phenomenology's method and mis-

sion (*Liebe und Person*, 42). Xiaofeng Liu also discusses the synthesis of phenomenological and theological methods of inquiry in Scheler's philosophy, stating that, in Scheler, the Augustinian "Theologia Cordis," an integral religious worldview that affirms the soul's immediate contact with the divine, acquires a new phenomenological basis (*Personwerdung*, 38).

12. Brandist makes a similar statement about Bakhtin's extension of the phenomenological method into the sphere of literary creation in the Dostoevsky study. According to Brandist, in *Problems of Dostoevsky's Art*, "the romantic idea of the artist's 'vision' is translated into the terms of a phenomenological 'intuition of essences' in which the 'formative principle' behind each character's discourse is objectified" (*The Bakhtin Circle*, 98). On Bakhtin and phenomenology see, for example, Craig Brandist, *The Bakhtin Circle*; B. Poole, "From Phenomenology to Dialogue"; Michael Gardiner, "A Very Understandable Horror of Dialectics: Bakhtin and Marxist Phenomenology," in *Materializing Bakhtin: The Bakhtin Circle and Social Theory*, ed. Craig Brandist and Galin Tihanov (London: Macmillan, 2000), 119–41; Michael Bernard-Donals, *Mikhail Bakhtin: Between Phenomenology and Marxism* (Cambridge: Cambridge University Press, 1994); and Matthias Freise, *Michail Bachtins philosophische Ästhetik der Literatur* (Frankfurt: Peter Lang, 1993).

13. Hence the sometimes disappointing refusal to probe the validity of certain philosophical propositions, which are conveniently proclaimed self-evident, presumably, in keeping with the phenomenological approach. See, for example, Leonardy's critique of Scheler's "Einstellung" (*Liebe und Person*, 36) and Edith Stein's claim that Scheler's work suffered because he did not subject the phenomenological method itself to critical scrutiny, affirming the same belief in revelation in his philosophy as in his private, deeply religious worldview (Stein, *Edith Steins Werke*, vol. 6, *Welt und Person: Beitrag zum Christlichen Wahrheitsstreben*, ed. L. Gelber [Freiburg: Verlag Herder, 1962], 11, 14). For a defense of Scheler's phenomenological method, see Peter H. Spader, *Scheler's Ethical Personalism: Its Logic, Development, and Promise* (New York: Fordham University Press, 2002), chap. 3.

14. See, for example, Leonardy, *Liebe und Person*, 26.

15. In proposing this innate foundation for empathy, Scheler has anticipated recent findings of developmental science based on studies of infant motor imitation and its link to human empathetic reactions that demonstrate that self-other connectedness is functional *at birth* (A. N. Meltzoff and M. K. Moore, "Explaining Facial Imitation: A Theoretical Model," *Early Development and Parenting* 6 [1997]: 179–92). As Jean Decety and Andrew N. Meltzoff point out, "few philosophers, prior to the discovery of newborn imitation took infant behavior as input into theories of human empathy" (Decety and Meltzoff, "Empathy, Imitation, and the Social Brain," in *Empathy: Philosophical and Psychological Perspectives*, ed. Amy Coplan and Peter Goldie [Oxford: Oxford University Press, 2011], 63),

but Scheler's acknowledgment of our innate relation to others makes him one of the few precocious philosophers deeply aware of this original social foundation that precedes the development of language and complex adult thought.

16. Such, for instance, is Bakhtin's reference to the "yet-to-be unity" of my internally valid self-image, rooted in my non-coincidence with myself. This unity constitutes a kind of "surplus" of knowledge, inaccessible to the other, who can never adequately grasp the absolute quality of my potential future. The loss of this essential "oneness with myself in the future" is fraught with disastrous consequences for the well-being of the personality (Bakhtin, "Author and Hero," 126).

17. See, for example, Charles Lock, "Bakhtin and the Tropes of Orthodoxy," in *Bakhtin and Religion: A Feeling for Faith*, ed. M. Felch and Paul J. Contino (Evanston, Ill.: Northwestern University Press, 2001), 97–119; and K. G. Isupov, "Uroki M.M. Bakhtina," in *M.M. Bakhtin: Pro et Contra*, ed. K. G. Isupov and D. K. Burlaka (St. Petersburg: Izdatel'stvo russkogo khristianskogo instituta, 2001), 7–44. The apophatic interpretation of Bakhtin's thought is part of a long-standing tradition. It seems that G. V. Florovsky, who expressed his appreciation of Bakhtin's *Problems of Dostoevsky's Art* (1929) in *The Ways of Russian Theology* (*Puti russkogo bogosloviia*), understood the thinker's work on Dostoevsky as apophatic in essence (see Isupov, "Uroki Bakhtina," 15). Isupov also ties Bakhtin to the apophatic tradition but describes the apophatic elements in his works as marginal and problematic ("Uroki Bakhtina," 15–23).

18. Randal Poole, "The Apophatic Bakhtin," in Felch and Contino, *Bakhtin and Religion: A Feeling for Faith*, 155.

19. See ibid., 159. Poole opposes the Bakhtinian person's joyful dependence on the other's consummating knowledge ("Author and Hero") to the aggressive "omniscience of the monological absolute consciousness" ascribed to the traditional novelist in the Dostoevsky study ("The Apophatic Bakhtin," 163). However, as we have seen, in the early Bakhtin, the self's surplus in relation to the consummated other becomes so enormous that it is precisely this knowledge that borders on omniscience and tends toward monologue. As will be shown later, the fear of the author's monologizing omniscience does not become a concern for Bakhtin until the Dostoevsky study, where he departs from many of his earlier postulates. This conceptual break is disregarded in Poole's otherwise insightful study.

20. For Bakhtin's use of the Incarnation image to symbolize the ideal act of consummation, see "Author and Hero" (56, 111).

21. Lock, "Bakhtin and the Tropes of Orthodoxy," 106.

22. Ibid., 114 and 109.

23. A similar criticism of Bakhtin's early concept of consummation is voiced by A. Kalygin, who states that, by viewing the consummated consciousness in the context of death, the Bakhtinian consummator silences any movement of spiritual becoming within it, in effect depriving it of life in the process (*Rannii*

Bakhtin, 61, 60). "The act of marking [the hero's] soul with the aesthetic seal of death transforms that very soul from within, making it arrested, constant, stable in its expressions," Kalygin writes (61), concluding that such consummation is incapable of capturing spiritual development (*stanovlenie*) in the other, the ostensible goal of the Bakhtinian author, stated in the beginning of his analysis of Pushkin's "Separation" in "Author and Hero" (60–61). Extending Kalygin's conclusions to the extraliterary, interpersonal aspect of *vzhivanie*, as an act of active empathy, of "authoring" our human others in everyday life, we may say that this type of (terminal) consummation arrests the other's spiritual development.

24. See also Alan Jacobs, "Bakhtin and the Hermeneutics of Love," in Felch and Contino, *Bakhtin and Religion: A Feeling for Faith*, 25–45.

25. Besides Batishchev's article, K. Isupov's and V. Makhlin's thoughtful criticism of Bakhtin's pre-dialogical and dialogical theories should be mentioned here. See Isupov's "Uroki Bakhtina" (esp. 29–33) and "Mikhail Bakhtin and Alexandr Meier," in *M. M. Bakhtin i filosofskaia kul'tura XX veka*, ed. A. P. Valitskaia and K. G. Isupov, vol. 1, part 2 (St. Petersburg, 1991), 60–70, esp. 65, 66; see also his "Smert' 'drugogo," in *Bakhtinologiia: Issledovaniia, perevody, publikatsii*, ed. A. P. Valitskaia et al. (St Petersburg: Aleteia, 1995), 103–116, and Makhlin's "Nasledie Bakhtina v kontekste zapadnogo postmodernizma," in *Bakhtin kak filosof*, ed. L. A. Gogoshvili and P. S. Gurevich (Moscow: Nauka, 1992), 206–20.

26. "Dialogizm ili polifonizm?" 127.

27. In *The Bakhtin Circle*, Brandist draws an analogy between ethical maturation described in this passage and the process of consolidating an independent authorial voice in Dostoevsky's novels, interpreted by Bakhtin as a responsible "emergence" from the sea of external alien discourses (95, 103).

28. Contemporary neuroscience validates this view of human development: studies of the infant brain have demonstrated that there is a stage of "emotion sharing" in early infancy, when perceptual action mapping, manifest in early motor imitation, facilitates the gradual process of distinguishing between the actions and emotional manifestations of the self and others (see, for example, Decety and Meltzoff, "Empathy, Imitation, and the Social Brain"). It is theorized that the gradual inhibiting and regulation of the imitation of others' (adults') movements and gestures performed by the infant's brain leads to the development of agency and a sense of knowing "whose actions and emotions belong to whom" (Decety and Meltzoff, "Empathy," 68; see also Fonagy et al., *Affect Regulation, Mentalization, and the Development of the Self* [New York: Other Press, 2002]).

29. A somewhat similar view of personal maturation in the world of shared psychic experiences, but defined in terms of discourse, is implicit in Bakhtin's *Discourse in the Novel*. While a child may naively apprehend another's (authoritative) discourse, for example, religious creed, as his own, as a responsible adult, he can no longer use the "unclaimed" or impersonal words about the world.

Instead he has to form a personal relationship with the inherited discourse, making it his own by stripping it of its external authority and making it internally or personally persuasive, Bakhtin states (*The Dialogic Imagination: Four Essays by M.M. Bakhtin*, ed. Michael Holquist, trans. Caryl Emerson and Michael Holquist [Austin, Tex.: University of Texas Press, 1981], 342, 345–46, 348).

30. Here the word "surplus" is my own description of the spiritual and psychic processes in question; it is not used by Scheler in this context, although elsewhere he does mention "ein unbegründbares Plus," the indescribable residue of personality that cannot be exhausted by the sum of its objectifiable characteristics (see, for example, *Sympathy*, *GW*, 7:168).

31. These expressions are used by Xiaofeng Liu in his discussion of Scheler's phenomenology of religion in a somewhat different context. Liu argues that for Scheler the "personalization" of the world (*Personwerdung*) is possible only through God's Incarnation. Through Christ God becomes a person and an individual and not simply a divine idea, Liu explains, interpreting Scheler's view of Incarnation (*Personwerdung*, 87–88). Moreover, for Scheler, the arrival of Christ changes the entire "experiential structure" of the world (*Personwerdung*, 88). However, Liu mistakenly interprets Incarnation as an act that *completely* eradicates the ontological difference between God and man in Scheler (86).

32. For the discussion of the "ontological delusion" in Scheler, see chapter 1.

33. See, for example, Bakhtin's "Work Notes of 1960s–early 1970s" (*Sobranie sochinenii*, 6:390–91; 411–13).

34. See, for example, *Ressentiment*, *GW*, 3:87; Ruth Coates notes a similar development in the concept of God in Bakhtin's oeuvre during the transition from the early period to the creation of the Dostoevsky book, stating that conflicting definitions of selfhood in *Problems of Dostoevsky's Art* reflect the philosophical crisis of Bakhtin's time, with its new, existentialist, definition of faith challenging the more conservative views (*Christianity in Bakhtin*, 92–100).

35. See, for example, his discussion of the significance of exteriorization and expression in the process of psychic and emotional individuation (Scheler, *Sympathy*, *GW*, 7:245).

36. Frings, *The Mind of Max Scheler*, 139.

37. A similarly dynamic reading of Incarnation as a mutual dialogical becoming of God and man has been recently proposed by Rowan Williams in his interpretation of Dostoevsky's theology, a reading informed by Williams's knowledge of both the Western and the Eastern Christian traditions, Russian religious thought, and the recently explicated religious subtext of Bakhtin's *PDP*. "[In the act of Incarnation], God determines to be God in the medium of the other," Williams writes, "in the medium of finite and material life, but of course does not cease to be God, and the fact of God's living in the medium of human existence drastically alters what is possible for human nature. While one cannot say with

any theological probity that this works the other way around in the same way (given the traditional commitment to the strict unchangeability of God's nature), it could nonetheless be said that at least what is possible for God to communicate of the divine is also altered in the incarnational encounter" (Williams, *Dostoevsky: Language, Faith and Fiction* [Waco, Tex.: Baylor University Press, 2008], 174–75).

38. "Man does not simply reproduce the ready-made, preexisting world of ideas contained in God before Creation," Scheler would write in *Philosophische Weltanschauung*, "he is the co-creator and co-founder of the ideational content which comes into being only in the process of his own becoming and the becoming of the world. . . . The status of humanity, which epitomizes free choice, bestows the superior honor of walking beside God, who realizes Himself through the world process, and of proudly carrying the banner of divinity through the storms of the world" (*GW*, 9:83–84).

39. On the level of author-hero relationship this is so, as Liisa Steinby explains, because "in *Problems of Dostoevsky's Poetics*, [Bakhtin] now claims that in a polyphonic novel, the architectonic of a work of art arises from its contents, namely the individuals who have their own views of the world and perform ethical actions in concrete situations. The form is no longer a 'gift' from the author, but the architectonic is now drawn directly from the persons acting in the ethical value-content of concrete events" ("Hermann Cohen and Bakhtin's Early Aesthetics," 246).

40. In the Dostoevsky study, where the parallel between the real life "authoring" of other consciousnesses and the inter-subjective activity of a literary author still obtains, although it is not as strong as in "Author and Hero," Dostoevsky the author is said to possess a non-essential, purely "information-bearing" surplus of vision in respect to his heroes (*PDP*, 73, 75). It is less clear what kind of visual advantages or disadvantages Dostoevsky's characters have in relation to *each other* in Bakhtin's view, but in *PDP* they do not possess the hopeful, grace-like surplus of knowledge the "I" has in relation to the "other" in Bakhtin's early works. However, in "Toward a Reworking of the Dostoevsky Book," Bakhtin seems to contemplate a return to a productive use of the surplus of vision, with its important role in guaranteeing the self's "extralocality" (*vnenakhodimmost'*) in relation to others (see *PDP*, 299).

41. The English translations of Bakhtin's *zavershenie* as "consummation" in the early works and "finalization" in *PDP*, seem to reflect the difference in the authorial evaluation of the same concept during different periods of Bakhtin's career (see *Art and Answerability* and *PDP*).

42. Coates, *Christianity in Bakhtin*, 88.

43. Compare, for example, Bakhtin's assessment of Raskolnikov as a virtually omniscient character, who "from the very beginning . . . already knows everything, takes everything into account, anticipates everything" (*PDP*, 74).

44. Similar questions have been posed by Caryl Emerson and Gary Saul Morson (see, for example, *Mikhail Bakhtin: Creation of a Prosaics*, 86, 251).

45. Such as, for example, Bakhtin's implicit judgment of the negative dialogicity characteristic of the Underground Man's consciousness, with its "bad infinity" (*durnaia beskonechnost'*) (*Sobranie sochinenii*, 6:60, compare also the "bad logical inconclusiveness" of a poorly constructed monological novel [*durnaia logicheskaiia bezyskhodnost'*] [*Sobranie sochinenii*, 6:40]).

46. This conclusion is implicit in Ruth Coates's analysis of *PDP*. According to Coates, the book puts forward two incompatible models of authoring, one based on the egoistical need for self-assertion and another emphasizing "the self-sacrificial, gracious element of authoring" (*Christianity in Bakhtin*, 96, 98–100). If the first model is prevalent among Dostoevsky's characters "authoring" each other, the second is chosen by Dostoevsky the author, Coates seems to suggest. In his interdisciplinary study of *PDP*, Brandist offers another possible solution. He argues that Bakhtin does provide an ethically productive alternative to the ultimately inconsequential dialogue of those characters, who, like Scheler's "heteropathic empathizers" cannot find a stable, unifying position outside of others, perpetually usurping other voices in their misguided search for selfhood. This ethically privileged mode of dialogic discourse, Brandist explains, is the "penetrative word," the initially monologic discourse which subdues the decentering, parasitic voices that perpetuate heteropathic dialogue, helping one find a genuine, ethically firm position outside others, which will eventually enable one to participate in authentic dialogue. While realistically depicting the socially prevalent "heteropathic" type of dialogue between his heroes, Bakhtin's Dostoevsky also shows his readers a path toward genuine dialogue, Brandist suggests. Furthermore, Dostoevsky himself takes this path as an author, using the model of the penetrative discourse to find a stable position outside his heroes without usurping or subjugating their voices (*The Bakhtin Circle*, 102–4). This is a compelling solution, but, in my view, Brandist overemphasizes the role of the penetrative word in the overall structure of Dostoevskian dialogue in its Bakhtinian interpretation, which is rather marginal. I tend to agree with Nina Perlina's argument that Bakhtin generally undervalues the productive uses of the authoritative word during his middle period (see "Bakhtin and Buber: Problems of Dialogic Imagination," 23; see also Morson and Emerson on Bakhtin's "dismissal of the creative uses of authoritative discourse" later in his career [*Mikhail Bakhtin: Creation of a Prosaics*, 220]).

47. In *Discourse in the Novel*, Bakhtin briefly reiterates his central argument about the twofold dialogism of Dostoevsky's narration as both a diverse collection of dialogically interconnected character-discourses and a remarkably "democratic" model of author / character relations. Here the two levels of dialogue are again emphatically brought together as equally respective of the sovereignty of another's discourse. Notably, it is precisely the fundamentally unresolved quality of the dialogic conflict between opposing discourses that seems to

be celebrated as a guarantor of their "free" and "open" status within the dynamic forum of competing words about the world (*Dialogic Imagination*, 349).

48. Isupov, "Smert' drugogo," 104.

49. A similar criticism was launched against Scheler, who, as Heinz Leonardy suggests, "had a gift for extracting the essential from a net of complicated [phenomenological] connections, and, as soon as he believed that essential something to be revealed, he immediately dropped it and turned to other potential discoveries" (*Liebe und Person*, 11). As noted above, this hastiness in defining the essential may, in part, be attributed to the phenomenological method itself as it was understood by Scheler and Bakhtin.

50. Isupov, "Smert' drugogo," 111. N. Bonetskaia also describes Bakhtinian consummation (*zavershenie)* as the death of the hero, who becomes an object ("veshch'") and loses any "subjective" or personal qualities in the process of receiving form from the consummating author (Bonetskaia, "Bakhtin's Aesthetics as a Logic of Form," in *The Contexts of Bakhtin: Philosophy, Authorship, Aesthetics* [Amsterdam: Harwood Academic Publishers, 1998], 85–87). I. N. Fridman echoes this criticism: "The gift of aesthetic grace turned out to be a posthumous one [in early Bakhtin]; there is no one to bestow it upon" (Fridman, "Nezavershennaia sud'ba estetiki zavershenia," in *M.M. Bakhtin kak filosof*, ed. L. A. Gogotishvili and P. S. Gurevich [Moscow: Nauka, 1992], 54, quoted in Kalygin, *Rannii Bakhtin*, 64).

51. See, for example, Bakhtin's *The Problem of Content, Material and Form*: "Forma vospolniaet vskiakoe sobytie i eticheskoe napriazhenie do polnoty sversheniia" ("The form completes each event and the concentration of ethical efforts associated with it to the level of fulfillment") (Bakhtin, *Voprosy literatury i estetiki: Issledovaniia raznykh let* [Moscow: Khudozhestvennaia literatura, 1975], 61, quoted in Bonetskaia, "Primechaniia k 'Avtoru i Geroiu,'" 250).

52. Bakhtin's interpreters almost invariably link consummation with Incarnation (see Coates, *Christianity in Bakhtin*, 21, 33–34, 49; and Morson and Emerson, *Mikhail Bakhtin: Creation of a Prosaics*, 61), while, to my knowledge, its connection with the Resurrection motif has not been explored.

53. Compare, for example, Kierkegaard's reference to loving oneself "in the truth and earnestness of eternity" (*Works of Love*, 429).

54. This determination must, of course, be made not from the point of view of any orthodox dogma but from that of the Schelerian-Bakhtinian theory of agapeistic dialogue, with its essentially proto-existentialist interpretation of the person of Christ and of Christ's "dialogical" mission (see chapter 1). In chapters 3–6, we will examine both positive and negative types of consummation in Dostoevsky, arguing for the relevance of this (revised) early Bakhtinian concept to Dostoevsky's religiously inflected ethics.

55. On the relationship between the Nietzschean ressentiment and Bakhtin's analysis of the characters' discourse in *Notes from Underground,* see chapter 3.

56. See Dostoevsky's notebooks for *The Devils* (*Polnoe sobranie sochinenii*

v tridtsati tomakh, 30 vols., ed. V. V. Vinogradov, G. M. Fridlender, and M. B. Khrapchenko [Leningrad: Nauka, 1972–90], 11:179, 180, 182). "Est' tol'ko dve initsiativy: ili vera, ili zhech'" ("There are only two initiatives: either to believe or to burn [everything]") (*PSS*, 11:182); "Esli pravoslavie vse, to i Rossiia vse. Esli zhe net, to luchshe szhech'" ("If orthodoxy is everything, then Russia is everything. If not, then it's better to burn [everything]") (*PSS*, 11:180).

57. Liu notes that in this Scheler's system is opposed to the Indic and Greek ontological models, according to which love results from one's knowledge of the subject. In the latter model, the act of salvation is achieved through knowledge, while in Scheler's interpretation of the Christian worldview, knowledge or revelation *follow* the saving act of love (*Personwerdung*, 88).

58. Compare Leonardy, *Liebe und Person*, 83.

59. It is evident from my analysis of Bakhtin's concepts of consummation and the surplus of vision that these efforts are not consistent on Bakhtin's part, being largely negated by the fact that the other's surplus of vision in relation to the self is virtually unlimited. However, the quotations displayed in this section exhibit precisely those aspects of Bakhtin's architectonics that are compatible with my revisions of the theory.

60. See Leonardy, *Liebe und Person*, 180.

CHAPTER THREE

1. A section of this chapter was published as "The Specter of Freedom: *Ressentiment* and Dostoevsky's *Notes from Underground*" in *Studies in East European Thought* 59 (2007): 119–40.

2. Note, for example, Scheler's interest in Vladimir Soloviev, a philosopher who had an important impact on Dostoevsky's thought in the 1870s and was beloved by Bakhtin (see, for example, Helmut Dahm, *Vladimir Solvyev and Max Scheler: Attempt at a Comparative Interpretation. A Contibution to the History of Phenomenology* [Dordrecht: Reidel, 1975]; Caryl Emerson, "Soloviev, the Late Tolstoy and the Early Bakhtin on the Problem of Shame and Love," *Slavic Review* 50 [1991]: 663–71; Aleksandar Mihailovic, *Corporeal Words: Mikhail Bakhtin's Theory of Discourse* [Evanston, Ill.: Northwestern University Press, 1997], esp. 11, 12, 29, 70–72, 140–47, 128–29; Steven Cassedy, *Flight from Eden: The Origins of Modern Literary Criticism and Theory* [Berkeley: University of California Press, 1990], 119–20). Now there is also more willingness to acknowledge Bakhtin's indebtedness to Dostoevsky precisely as a philosopher of both ethics and aesthetics (see, for example, K. G. Isupov, "Ot estetiki zhizni k estetike istorii [Traditsii russkoi filosofii u M. M. Bakhtina]," in Gogotishvili and Gurevich, *M.M. Bakhtin kak filosof*, esp. 69–70; Isupov, "Smert' drugogo," 107–9).

3. Feodor Dostoevsky, *Polnoe sobranie sochinenii v tridtsati tomakh*, 30 vols., ed. V. V. Vinogradov, G. M. Fridlender, and M. B. Khrapchenko (Lenin-

grad: Nauka, 1972–90), my translation. Hereafter this collected edition will be referenced in the text as *PSS*, followed by the volume and page number, separated by a colon. Volume number may be omitted if the same novel is continuously quoted in a chapter or section dedicated solely or chiefly to its analysis. If that is the case, the volume number will be given in a note and only the page number will subsequently appear in the text following quotations from this particular work. Volumes 28, 29, and 30 are each separated into two books. When these volumes are cited, the book number will appear after the volume number, separated by a period, for example, *PSS*, 28.2:251.

4. Bakhtin cites a similar depiction of the "ontological gulf" in its Dostoevskian definition in the writer's letter to Kovner: "If I justify you in my own way in my heart (as I invite you to justify me), then it is still better if *I* justify you rather than you justify yourself" (*PSS*, 29.2:139–40, italics in text, quoted in Bakhtin, *PDP*, 256–57).

5. For Vyacheslav Ivanov's explication of Dostoevsky's "Thou art" principle, in which he sees one of Dostoevsky's major philosophical mottos, see Ivanov, *Freedom and the Tragic Life: A Study in Dostoevsky*, trans. Norman Cameron, ed. S. Konovalov (London: Noonday, 1952), 26–28. As Robert Louis Jackson notes, Ivanov's observations on the significance of the "Thou art" principle became a foundation for Bakhtin's model of Dostoevsky's poetics (R. L. Jackson, *Dialogues with Dostoevsky*, 252).

6. Indeed, as Bakhtin emphasizes in *PDP*, "for a correct understanding of Dostoevsky's [artistic] plan[s] it is very important to consider the value he placed on the role of the other person as another" (256).

7. Note, for example, Myshkin's "proniknovenie" ("penetration [into other minds]"), his "pristal'nyi," "pronitsaiushchii vzgliad" ("searching, penetrative gaze") (*PSS*, 9:278; *PSS*, 8:6, 138), Tikhon's "pronitsaiushchii dushu golos" ("voice that penetrates the soul") (*PSS*, 11:30), Alyosha's penetrating words (*PSS*, 15:39), and the notion of "penetrative" sociopolitical ideas, afloat in the air, in Dostoevsky's journalistic writings ("pronitsaiushchaia ideia," see, for example, *PSS*, 21:16), and so on. Compare also Vyacheslav Ivanov's and Bakhtin's use of this characteristic Dostoevskian word as a theoretical concept ["proniknovenie"; "proniknovennoe slovo" ("penetrative word")], see, for example, Ivanov, *Freedom and the Tragic Life*, 26–27; Bakhtin, *PDP*, 10, 242, 249–50.

8. This is why Dmitry Chizhevsky could say that a Dostoevskian soul is capable of comprehending anything, "[In Dostoevsky] a person's soul is in principle open to anything, capable of understanding anything" ("dushe cheloveka v printsipe vse dostupno, vse poniatno") (Chizhevsky, "Dostoevsky psikholog," in *O Dostoevskom: Sbornik statei pod redaktsiei A.L. Bema*, ed. A. L. Bem, 2 vols. [Prague, 1933], 2:57), and Bakhtin states, with some exaggeration, that a Dostoevskian hero understands everyone else's truth "perfectly" (*PDP*, 73). I would object that the hero's understanding of "another truth" and of another soul is

never perfect, but the scholars are correct in acknowledging the fundamental openness of a Dostoevskian soul and the *ontological reality* of live-entering in Dostoevsky, based precisely on the reality of Christ's undertaking. (In this sense, it is quite different from the kind of intersubjectivity we see, for example, in Tolstoy, where the notion of emotional understanding is usually based on the *identity* of the shared experience and not on an active, imaginative participation in another's life, as in Dostoevsky. Compare, for example, Pozdnyshev's statement in "The Kreutzer Sonata" that "he who has not lived through it [his murderous experience] cannot understand" [Tolstoy, *Sobranie sochinenii*, 12:196], or Anna Karenina's: "To forgive [Kitty] would have to live through what I have lived through" [*Sobranie sochinenii*, 9:291]).

9. The concept of ressentiment is not explicitly mentioned in Shestov's study, but it is clear that the author refers to this Nietzschean notion when he critiques the value of humanitarian pity, contending that the man of the forties undertook to "serve the humblest man" not out of genuine compassion but merely to turn away from his own spiritual emptiness, seeking consolation for himself in consoling his "humble brother" (Lev Shestov, "Dostoevsky and Nietzsche: The Philosophy of Tragedy," in *Essays in Russian Literature: The Conservative View: Leontiev, Rozanov, Shestov,* ed. Spencer E. Roberts [Athens: Ohio University Press, 1968], 29). In Nietzsche, ressentiment "love" is characterized by precisely such turning away from one's own self to conceal its impotence and emotional bankruptcy (see, for example, *Genealogy of Morals*).

10. Richard H. Weisberg has applied Scheler's concept of ressentiment to *Notes from Underground* in his 1984 book *The Failure of the Word: Protagonist as Lawyer in Modern Fiction*, but, in my opinion, his analysis of underground psychology is fragmentary and somewhat superficial (see Weisberg, *The Failure of the Word: The Protagonist as Lawyer in Modern Fiction* [New Haven, Conn.: Yale University Press, 1984]). In *Rancor against Time: The Phenomenology of "Ressentiment"* (Hamburg: Felix Meiner Verlag, 1980), Richard Ira Sugarman also discusses both *Notes from Underground* and Scheler's *Resssentiment*, but in this work the two texts, presented as alternative philosophical considerations of the same phenomenon, are examined independently from each other, in separate chapters.

11. Nietzsche, *The Complete Works of Friedrich Nietzsche*, 13:32.

12. The concept of *ressentiment* is developed by Scheler (much more fully than in Nietzsche's work) in *Ressentiment* and *The Nature of Sympathy* ("Das Ressentiment im Aufbau der Moralen" [originally published in 1912] and *Wesen und Formen der Sympathie*) and, as a peculiar inversion of empathy, presents an important addition to his study of love and fellow feeling discussed in chapters 1 and 2. See Scheler, *GW*, vol. 3, and *GW*, vol. 5. In this chapter Scheler's works are cited from their translated editions, unless otherwise indicated.

13. Hereafter references to *Notes from Underground* will be made in the

text, accompanied by the page number in Michael Katz's translation (Dostoevsky, *Notes from Underground*, trans. and ed. Michael R. Katz [New York: Norton, 1989]), which is followed by the semicolon and the page number in the Collected Works edition, *Polnoe sobranie sochinenii v tridtsati tomakh* (*PSS*), vol. 5. Michael Katz's excellent translation, used throughout the chapter, is occasionally revised for greater accuracy.

14. Bernstein, *Bitter Carnival*, 90.

15. Nietzsche, *The Complete Works of Friedrich Nietzsche*, 13:34.

16. William Holdheim's translation of Scheler's *Ressentiment* is used in this chapter (Scheler, *Ressentiment*, ed. Lewis A. Coser, trans. William W. Holdheim [New York: Free Press of Glencoe, 1961]).

17. Resorting to Scheler's own frequently used expression, we may call it a situation rich in ressentiment potential to distinguish it from a fully developed ressentiment attitude.

18. Shestov, "Dostoevsky and Nietzsche," 13.

19. Ibid., 13.

20. Note the preceding reference to the idealism of the 1840s as the source of the character's irrational predilection for the ideal values, which makes his life in the rigidly rationalistic, "ideal-less" universe governed by natural laws so acutely painful: "But let's say that the crystal building is a hoax, that, according to the laws of nature, it shouldn't exist, and that I've invented it only out of my own stupidity, *as a result of certain antiquated, irrational habits of my generation*" (Dostoevsky, *Notes*, 25; *PSS*, 120).

21. Edward Wasiolek, *Dostoevsky: The Major Fiction* (Cambridge, Mass.: MIT Press, 1964), 42.

22. The objective truth or falsity of the chosen view of reality has no bearing on the formation of a ressentiment attitude. As long as the subject wholeheartedly believes in the validity of his truth and is fundamentally unconcerned with the values of the opposite system, he is free from ressentiment. Ressentiment results from a conscious (or semi-conscious) manipulation of one's own value system, when the choice of an existential program is motivated by the wish to "spite" the desired but unattainable values. In this case, the subject's *consciousness* of the falsity of the chosen belief, which exists on some level of the psychic processes, becomes an indicator of a ressentiment delusion. If that is the case, the subject is never entirely free from the authority of the rejected values.

23. Nietzsche, *The Complete Works of Friedrich Nietzsche*, 13:30.

24. My translation, corresponding passage in Katz's translation is in *Notes*, 25.

25. Literally: "gave so-and-so the fig" ("pokazal takomu-to kukish [figu]")—a rude gesture common in several Slavic cultures, consisting of putting the thumb between clenched fingers.

26. This shift seems to take place when the hero becomes acutely conscious

of his enslavement to the laws of nature, when he, so to speak, finds himself in direct proximity to "the wall." Note the ominous presence of the wall image in the passages above: "Only jackasses and their mongrels put on a brave face and only until they come up against *a wall* [do izvestnoi *steny*]" (*Notes*, 30; *PSS*, 125); "you feel that you've reached the last limit [literally, "the last *wall*": do poslednei *steny* doshel]" (*Notes*, 6; *PSS*, 102).

27. David Booth, "Ressentiment and Constructive Theology: Positive Uses of Nietzsche's Critique of Christianity" (Ph.D. diss., University of Chicago, 1984), 51.

28. In his Schelerian analysis of *Notes from Underground*, Weisberg goes as far as to claim that in the paltry Zverkov the Underground Man encounters true beauty and in the puny official Anton Antonovich—genuine power. According to Weisberg, these characters not only arouse the hero's "existential envy" but represent genuine values (*The Failure of the Word*, 39).

29. Robert Louis Jackson, who notes that "absolute chance," chosen as a paradoxical "strategy" of the underground revolt, "is indistinguishable from absolute necessity," is one of such scholars, whose criticism targets the fundamentally reactive nature of the Underground Man's protest (*The Art of Dostoevsky: Deliriums and Nocturnes* [Princeton, N.J.: Princeton University Press, 1981], 186). Similar views are also expressed by Edward Wasiolek (*Dostoevsky: The Major Fiction*) and Joseph Frank (see his *Dostoevsky: The Stir of Liberation 1860–1865* [Princeton, N.J.: Princeton University Press, 1986]).

30. Weisberg, *The Failure of the Word*, 39.

31. Shestov, "Dostoevsky and Nietzsche," 62.

32. Nietzsche, *The Complete Works of Friedrich Nietzsche*, 13:37.

33. Ibid.

34. In modern German, "scheel ansehen" means "to look askance or disparagingly at somebody."

35. Nietzsche, *The Complete Works of Friedrich Nietzsche*, 13:37.

36. "Placing them above myself."

37. We should note that Scheler's position on the status of the rejected values in the ressentiment worldview is somewhat ambiguous: in the beginning of his study he states that the negated values are still felt as positive by the man of ressentiment, although they are "overcast by the false values and can shine through only dimly" (*Ressentiment*, 60). However, later in his discussion, the author seems to imply that the accomplishment of "the sublime revenge" of ressentiment consists in complete obliteration of the original value system from consciousness. "[The ressentiment revenge] is sublime, for the impulses of revenge against those who are strong, healthy, rich, or handsome now disappear entirely. *Ressentiment* has brought deliverance from the inner torment of these affects," because the hated values are no longer perceived as worthy possessions even on the deepest level of consciousness (*Ressentiment*, 76–77). It seems that

Scheler views ressentiment as a process consisting of several stages: in its initial phase ressentiment is characterized by the state of "transparency," when the "sweet grapes" are still recognized as such on the conscious (or perhaps, semi-conscious) level, while the accomplishment of the "sublime revenge" signals the transition to the stage of "organic mendacity" ("organische Belogenheit") (see *Ressentiment*, 77–78).

38. Compare the hero's famous utterance: "*Luchshe* soznatel'naia inertsiia!" ("Conscious inertia is *better*!") (*Notes*, 26; *PSS*, 121).

39. For instance, awakening in the cellar-like room of the brothel next to Liza, the hero feels as if buried in the underground: "A dismal thought was conceived in my brain and spread throughout my whole body like a nasty sensation, such as one feels upon entering a damp, mouldy *underground cellar* [*v podpol'e*, syroe i zatkhloe]" (*Notes*, 60; *PSS*, 152). He prophesies a similar "burial alive" for Liza: "as you're breathing your last, they'll shove you into the filthiest corner of *the cellar* [v samyi smradnyi ugol *v podvale*]" (70; *PSS*, 161). "No, Liza, you'd be lucky if you died quickly of consumption somewhere in a corner, *in a cellar* [*v podvale*], like the other girl," he tells Liza after relating the chilly tale of a prostitute's death in a basement apartment (*Notes*, 69; *PSS*, 161).

40. Anders Nygren, *Agape and Eros*, trans. Philip S. Watson (Chicago: University of Chicago Press, 1982), 215.

41. Wasiolek, *Dostoevsky: The Major Fiction*, 53.

42. "To be loved, a person needs to hide himself. The minute he shows his face love disappears," Ivan says to Alyosha in *The Brothers Karamazov* (*PSS*, 14:215).

43. For other interpretations exploring the religious meanings of *Notes from Underground*, see Olga Meerson, "Old Testament Lamentation in the Underground Man's Monologue: A Refutation of the Existentialist Reading of *Notes from Underground*," *Slavic and East European Journal* 36, no. 4 (1992): 317–22; and Carol A. Flath, "Fear of Faith: The Hidden Religious Message of *Notes from Underground*," *Slavic and East European Journal* 37, no. 4 (1993): 510–29.

CHAPTER FOUR

1. All references to *Notes from the House of the Dead*, cited in text as *House of the Dead*, are to Jessie Coulson's translation (Dostoevsky, *Memoirs from the House of the Dead*, trans. Jessie Coulson [London: Oxford University Press, 1965]), unless otherwise indicated. Following the page number in Coulson's translation, the corresponding page number in the collected works edition, *PSS*, vol. 4, is provided after a semicolon. Coulson's translation is occasionally emended for greater accuracy.

2. As many recent publications have underscored, this semi-autobiographical novel has a special status in Dostoevsky's oeuvre, as it reveals "an atypically rigid

sense of class consciousness" for Dostoevsky's heroes (Robin Feuer Miller, *Dostoevsky's Unfinished Journey* [New Haven, Conn.: Yale University Press, 2007], 26; see also Donna Tussing Orwin, *Consequences of Consciousness: Turgenev, Dostoevsky, Tolstoy* [Stanford, Calif.: Stanford University Press, 2007]; Nancy Ruttenburg, *Dostoevsky's Democracy* [Princeton, N.J.: Princeton University Press, 2008] and Ruttenburg, "Dostoevsky's Estrangement," in *Poetics Today* 26, no. 4 [2005]: 719–51). It is also arguably a major work in which Dostoevsky engages most closely with peasant characters.

3. Alexander Burry insightfully notes that passages such as quoted here, where Goryanchikov speculates about his fellow prisoners' hidden thoughts by scrutinizing their enigmatic countenances and often ambiguous gestures, are "deliberately underreported," which "encourages readers to fill in what may be hidden behind these 'scowling brows and excessively cheerful faces'" (Burry, *Multi-Mediated Dostoevsky: Transposing Novels into Opera, Film, and Drama* [Evanston, Ill.: Northwestern University Press, 2011], 81). This emphatic restraint in exposing the convict's inner world, in "peeking into his soul," which, as Burry observes, contrasts sharply with the narrator's detailed depiction of the peasant speech, prison folklore, and other objectified or "ethnographic" characteristics of the prison population, is indeed consistent throughout the novel and points to Dostoevsky's larger theme, namely, the impossibility of fully knowing another soul, a postulate that, however, does not preclude his agapeistic heroes from seeking communion with others.

4. R. L. Jackson, *The Art of Dostoevsky*, 44–45.

5. Lanz's translation of "The Peasant Marey" is cited in this chapter (see Dostoevsky, *A Writer's Diary*, trans. Kenneth Lantz, intro. Gary Saul Morson, 2 vols. [Evanston, Ill.: Northwestern University Press, 1993]), abbreviated as *WD*, followed by a page number in that edition and, after a semicolon, a reference to volume and page numbers in *PSS*. In Lantz's translation, page numbers run consecutively throughout the two volumes, therefore the volume number is not given.

6. All references to *The Idiot* (*Idiot*) in chapters 4 and 5 are to David Magarshack's translation (Dostoevsky, *The Idiot*, trans. David Magarshack [London: Penguin Books, 1955]), unless otherwise indicated. Hereafter the first number in the parenthetical note will refer to the page number in Magarschack's translation, while the number after the semicolon references the corresponding page number in the collected works edition, *PSS*, vol. 8. When it is clear from the context that the reference is to *The Idiot*, the volume number in *PSS* is omitted. Magarshack's translation is occasionally modified for greater accuracy.

7. In her *Dostoevsky's Unfinished Journey*, Robin Miller also draws a link between these two episodes that demonstrate the narrators' ethically motivated suspension of judgment in view of our ultimate inability to "peer into [the others'] hearts" (78). In Miller's analysis the two passages are seen as examples of framed parables and are brought together to illuminate the structure and mean-

ing of conversion and near-conversion experiences in Dostoevsky's prose. In these two parables "good and evil are intimately intertwined," Miller observes, "and their very intertwining serves to strengthen the good rather than the evil" (*Dostoevsky's Unfinished Journey*, 78).

8. Bakhtin extends the same interpretation to a somewhat similar scene in *The Brothers Karamazov*, where Lise questions Alyosha's "unauthorized" peeking into Captain Snegiryov's soul (*PDP*, 59–60). Alan Jacobs, who discusses Bakhtin's analysis of the scene to illustrate the philosopher's concept of love, suggests that Bakhtin's ethical concerns are not necessarily identical with Dostoevsky's. According to Jacobs, Dostoevsky disagrees with Lise's criticism: countering it with Alyosha's response (that there is no scorn or condescension in their examination of the captain's soul, because they are themselves "just like" the captain [*PSS*, 14:197]); the author actually emphasizes the bond of common humanity between characters (see Jacobs, "Bakhtin and the Hermeneutics of Love," 29–30). Alyosha's confident awareness of this fundamental bond with his interlocutors allows him to approach the other's soul with greater moral certainty, Jacobs concludes (29–30). I find Jacobs's interpretation rather convincing in the case of the Lise-Alyosha exchange in *The Brothers Karamazov*, where Dostoevsky seems to give a different, somewhat revised, answer to the moral dilemma first posed in *The Idiot*. In the context of Jacobs's concerns, Bakhtin's uniform interpretation of both conversations, that between Aglaya and Myshkin and between Lise and Alyosha, may need to be revised. However, in *The Idiot*, the problem of maintaining certain spiritual and moral "chastity" in relation to another's soul remains very relevant till the end of the novel, and the disappointing lack of such ideal chastity is felt acutely by Myshkin in himself and others. In this sense, Aglaya's criticism of the Prince is harder to discount than Lise's reproach of Alyosha.

9. This expression is used by Edward Wasiolek to describe Myshkin's ethical transgression against Rogozhin in the scene preceding his attack on the Prince (*Dostoevsky: The Major Fiction*, 106).

10. In her detailed study of the characters' speech patterns in *The Idiot*, Brigitte Schultze notes the special status and frequency of the word "almost" (*pochti*) in Myshkin's utterances as a characteristic expression of his extreme caution in using his word to judge or define others (Schultze, *Der Dialog in F. M. Dostoevskijs "Idiot,"* [Munich: Verlag Otto Sagner], 83). I would add that the word "almost" often serves as a positive loophole, an opening into another character's view of the problem, which allows Myshkin to enter other minds and to mediate freely between discourses.

11. Wasiolek, *Dostoevsky: The Major Fiction*, 106. Wasiolek treats Myshkin's behavior in the scene as a crisis of faith, an episode symbolically equivalent to Alyosha's momentary betrayal of Father Zosima in *The Brothers Karamazov* (book 7, chapter 1) (*Dostoevsky: The Major Fiction*, 105–6), while Romano Guardini provides a more specific religious reference, interpreting Myshkin's

spiritual test as an allusion to Christ's Temptation of the Abyss. Myshkin succumbs to the temptation precisely where Christ remains firm and unwavering, so that, in the process of symbolic interpretation, Dostoevsky's reader may attribute the ultimate glory to Myshkin's divine referent, Guardini concludes (*Religiöse Gestalten in Dostojewskijs Werk: Studien über den Glauben* [Munich: Kösel Verlag, 1977], 402). It is implicit in Galina Ermilova's interesting interpretation of *The Idiot* that the scene is a symbolic enactment of the procession of the Cross, just as the entire novel symbolically commemorates Christ's journey from Bethany to Jerusalem and to Golgotha during passion week, Ermilova suggests (see "Tragediia 'russkogo Khrista' ili o 'neozhidannosti okonchaniia 'Idiota,'" in *Roman F.M. Dostoevskogo "Idiot": Sovremennoe sostoianie izucheniia*, ed. T. Kasatkina [Moscow: Nasledie, 2001], 446–61). In a very different treatment of the episode, T. Kasatkina explains Myshkin's behavior quite literally as a demonic possession ("Rol' khudozhestvennoi detali i osobennosti funktsionirovaniia slova v romane F. M. Dostoevskogo 'Idiot,'" in Kasatkina, *Roman F.M. Dostoevskogo "Idiot,"* 60–99). For more on the religious significance of Myshkin's tragic journeys through Petersburg, see chapter 5.

12. V. A. Tunimanov, *Tvorchestvo Dostoevskogo 1854–1862* (Leningrad: Nauka, 1980), 93.

13. Nancy Ruttenburg arrives at a similar interpretation when she examines the bathhouse scene, where the threshold perspective is yielded by the metaphors of hell emphatically used by the narrator (*House of the Dead*, 145; *PSS*, 98) and this transitional space similarly encourages a view of oneself as *other*. At the entrance to the bathhouse Goryanchikov encounters "bare life: one hundred naked men packed into a room twelve paces by twelve connected by their filth," Ruttenburg writes, "their animal joy in the sensual pleasure of the bath" (*Dostoevsky's Democracy*, 161). "Standing at the entrance to the bath house, wearing only his fetters, subjected to what Merleau-Ponty calls the 'complementary vision [. . . of] myself seen from without, such as another would see me,' Goryanchikov offers an apt example of one 'installed in the midst of the visible, occupied in considering it from a certain spot'" (Ruttenburg, *Dostoevsky's Democracy*, 161; Merleau-Ponty's passage quoted here is from *The Visible and the Invisible,* ed. Claude Lefort, trans. Alphonso Lingis [Evanston, Ill.: Northwestern University Press, 1968], 134).

14. R. L. Jackson, *The Art of Dostoevsky*, 123.

15. Ibid., 139

16. Literally, "even if I were the most convicted of convicts [*bud' ia razarestant*], sentenced to eternity" (*PSS*, 2, 7:207).

17. R. L. Jackson, *The Art of Dostoevsky*, 44–45.

18. Dostoevsky, *PSS*, 28.1:170, quoted in Jackson, *The Art of Dostoevsky*, 45.

19. Miller, *Dostoevsky's Unfinished Journey*, 29.

20. R. L. Jackson, *The Art of Dostoevsky*, 7.

21. Miller, *Dostoevsky's Unfinished Journey*, 28.

22. R. L. Jackson, *The Art of Dostoevsky*, 44–45.

23. For observations on the significance of Russianness in the interior narrator's valuation of his peasant others in *The House of the Dead* in the context of Dostoevsky's imperial consciousness and the problematic national stereotypes present in the novel, see Anne Dwyer's "Dostoevsky's Prison House of Nation(s): Genre Violence in *Notes from the House of the Dead*," *Russian Review* 71 (2012): 209–25. Dostoevsky's own allegedly chauvinistic behavior in prison, especially in regard to its Polish population, was reported by Szymon Tokarzewski, the novelist's fellow prisoner in the Omsk stockade, in his memoir *Siedem lat katorgi: Pamiętniki 1846–1857*, 2nd ed. (Warsaw: Gebethner and Wolff, 1918).

24. Another interpretation that capitalizes on the ineradicable distance between Goryanchikov and his fellow inmates is Nancy Ruttenburg's ("Dostoevsky's Estrangement" [2005]; *Dostoevsky's Democracy* [2008]). Ruttenburg sees the work's main aesthetic achievement in capturing the stinging shock of the interior narrator's painful estrangement from the peasant convicts and in using this ever-present distance to expose the hero's deficiency of sight in respect to his peasant other. Far from being a record of a fully consummated conversion resulting in a communion with the peasant convict, the narrative reveals the "epistemological and ideological value . . . of estrangement as a means of defamiliarizing one's own habitual blindness in order to see one's own non-seeing," Ruttenburg asserts ("Dostoevsky's Estrangement," 741; see also *Dostoevsky's Democracy*, 33, 90). While I also emphasize the character's and the author's uses of (ontological) distance in the novel, my assessment of Goryanchikov's dialogical efforts is more optimistic. I argue that Goryanchikov begins to achieve an active understanding of his fellow convicts and hence to overcome his "optical illusion" precisely when he fully acknowledges the substantial existential gulf separating the two parties. It is consistent with her vision of ineradicable estrangement that Ruttenburg seems to take literally Goryanchikov's statement that, to understand the phenomenon of crime (and the peasant criminal inhabiting the House of the Dead), the Russian nobleman must be "turned 'actually and in fact' into one of the common people" (*Dostoevsky's Democracy*, 43) as well as Dostoevsky's later journalistic calls for "therapeutic merging" with the people (*Dostoevsky's Democracy*, 80). If Goryanchikov's goal is indeed no less than to "turn into" the peasant convict, then all his efforts both during and after incarceration do, in fact, come to naught: in this sense, he indeed "tried and failed to gain access to the psyche of the peasant convict," as Ruttenburg concludes (*Dostoevsky's Democracy*, 69). But, as I argue, such ultimately depersonalizing identification is never a spiritual goal for Dostoevsky, nor for his protagonist in *House of the Dead*, although forced "democratization" is part of the hero's inescapable social *reality* in Siberia, as he is traumatically stripped of his class privileges in punishment for his crime. Instead of a call to "become" the peasant convict, rhetorically

extended to both the hero and the reader with the ambition of procuring the first-person perspective of the peasant's otherwise inscrutable psyche, as Ruttenburg sees it, I read this statement as an a priori acknowledgment of the limits of understanding. It is a sociopolitical variant of "I cannot peer into [another's] soul after all," which, as we saw in "The Peasant Marey" and *The Idiot*, was a necessary precondition for, rather than an insurmountable obstacle to, morally productive understanding, always based on *partial* knowledge in Dostoevsky. For that reason, Goryanchikov-Dostoevsky's spiritual task cannot be defined as the nobleman's "ideologically desirable . . . principled transformation into the peasant" (*Dostoevsky's Democracy*, 66). Although I agree with Ruttenburg's general thesis that the hero's conversion is not conclusive (90, 33), it is so certainly not because he fails to reach that radical goal, which, I would argue, was never set in the first place, and is, in fact, inimical to the author's and the protagonist's personalist ethics. In my opinion, instead of "turning into" the Russian peasant, Dostoevsky's partly autobiographical hero in *The House of the Dead* "turns toward" him, dialogically, as Robin Miller more aptly puts it in *Dostoevsky's Unfinished Journey* (4).

In some ways similar to Ruttenburg's interpretation is Donna Orwin's Tolstoyan take on empathy in *The House of the Dead* in her *Consequences of Consciousness* (2007). "Empathy for the lot of the convicts depends on the narrator's assimilation through imagination of their inner life to his own," Orwin writes. "This means that to understand them even to the extent that he does, he must have the *same* experiences and feelings as they do" (124). While I agree with Orwin that Dostoevsky emphasizes the impossibility of wholly joining in with another psyche (124), once again, this acknowledgment of the ontological asymmetry between persons does not result in a *replicative* view of empathy for Dostoevsky, which is Orwin's conclusion. As I have tried to demonstrate here and in the rest of this study, quite the opposite is true: for Dostoevsky, in contrast to Tolstoy, authentic empathy is always imaginative and creative in its very essence precisely because of its Christological basis.

25. R. L. Jackson, *The Art of Dostoevsky*, 68. In a similar vein, Robin Miller eloquently underscores the religious aspect of Dostoevsky-Goryanchikov's spiritually deepened understanding of his peasant *other* in *The House of the Dead*: Dostoevsky's "turning toward the people" was an essential part of his own conversion experience, leading to a deepened embrace of his native Orthodoxy after his mock-execution, Miller remarks (*Dostoevsky's Unfinished Journey*, 4).

26. For instance, Joseph Frank sees this notable omission as one of the intriguing "anomalies of *The House of the Dead*" (*Dostoevsky: The Years of Ordeal, 1850–1859* [Princeton, N.J.: Princeton University Press, 1983], 114). This view is also shared by Gary Saul Morson ("Introductory Study: Dostoevsky's Great Experiment," introduction to *A Writer's Diary I: 1873–1876*, by Feodor Dostoevsky, trans. Kenneth Lantz [Evanston, Ill.: Northwestern University Press], 1–117). Robin Miller suggests that Dostoevsky's conversion has happened long

before his prison years, in the immediate aftermath of the author's own life-changing scaffold moment, and this essentially timeless lived experience was "spread out" throughout his artistic career to create many inspiring, if open-ended and reversible, moments of conversion epiphanies for his heroes, including Goryanchikov (*Dostoevsky's Unfinished Journey*, see, e.g., 28, 155). Nancy Ruttenburg classifies Goryanchikov's experience as an interrupted or "unconsummated" conversion (*Dostoevsky's Democracy*, 33, 90).

27. Guardini, *Religiöse Gestalten*, 411–13.

28. Ibid., 411–12; here and throughout translation of Guardini's text is my own.

29. In this context, Bakhtin's remark on the connection between the temporality of gambling and that of prison life in Dostoevsky's novels is of interest. "The *time* of penal servitude and the time of gambling are—for all their profound differences—an identical *type of time*, similar in general to the time of crisis," Bakhtin writes (*PDP*, 172, italics in text). For Bakhtin, both gamblers and convicts represent "carnivalized collectives" by virtue of their markedly peripheral status, located as they are on the extreme exterior of normal or biological time (*PDP*, 172). However, as Bakhtin describes him, the gambler can be compared to both a man on the scaffold (*The Idiot*) and the one in prison (*House of the Dead*)—about to die (in case of a loss), or to be resurrected (in case of a sudden win). In *The House of the Dead*, the prisoners with long sentences could be compared to those daredevil gamblers who stake everything on their game not because they are hoping to win big, but rather because they do not value their "capital" and thus feel they have nothing to lose. The convicts recklessly "gamble away" their time in prison the same way they ostentatiously squander their possessions, to emphasize that the only time that is endowed with value, that really counts, is the time *after* their release.

30. The narrator's lack of attention to the "middle" period of his prison experience in the memoir, insightfully noted by Miller (*Dostoevsky's Unfinished Journey*) and Orwin (*Consequences of Consciousness*), is another expression of this dominant threshold temporality in the novel. Like Raskolnikov in the epilogue to *Crime and Punishment*, Goryanchikov describes primarily the first year of his imprisonment, telescoping the rest of his time in *katorga*, Miller observes (43). Donna Orwin notes that the first six chapters, "ostensibly covering only a single month of the narrator's ten years in the camp, take up more than a quarter of his narrative" (*Consequences of Consciousness*, 122). Part 1, which ends with the Christmas theatricals, takes up well over half of the narrative but covers only the first year. Orwin, who reads *Notes from the House of the Dead* as a Bildungsroman of sorts, ascribes this heavy focus on the hero's first impressions to Dostoevsky's wish to document Goryanchikov's formative *learning* experiences: we pay more attention to the new and learn from it, Orwin explains (122). In my interpretation, which takes stock of the novel's consistent chthonic symbolism, this selective coverage is remarkable for its omission of "the time in the middle,"

that is, of diachronically stretched time: the narrator's gaze momentarily rests on the immediate transitional experience following his symbolic death (imprisonment), impatiently rushing over to the longed-for moment of resurrection (release from prison), passionately anticipated by all convicts. In this sense, this narrative choice echoes the convicts' general refusal to be at home in the house of the dead, to truly "inhabit" their time in *katorga*.

31. "*Perhaps there is such a person*, who had been read a death sentence, put through a torment [of standing on the scaffold], and then told 'you are pardoned, go!' *Well, that kind of a person could, perhaps, tell us*," Myshkin muses teasingly, as he first approaches the topic of execution in his most unusual small talk with General Epanchin's astonished butler in part 1, chapter 2 (*Idiot*, 46; *PSS*, 21, translation emended). How much Dostoevsky's own life experiences are taken into account by modern readers in interpreting *The House of the Dead* depends on how we define the genre of this somewhat unusual work, which I view as a semi-autobiographical novel. Critics' definitions of the work's genre have differed widely in the twentieth and twenty-first century, as a testament to its ambiguous, liminal generic status: Frank compares it to similarly titled "notes" (*zapiski*) of Ivan Turgenev and Sergei Aksakov that blend fictional storytelling, personal recollections, and ethnographic observations in a loose, sketch-like form (*The Stir of Liberation*, 216–17); Miller and Dwyer compare it to a Gothic novel, each proposing her own list of features that distinguish this novel from a Gothic proper (Miller, *Dostoevsky's Unfinished Journey*, 23; Dwyer, "Dostoevsky's Prison House of Nation(s)," 223–24); Orwin treats it as a novel of education (*Consequences of Consciousness*, 122); while Burry terms it "a fictional memoir" (*Multi-Mediated Dostoevsky*, 213). While today's readership may find itself understandably distanced from Dostoevsky's biography, Dostoevsky's contemporaries certainly read the work in the immediate context of his well-known experience of exile, imprisonment, and mock-execution, a link my interpretation also maintains. According to various sources, the majority of contemporary readers saw the work as a thinly disguised account of the writer's *katorga* experience (Frank, *The Stir of Liberation*, 219).

32. Besides Dostoevsky's personal experience on the scaffold that likely informs these empathically reconstructed scenes, Victor Hugo's *The Last Day of a Condemned Man* (1829) should be mentioned as a key *literary* source here. Dostoevsky had referenced the novel, one of his brother's favorites, in a conversation with a fellow Petrashevets as he awaited execution in the Semionovsky Square and placed an imprecise quotation from the text ("On voit le soleil" / "One can see the sun" [in prison]") in a letter to Mikhail written immediately after the ordeal (see, for example, Frank, *The Stir of Liberation*, 24; *PSS*, 28.1:162). The special synchronic temporality of Myshkin's intensely narrated "mini-chronicles" of his imaginary prisoner's execution and several details of the prisoner's journey to the scaffold recall Hugo's novel (Liza Knapp, *The Annihilation of Inertia:*

Dostoevsky's Metaphysics [Evanston, Ill.: Northwestern University Press, 1996], 68–69). Dostoevsky's continued interest in Hugo's innovative literary technique in rendering characters' thought processes with maximum immediacy is documented in his preface to *The Meek One* (1876), where *The Last Day of a Condemned Man* is mentioned as a predecessor of the Russian writer's own experimentation with what would later become known as stream-of-consciousness narration (*PSS*, 24:6).

33. Vyacheslav Ivanov describes a similar enhancement of vision in his interpretation of Dostoevsky's own scaffold experience during his mock execution. "It may be that during those moments when, at the place of execution, Dostoevsky looked into the eyes of death, he underwent a sudden and decisive transformation of the soul—a beautiful death, followed by the unexpected gift of divine mercy to his corporeal shell . . . in these moments of preparedness for death he felt that his soul had overrun death and knew itself alive . . . [His] personality was thus forcibly extracted from the conditions of its earlier existence and became conscious of its own true substance" (Ivanov, *Freedom and the Tragic Life*, 26–27). It is implicit in Ivanov's interpretation that knowing his soul as *other*, as a metaphysical entity, not fully realized in the empirical reality, endowed Dostoevsky with a deep understanding and appreciation of otherness as an ontological category. This allowed the artist to create partial "doubles" of his miraculously enriched personality in the guise of his many characters, Ivanov concludes, and to grant these characters unprecedented freedom in the world of his novels (Ivanov, *Freedom and the Tragic Life*, 26–27; see also Anna Lisa Crone, "Polyphony in the Prose of Vjaceslav Ivanov: A Preliminary Consideration," in *Cultura et Memoria: Atti del terzo simposio internationale dedicato a Vjaceslav Ivanov I: Testi in italiano, francese, inglese*, ed. Fausto Malcovati [Florence: La Nuova Italia, 1988], 108–9).

34. R. L. Jackson, *The Art of Dostoevsky*, 68.

35. In Nancy Ruttenburg's interpretation, which minimizes Goryanchikov's hopeful sense of resurrection at the end of "Scenes from the House of the Dead," the frame narrator's inability to fathom the sullen, socially withdrawn Goryanchikov mirrors Goryanchikov's own failure to understand his reluctant interlocutors, the peasant convicts, *inside* the novel's frame and to sustain a meaningful conversation with them (*Dostoevsky's Democracy*, 69).

36. Morson, "Introductory Study," 25.

CHAPTER FIVE

1. See, for example, Dostoevsky's letter to S. A. Ivanova from January 1, 1868, and his letters to K. P. Pobedonostsev from May 19, 1879, and to N.A. Liubimov from June 11 and August 19, 1879, where such concerns are expressed (*PSS*, 28.2: 251, *PSS*, 30.1:66, 68, 102).

2. A. S. Dolinin, introduction to *F.M. Dostoevskii: Pis'ma I: 1832–1867*, by Feodor Dostoevsky, ed. A. S. Dolinin, vol. 1 (Moscow: Gosudarstvennoe Izdatel'stvo, 1928), 13. As Leonid Grossman puts it, "All of Dostoevsky's [post-Siberian] works are dedicated to the problem of Christ in contemporary life" (L. P. Grossman, "Put' Dostoevskogo," in *Tvorchestvo Dostoevskogo: Sbornik statei i materialov*, ed. L. P. Grossman [Odessa: Vseukrainskoe Gosudarstvennoe Izdatel'stvo, 1921], 100). A number of other critics also emphasize a cumulative and sustained effort on Dostoevsky's part to depict a philosophically and artistically successful ideal type. For example, P. M. Bitsilli suggests that all of Dostoevsky's works combined achieve the goal intended for his unrealized *Life of a Great Sinner*, namely, that of depicting an archetypal everyman (Bitsilli, "Pochemu Dostoevskii ne napisal 'Zhitiia velikogo greshnika,'" in *O Dostoevskom: Sbornik statei pod redaktsiei A.L. Bema*, ed. A. L. Bem, 2 vols. [Prague: Sklad Izdatel'stvo F. Svoboda, 1933], 2:30). In a similar vein, Dmitry Chizhevsky suggests that Dostoevsky achieves a greater and greater synthesis of the hero's otherworldly and human tasks as the author continues to refine his positive type throughout his artistic career ("Dostoevskii psikholog," 71). For other discussions of Dostoevsky's ideal characters and the author's special mission in defining a new positive type in Russian and world literature see, for example, R. Pletnev, "Serdtsem mudrye (O 'startsakh' u Dostoevskogo)," in Bem, *O Dostoevskom: Sbornik statei*, 2:73–92; Simon O. Lesser, "Saint and Sinner: Dostoevsky's 'Idiot,'" *Modern Fiction Studies* 4 (1958): 211–24; Murray Krieger, "Dostoevsky's 'Idiot': The Curse of Saintliness," in *Dostoevsky: A Collection of Critical Essays*, ed. Rene Wellek (Englewood Cliffs, N.J.: Twentieth Century Views, 1962), 39–52; Robert Bird, "Refiguring the Russian Type: Dostoevsky and the Limits of Realism," in *A New Word on "The Brothers Karamazov,"* ed. Robert Louis Jackson (Evanston, Ill.: Northwestern University Press, 2004), 17–30; Nina Perlina, *Varieties of Poetic Utterance: Quotation in "The Brothers Karamazov"* (Lanham, Md.: University Press of America, 1985), esp. 17, 43–44, 191–94; Diane Oenning Thompson, *"The Brothers Karamazov" and the Poetics of Memory* (Cambridge: Cambridge University Press, 1991), esp. 89–116, 273–75, 312–18.

3. I am responding to Avril Pyman's statement about Dostoevsky's positive characters, who, according to the critic, "go farther than any characters I know in the 19th century as a whole to make the good attractive" ("Dostoevsky in the Prism of the Orthodox Semiosphere," in Pattison and Thompson, *Dostoevsky and the Christian Tradition*, 112).

4. Romano Guardini's reading of the novel in *Religiöse Gestalten in Dostojewskijs Werk* largely reflects the first line of interpretation (see also G. K. Schchennikov, *Tselostnost' Dostoevskogo* [Ekaterinburg: Izdatel'stvo Ural'skogo Universiteta, 2001]), while Vyacheslav Ivanov (*Freedom and the Tragic Life*) and the majority of the twenty-first-century scholarship on *The Idiot* tend toward the

second answer (see, for example, Williams, *Dostoevsky: Language, Faith, and Fiction*; Sarah Young, *Dostoevsky's "The Idiot" and the Ethical Foundation of Narrative: Reading, Narrating, Scripting* [London: Anthem, 2004]; Sergei Bocharov, "'O bessmyslennaia vechnost'!' Ot 'Nedonoska' k 'Idiotu,'" in Kasatkina, *Roman F.M. Dostoevskogo "Idiot": Sovremennoe sostoianie izucheniia*, 111–36; Evgenii Trofimov, "Obraz Myshkina v pervoi chasti romana 'Idiot,'" ibid., 239–49; Andrei Manovtsev, "Svet i soblazn," ibid., 250–90; Dennis Patrick Slattery, *The Idiot, Dostoevsky's Fantastic Prince: A Phenomenological Approach* [New York: Peter Lang, 1983]).

5. See chapters 1 and 2.

6. Frank, *Dostoevsky: The Miraculous Years, 1865–1871* (Princeton, N.J.: Princeton University Press, 1995), 318.

7. See, for example, *Idiot*, 68; *PSS*, 39, *Idiot*, 137; *PSS*, 98, *Idiot*, 363; *PSS*, 290.

8. Thus, in my usage, *consummation* is by no means identical with Bakhtin's reifying and unfair "finalization" (*zavershenie*), as it is used in *PDP*. Rather, *consummation* is utilized as a conceptual tool of Bakhtin's early, architectonic period, revised and enriched through Scheler's related philosophical concepts in chapters 1 and 2 of this study.

9. Such accusations seem to be commonplace in the new wave of criticism on *The Idiot*, where Myshkin's activity is interpreted as a blatant perversion of the Christian message, a replacement of love with merely sentimental, despiritualized empathy (e.g., Manovtsev, "Svet i soblazn," 278; Trofimov, "Obraz Myshkina v pervoi chasti romana 'Idiot,'" 246; see also Slattery, *"The Idiot," Dostoevsky's Fantastic Prince*, 213).

10. Paul Tillich, *Systematic Theology*, 3 vols. (Chicago: University of Chicago Press, 1951–63), 1:283.

11. Tillich, *Love, Power, and Justice: Ontological Analyses and Ethical Applications* (New York: Geoffrey Cumberlege, Oxford University Press, 1954), 115.

12. Tillich, *Systematic Theology*, 1:283. In a similar vein, according to Anders Nygren, "Only that love which pronounces judgment on all that is not love is in the deepest sense a restoring and saving love" (*Agape and Eros*, 104). On the compatibility of love and forgiveness with (constructive) judgment also see Barth, *Evangelical Theology*, 93; and Kierkegaard, *Works of Love*, 110–11. Defined as "judgment against not-love," the concept of judgment seems compatible with Bakhtinian *consummation*, precisely as a means of preserving love's *active surplus* in the process of empathetic understanding. If developed, it could become a useful addition to Bakhtin's architectonics, since, as noted by critics, judgment remains an "undeveloped Christian motif" in Bakhtin's work (see, for example, Coates, *Christianity in Bakhtin*, 21, 50).

13. The difference between Nastasia Filippovna's particular case of ressentiment and that exhibited by the Underground Man seems to result from the fact

that the characteristic balance of ressentiment aggression, always affecting both the *self* and the *other*, is "tilted" toward the self in Nastasia Filippovna's case and toward the other in the case of the Underground Man.

14. For Bakhtin's discussion of the process of self-objectification and the crucial differences in experiencing the "I-for-myself" and the "I-for-another" see "AH," 38.

15. In this context, it is significant that in the notebooks for *The Idiot* there are rather frequent mentions of the Prince's ability to judge others and to affect positive change by doing so. The references to the hero's productive judgment ("sud kniazia" [*PSS*, 9:280, 278, 279]; "osuzhdenie kniazem" [*PSS*, 9:278]; "raz"iasnenie kazhdomu sebia samogo" [*PSS*, 9:280] / "the Prince's judgment [of others]"; "the Prince's explanation of each character") seem to coincide with a vision of a more effective, "useful" hero in the notes, helpful to many major characters and capable of "rehabilitating" the heroine (see, for example, *PSS*, 9: 278–80).

16. Compare, for example, the devastating spiritual effects of Stavrogin's absolute pride on those driven to actual or virtual suicide by his profound existential detachment, intensely provoking precisely by virtue of its absolute and, as it were, innate quality.

17. Guardini, *Religiöse Gestalten*, 322.

18. The fundamental psychological correctness of Aglaya's judgment has been acknowledged by critics (see, for example, Malcolm V. Jones, "Sisters and Rivals: Variation on a Theme in Dostoevskii's Fiction," in *Die Wirklichkeit der Kunst und das Abenteuer der Interpretation: Festschrift für Horst-Jürgen Gerigk*, ed. K. Manger [Heidelberg: Universitätsverlag C. Winter, 1999], 163).

19. This disregard of the heroine's own ethical concerns at the moment of passionate indignation has also been noted by Sarah Young (*Dostoevsky's "The Idiot" and the Ethical Foundation of Narrative*, 65).

20. See chapter 1; also see Bakhtin's *TPA* (15) and Scheler's *The Nature of Sympathy* (e.g., *GW*, 7:70, 81); in *PDP* Bakhtin also notes Myshkin's lack of a specific "place" in life but does not link it with the challenges of his empathetic experiences. "One might say that Myshkin is not able to enter into life completely, cannot become completely embodied, cannot accept any definiteness in life that would limit a personality," Bakhtin writes (*PDP*, 173), but does not show how this characteristic feature impacts the Prince's ability to practice active love and empathy.

21. The devastating toll Nastasia Filippovna's pain takes on the Prince reveals the emotional costs and spiritual challenges inherent in agapeistic compassion. Cases of such intense emotional involvement with the empathized suffering, which is not limited to loveless emotional contagion but may also occur in loving compassion, suggest that Scheler may be oversimplifying the process

by stating that in authentic compassion (*Mitgefühl*) the empathized emotional state is given entirely in the other (see *GW*, 7:52–53). In this context, Matthias Schlossberger's criticism of Scheler's "purist" depiction of empathy may be relevant. Contrary to Scheler's belief, our empathized feelings do "feel like something," Schlossberger suggests. According to Schlossberger, in actuality, we do partake of the sufferer's emotional state, at least to some degree, be it because empathy itself presupposes such emotional participation or because it does not appear isolated and is always mixed in with some amount of emotional infection (Schlossberger, "Das Mitgefühl als Gefühl," in *Vernunft und Gefühl: Schelers Phänomenologie des emotionalen Lebens*, ed. Christian Bermes, Wolfhart Henckmann, and Heinz Leonardy [Wurzburg: Königshausen & Neumann, 2003], 49). The fact that one can indeed become emotionally overwhelmed by the sufferer's pain makes an active compassionate response especially challenging: one must often struggle to retain the hopeful surplus of vision in respect to the sufferer before his pain becomes equally debilitating for the empathizer. The moral-practical necessity of separating oneself from another's pain is corroborated by contemporary research in neuroscience: from the point of view of current neuro-scientific theories of empathy, Myshkin's exceptionally sensitive perception of Nastasia's suffering is a hindrance to compassion, rather than an advantage. "Maxing out" on accuracy in knowing what the other is experiencing may be detrimental to delivering much-needed help, some studies have shown, because the overly sensitive empathizer is often paralyzed by personal distress in her efforts to ease the pain (Liesbet Goubert et al., "Perceiving Others in Pain: Experimental and Clinical Evidence on the Role of Empathy," in *The Social Neuro-Science of Empathy*, ed. Jean Decety and William Ickes [Cambridge, Mass.: MIT Press, 2009], 156; S. D. Hodges and K. J. K. Klein, "Regulating the Costs of Empathy: The Price of Being Human," *Journal of Socio-Economics* 30 [2001]: 437–52). Rather, observers with just average empathetic accuracy, that is, those who have a general sense of knowing that the other is in pain, but are not emotionally overcome by it, may be the most effective in aiding the sufferer, data suggest (Goubert et al., "Perceiving Others in Pain," 156; L. Goubert et al., "Facing Others in Pain: The Effects of Empathy," *Pain* 118 [2005]: 285–88).

22. See, for example, "AH," 111.

23. See, for example, Bakhtin's observations on the phenomenological significance of confession and absolution ("AH," 57).

24. Here my interpretation differs significantly from Sarah Young's assessment of the heroine's "scripting" of her own fate in *Dostoevsky's "The Idiot" and the Ethical Foundations of Narrative* (2004). Following Bakhtin's conclusions in *PDP* that Nastasia Filippovna "does not know her own final word about herself" (*PDP*, 234), Young states that Nastasia Filippovna's activity is directed at keeping herself radically unfinalized or "unconsummated," while I argue that, frustrated

in her search for positive consummation, the heroine finalizes her own self most violently (see Young, *Dostoevsky's "The Idiot" and the Ethical Foundations of Narrative*, esp. 63–74).

25. Compare, for example, David M. Bethea's interpretation in *The Shape of Apocalypse in Modern Russian Fiction* (Princeton, N.J.: Princeton University Press, 1989).

26. In the notebooks Nastasia Filippovna's spiritual renewal is referred to as "vosstanovlenie," "reabilitatsiia," "perevospitaniie," "voskreseniie"—*rehabilitation*, *reformation*, and *resurrection* (see *PSS*, 9:245, 251). It is evident from the notebooks that the hero's central mission consists precisely in "resurrecting" the heroine, "vosstanovit' i voskresit' cheloveka" ("to rehabilitate and resurrect a person"), a task that attains not merely ethical but also spiritual significance (*PSS*, 9:264). The test of his Christlike love is the spiritual renewal of one remarkably challenging soul: "The Prince announces upon marrying Nastasia Filippovna that *resurrecting* one person is better than performing all the heroic deeds of Alexander the Great" ("luchshe odnu *voskresit'* . . .") (*PSS*, 9:268).

27. The pattern of leading and following is also sustained in the beginning of the episode 1, with Rogozhin leading Myshkin through the dark labyrinth of his house ultimately to receive a blessing from Rogozhin's mother. Compare: episode 1: "They passed through the same rooms that the Prince had passed through, *Rogozhin walking a little in front and the Prince behind him*" ("*Rogozhin shel nemnogo vperedi, kniaz' za nim*") (*Idiot*, 235; *PSS*, 181); episode 2: "Lev Nikolaevich, *follow me*, old man [stupai brat *za mnoi*], I need you" (*Idiot*, 607; *PSS*, 500).

28. Some of the similarities between the two chapters have been noted by critics. For example, Dennis Slattery notes the similarity of the heroes' two meetings at the hotel (*The Idiot, Dostoevsky's Fantastic Prince*, 202–3), while Jacques Catteau remarks that in the final chapter "the strange walk, with [Myshkin and Rogozhin] on opposite pavements, begins again—like a musical theme in reverse," for this time they are moving in the opposite direction (Catteau, *Dostoevsky and the Process of Literary Creation*, trans. Audrey Littlewood [Cambridge: Cambridge University Press, 1989], 352).

29. For a discussion of the motif of vision and its mythical implications in *The Idiot*, see I. R. Arkhundova, "'Voploshchenie khaosa i nebytiia' (Parfen Rogozhin—demon smerti ili personifikatsiia sud'by)," in Kasatkina, *Roman F.M. Dostoevskogo "Idiot": Sovremennoe sostoianie izucheniia*, 364–89; and A. B. Krinitsyn, "O spetsyfike vizual'nogo mira u Dostoevskogo i semantike 'videniia' v romane 'Idiot,'" ibid., 170–205.

30. Note also the connection of these gestures with that of Rogozhin's mother blessing their brotherhood with the sign of the cross and the reinforcement of this symbolic link by Myshkin's comment after the attack: "Before Parfyon had time to touch her, the old woman *raised her right hand*, put three

fingers together and devoutly made the sign of the cross three times over the Prince" [*Idiot*, 240]; "Why did you take me to your mother then? Did you think *that would hold back your hand*? . . . *If you hadn't raised your hand* against me then (which God averted), what would I have been to you now?" (*Idiot*, 377). ("Starushka, prezhde chem Parfen uspel vziat'sia, *podniala svoiu pravuiu ruku*, slozhila pal'tsy v tri persta i tri raza nabozhno perekrestila kniazia" [*PSS*, 185]; "Dlia chego ty menia k starushke togda vodil? *Svoiu ruku etim dumal sderzhat'*? . . . *Ne podymi ty ruku* togda na menia (kotoruiu Bog otvel), chem by ia teper' pred toboi okazalsia?" [*PSS*, 303]). These emphatic repetitions of raising one's hands (*ruki* / *ruku*)—to either make the sign of the cross / embrace someone or to aim a knife at them—are an extended reference to the parable-like (cautionary?) tale Myshkin tells Rogozhin during the same visit before the attack, about a man who kills a friend with a knife, but not before saying a prayer and making the sign of the cross.

31. In *Dostoevsky, Language, Faith and Fiction*, Rowan Williams writes that "Myshkin *never* seems to turn full-face to his interlocutors, despite the appearance of utter transparency" (125). As my detailed analysis of the sometimes ambivalent "dialogue" of glances exchanged between Rogozhin and Myshkin demonstrates, this is clearly an exaggeration, and the Prince's communication pattern is more complex, but, among Dostoevsky's saintly heroes, Myshkin is certainly guiltier of evading direct interaction with his peers than others. The Prince is certainly less consistent in maintaining direct addressivity with other characters than Alyosha Karamazov, an issue that will be discussed in more detail in the next chapter.

32. Compare Myshkin's sermon-like internal dialogue during his shameful flight from Rogozhin, eulogizing the value of open and direct encounters with one's neighbors (*Idiot*, 247–49; *PSS*, 191–94, discussed earlier, in chapter 4).

33. A. B. Krinitsyn notes that Myshkin's gesture of turning Rogozhin to the light is analogous to his earlier gesture of turning Nastasia Filippovna's portrait "to the window, closer to the light," also to "read" it better (*PSS*, 68; Krinitsyn, "O spetsifike vizual'nogo mira," 195).

34. Parallel passages are underscored, marked with italics, bald script, and a matching letter to indicate textual correspondences. The English translation of the table is provided below.

35. As Dostoevsky scholars have long pointed out, these utterances are close to Pilate's "Behold the Man": "Se Chelovek" (John 19:5) (see *PSS*, 9:452). In this context, Dostoevsky's observation in the notebooks for *The Idiot* that man is perhaps most real in the character of the Idiot ("Mozhet byt', v Idiote chelovek-to bolee deistvitelen" (*PSS*, 9:276), may also be read in the context of the specific meaning of "Chelovek": for Dostoevsky, man is most real in Christ, because Christ shows humanity its spiritual possibilities (see also a similar statement in the notebooks to *The Devils* [*PSS*, 11:112]).

36. Guardini, *Religiöse Gestalten*, 418.

37. See Ermilova, "Tragediia russkogo Khrista," 448.

38. One level of meaning behind this symmetry may be attributed to a realistic depiction of the hero's illness. Interestingly enough, the peculiar déjà vu effect conveyed to the reader in the novel's final chapter may be akin to a characteristic side effect of epilepsy. According to recent research, many epileptics experience the déjà vu effect, a phenomenon perceived as rare and strange by healthy people, on a regular basis (see Michael D. Lemonick, "Explaining Déjà vu," *Time* [August 20, 2007]: 50–51; and Thomas J. McHugh et al., "Dentate Gyrus NMDA Receptors Mediate Rapid Pattern Separation in the Hippocampal Network," *Science* 317, no. 94 [2007]: 94–99). For a discussion of the medically valid features of epilepsy depicted in *The Idiot,* see also Nikolai Bogdanov, "'Sviashchennaia bolezn' kniazia Myshkina—Morbus Sacer Fedora Dostoevskogo," in Kasatkina, *Roman F.M. Dostoevskogo "Idiot": Sovremennoe sostoianie izucheniia*, 337–57; and Toni Miksanek, "Dostoevsky's *The Idiot* and Psychic Disorders in Epilepsy," *Perspectives in Biology and Medicine* 25, no. 2 (1982): 231–37.

39. Guardini, *Religiöse Gestalten*, 402.

40. In terms of contemporary psychology, based on the latest findings of neuroscience, the label "compassion fatigue" would be somewhat appropriate here, if we were to diagnose Myshkin's spiritual problem from the psychobiological point of view. This phenomenon, first introduced by C. Joinson ("Coping with Compassion Fatigue," *Nursing* 4 [1992]: 116–21), is described as a "state of reduced capacity for [active] compassion as a consequence of being exhausted from absorbing the suffering of others" (Olga Klimecki and Tania Singer, "Empathic Distress Fatigue rather than Compassion Fatigue? Integrating Findings from Empathy Research in Psychology and Social Neuroscience," in *Pathological Altruism*, ed. Barbara Oakley et al. [Oxford: Oxford University Press, 2012], 368). Recent psychological and neuroscientific examinations of the phenomenon that voice the same concerns about empathetic over-identification that had been expressed by Scheler and Bakhtin more than half a century earlier conclude that the empathizer's loss of autonomy results in pathological behavior that impairs her capacity to help and often proves harmful to the object of empathy. In several thought-provoking studies the phenomenon was recently linked with "pathological empathy" and pathological, ultimately pernicious altruism (see, for example, Klimecki and Singer, "Empathic Distress Fatigue"; C. Figley, "Compassion Fatigue: Psychotherapists' Chronic Lack of Self Care," *Journal of Clinical Psychology* 58 [2002]: 1433–41; B. M. Sabo, "Compassion Fatigue and Nursing Work: Can We Accurately Capture the Consequences of Caring Work?" *International Journal of Nursing Practice* 12 [2006]:136–42; see also Barbara Oakley, *Cold-Blooded Kindness: Neuroquirks of a Codependent Killer, or Just Give Me a Shot at Loving You, Dear, and Other Reflections on Helping That Hurts* [Amherst, N.Y.: Prometheus Books, 2011]; and Oakley et al., *Pathological Altruism*).

41. Shestov, "Dostoevsky and Nietzsche," 166.

42. In Scheler's system the first "transgression" of empathy is called the "idiopathic" form of unitary feeling (*GW*, 7: 20) (compare Bakhtin's description of the phenomenon in terms of literary theory: the author takes complete possession of the hero ["AH," 20]) and the second one—the "heteropathic" form of unitary feeling (*GW*, 7:21) (compare Bakhtin's: the hero takes possession of the author ["AH," 17]).

43. Ivanov, *Freedom and the Tragic Life*, 90, 91.

44. Bocharov, "'O bessmyslennaia vechnost'!' Ot 'Nedonoska' k 'Idiotu,'" 132. This view seems to be at least partly shared by Rowan Williams, who, in a recent study of Dostoevsky's religious vision, notes Myshkin's difficulty in establishing his own distinct place among others and their discourses and in controlling his "self-presentation" to his interlocutors, which leads to a failure to take responsibility for his words and actions (*Dostoevsky: Language, Faith and Fiction*, see, e.g., 124, 125, 145). Williams refers provocatively to Myshkin's "'undialectical' or unfallen goodness" (145), which he sees as destructive, also suggesting that this would-be Christ has somehow foregone Incarnation.

45. Bitsilli, "Pochemu Dostoevsky ne napisal 'Zhitiia velikogo greshnika,'" 28.

46. Guardini, *Religiöse Gestalten*, 405.

47. See "AH," 111, 56; for similar conclusions in Scheler's philosophy see *GW*, 12:160, *GW*, 9:83, *GW*, 7:78, 103.

48. See Guardini, *Religiöse Gestalten*, 405, 414.

49. In this context, it is relevant that in Scheler's theory Incarnation provides a specific *form* in which spirit can live actively and be effective; for Scheler, this concrete form is that of a "person" (see, for example, *GW*, 10:63–64, *GW*, 2:294; Leonardy, *Liebe und Person*, 129). In distinguishing between love as *affect* and love as an *act*, the latter expressed through concrete, responsible deeds of caring, or active empathy, Scheler also provides an important philosophical basis for explaining Myshkin's dilemma. In early Bakhtin the notion of endowing the other with "the gift of form" is also extremely important and linked with the notion of Incarnation (see, for example, "AH," 24, 5). For both thinkers, the process of active empathy entails giving love a specific form, as was implicitly shown in chapters 1 and 2.

50. Some critics correctly point out that other characters in the novel actively contribute to Myshkin's failure. See, for example, Karen Stepanian's claim that the lack of "sobornost'" in the characters' response to Myshkin's love impacts the outcome of his spiritual quest (Stepanian, "Iurodstvo i bezumie, smert i voskresenie, bytie i nebytie v romane 'Idiot,'" in Kasatkina, *Roman F.M. Dostoevskogo "Idiot": Sovremennoe sostoianie izucheniia*, 144) and Ermilova's observation about the lack of an adequate answer to Myshkin's offerings: "No energy issues from the characters' answering 'gestures.' The lack of response on Nastasia Filippovna's part is amazing in this respect" (Ermilova, "Tragediia 'russkogo Khrista' ili o neozhidannosti okonchaniia 'Idiota,'" 459). See also Frank Seeley

on Aglaya's share of responsibility for the novel's final catastrophe (*From the Heyday of the Superfluous Man to Chekhov: Essays on 19th Century Russian Literature* [Nottingham, Eng.: Astra, 1994], 140–48).

51. George Steiner, *Tolstoy or Dostoevsky: An Essay in the Old Criticism* (Chicago: University of Chicago Press, 1959), 313.

52. For example, Olga Meerson reminds Dostoevsky's readers that the logic of redemption through Christ's sacrifice is unique because Christ is unique and not "typological," thus, in the absence of Christ, this logic inevitably turns into a caricature (Meerson, "Khristos ili 'Kniaz'-Khristos? Svidetel'stvo generala Ivolgina," in Kasatkina, *Roman F.M. Dostoevskogo "Idiot": Sovremennoe sostoianie izucheniia*, 47). She illustrates her thesis by reading General Ivolgin's absurd story of Private Kolpakov's "resurrection" as a carnivalized or travestied allusion to Christ's mission of redemption meant to warn the reader against a too-literal, Christological reading of another character's "story," that of the saintly Prince Myshkin ("Khristos ili 'Kniaz'-Khristos?" 56). Meerson's reading of General Ivolgin's "witness account" is witty and insightful, but, in my opinion, it does not negate the symbolic level of (Christological) signification inherent in Myshkin's image.

53. In Dostoevsky's *Diary of a Writer* and various notebooks one often encounters a juxtaposition between a belief in Christian teachings and that in the person of Christ, "the incarnated ideal." The Russian people may be ignorant of the Christian doctrine, but they know it inwardly (by means of "serdechnoe znanie"), through understanding the *person* of Christ and his sacrificial love, Dostoevsky argues in *Diary of a Writer* (*PSS*, 21:38). In notebooks for *The Devils* we come across the theme of *imitatio Christi*, "podrazha[nie] sovershenstvu etogo *obraza* [Khrista]" ("imitation of the perfection of [Christ's] *image*") (*PSS*, 11:113), through *personal* following as a "natural" spiritual undertaking, "possible" for the entire humanity precisely because the emergence of Christ is itself proof of the reality of his ideal: "ideal byl vo ploti, a stalo byt' ne nevozmozhen i dostizhim vsemu chelovechestvu" ("the ideal was in the flesh, therefore it is not impossible but achievable for the entire humanity") (*PSS*, 11:112). In this context, the characters' call for everyone to "become Christlike" ("Voobrazite, chto vse Khristy"; "predpolozhit', chto vse Khristy" / "Imagine that everyone is [a] Christ") (*PSS*, 11:106, 192–93) is quite consistent with the *reality* of the Christian ideal in Dostoevsky's thought. And although some of these utterances belong to spiritually tormented, morally problematic characters, who are still searching for a firm ideological stance vis-à-vis God and are by no means the reader's moral or spiritual compasses, the belief in the reality of Christ (or at least, the necessity of such a belief), expressed here is certainly shared by Dostoevsky. It is interesting that the proposition "suppose we all become Christlike," which, for some theologians, serves as an argument against issuing "the absolute blank check" to the other in the practice of Christian love (as in: what would happen if we all sac-

rificed ourselves for each other? a global suicide? See, e.g., Gene Outka, *Agape: An Ethical Analysis* [New Haven, Conn.: Yale University Press, 1972], 276; and Kurt Baier, *The Moral Point of View* [Ithaca, N.Y.: Cornell University Press, 1958], 196–97), is accepted without hesitation by Dostoevsky. In *The Idiot*, with Myshkin's and Nastasia's simultaneous attempts at self-sacrifice, one may see an artistic enactment of this theological "test of feasibility," an attempt at answering the question of what would happen if all sacrificed themselves for the others' sake. Although the practical reality of this poorly coordinated mutual sacrifice is problematic in the novel, many readers feel that the soundness of the sacrificial *ideal* remains uncompromised.

54. Andrey Manovtsev suggests that the Prince "blocks" the real Christ from the many souls in need of Christian salvation in the novel ("Svet i soblazn," 268). See also Meerson, "Khristos ili 'Kniaz'-Khristos" and Trofimov, "Obraz Myshkina."

55. Guardini, *Religiöse Gestalten*, 414.

56. Here the hero appears as an effective "doer" ("[he] is firm in action [*tverd v dele*]," "useful" [*PSS*, 9:227, 259]), while the major characters' fundamental need in the Prince is emphasized. The hero's usefulness in ministering to his needy neighbors is celebrated with quiet joy: "But the joyful realization of being useful fills him"; "The Prince's quiet joy at being useful" (*PSS*, 9:257, 259); but also: "impotence to help [others]," which anticipates the Prince's predicament in the novel in its final form (*PSS*, 9:241). See also *PSS*, 9:252, 278.

CHAPTER SIX

1. My assessment of Alyosha Karamazov as one of Dostoevsky's most successful ideal heroes is shared by a long list of scholars. Among them are Diane Oenning Thompson, Dmitry Chizhevsky, Viacheslav Ivanov, and Romano Guardini. If Ivanov describes Alyosha as "the one who would do Christ's work" (*Freedom and the Tragic Life*, 157) and Chizhevsky admits Dostoevsky's continual progress in renegotiating the ideal of Christian personhood, without, however, noting a contrast between Alyosha and Myshkin ("Dostoevskii psikholog," 71), Thompson is perhaps the closest to my position in her assessment of Alyosha as Dostoevsky's most authentic Christological hero. According to Thompson, *The Brothers Karamazov*, "more than any other of Dostoevsky's works, bears evidence of [his intended] ideal artistic project [a book about Christ] coming to fruition," while Alyosha is "the only Urbild [of Christ] truly realized in the novel" (Thompson, *"The Brothers Karamazov" and the Poetics of Memory* [Cambridge: Cambridge University Press, 1991], 318; 308). For more critical evaluations of Alyosha's spiritual accomplishments, see, for example, Olga Meerson, *Dostoevsky's Taboos* (Dresden: Dresden University Press, 1998), 183–209; James Rice, "The Covert Design of *The Brothers Karamazov*: Alesha's Pathology and Dialectic," *Slavic Review* 68, no. 2 (2009): 355–75; and Carol Apollonio, *Dostoevsky's*

Secrets: Reading against the Grain (Evanston, Ill.: Northwestern University Press, 2009), 157, 163–64.

2. All quotations from *The Idiot* and *The Brothers Karamazov* in this chapter are given in my own translation and all references are to the collected works edition (*PSS*). For the sake of clarity, quotations from *The Idiot* and *The Brothers Karamazov* are followed by the volume number in *PSS* (vol. 8 and vols. 14 and 15, respectively) and the page numbers in that edition, separated by a colon.

3. We shall recall that, in notes for *The Idiot*, Dostoevsky defines the Prince's task in the novel as that of "rehabilitating and resurrecting a person": "*vosstanovit' i voskresit' cheloveka*" (*PSS*, 9:264). It is clear that in the final version of the novel Nastasia Filippovna remains "the one person" whose resurrection may validate the hero's Christlike status; she is certainly a character most in need of his ministry: "resurrecting one person is better than performing all the heroic deeds of Alexander the Great" ("luchshe odnu voskresit'"), Dostoevsky writes in the notebooks for *The Idiot* (*PSS*, 9:268). On the other hand, Myshkin's mission can be read more broadly as well, as that of resurrecting a human being (the Dostoevskian "man in man," *chelovek v cheloveke*) in each of his neighbors. The majority of current Russian scholars tend to see in the Pavlovsk passage not a solemn allusion to the Gospel episode, but a perversion or, at best, a parody of Gethsemane (see, for example, Karen Stepanian, *Iavlenie i dialog v romanakh F. M. Dostoevskogo* [St. Petersburg: Kniga, 2009], 174; Tatiana Kasatkina, *O tvoriashchei prirode slova: Ontologichnost' slova v tvorchestve F. M. Dostoevskogo kak osnova "realizma v vysshem smysle"* [Moscow: IMLI RAN, 2004], 256). I disagree with such a negative reading of Myshkin's mission in the novel.

4. Thompson, *"The Brothers Karamazov" and the Poetics of Memory*, 318.

5. "The Elder has sent me to appease and unite [others]," Alyosha reminds himself in book 6, chapter 6, as he deliberates on the best course of action to help both of his brothers (*PSS*, 14:178).

6. See my analysis of Myshkin's experience of time in chapter 5 of this book, as well as relatively recent medical findings pointing to the merging of the past, present, and future in the consciousness of epileptics. One example of such peculiar experience of time is the phenomenon of déjà vu often reported by epileptics (Lemonic, "Explaining Déjà vu," 51; also see McHugh, "Dentate Gyrus NMDA Receptors"). Myshkin's excessive absentmindedness and detachment from his surroundings during the episode makes Mrs. Epanchin suspect an epileptic attack (a "pripadok"), and his vacant stare at Aglaya that frightens her is consistent with epileptic symptoms.

7. "This first vision [Rogozhin] could be the harbinger and forerunner of a second vision [Nastasia Filippovna]," the narrator states enigmatically less than a page later, describing Myshkin's growing fear: "How could he have forgotten about the possibility of that meeting when he had set out for the pleasure gardens?" (*PSS*, 8:288).

8. Nadine Natov needs to be credited for pointing out the great multiplicity of temptation episodes in *The Brothers Karamazov* (see "The Ethical and Structural Significance of the Three Temptations in *The Brothers Karamazov*," *Dostoevsky Studies* 8 [1987]: 3–43). Drawing on Vladimir Soloviev's conclusions in *Lectures on Godmanhood*, a work in many ways inspired by Dostoevsky's theology, Natov interprets Christ's temptations as part of a complex process of his unification with God, and then points to Alyosha's temptations as a sign of his Christian calling. In a similar vein, Diane Thompson points out that Alyosha's temptations, as an evocation of the three temptations of Christ, are an essential element of a saint's journey in the hagiographic genre (*"The Brothers Karamazov" and the Poetics of Memory*, 200).

9. N. P. Antsiferov, *Problemy urbanisma v russkoi khudozhestvennoi literature* (Moscow: IMLI RAN, 2009), 269–86.

10. Ibid., 274.

11. See Morson and Emerson, *Mikhail Bakhtin: Creation of a Prosaics*, 61, 66, 91.

12. This hopeful "resolution" or *consummation* proposed by Dostoevsky's *homo amans* is similar to what Sarah Young calls Myshkin's "active script" to save Nastasia Filippovna by inducing her to "rewrite" the scenario of her life according to his spiritually affirming vision of her better, ideal self (*Dostoevsky and the Ethical Foundation of Narrative*, 109). This yet unrealized, productive *consummation*, posited before a Dostoevskian dialogist as a task, is what Arpad Kovacs also sees behind Myshkin's interference in the fate of Nastasia Filippovna, namely, it is the necessity to realize "in practice . . . those principles of life which had found expression in his external monologues" (Kovacs, "The Poetics of *The Idiot*: On the Problem of Dostoevsky's Thinking about Genre," in *Critical Essays on Dostoevsky*, ed. Robin Feuer Miller [Boston: G.K. Hall, 1986], 117).

13. Within the framework of personalist philosophy used in my analysis, this dichotomy may be seen as an opposition between the *personal* and the objectifying, *im*personal view of human nature that replaces the individual ineffable with a predetermined, psychologically or socially finalized human "type." Or, from a literary standpoint, these two different types of *zavershenie* (or *razreshenie*) could be seen as the marks of two competing generic traditions structuring some of Dostoevsky's works: the criminal novel and hagiography, each with its own tradition of narrative closure. The latter view is likely to be endorsed by those who approach Dostoevsky with the help of Bakhtin's theory of genre, for example, Gary Saul Morson, who claims that Dostoevsky's Christological hero is actually "a generic refugee" in the nineteenth-century realist novel from the realm of hagiography ("The God of Onions: *The Brothers Karamazov* and the Mythic Prosaic," in *A New Word on "The Brothers Karamazov,"* ed. Robert Louis Jackson [Evanston, Ill.: Northwestern University Press, 2004], 112). The fact that in Dostoevsky's works the logic of plot development and that of the

characters' metaphysical development are two separate, not necessarily coinciding forces is routinely noticed by critics: as Robin Feuer Miller elegantly puts it, in Dostoevsky, "a metaphysical riddle is [usually] superimposed on a mystery plot" (*"The Brothers Karamazov": The Worlds of the Novel* [New York: Twayne, 1992], 93). In my analysis, it is important to emphasize that in Dostoevsky the *essential*, sometimes paradoxical, definition of the heroes, which often emerges in opposition to the objectifying mechanisms of plot development and closure, is the *personal* definition, understood by Dostoevsky in the context of the Christian concept of personhood. Thus, I would modify Bakhtin's statement that "dialogue is *always* external to the plot in Dostoevsky" (*PDP*, 252), saying instead that *agapeistic dialogue*, that is, those psycho-spiritual investigations that seek out one's morally productive, non-objectifying, and uniquely personal definition, *may* indeed be outside of, or even in conflict with, the plot in Dostoevsky.

14. One obvious reason for this difference between the two heroes is that Prince Myshkin, the longtime resident of Switzerland, "has no stable connection to the [Russian] soil," a lack that has been seen as problematic by some critics in the context of Dostoevsky's own enthusiasm for the "philosophy of the soil"("pochvinnichestvo") (Pletnev, "Serdtsem mudrye," 75). On the other hand, Dostoevsky's "earthier" last saint, Alyosha Karamazov, is well grounded in a concrete place, *rooted* in provincial Russia. According to Zenkovsky, in Alyosha one finds a Christian transfiguration of that sometimes pernicious "force of Karamozovian *baseness*" ("sila *nizosti* Karamazovskoi") which effectively grounds the youngest Karamazov, binding him to the world at large and to the Russian soil (V. V. Zenkovsky, "Fedor Pavlovich Karamazov," in Bem, *O Dostoevskom: Sbornik statei pod redaktsiei A.L. Bema*, 2:110).

15. The motif of recognition is, of course, of major importance in *The Brothers Karamazov* precisely because of its Christological symbolism. In this context, it is significant that Christ in Ivan's legend is immediately recognized by everyone but the unbelieving Grand Inquisitor, who asks incredulously: "Is it you? You?" (*PSS*, 14:228). The mutual recognition of Myshkin and Nastasia Filippovna, discussed in chapter 5, certainly belongs to the same symbolic cluster in Dostoevsky's semiotic system, but in *The Brothers Karamazov* Alyosha achieves a much wider recognition as "the one who does Christ's work," as Viacheslav Ivanov aptly puts it (*Freedom and the Tragic Life*, 157). For an intriguing, if not fully developed, suggestion that Myshkin does not allow himself to be truly seen or recognized by others, "despite the appearance of utter transparency," a feature that likens him to Stavrogin, see Williams, *Dostoevsky: Language, Faith and Fiction*, 125 (see also 124, 145).

16. As I demonstrate in chapters 4 and 5, one of the reasons Myshkin is unable to face Rogozhin in the notorious "stalking" scene (part 2, chapter 5), to unambiguously identify the pair of "those eyes" and to look into them directly, is because in his over-identification with Rogozhin the Prince ultimately loses all

sense of his own identity and agency. Here the hero's predicament reflects the perils of passive empathy that are beginning to be discussed more and more in current psychological and philosophical literature on the subject. For example, Peter Goldie's recent objections to the "empathetic perspective shifting," that is, seeing the world from the perspective of the other that usurps the agent's own point of view, have to do with such agent's impaired capacity to interact or dialogue with the object of his empathy (Goldie, "Anti-Empathy," in *Empathy: Philosophical and Psychological Perspectives*, ed. Amy Coplan and Peter Goldie [Oxford: Oxford University Press, 2011], 302–17). "If A is engaged in empathetic perspective shifting with B, he is . . . imagining *being* B, so obviously A cannot imagine *meeting* B," Goldie argues (303, italics in text). Indeed, Myshkin cannot *meet* Rogozhin in the notorious episode preceding the murder attempt, because he has *become* Rogozhin. As we shall see, Alyosha, who withstands the temptation to over-identify with others, is more comfortable facing these others in direct dialogical encounters.

17. Alyosha's need to *see* his oldest brother in person before completing various assignments related to Dmitry is repeatedly expressed in the novel. Compare: "Katerina Ivanovna's errand [to visit Captain Snegiryov] was for Ozernaia Street, and brother Dmitry happened to live on the way, not far from Ozernaia Street, in an alley. Alyosha decided to stop by at his place in any case before going to the Captain's. He had suspected that his brother might be deliberately hiding from him now, *but it was imperative that he find him*" [no *vo chto by to ni stalo, nado bylo ego razyskat'*] (*PSS*, 14:179); "With his whole being Alyosha desired to be at the monastery, with his 'great' dying Elder, *but the need to see Dmitry won over everything else*" [*no potrebnost' videt' Dmitriia peresilila vse*] (*PSS*, 14:202–3). It is thus not accidental that the only time Alyosha experiences a fall from faith analogous to Prince Myshkin's in part 2, chapter 5 of *The Idiot*, its most pernicious consequence is precisely forgetting about his brother Dmitry. By doing so, Alyosha neglects to follow Zosima's last admonition *to see* his oldest brother: "Have you been home and *seen* your brother?" ("Byl li u svoikh i *videl* li brata?"), the Elder asks with urgency during his last conversation with Alyosha (*PSS*, 14:258). Equally significant is that during his short-lived rebellion, caused by the notorious "odor of corruption," Alyosha, like Myshkin in part 2, chapter 5 of *The Idiot*, averts his eyes from his interlocutors and refuses to face them. "Have you, too, fallen into temptation?" (*PSS*, 14:305), Paisy asks with sadness, when he notices Alyosha's disappointment and shame after Father Ferapont publicly denies Zosima's sanctity on the "evidence" of his body's rapid decay: "'Could it be that even you are with those of little faith?' Alyosha stopped and glanced at Paisy somehow indefinitely, but then once again quickly *turned his eyes away and looked at the ground. He was standing sideways and did not turn his face toward his interlocutor*" (*PSS*, 14:305). The same happens in the following scene, when Alyosha avoids Rakitin's eyes (*PSS*, 14:308) and, minutes later,

accepts his challenge to eat sausage and to visit the temptress Grushenka, that is, indeed succumbs to a temptation, as Paisy had suspected. However, this temporary avoidance of face-to-face contact is not generally characteristic of Alyosha, who, unlike Myshkin, fully recovers his capacity for active, dialogical empathy after his brief fall from faith.

18. Following A. Boyce Gibson (*The Religion of Dostoevsky* [Philadelphia: Westminster, 1974], 121), Rowan Williams also calls attention to this passage, noting that "Myshkin is described as not wanting to confront what is going on in his mind and feelings" (*Dostoevsky: Language, Faith and Fiction*, 258). According to Williams, "it is hard to avoid the conclusion that he [Myshkin] has no equipment for making that kind of sense, and so for presenting himself in relation to the conversation of others" (125; see also Gibson, 121, quoted in Williams, 258). Neither of the critics notice Dostoevsky's return to the positive hero's confrontation with a "frightful thought" in *The Brothers Karamazov*, where essentially the same situation receives a different resolution and a suggested alternative to the earlier novel is signaled by the similarity in wording, as I demonstrate.

19. Rowan Williams equates Myshkin's difficulty with acknowledging and engaging with *evil* with his ineffectiveness as a propagator and representative of *the good* in the world of the novel: "for Dostoevsky, the good is neither knowable nor effective if it is not engaged historically and specifically with its opposite," Williams writes, hinting at Myshkin's lack of such responsible engagement (*Dostoevsky: Language, Faith and Fiction*, 145). Williams links Myshkin's hesitation to confront evil with the character's "unfallen goodness," which, he argues, is ultimately pernicious (145).

20. "Nel'zia bylo ne dumat'" could also mean "it was impossible not to think," but this latter meaning would be more accurately rendered as "nevozmozhno bylo ne dumat'," and the context strongly suggests my reading of the sentence. In the context of Alyosha's life philosophy, "nel'zia" here signifies a moral imperative, rather than a mere impossibility, as my close reading of the passage shows.

21. For a discussion of this Schelerian concept, namely, the spiritual-practical process of assessing another's essential inner being in the act of active empathy, see Scheler, *GW*, 7:130 and chapter 2, section 5 of the present study ("Reading between the Lines: The Practice of Active Empathy").

22. See my analysis of Prince Myshkin's problematic attempt to enter Rogozhin's soul preceding his attack on the Prince in chapters 4 and 5 of this study.

23. Katerina Ivanovna's ressentiment "love" for Dmitry results in the constant perpetuation of emotional violence between the two, for it is inspired by a repressed wish to pay Dmitry back for the original insult suffered from him—his indecent proposal, accepted by the desperate Katerina to save her father. Alyosha's exposure of this "nadryv" (self-laceration) as such may be seen as an example of what Anders Nygren calls "judgment against that which is not love"

(*Agape and Eros*, 104) and Paul Tillich terms "the negation of the negation of love" (*Love, Power, and Justice*, 115). As was shown in my analysis of *The Idiot* in chapter 5, such constructive judgment, compatible with agape, was largely absent in Prince Myshkin's treatment of Nastasia Filippovna.

24. This act of positive *wishing* ("zhelanie / pozhelanie [chego-to komu-to]"), inspired by love, is, of course, juxtaposed to Ivan's hateful wish for his father's death. "I reserve the right to *wish* [for anything]" ("'pravo *zhelanii* ostavliaiu za soboi") (*PSS*, 15:49); "in my *wishes*, in this case, I reserve complete freedom for myself" ("v *zhelaniiakh* moikh ia ostavliaiu za soboiu v dannom sluchae polnyi prostor") (*PSS*, 14:132), Ivan tells Alyosha. While Alyosha wishes for the positive resolution of his family's conflicts, accomplished *internally* through the work of love and compassion, Ivan is wishing for the catastrophic, *external* consummation of the story, already prepared by the novel's criminal intrigue: instead of actively contributing to a "resolution," Ivan is prepared to allow the expected villain (Dmitry) to supply the denouement. The struggle between two possible resolutions, or two kinds of consummation (*razreshenie* [*konfliktov*]), mentioned earlier in chapter 6 as a characteristic situation encountered by Dostoevsky's Christlike empathizers, is once again evident in this emphatic minimal pair.

25. As Robin Miller insightfully notes in regard to a different passage, in his deeply personal conversations with others, Alyosha functions as a "canny intermediary between [different] parts of the [interlocutor's] self, a kind of spiritual therapist" (*"The Brothers Karamazov": The Words of the Novel*, 86). This is indeed one of the key functions he performs as a consummator of Ivan, Dmitry, Kolya Krasotkin, and others.

26. In the tradition of Dostoevsky's agapeistic consummation, Alyosha's "not you!" belongs in the same paradigm as his earlier statements to his father: "I believe that you are *not* merely a buffoon" ("Veriu, chto [Vy] *ne vsego tol'ko* shut") (*PSS*, 14:123); "You are *not* an evil man, but a twisted (distorted) one" ("*Ne* zloi vy chelovek, a iskoverkannyi") (*PSS*, 14:158), and Prince Myshkin's "antidefinition" of Nastasia Filippovna: "You are *not* the sort of woman you are pretending to be" ("*Razve vy takaia*, kakoiu teper' predstavlialis'?" [*PSS*, 8:99]). All of these statements affirm the deeply personal, unfinalizable essence of human individuality by defending it from objectifying labels that are rejected (and grammatically negated: *ne* shut! *ne* zloi! *ne* kurtizanka! *ne* ubiitsa! / *not* a buffoon! *not* evil! *not* a courtesan! *not* a murderer!) in favor of what Scheler would call one's "Individual Ineffable." Our analysis shows that, in comparison to Myshkin's similarly intended affirmations through negation, Alyosha's words are markedly more confident and seem to better reach his addressees.

27. For widely differing opinions on the nature of Ivan's responsibility for the crime see, for example, Bakhtin, *PDP*, 259, 221–22; Vladimir Kantor, "Pavel Smerdyakov and Ivan Karamazov: The Problem of Temptation," in Pattison and Thompson, *Dostoevsky and the Christian Tradition*, 189–225; and V. E.Vetlovskaia,

Roman F. M. Dostoevskogo "Brat'ia Karamazovy" (Saint Petersburg: Pushkinskii Dom, 2007), 88–97.

28. As Vladimir Kantor points out, in his moral-metaphysical self-renewal, Ivan faces a triple task: he has to (1) realize the bankruptcy of his ideological stance (the idea of "Mangodhood"), and (2) acknowledge his share of responsibility in the murder for propagating his pernicious "idea," enacted by Smerdyakov, but, at the same time, (3) realize that his potential is not exhausted by this bankrupt idea (Kantor, "Pavel Smerdyakov and Ivan Karamazov," 213). In his consummation of Ivan, which takes place throughout the entire novel, Alyosha, indeed, pays attention to all three parts of this difficult task.

29. For a relevant discussion of the dangers of premature forgiveness that precedes, and ultimately supersedes, repentance, see Nathan Rosen's "Ivan Karamazov on Killing the Father," in *Die Brüder Karamazow: Dostojewskijs letzter Roman in heutiger Sicht: elf Vorträge des IX Symposiums der Internationalen Dostojewskij-Gesellschaft*, ed. Horst-Jürgen Gerigk [Dresden: Dresden University Press, 1997], esp. 156–58.

30. It is important that Alyosha does not deny that Ivan has indeed *desired* their father's death, and even his murder, as he himself admits to Ivan during their earlier meeting: "'Do you remember when, after dinner, Dmitry broke into the house and gave father a beating and afterwards I told you in the yard that I reserved "the right to desire" [anything in the world] . . . tell me, did you think that I wished for father's death?' 'I did,' Alyosha replied softly. . . . 'But didn't you also think that what I wished for was precisely that "one viper should eat another" . . . and the sooner the better?' . . . 'Forgive me, I did think that too,' whispered Alyosha and fell silent, without adding a single 'mitigating circumstance'" (*PSS*, 15:49). The "not you!" dialogue is an important continuation of and follow-up to this earlier conversation and part of Alyosha's continual effort to help his brother in the process of moral renewal, without doing the work of moral renewal for him.

31. Compare, for example, the arch-narrator's oblique references to Ivan's future, passionately renewed romance with Katerina Ivanovna, which "could serve as an outline *of another tale, of a different novel*, which I may or may not undertake at some point in time" (*PSS*, 15:48).

32. While the near identity of Alyosha's and Smerdyakov's utterances has been noticed by critics, who correctly attribute the startling difference in meaning to the speakers' different accentuation (see, for example, Miller, *"The Brothers Karamazov": The Worlds of the Novel*, 119; see also Bakhtin's interpretation of Alyosha's words to Ivan as a re-accentuation of Ivan's internal dialogue, directly opposed to the devil's accentuation of it [*PDP*, 256, 222]), it is the important *reversal* in the order of condemning and vindicating statements, pointed out in my analysis, that results in the opposite accentuation of the two "testaments." After all, Alyosha's and Smerdyakov's concluding verdicts to Ivan are,

respectively, "it wasn't you" ("*ne ty* [ubil]!" [*PSS*, 15:40]) and "*you* are the one who killed [Feodor Pavlovich]"; "the main murderer is no one but *you*" ("*vy-to* i ubili!"; "glavnyi ubivets vo vsem zdes' edinyi *vy-s*" [(*PSS*, 15:59, 63]).

33. In Carol Apollonio's opinion, Smerdyakov, with his unceasing argumentation and treacherous use of language, represents "the absurdity of language taken to its ultimate limit," and his final word to Ivan represents the extreme of this evil verbosity, slander: "His terrifying final speech serves to keep Ivan in the hell of his internal intellectual torment, his (their) blame of himself," Apollonio writes (*Dostoevsky's Secrets: Reading against the Grain*, 162).

34. Bakhtin acknowledges Myshkin's "deep and fundamental horror at speaking a decisive and ultimate word about another person" (*PDP*, 242).

35. Announced as a word of God, merely heralded by Alyosha, this "last word" is an example of what Diane Thompson would describe as a positive authoritative word in Dostoevsky, compatible with polyphonic discourse. According to Thompson, in *The Brothers Karamazov*, Alyosha is a carrier of such discourse, representing "what Christ really stood for—the authoritative word made internally persuasive through Him" (*"The Brothers Karamazov" and the Poetics of Memory*, 194). In *Varieties of Poetic Utterance*, Nina Perlina also examines Dostoevsky's use of the authoritative word, which, in her interpretation, is not inimical to dialogue and polyphony. Perlina argues that Alyosha is marked as a positive, Christological hero through his successful selection and assimilation of another's authoritative word (mostly the biblical Word and the word of Father Zosima), which he then makes palatable and accessible to others by "translating" it into morally productive action (see, for example, 17). In my view, the greater authority of Alyosha's dialogically addressed word, in comparison to Prince Myshkin's, also renders Alyosha more *active* in his communicative endeavors.

36. Summarizing the short biography of his "main hero" in *The Brothers Karamazov*, the narrator tells us that, in his youth, Alyosha himself exemplified this tendency, wishing to devote no less than his whole soul to the propagation of his newly found truth, and eager to sacrifice everything, even his life, for it. Noting that Alyosha's choice of vocation was motivated by the same extremist "desire for immediate heroism" (*zhazhdoi skorogo podviga*), the narrator contends that giving one's life may sometimes be the easiest form of sacrifice. Devoting five or six years of this life to difficult studies in order to prepare oneself for a lifelong service to the same ideal would be a more responsible and productive sacrifice, the narrator suggests, yet most of the impatient young idealists who are ready to perform the first "podvig" (heroic feat) are unwilling to endure the latter (*PSS*, 14:25, 54). A similar distinction between ostentatious gestures that display one's spiritual largesse but do not lead to any real spiritual growth and the prosaic, arduous, and private work of spiritual self-renewal is made in the chapter "At Tikhon's" in *The Devils* and in Dostoevsky's notebooks for *The Devils*, when Tikhon attempts to dissuade Stavrogin (and his predecessor in the

notebooks, the character named "the Prince") from going public with his terrible confession. Instead, the bishop proposes that he opt for private, lifelong penance. Instead of the "sublime heroism" (*vysshii podvig*) the bishop in the notebooks for *The Devils* demands a "more difficult" form of heroism ("trudneishii [podvig]") from the Prince, namely, that of daily moral-spiritual labor ("trud pravoslavnyi") (*PSS*, 11:195). According to the bishop, "one shouldn't take a leap, but instead should restore a human being within oneself" through daily self-betterment (*PSS*, 11:195), a solution that is fundamentally similar to the one suggested by Alyosha to Mitya in the "Epilogue" of *The Brothers Karamazov*. Because, as a spiritually motivated rejection of *skoryi podvig*, Alyosha's advice is quite consistent with Zosima's teachings (see, for example, *PSS*, 14:54) and with the authorial pronouncements on the subject, I think that Alyosha is sincere in his counseling, hence: "I say it to you once and for all [*raz navsegda*]." As such, Mitya's comparison of Alyosha's reasoning to Jesuit thinking notwithstanding, the hero's advice cannot simply be dismissed as a half-hearted pat on the back, a white lie to make Mitya feel better in his hopeless misery, as some critics have suggested (see, for example, Victor Terras, *Reading Dostoevsky* [Madison: University of Wisconsin Press, 1998], 137). For a positive interpretation of Alyosha's Jesuitical "casuistry" in the episode, generally consonant with my interpretation of Alyosha's consummating activity, see Paul Contino's "Dostoevsky and the Ethical Relation to the Prisoner," *Renascence: Essays on Values in Literature* 48, no. 4 (Summer 1996): esp. 237–74.

37. The descriptions of Ippolit and Snegiryov during their similarly motivated outbursts are consonant with each other: both heroes are extremely pale, with distorted faces and crooked smiles: Ippolit is portrayed "with an embarrassed, crooked and wandering smile on his trembling lips" ("[s] poteriannoi, iskrivlennoi i polzuchei usmeshk[oi] na vzdragivaiushchikh gubakh") (*PSS*, 8:249); Snegiryov is given to fits of similarly distorting laughter: "s iskrivlenn[ym] smekh[om] v litse" (*PSS*, 14:193); about to throw away the money, he springs at Alyosha "looking like a man who decided to jump off a cliff, but at the same time as if also smiling with his lips only" ("s vidom reshivshegosia poletet' s gory, i v to zhe vremia gubami kak by i ulybaias'") (*PSS*, 14:192). Snegiryov's impressionistic description earlier in the chapter is especially evocative of Ippolit's and reads like a deliberate quotation from the earlier novel: "*Each and every part of his* [Snegiryov's] *face moved and twitched*; he looked [at Alyosha] with extreme defiance. He seemed beside himself" (*PSS*, 14:183) compare: "Ippolit quickly turned around with most ferocious anger, and *each and every part of his face seemed to be quivering and speaking*" (*PSS*, 8:249) ("*Kazhdaia chertochka na ego litse* [na litse kapitana] *khodila i dergalas'*, gliadel zhe s chrezvychainym vyzovom. On kak by byl v isstuplenii" [*PSS*, 14:183] // "Ippolit bystro obernulsia s samoiu beshenoiu zloboi, i *kazhdaia chertochka na litse ego, kazalos', trepetala i govorila*" [*PSS*, 8:249]). These close textual correspondences signal to the reader

that here Dostoevsky deliberately revisits a psychological situation familiar to his audience from an earlier novel, and discussed in my analysis of *The Idiot* in chapter 4—a positive hero's confrontation with an extremely sensitive, self-lacerating interlocutor, reluctant to accept sympathy and charity from others. As we can see, the outcome of the protagonist's efforts is somewhat different in *The Brothers Karamazov*: a different Christlike hero suggests a different solution.

38. Scheler gives an example of two parents grieving for their child to illustrate a "joint feeling" ("das unmittelbare Mitfühlen," sometimes also translated as "immediate community of feeling" [see, for example, Scheler, *The Nature of Sympathy*, 13]): the two "feel and experience in common not only the same value-situation but also the same keenness of emotion in regard to it," Scheler writes (*The Nature of Sympathy*, 13, Peter Heath's translation). He then contrasts the parents' friend's empathy with them (classified as fellow-feeling / "Mitfühlen" or "Mitgefühl") with their mutual feeling of grief, to illustrate the phenomenological distinctiveness of joint feeling: while the couple's friend "understands" their grief, the parents don't need to understand each other, they are conjoined in one unitary feeling of grief (*GW*, 7: 23; *The Nature of Sympathy*, 13). Captain Snegiryov and his son are likely experiencing such a joint feeling of shared humiliation when Dmitry insults both of them; at least this seems to be Snegiryov's understanding of it, for he claims to be the only one with direct knowledge of Ilyusha's suffering ("what he suffered through . . . only God Himself knows and I" [*PSS*, 14:235]). However, one should note that Ilyusha's emotional focus is almost exclusively on *his father's* pain and humiliation, especially after the assault, and thus also necessarily involves fellow-feeling (*Mitgefühl*) in relation to his father. In this case, his father's suffering and Ilyusha's commiseration with his father's suffering are two phenomenologically different facts. For an excellent overview of Scheler's taxonomy of empathetic feelings see Frings, *The Mind of Max Scheler*, 92–95. For a recent, detailed, and sophisticated discussion of the community of feeling ("das unmittelbare Mitfühlen" or "Miteinanderfühlen") and its relation to other types of empathy see Angelika Krebbs, "The Phenomenology of Shared Feeling," *Appraisal* 8, no. 3 (2011): 35–50.

39. Here my assessment of Alyosha's respect for and encouragement of the other's dialogical *activity* agrees with Paul Contino's characterization of Alyosha, inspired by Bakhtin's reflections on the challenges of dialogical freedom. According to Contino, Alyosha is "an attentive, *kenotic* confessor" whose "words are not imposed from above" ("Dostoevsky and the Ethical Relation to the Prisoner," 272, italics in text). As Contino insightfully points out in his discussion of Mitya's planned escape in the epilogue, Alyosha "attentively *wishes* with his brother [Dmitry], but will not decide for him" (272, italics in text).

40. "Sovsem gotovoe" (*PSS*, 5:133); we shall recall that in *Notes from Underground* the narrator uses this derogatory epithet to denote passively received ideological goods, as opposed to values and convictions freely chosen by each

individual consciousness. For example, the Underground Man mocks his purely theoretical dreams of future activity for the good of all, "beneficent, beautiful, and, most of all, *ready-made* (what kind of activity precisely I never knew, but, most of all, it had to be ready-made" (*Notes*, 39; *PSS*, 5:133, italics in text). Although Dostoevsky does not use this particular term to describe it, the compulsory happiness reigning inside the ominous Crystal Palace belongs in the same category and could also be aptly called "ready-made."

41. See, for example, Karen Stepanian, *Iavlenie i dialog v romanakh F. M. Dostoevskogo*, 182.

42. Rowan Williams wittily refers to the sexual temptation prepared for Alyosha by the devious Rakitin in the "Onion" chapter as "a kind of correlative to the loss of his [Alyosha's] spiritual or theological virginity that has occurred after Zosima's death" (*Dostoevsky: Language, Faith and Fiction*, 179).

43. Or "pear," as suggested by Grushenka's juicy, sexually evocative name. Grushenka's curvy, bottom-heavy shape, her intense sexual energy and obvious connection to the soil and the elemental forces of life and fertility, that is akin to the ambiguous but ultimately redeeming "force of Karamazovian baseness," encourage her identification with this suggestive fruit. The structural similarity between the feminine nouns "l*u*kov*ka*" (little onion) and "gr*u*shen'*ka*" (little pear), with their equal number of syllables, identical stress on the "-u" (-oo sound) of the first syllable and the identical suffixes (-ka), underscore the visual similarity between the two fruits of the earth. That Grushenka herself is a kind of "lukovka," a spiritually meaningful, yet tangible, earthy, and potentially endlessly fruitful gift to others, and not merely a giver of "lukovki," is certainly a significant aspect of this immensely rich parable that, along with its many other symbolic functions, endorses the importance of the interpenetration of life and spirit in the novel, a key value in late Dostoevsky. While Alyosha, having remained a virgin through his ostensible temptation in the Onion chapter, importantly loses his fear of eros in the scene, acknowledging the erotic as he allows his seductress to sit on his lap and no longer regarding the sexy Grushenka as a "strashnaia" (fear-inducing, terrible) woman, Dmitry will be the recipient of all of Grushenka's gifts, body and soul. For insightful reflections on Grushenka's role in Alyosha's spiritual renewal, as someone who both initiates him into the realm of eros and diverts his awakened sexual desire elsewhere, see Williams, *Dostoevsky: Language, Faith and Fiction*, 179–80.

44. Morson, "The God of Onions: *The Brothers Karamazov* and the Mythic Prosaic," in R. L. Jackson, *A New Word on "The Brothers Karamazov*,*"* 114, italics in text. In her excellent study of conversion in Dostoevsky, Robin Miller echoes Morson's emphasis on *sharing* the redemptive experience in this important scene. "Who has given whom an onion?" Miller asks, "or, does the successful giving of the onion depend, as in the parable, wholly on mutuality, on shared responsibility? The angel holds out the onion to the sinner, and the other sinners

hold on to her. No one must let go of it or push anyone else away. Grushenka's story literalizes Zosima's idea about the chain of interconnectedness among all things" (*Dostoevsky's Unfinished Journey*, 83).

45. For example, Alyosha responds to Rakitin's reference to Grushenka as "publichnaia devka" (prostitute) when he asks, "Is she really *that sort* of woman?" ("da razve ona *takaia*?") (*PSS*, 14:77); in an early interior dialogue, before his firsthand encounters with Grushenka, Alyosha himself calls her "that terrible woman" ("eta strashnaia zhenshchina"), a definition most certainly influenced by the public perception of the heroine (*PSS*, 14:132).

46. Diane Thompson has pointed out that Dostoevsky omits the concluding verse of the biblical account of the miracle that contains this information (*"The Brothers Karamazov" and the Poetics of Memory*, 302), but, in my opinion, the reader's knowledge of the full Gospel text is relied upon to suggest the passage's relevance to the novel's events.

47. The importance of Grushenka's positive authorial valuation in *The Brothers Karamazov*, which represents Dostoevsky's revised vision of Christian love as a union of agape and eros, a vision that differs significantly from the ideal of love posited in *The Idiot* or *Crime and Punishment*, is beginning to be acknowledged by critics (see, for example, Paul Friedrich, "Grushenka," *Dostoevsky Studies* 11 [2007]: 38–55; see also Leonard J. Stanton, *The Optina Pustyn Monastery in the Russian Literary Imagination: Iconic Vision in Works by Dostoevsky, Gogol, Tolstoy and Others* [New York: Peter Lang, 1995], 196–201).

48. There is one notable exception to this general pattern: Smerdyakov, who is initially disguised as a minor actor in the novel's cast, but ultimately emerges as a key player in its drama. Intellectually drawn to Ivan, Smerdyakov shows no interest in Alyosha and, according to Feodor Pavlovich, even "despises" him more than the other members of the Karamazov clan (*PSS*, 14:122). Smerdyakov's indifference or even hostility to Alyosha may be due to the fact that he represents the opposite metaphysical pole in the novel, the axis of evil, but Alyosha's lack of attention to his half-brother also needs to be noted. Alyosha's failure to acknowledge Smerdyakov as a brother and neighbor in a Christian sense, explored in Olga Meerson's excellent studies, is perhaps the most troubling failure of love in this otherwise positive, loving character (see Meerson's *Dostoevsky's Taboos*, 183–209, and *Personalizm kak poetika: Literaturnyi mir glazami ego obitatelei* [St. Petersburg: Pushkinskii Dom, 2009], 273–329; see also Gary Saul Morson, "Verbal Pollution in *The Brothers Karamazov*," in *Critical Essays on Dostoevsky*, ed. Robin F. Miller [Boston: G.K. Hall, 1986], 241, where he argues that even Alyosha contributes to the tragedy by refusing to recognize a brother in Smerdyakov and thus exacerbates his bitter resentment against the family).

49. As Bakhtin notes, "*All* decisive encounters of man with man, consciousness with consciousness, always take place in Dostoevsky's novels 'in infinity' and 'for the last time'" (*PDP*, 177). Bakhtin connects this symbolically universalized

space-time with the chronotope of the mystery play and of carnival (*PDP*, 177). In the context of my argument, it is important that this characteristic feature of ultimate dialogue in Dostoevsky is consistently associated with Alyosha, the most popular and beloved *addressee* not only in his own novel, but, arguably, in all of Dostoevsky's fiction.

50. Alyosha's singularity has been noted by critics and is supported by many other examples in the text. As Diane Thompson points out, Miusov calls Alyosha "perhaps *the only man in the world* who, left alone, would be immediately taken care of" (*PSS*, 14:20, quoted in Thompson, *"The Brothers Karamazov" and the Poetics of Memory*, 313); both Grushenka and Katerina Ivanovna await his and only his judgment, while Feodor Pavlovich calls him "his *only* son," *the only person* of whom he is not afraid (*PSS*, 14:130) and *the only one* with whom he has experienced moments of kindness (*PSS*, 14:158). To highlight the Christological significance of Alyosha's singularity, Thompson quotes Jean Starobinsky, for it is "Jesus, the permanent hero of the evangelical narrative, [who is] the immutable representative of the singular," Starobinsky suggests (Starobinsky, "The Struggle with Legion," *New Literary History* 4 [1973]: 342, quoted in Thompson, *"The Brothers Karamazov" and the Poetics of Memory*, 314).

51. For the significance of affirming the others' existence in Dostoevsky's world, see Viacheslav Ivanov's reflections on the "Thou Art" (*Ty esi*) principle in Dostoevsky in *Freedom and the Tragic Life*, 26–28.

52. "This third one is God, sir, that very Providence, sir, it is here *next* to us, sir [*podle* nas-s], but don't look for it, you won't find it," Smerdyakov tells Ivan with profound sadness on the eve of his suicide (*PSS*, 15:60).

53. For a discussion of "the absolute Robinson Crusoe" and his significance in Scheler's phenomenology of emotions, see chapter 2 of the present study.

54. Stavrogin has no neighbors (*keine Nächsten*) in the Christian sense, Guardini implicitly suggests, and "he cannot come to another person and no one can come to him, for it is the heart that creates closeness [*Nähe*]," a spiritual organ this Dostoevskian pretender seems to lack (Guardini, *Religiöse Gestalten in Dostojewskijs Werk*, 319). In this context, it is also significant that in the drafts of *The Devils*, Dostoevsky gives Stavrogin the following characteristic remark, as he confesses to the priest Feodosii, Tikhon's predecessor in the early versions of the novel: "I hate my fellow men [literally: my neighbors]. And I will, most likely, come to hate you if you will always be *next* to me" ("*Blizhnego* ia nenavizhu. I vas, naverno, voznenavizhu, esli vy budete vechno *podle* menia") (*PSS*, 11:305).

55. Chizhevsky, "Dostoevskii psikholog," 71.

56. Another affirmation of Alyosha's competency as a *homo amans* is Grushenka's "I had waited my whole life for *someone like you* [*takogo kak ty*], I waited and knew that someone would come and forgive me. I believed that someone would love *even someone like me* [chto *i menia kto-to poliubit*], me, a nasty creature, not just for that shameful reason [that is, for Grushenka's sex

appeal]" (*PSS*, 14:323). The similarity between these words and Nastasia Filippovna's confession to Myshkin in part 1 points to another situation in *The Idiot* revisited in *The Brothers Karamazov*, namely, the Christlike hero's ministering to an abused, "fallen" woman, released from the objectifying labels attributed to her by society through his agapeistic love, once again, with a happier ending in the later novel.

57. The old Karamazov certainly does not lack the capacity to feel; in fact, he has an intense and stormy emotional life. Feodor Pavlovich is obviously capable of erotic attachments and facile sentiment ("He was sentimental; he was mean and sentimental" [*PSS*, 14:24]), but it is unacquisitive, disinterested, and morally relevant love that I, and the narrator, have in mind here when emphasizing the newness of this feeling to "someone like" Feodor Pavlovich. It is love that has no ulterior motive, love not "for the sake of" anything else, "[liubov'] 'ni za chto,'" as Grushenka puts it in "An Onion" (*PSS*, 14:320), that had been alien to Feodor Pavlovich before Alyosha's arrival. When speaking of the uniqueness of their love for Alyosha or of Alyosha's love for them, the characters usually stress the agapeistic nature of the feeling: Mitya contrasts "vlublennost'," his erotic infatuation with Grushenka, a love compatible with hatred, with his "genuine" love for Alyosha: "for in the whole world, genuinely [po-nastoiashchemu] . . . ge-nu-ine-ly (listen! listen!) I love only you" (*PSS*, 14:96); Grushenka tells Alyosha that he is the only person whose love for her is not sexually motivated: importantly, Alyosha loves her "not for that shameful reason" ("ne za odin tol'ko sram") (*PSS*, 14:323). The same distinction between acquisitive and unacquisitive love is made by the narrator in the case of Feodor Pavlovich, who actively experiences the latter only through Alyosha. Before Alyosha's arrival, he "loved only filth [odnu lish' skvernu]," that is, the extremes of debauchery, the narrator reports (*PSS*, 14:87). For valuable observations on the spiritual relevance of Feodor Pavlovich's unstoppable sexual drive, see Zenkovsky, "Fedor Pavlovich Karamazov" and Rosen, "Ivan Karamazov on Killing the Father."

58. Guardini, *Religiöse Gestalten*, 140.

59. David S. Cunningham, "*The Brothers Karamazov* as Trinitarian Theology," in R. L. Jackson, *A New Word on "The Brothers Karamazov,"* 138.

60. Robert Bird, "Refiguring the Russian Type: Dostoevsky and the Limits of Realism," in R. L. Jackson, *A New Word on "The Brothers Karamazov,"* 27.

61. Thompson, *"The Brothers Karamazov" and the Poetics of Memory*, 308.

62. The immense suffering of sinners in hell would not be mitigated even if the virtuous in heaven were to forgive them and call them to join themselves, Zosima claims in "On Hell and Hellfire: A Mystical Reflection." Instead, such acceptance would only intensify the sinners' suffering, "for it would invoke in them even more intensely the fiery thirst for *reciprocal, active and grateful love*" ("vozbudilo by v nikh plamen' zhazhdy *otvetnoi, deiatel'noi i blagodarnoi liubvi*"), the love they had chosen not to practice when they were alive (*PSS*, 14:293). This

unrelenting spiritual torment over the lost opportunity to respond to love, and not the physical suffering, as is sometimes presumed, is the essence of hell, Zosima maintains. A similar view of ultimate suffering is voiced by Father Tikhon in the notebooks for *The Devils*: "I imagine it [hell] this way: the soul will wander and will see its sin, and not the way it sees it now, but in its entirety, and it will see that God is opening His embrace toward it . . . , and [the soul] will become indignant and will itself demand punishment and will seek it, and, instead, *it will be answered by love, and that is precisely its hell* [*a ei* (dushe) *otvechaiut liubov'iu—i v etom ad ee*]. *The consciousness of unfulfilled love must be the most terrible thing, and that is what hell is*" ("*Soznanie liubvi neispolnennoi dolzhno byt' vsego uzhasnee, i v etom-to ad ee i est'*") (*PSS*, 11:190).

63. "But how much love, o Lord, how much love I would feel in these dreams of mine, in these 'escapes into all that is sublime and beautiful,'" the Underground Man confesses, "although it was fantastic love, love never applied to anything human, but there was such an abundance of it that later, in practice, I felt no need to apply it: that would have been an unnecessary luxury" (*PSS*, 5:133; *Notes*, 39).

64. For an explication of the various ways Alyosha uses Zosima's lessons and sayings in his talks with his own disciples, see Perlina, *Varieties of Poetic Utterance*, for example, 44, 184,192. By analyzing many instances of Alyosha's successful assimilation of Zosima's authoritative word, Perlina demonstrates that, in the course of the novel, "the borders between Zosima's quoted discourse and Alyosha's original utterances gradually disappear" (*Varieties of Poetic Utterance*, 22).

65. Alyosha is said to be "the spitting image" of his mother ("toch'-v-toch' kak ona") (*PSS*, 14:127), not only in his appearance, but also in his gestures and movements, when he reacts to Feodor Pavlovich's sadistically embellished recollection of abusing his second wife, the shrieker Sophia: "His [Alyosha's] extraordinary likeness to his mother especially struck the old man" (*PSS*, 14:127). It is for Alyosha's countenance (*lik*), a spiritual-bodily entity in Zosima's usage, connotative of Christian personhood (*lichnost'*) and contrasted with the bodily "face" (*litso*), that the Elder came to love him and to bless him for his spiritual journey (*PSS*, 14:259). Alyosha's "lik" resembles Zosima's long-deceased brother Markel, the person whose Christian humility in the face of death and love of the world had inspired Zosima's own choice of spiritual vocation: "[his [Alyosha's] countenance [*lik ego*] was, as it were, a reminder and a prophecy to me," Zosima confesses shortly before his death, "without resembling him [Markel] much physically [*litsom*], but just slightly so, Aleksei seemed so like him spiritually, that many a time I treated him directly as that other youth, my brother, who has mysteriously come to me at the end of my journey for some kind of remembrance and communion [*proniknovenie*], so that I was even surprised at myself and at that strange dream of mine" (*PSS*, 14:259).

66. In spite of his reputation as "the early lover of humanity" (*PSS*, 14:17),

before Zosima's death, Alyosha's love was indeed somewhat disproportionately concentrated on one, albeit very special, person, as the narrator notes guardedly: "The fact is that all of the love contained in his young and pure heart 'for everyone and everything,' at that time and all of the previous year, was, as it were, concentrated mostly, at least in its most intense impulses, on one being, and perhaps even wrongly so—on his beloved Elder, now deceased" (*PSS*, 14:306). As concerned as Alyosha is about ending the strife in his family, the Elder takes precedence over these needs, the narrator tells us in book 1: "Without doubt, he [Alyosha] was very concerned in his heart about ending all of these family feuds. Nevertheless, his main care was about the Elder" (*PSS*, 14:31) Alyosha's fateful neglect of his family because of the Elder's posthumous disgrace may be seen as a consequence of this unfortunate "hoarding" of love in the first half of the novel, of lavishing it on one person at the expense of others. We may say that, on the day of his death, Zosima's decaying body indeed "blocked the entire world" from Alyosha, as the Russian proverb has it ("ves' svet zaslonil"), including his brothers Dmitry and Ivan and his vulnerable father, all in need of his saving love. This behavior is, of course, contrary to Zosima's own teachings, and thus represents a temptation of agape. In this context, perhaps the most important practical effect of Alyosha's conversion ("Cana of Galilee"), which marks his ultimate triumph over temptation, is the release of his agape after Zosima's death, its fruitful *dispersal* among many needful neighbors, which illustrates one of the meanings of the novel's epigraph (John 12:24).

67. As we noted in chapter 5, after the end of part 1, Myshkin's revealed internal dialogues have little relevance to his "external," that is, actual, dialogues with Rogozhin and Nastasia Filippovna, and this imbalance between the internal and the external components of *vzhivanie* is a key difference between him and Alyosha. This characteristic abstractness of Myshkin's inner word, its separation from action (and from personal inter-*action*) explains the gradual weakening of his external dialogical word in *The Idiot*, noted by Arpad Kovacs: "the predominance of external monologue" gives way to "a preponderance of inner monologue" (I would say "dialogue" in both cases) in Myshkin's discourse as the novel progresses, Kovacs observes ("The Poetics of *The Idiot*," 121).

68. The narrator reports: "All his art in this matter consisted in the fact that he brought them [the boys] to Ilyusha [svel ikh . . . s Iliushei] one by one, without mushy sentimentality [bez teliach'ikh nezhnostei] and making it look as though it all happened inadvertently and spontaneously" (*PSS*, 14:485). Travis P. Kroeker and Bruce K. Ward note the same, actively dialogical strategy on Alyosha's part in respect to Kolya Krasotkin, whom Alyosha never coerces into a friendship with himself or Ilyusha (Kroeker and Ward, *Remembering the End: Dostoevsky as Prophet of Modernity* [Boulder, Colo.: Westview, 2001], 217, 219); instead, Alyosha lets Kolya come to him "on Kolya's own swaggering terms" (219). Alyosha neither judges Kolya, nor flatters him, the way Captain Snegiryov

does, but rather listens respectfully to his often silly, politically provocative but misinformed chatter, before providing a disarmingly honest response as Kolya's equal (*Remembering the End*, 219).

69. Guardini uses this epithet in relation to Stavrogin, but, in my opinion, it is also applicable to Prince Myshkin, the character genetically linked to Stavrogin, as the notebooks for *The Idiot* demonstrate. "Stavrogin is not in possession of himself and for that reason cannot give (literally: 'gift') himself to others [*so daß er sich selbst nicht schenken kann*]," Guardini writes (*Religiöse Gestalten*, 318). "He is unreachable. He cannot offer himself to others [*er ist unschenkbar*]; he cannot give of himself, nor belong to anyone" (319).

70. Dmitry, Grushenka, Zosima, and Lise Khokhlakov all unambiguously profess their love for the youngest Karamazov, while both Ivan Karamazov and Kolya Krasotkin refer to their confessions to Alyosha, with gentle irony, as "declaration[s] of love" ("priznani[ia] v liubvi") (*PSS*, 14:240, 504), making this an important motif in the novel. These individual "declarations of love" are reinforced by a choral "We love you, Karamazov!" uttered by the twelve boys in the novel's final scene featuring an informal wake for Ilyusha at the stone (*PSS*, 15:509; for the religious significance of this utterance and of the entire scene see Robert Louis Jackson, "Alyosha's Speech at the Stone: The Whole Picture," in R. L. Jackson, *A New Word on "The Brothers Karamazov,"* 234–53).

CONCLUSION

1. "My dva sushchestva i soshlis' v bespredel'nosti . . . v poslednii raz v mire" ("We are two beings and have come together in infinity . . . for the last time in the world") (*PSS*, 10:195).

2. We shall recall that it is the Underground Man who first anticipates Ivan Karamazov's difficulty of putting his theoretical love for humanity into practice when the former wittily describes his woefully inadequate, "fantastic love," nurtured by the romantic ideals of the sublime and the beautiful, so abundant that it could hardly be applied to anything human (*PSS*, 5:133, see chapter 3 of this study).

3. Guardini, *Religiöse Gestalten*, 22.

4. My use of "formal structure" here can, of course, in no way be equated with the meaning the Russian Formalists would impart to the words "form" and "formal": I am simply referring to the concrete "out-in-out-again" structure or mental acrobatics of *live-entering* detailed in Bakthin's early works. As was pointed out in chapters 1 and 2, Bakhtin was careful to define his "architectonic *form*" in terms inimical to aesthetic and philosophical formalism. As Liisa Steinby rightly notes, in his original description of "architectonic form" Bakhtin "does not only distance himself from the Russian Formalists but also from the Neo-Kantian search for universally valid forms" ("Hermann Cohen and Bakhtin's Early Aesthetics," 243).

5. An emphatic rejection of empathy as an irrelevant and presumably discredited response to the massive, utterly dehumanizing suffering in Stalin's gulags is widespread in the starkly unsentimental *Kolyma Tales* (1954–73), while Hannah Arendt's *Eichmann in Jerusalem* (1963) presents a similarly motivated attempt at reevaluating the role of empathy in a totalitarian world, scrutinizing the way Himmler, Eichmann, and other Nazi officials used (affective) empathy to both prepare the artfully staged demise of their victims and to ensure the efficient perpetuation of mass killings that would not be hindered by the unavoidable "animal pity" felt by Nazi soldiers as they carried out their murderous duties (Arendt, *Eichmann in Jerusalem: A Report on the Banality of Evil* [New York: Penguin Books, 1994], 106, 108–9). For thought-provoking discussions of Arendt's implicit critique of empathy, or rather of the totalitarian "uses" of the empathetic instinct for murderous purposes, see Lou Agosta, *Empathy in the Context of Philosophy* (London: Palgrave Macmillan, 2010), 72–76; and Tudor, *Compassion and Remorse*, 48–49; see also Augustine Bannigan's related reflections on the role of presumably empathy-based pathological obedience in mobilizing the population for mass killings in late twentieth-century Rwanda ("Genocide: From Pathological Altruism to Pathological Obedience," in Oakley et al., *Pathological Altruism*). Susan Sontag's *Regarding the Pain of Others* (New York: Picador, 2003) is another provocative questioning of the effectiveness of empathy in responding to mass violence, as are Emmanuel Levinas's reflections on the value of suffering and co-suffering in a post-Auschwitz world in "Useless Suffering" (in *The Provocation of Levinas: Rethinking the Other*, ed. Robert Barnasconi and David Wood, trans. R. Cohen [London: Routledge, 1988], 156–67; see also E. Ann Kaplan, "Empathy and Trauma Culture: Imaging Catastrophe," in Coplan and Goldie, *Empathy: Philosophical and Psychological Perspectives*, 255–76.). In all of these still pressingly relevant discussions the distinction between "pure" or passive empathy and the *active*, responsible kind, proposed by Scheler and Bakhtin in the first half of the twentieth century and implicitly or explicitly suggested by each of the authors, becomes a crucial barometer of the agent's moral efficacy. The possibility of practically sustaining such responsible empathy in the face of radical depersonalization characteristic of totalitarian states is another matter, but here the *normative* nature of Scheler's and Bakhtin's concepts of intersubjectivity, underscored by these two idealistic, but by no means naive personalist thinkers, may guard against facile optimism in assessing the practical reality of empathetic communication in today's world.

6. See, for example, Meltzoff and Moore, "Explaining Facial Imitation"; Jean Decety and Andrew N. Meltzoff, "Empathy, Imitation, and the Social Brain," in Coplan and Goldie, *Empathy: Philosophical and Psychological Perspectives*, 60–63.

7. G. Rizzolatti et al., "Premotor Cortex and the Recognition of Motor Actions," *Cognitive Brain Research* 3 (1996): 131–34; V. Gallese et al., "Action Recognition in the Premotor Cortex," *Brain* 119, no. 2 (1996): 593–609; T. Singer

et al., "Empathy for Pain Involves the Affective but Not Sensory Components of Pain," *Science* 303, no. 5661 (2004): 1157–62; P. I. Jackson et al., "How Do We Perceive the Pain of Others? A Window into Neural Processes Involved in Empathy," *NeuroImage* 2 (2004): 771–79; I. Morrison et al., "Vicarious Responses to Pain in Anterior Cingulate Cortex: Is Empathy a Multisensory Issue?" *Cognitive, Affective, Behavioral Neuroscience* 4 (2004): 270–78.

8. See Alvin E. Goldman, "Two Routes to Empathy: Insights from Cognitive Neuroscience," in Coplan and Goldie, *Empathy: Philosophical and Psychological Perspectives*, 31–44; K. Stueber, *Rediscovering Empathy: Agency, Folk Psychology, and the Human Sciences* (Cambridge, Mass.: MIT Press, 2006); K. Shanton and A. I. Goldman, "Simulation Theory," *Wiley Interdisciplinary Reviews: Cognitive Science* 1, no. 4 (2010): 527–38.

9. Goldman, "Two Routes to Empathy," 44; Marco Iacoboni, "Within Each Other: Neural Mechanisms for Empathy in the Primate Brain," in Coplan and Goldie, *Empathy: Philosophical and Psychological Perspectives*, 46; L. Q. Uddin et al., "The Self and Social Cognition: The Role of Cortical Midline Structures and Mirror Neurons," *Trends in Cognitive Sciences* 11 (2007): 153–57.

10. Amy Coplan, "Understanding Empathy: Its Features and Effects," in Coplan and Goldie, *Empathy: Philosophical and Psychological Perspectives*, 16. See also Klimecki and Singer, "Empathic Distress Fatigue"; Goubert et al., "Facing Others in Pain: The Effects of Empathy"; Hodges and Klein, "Regulating the Costs of Empathy."

11. Barbara Oakley, *Cold-Blooded Kindness: Neuroquirks of a Codependent Killer, or Just Give Me a Shot at Loving You, Dear, and Other Reflections on Helping That Hurts* (Amherst, N.Y.: Prometheus Books, 2011).

12. A. Bartels and S. Zeki, "The Neural Basis of Romantic Love," *Neuroreport* 11 (2000): 3829–34; Bartels and Zeki, "The Neural Correlates of Maternal and Romantic Love," *NeuroImage* 21 (2004): 1155–66; see also Klimecki and Singer, "Empathic Distress Fatigue," 376.

Works Cited

Agosta, Lou. *Empathy in the Context of Philosophy*. London: Palgrave Macmillan, 2010.

Antsiferov, N. P. *Problemy urbanisma v russkoi khudozhestvennoi literature*. Moscow: IMLI RAN, 2009.

Apollonio, Carol. *Dostoevsky's Secrets: Reading against the Grain*. Evanston, Ill.: Northwestern University Press, 2009.

Arendt, Hannah. *Eichmann in Jerusalem: A Report on the Banality of Evil*. New York: Penguin Books, 1994.

Arkhundova, I. R. "'Voploshchenie khaosa i nebytiia' (Parfen Rogozhin—demon smerti ili personifikatsiia sud'by)." In *Roman F.M. Dostoevskogo "Idiot": Sovremennoe sostoianie izucheniia*, edited by T. A. Kasatkina, 364–89. Moscow: Nasledie, 2001.

Avtonomova, Natalia. *Otkrytaia struktura: Iakobson—Bakhtin—Lotman—Gasparov*. Moscow: ROSSPEN, 2009.

Bagshaw, Hilary B. P. *Religion in the Thought of Mikhail Bakhtin: Reason and Faith*. Surrey, Eng.: Ashgate, 2013.

Baier, Kurt. *The Moral Point of View*. Ithaca, N.Y.: Cornell University Press, 1958.

Bakhtin, Mikhail. *Art and Answerability: Early Philosophical Essays by M.M. Bakhtin*. Edited by Mikhail Holquist and Vadim Liapunov. Translated by Vadim Liapunov. Austin: University of Texas Press, 1990.

———. *Besedy s V.D. Duvakinym*. Edited by S. G. Bocharov et al. Moscow: Soglasie, 2002.

———. *The Dialogic Imagination: Four Essays by M.M. Bakhtin*. Edited by Michael Holquist. Translated by Caryl Emerson and Michael Holquist. Austin: University of Texas Press, 1981.

———. *Problems of Dostoevsky's Poetics*. Edited and translated by Caryl Emerson. Introduction by Wayne C. Booth. Minneapolis: University of Minnesota Press, 1984.

———. *Sobranie sochinenii v semi tomakh*. Edited by S. G. Bocharov et al. 7 vols. Moscow: Russkie Slovari, 1996–.

———. *Toward a Philosophy of the Act*. Translated by Vadim Liapunov. Edited by Vadim Liapunov and Michael Holquist. Austin: University of Texas Press, 1993.

———. *Voprosy literatury i estetiki: Issledovaniia raznykh let*. Moscow: Khudozhestvennaia literatura, 1975.

Bannigan, Augustine. "Genocide: From Pathological Altruism to Pathological Obedience." In *Pathological Altruism*, edited by Barbara Oakley et al., foreword by Francisco J. Ayala, 225–36. Oxford: Oxford University Press, 2012

Bartels, A., and S. Zeki. "The Neural Basis of Romantic Love." *Neuroreport* 11 (2000): 3829–34.

———. "The Neural Correlates of Maternal and Romantic Love." *NeuroImage* 21 (2004): 1155–66.

Barth, Karl. *Church Dogmatics*. Vol. 3, part 2. Translated by G. W. Bromiley et al. Edinburgh: T&T Clark, 1960.

———. *Evangelical Theology, an Introduction*. Translated by Grover Foley. New York: Holt, Rinehart and Winston, 1963.

Batishchev, G. S. "Dialogizm ili polifonizm? (Antitetika v ideinom nasledii M. M. Bakhtina)." In *M.M. Bakhtin kak filosof*, edited by L. A. Gogotishvili and P. S. Gurevich, 123–41. Moscow: Nauka, 1992.

Baxter, Leslie A. *Voicing Relationships: A Dialogic Perspective*. Los Angeles: Sage, 2011.

Bem, A. L., ed. *O Dostoevskom: Sbornik statei pod redaktsiei A.L. Bema*. Vol. 2. Prague: Sklad izd. F. Svoboda, 1933.

Bergson, Henri. *Creative Evolution*. Translated by Arthur Mitchell. New York: Modern Library, 2011.

———. *Matter and Memory*. Translated by Nancy Margaret Paul and W. Scott Palmer. London: G. Allen and Unwin, 1978.

———. *Time and Free Will: An Essay on the Immediate Data of Consciousness*. Translated by F. L. Pogson. Mineola, N.Y.: Dover, 2001.

Bermes, Christian, Wolfhart Henckmann, and Heinz Leonardy, eds. *Vernunft und Gefühl: Schelers Phänomenologie des emotionalen Lebens*. Wurzburg: Königshausen & Neumann, 2003.

Bernard-Donals, Michael. *Mikhail Bakhtin: Between Phenomenology and Marxism*. Cambridge: Cambridge University Press, 1994.

Bernstein, Michael André. *Bitter Carnival: Ressentiment and the Abject Hero*. Princeton, N.J.: Princeton University Press, 1992.

———. "The Poetics of Ressentiment." In *Rethinking Bakhtin: Extensions and Challenges*, edited by Gary Morson and Caryl Emerson, 197–224. Evanston, Ill.: Northwestern University Press, 1989.

Bethea, David M. *The Shape of Apocalypse in Modern Russian Fiction*. Princeton, N.J.: Princeton University Press, 1989.

Bird, Robert. "Refiguring the Russian Type: Dostoevsky and the Limits of Realism." In *A New Word on "The Brothers Karamazov,"* edited by Robert Louis Jackson, 17–30. Evanston, Ill.: Northwestern University Press, 2004.

Bitsilli, P. M. "Pochemu Dostoevsky ne napisal 'Zhitiia velikogo greshnika.'" In *O Dostoevskom: Sbornik statei pod redaktsiei A.L. Bema*. Edited by A. L. Bem, vol. 2: 25–30. Prague: Sklad izd. F. Svoboda, 1933.

Bocharov, Sergei. "'O bessmyslennaia vechnost'!' Ot 'Nedonoska' k 'Idiotu.'" In Kasatkina, *Roman F.M. Dostoevskogo "Idiot": Sovremennoe sostoianie izucheniia*, 111–36.

Bogdanov, Nikolai. "'Sviashchennaia bolezn' kniazia Myshkina—Morbus Sacer Fedora Dostoevskogo." In Kasatkina, *Roman F.M. Dostoevskogo "Idiot": Sovremennoe sostoianie izucheniia*, 337–57.

Bonetskaia, Natalia. "Bakhtin's Aesthetics as a Logic of Form." In *The Contexts of Bakhtin: Philosophy, Authorship, Aesthetics*, edited by David Shepherd, 83–94. Amsterdam: Harwood Academic, 1998.

———. "Primechaniia k 'Avtoru i Geroiu': Prodolzhenie (k izdaniiu 'Estetika slovesnogo tvorchestva')." In *Bakhtinologiia: Issledovaniia, perevody, publikatsii*, edited by A. P. Valitskaia et al., 248–87. St. Petersburg: Aleteia, 1995.

Booth, David. "*Ressentiment* and Constructive Theology: Positive Uses of Nietzsche's Critique of Christianity." Ph.D. diss., University of Chicago, 1984.

Brandist, Craig. *The Bakhtin Circle: Philosophy, Culture and Politics*. London: Pluto, 2002.

Breikin, O. B. "Filosofia postupka M. Bakhtina i problema absoluta." In Valitskaia et al., *Bakhtinologiia: Issledovaniia, perevody, publikatsii*, 217–24.

Burry, Alexander. *Multi-Mediated Dostoevsky: Transposing Novels into Opera, Film, and Drama.* Evanston, Ill.: Northwestern University Press, 2011.

Cassedy, Steven. *Flight from Eden: The Origins of Modern Literary Criticism and Theory*. Berkeley: University of California Press, 1990.

Catteau, Jacques. *Dostoevsky and the Process of Literary Creation*. Translated by Audrey Littlewood. Cambridge: Cambridge University Press, 1989.

Chizhevsky, Dmitry. "Dostoevsky psikholog." In Bem, *O Dostoevskom: Sbornik statei pod redaktsiei A.L. Bema*, vol. 2: 51–72.

Coates, Ruth. *Christianity in Bakhtin: God and the Exiled Author*. Cambridge: Cambridge University Press, 1998.

———. "The First and the Second Adam in Bakhtin's Early Thought." In *Bakhtin and Religion: A Feeling for Faith,* edited by Susan M. Felch and Paul J. Contino, 63–78. Evanston, Ill.: Northwestern University Press, 2001.

Cohen, Hermann. *Aesthetik des reinen Gefühls*. 2 vols. Berlin: B. Cassirer, 1912.

Contino, Paul J. "'Descend That You May Ascend': Augustine, Dostoevsky, and the Confessions of Ivan Karamazov." In *Augustine and Literature*, edited by Robert P. Kennedy, Kim Paffenroth, and John Doody, 179–214. New York: Lexington Books, 2006.

———. "Dostoevsky and the Ethical Relation to the Prisoner." *Renascence: Essays on Values in Literature* 48, no. 4 (Summer 1996): 259–78.

Coplan, Amy. "Understanding Empathy: Its Features and Effects." In *Empathy: Philosophical and Psychological Perspectives*, edited by Amy Coplan and Peter Goldie, 3–18. Oxford: Oxford University Press, 2011.

Coplan, Amy, and Peter Goldie, eds. *Empathy: Philosophical and Psychological Perspectives*. Oxford: Oxford University Press, 2011.

Crone, Anna Lisa. "Polyphony in the Prose of Vjaceslav Ivanov: A Preliminary Consideration." In *Cultura et Memoria: Atti del terzo simposio internationale dedicato a Vjaceslav Ivanov I: testi in italiano, francese, inglese*, edited by Fausto Malcovati, 97–109. Florence: La Nuova Italia, 1988.

Cunningham, David S. "*The Brothers Karamazov* as Trinitarian Theology." In *A New Word on "The Brothers Karamazov,"* edited by Robert Louis Jackson, 134–55. Evanston, Ill.: Northwestern University Press, 2004.

Currie, Gregory. "Empathy for Objects." In Coplan and Goldie, *Empathy: Philosophical and Psychological Perspectives*, 82–95.

Cusinato, Guido. "Eros und Agape bei Scheler." In *Vernunft und Gefühl: Schelers Phänomenologie des emotionalen Lebens*, edited by Christian Bermes, Wolfhart Henckmann, and Heinz Leonardy, 93–108. Wurzburg: Königshausen & Neumann, 2003.

Dahm, Helmut. *Vladimir Solovyev and Max Scheler: Attempt at a Comparative Interpretation. A Contribution to the History of Phenomenology*. Dordrecht: Reidel, 1975.

Decety, Jean, and Andrew N. Meltzoff. "Empathy, Imitation, and the Social Brain." In Coplan and Goldie, *Empathy: Philosophical and Psychological Perspectives*, 58–81.

Dolinin, A. S. Introduction to *F.M. Dostoevskii: Pis'ma I: 1832–1867*, by Feodor Dostoevsky, vol. 1: 1–36. Edited by A. S. Dolinin. Moscow: Gosudarstvennoe izdatel'stvo, 1928.

Dostoevsky, Feodor. *The Brothers Karamazov*. Edited by Ralph E. Matlaw. Translated by Constance Garnett, revised by Ralph Matlaw. New York: Norton, 1976

———. *The Idiot*. Translated by David Magarshack. London: Penguin Books, 1955.

———. *Memoirs from the House of the Dead*. Translated by Jessie Coulson. London: Oxford University Press, 1965.

———. *Notes from Underground*. Translated and edited by Michael R. Katz. New York: Norton, 1989.

———. *Polnoe sobranie sochinenii v tridtsati tomakh*. 30 vols. Edited by V. V. Vinogradov, G. M. Fridlender, and M. B. Khrapchenko. Leningrad: Nauka, 1972–90.

———. *A Writer's Diary*. Translated by Kenneth Lantz. Introduction by Gary Saul Morson. 2 vols. Evanston, Ill.: Northwestern University Press, 1993.

Dwyer, Anne. "Dostoevsky's Prison House of Nation(s): Genre Violence in *Notes from the House of the Dead.*" *Russian Review* 71 (2012): 209–25.

Emerson, Caryl. *The First Hundred Years of Mikhail Bakhtin*. Princeton, N.J.: Princeton University Press, 1997.

———. "Russian Orthodoxy and the Early Bakhtin." *Religion and Literature* 22, no. 2–3 (Summer-Autumn 1990): 109–30.

———. "Soloviev, the Late Tolstoy and the Early Bakhtin on the Problem of Shame and Love." *Slavic Review* 50 (1991): 663–71.

Erdmann, Benno. *Grundzüge der Reproduktionspsychologie*. Berlin: W. de Gruyter, 1920.

Ermilova, Galina. *Taina kniazia Myshkina: O romane Dostoevskogo "Idiot."* Ivanovo: Ivanovo University Press, 1993.

———. "Tragediia 'russkogo Khrista' ili o neozhidannosti okonchaniia 'Idiota.'" In Kasatkina, *Roman F.M. Dostoevskogo "Idiot": Sovremennoe sostoianie izucheniia*, 446–61.

Felch, Susan M., and Paul J. Contino, eds. *Bakhtin and Religion: A Feeling for Faith*. Evanston, Ill.: Northwestern University Press, 2001.

Figley, C. "Compassion Fatigue: Psychotherapists' Chronic Lack of Self Care." *Journal of Clinical Psychology* 58 (2002): 1433–41.

Flath, Carol A. "Fear of Faith: The Hidden Religious Message of *Notes from Underground.*" *Slavic and East European Journal* 37, no. 4 (Winter 1993): 510–29.

Fonagy, P., et al. *Affect Regulation, Mentalization, and the Development of the Self*. New York: Other, 2002.

Frank, Joseph. *Dostoevsky: The Miraculous Years, 1865–1871*. Princeton, N.J.: Princeton University Press, 1995.

———. *Dostoevsky: The Stir of Liberation, 1860–1865*. Princeton, N.J.: Princeton University Press, 1986.

———. *Dostoevsky: The Years of Ordeal, 1850–1859*. Princeton, N.J.: Princeton University Press, 1983.

Freise, Matthias. *Michail Bachtins philosophische Ästhetik der Literatur*. Frankfurt am Main: Peter Lang, 1993.

Fridman, I. N. "Nezavershennaia sud'ba estetiki zaversheniia." In Gogotishvili and Gurevich, *M.M. Bakhtin kak filosof*, 51–67.

Friedrich, Paul. "Grushenka." *Dostoevsky Studies* 11 (2007): 38–55.

Frings, Manfred. *The Mind of Max Scheler*. Milwaukee, Wis.: Marquette University Press, 1997.

Frisby, David. *The Alienated Mind: The Sociology of Knowledge in Germany, 1918–1933*. 2nd ed. New York: Routledge, 1992.

Gallese, V., et al. "Action Recognition in the Premotor Cortex." *Brain* 119, no. 2 (1996): 593–609.

Gardiner, Michael. "'A Very Understandable Horror of Dialectics': Bakhtin and Marxist Phenomenology." In *Materializing Bakhtin: The Bakhtin Circle and*

Social Theory, edited by Craig Brandist and Galin Tihanov, 119–41. London: Macmillan, 2000.

Gasché, Rodolphe. "A Material *A Priori*? On Max Scheler's Critique of Kant's Formal Ethics." *Philosophical Forum* (2010): 113–26.

Gasparov, M. L. "Istoriia literatury kak tvorchestvo i issledovanie: sluchai Bakhtina." In *Russkaia literatura XX–XXI vekov: Problemy teorii i metodologii izucheniia: Materialy mezhdunarodnoi nauchnoi konferentsii 10–11 noiabria 2004 goda*, edited by S. I. Kormilov, 8–10. Moscow: Izdatel'stvo Moskovskogo universiteta, 2004.

———. *Izbrannye trudy*. 4 vols. Moscow: Iakyki russkoi kul'tury, 1997.

Gibson, A. Boyce. *The Religion of Dostoevsky*. Philadelphia: Westminster, 1974.

Givens, John. "A Narrow Escape into Faith? Dostoevsky's *Idiot* and the Christology of Comedy." *Russian Review* 70 (January 2011): 95–117.

Gogotishvili, L. A., and P. S. Gurevich, eds. *M.M. Bakhtin kak filosof*. Moscow: Nauka, 1992.

Goldie, Peter. "Anti-Empathy." In Coplan and Goldie, *Empathy: Philosophical and Psychological Perspectives*, 302–17.

Goldman, Alvin E. "Two Routes to Empathy: Insights from Cognitive Neuroscience." In Coplan and Goldie, *Empathy: Philosophical and Psychological Perspectives*, 31–44.

Goubert, Liesbet, Kenneth D. Craig, and Ann Buysse. "Perceiving Others in Pain: Experimental and Clinical Evidence on the Role of Empathy." In *The Social Neuro-Science of Empathy*, edited by Jean Decety and William Ickes, 153–65. Cambridge, Mass.: MIT Press, 2009.

Goubert, L., et al. "Facing Others in Pain: The Effects of Empathy." *Pain* 118 (2005): 285–88.

Grossman, L. P. "Put' Dostoevskogo." In *Tvorchestvo Dostoevskogo: Sbornik statei i materialov*, edited by L. P. Grossman, 83–108. Odessa: Vseukrainskoe gosudarstvennoe izdatel'stvo, 1921.

Guardini, Romano. *Religiöse Gestalten in Dostojewskijs Werk: Studien über den Glauben*. Munich: Kösel Verlag, 1977.

Haardt, Alexander. "Ethische und ästhetische Persönlichkeit: Zum Verhältnis des Ethischen und Ästhetischen bei Sören Kierkegaard und Michail Bachtin." *Studies in East European Thought* 61 (2009): 165–79.

Hartmann, Eduard von. *Philosophie des Schönen: Zweiter systematischer Theil der Äesthetik*. Karben: Petra Wald, 1998.

Hartmann, Nicolai. *Ethik*. Berlin: W. de Gruyter, 1926.

———. *Grundzüge einer Metaphysik der Erkenntnis*. Berlin: W. de Gruyter, 1926.

Hirschkop, Ken. "Is Dialogism for Real?" In Shepherd, *The Contexts of Bakhtin: Philosophy, Authorship, Aesthetics*, 183–95.

Hodges, S. D., and K. J. K. Klein. "Regulating the Costs of Empathy: The Price of Being Human." *Journal of Socio-Economics* 30 (2001): 437–52.

Howe, David. *Empathy: What It Is and Why It Matters*. New York: Palgrave Macmillan, 2013.

Iacoboni, Marco. "Within Each Other: Neural Mechanisms for Empathy in the Primate Brain." In Coplan and Goldie, *Empathy: Philosophical and Psychological Perspectives*, 45–57.

Isupov, K. G. "Mikhail Bakhtin i Aleksandr Meier." In *M. M. Bakhtin i filosofskaia kul'tura XX veka: Problemy Bakhtinologii; Sbornik nauchnykh statei*, edited by A. P. Valitskaia and K. G. Isupov, vol. 1, part 2: 60–70. St. Petersburg, Rosskiiskii gosudarstvennyi pedagogicheskii universitet, 1991.

———."Ot estetiki zhizni k estetike istorii (Traditsii russkoi filosofii u M. M. Bakhtina)." In Gogotishvili and Gurevich, *M.M. Bakhtin kak filosof*, 68–82.

———."Smert' 'drugogo.'" In Valitskaia et al., *Bakhtinologiia: Issledovaniia, perevody, publikatsii*, 103–16.

———."Uroki M.M. Bakhtina." In *M.M. Bakhtin—pro et contra: Lichnost' i tvorchestvo M. M. Bakhtina v otsenke russkoi i mirovoi gumanitarnoi mysli; antologiia*, edited by K. G. Isupov and D. K. Burlaka, 7–44. St. Petersburg: Izdatel'stvo Russkogo Khristianskogo gumanitarnogo instituta, 2001.

Ivanov, Vyacheslav. *Freedom and the Tragic Life: A Study in Dostoevsky*. Translated by Norman Cameron. Edited by S. Konovalov. London: Noonday, 1952.

Jackson, P. I., et al. "How Do We Perceive the Pain of Others? A Window into Neural Processes Involved in Empathy." *NeuroImage* 2 (2004): 771–79.

Jackson, Robert Louis. "Alyosha's Speech at the Stone: The Whole Picture." In R. L. Jackson, *A New Word on "The Brothers Karamazov,"* 234–53.

———. *The Art of Dostoevsky: Deliriums and Nocturnes*. Princeton, N.J.: Princeton University Press, 1981.

———. *Dialogues with Dostoevsky: The Overwhelming Questions*. Stanford, Calif.: Stanford University Press, 1993.

———, ed. *A New Word on "The Brothers Karamazov."* Introduction by Robin Miller. Evanston, Ill.: Northwestern University Press, 2004.

Jacobs, Alan. "Bakhtin and the Hermeneutics of Love." In Felch and Contino, *Bakhtin and Religion: A Feeling for Faith*, 25–45.

Joinson, C. "Coping with Compassion Fatigue." *Nursing* 4 (1992): 116–21.

Jones, Malcolm V. "Sisters and Rivals: Variation on a Theme in Dostoevskii's Fiction." In *Die Wirklichkeit der Kunst und das Abenteuer der Interpretation: Festschrift für Horst-Jürgen Gerigk*, edited by K. Manger, 159–69. Heidelberg: Universitätsverlag C. Winter, 1999.

Kalygin, Aleksandr. *Rannii Bakhtin: Estetika kak preodolenie etiki: Egopersonalism, liricheskii geroi i edinstvo esteticheskikh teorii*. Moscow: RGO, 2007.

Kantor, Vladimir. "Pavel Smerdyakov and Ivan Karamazov: The Problem of Temptation." In *Dostoevsky and the Christian Tradition*, edited by George Pattison and Diane Oenning Thompson, 189–225. Cambridge: Cambridge University Press, 2001.

Kaplan, E. Ann. "Empathy and Trauma Culture: Imaging Catastrophe." In Coplan and Goldie, *Empathy: Philosophical and Psychological Perspectives*, 255–76.

Kasatkina, Tatiana. *O tvoriashchei prirode slova: Ontologichnost' slova v tvorchestve F.M. Dostoevskogo kak osnova "realizma v vysshem smysle."* Moscow: IMLI RAN, 2004.

———. "Rol' khudozhestvennoi detali i osobennosti funktsionirovaniia slova v romane F. M. Dostoevskogo 'Idiot.'" In Kasatkina, *Roman F.M. Dostoevskogo "Idiot": Sovremennoe sostoianie izucheniia*, 60–99.

———, ed. *Roman F.M. Dostoevskogo "Idiot": Sovremennoe sostoianie izucheniia*. Moscow: Nasledie, 2001.

Kelly, Eugene. "Zu Schelers Begriff der Philosophie." In Bermes et al., *Vernunft und Gefühl: Schelers Phänomenologie des emotionalen Lebens*, 121–34.

Kierkegaard, Søren. *Works of Love*. Edited and translated by Howard V. Hong and Edna H. Hong. Princeton, N.J.: Princeton University Press, 1995.

Klimecki, Olga, and Tania Singer. "Empathic Distress Fatigue rather than Compassion Fatigue? Integrating Findings from Empathy Research in Psychology and Social Neuroscience." In *Pathological Altruism*, edited by Barbara Oakley, Ariel Knafo, Guruprasad Madhavan, and David Sloan Wilson, 368–83. Oxford: Oxford University Press, 2012.

Knapp, Liza. *The Annihilation of Inertia: Dostoevsky's Metaphysics*. Evanston, Ill.: Northwestern University Press, 1996.

Kovacs, Arpad. "The Poetics of *The Idiot*: On the Problem of Dostoevsky's Thinking about Genre." In *Critical Essays on Dostoevsky*, edited by Robin Feuer Miller, 116–26. Boston: G.K. Hall, 1986.

Kozhinov, V. V. "Kak pishut trudy, ili proiskhozhdenie nesozdannogo avantiurnogo romana." *Dialog, Karnaval, Khronotop* no. 1 (1992): 109–22.

Krebbs, Angelika. "The Phenomenology of Shared Feeling." *Appraisal* 8, no. 3 (March 2011): 35–50.

Krieger, Murray. "Dostoevsky's 'Idiot': The Curse of Saintliness." In *Dostoevsky: A Collection of Critical Essays*, edited by Rene Wellek, 39–52. Englewood Cliffs, N.J.: Twentieth Century Views, 1962.

Krinitsyn, A. B. "O spetsyfike vizual'nogo mira u Dostoevskogo i semantike 'videnii' v romane 'Idiot.'" In Kasatkina, *Roman F.M. Dostoevskogo "Idiot": Sovremennoe sostoianie izucheniia*, 170–205.

Kroeker, Travis P., and Bruce K. Ward. *Remembering the End: Dostoevsky as Prophet of Modernity*. Boulder, Colo.: Westview, 2001.

Lemonick, Michael D. "Explaining Déjà vu." *Time*, August 20, 2007, 50–51.

Leonardy, Heinz. *Liebe und Person: Max Schelers Versuch eines "phänomenologischen" Personalismus*. The Hague: Martinus Nijhoff, 1976.

Lesser, Simon O. "Saint and Sinner: Dostoevsky's 'Idiot.'" *Modern Fiction Studies* 4 (1958): 211–24.

Levinas, Emmanuel. "Useless Suffering." Translated by R. Cohen. In *The Provocation of Levinas: Rethinking the Other*, edited by Robert Bernasconi and David Wood, 156–67. London: Routledge, 1988.

Lipps, Theodor. *Ästhetik: Psychologie des Schönen und der Kunst*. 2 vols. Hamburg: Voss, 1903–6.

———. *Die ethischen Grundfragen: Zehn Vorträge*. Hamburg: Voss, 1899.

Liu, Xiaofeng. *Personwerdung: Eine theologische Untersuchung zu Max Schelers Phänomenologie der "Person-Gefühle" mit besonderer Berücksichtigung seiner Kritik der Moderne*. Bern: Peter Lang, 1996.

Lock, Charles. "Bakhtin and the Tropes of Orthodoxy." In Felch and Contino, *Bakhtin and Religion: A Feeling for Faith*, 97–119.

Makhlin, V. L. "Nasledie M.M. Bakhtina v kontekste zapadnogo postmodernizma." In Gogoshvili and Gurevich, *Bakhtin kak filosof*, 206–20.

Manovtsev, Andrei. "Svet i soblazn." In Kasatkina, *Roman F.M. Dostoevskogo "Idiot": Sovremennoe sostoianie izucheniia*, 250–90.

McHugh, Thomas J., et al. "Dentate Gyrus NMDA Receptors Mediate Rapid Pattern Separation in the Hippocampal Network." *Science* 317, no. 94 (2007): 94–99.

Meerson, Olga. *Dostoevsky's Taboos*. Dresden: Dresden University Press, 1998.

———. "Khristos ili 'Kniaz''-Khristos? Svidetel'stvo generala Ivolgina." In Kasatkina, *Roman F.M. Dostoevskogo "Idiot": Sovremennoe sostoianie izucheniia*, 42–59.

———. "Old Testament Lamentation in the Underground Man's Monologue: A Refutation of the Existentialist Reading of *Notes from Underground*." *Slavic and East European Journal* 36, no. 4 (Autumn 1992): 317–22.

———. *Personalizm kak poetika: Literaturnyi mir glazami ego obitatelei*. St. Petersburg: Pushkinskii Dom, 2009.

Meltzoff, A. N., and M. K. Moore. "Explaining Facial Imitation: A Theoretical Model." *Early Development and Parenting* 6 (1997): 179–92.

Merleau-Ponty, Maurice. *The Visible and the Invisible*. Edited by Claude Lefort. Translated by Alphonso Lingis. Evanston, Ill.: Northwestern University Press, 1968.

Mihailovic, Aleksandar. *Corporeal Words: Mikhail Bakhtin's Theory of Discourse*. Evanston, Ill.: Northwestern University Press, 1997.

Miksanek, Toni. "Dostoevsky's *The Idiot* and Psychic Disorders in Epilepsy." *Perspectives in Biology and Medicine* 25, no. 2 (Winter 1982): 231–37.

Miller, Robin Feuer. *"The Brothers Karamazov": Worlds of the Novel*. New York: Twayne, 1992.

———. *Dostoevsky's Unfinished Journey*. New Haven, Conn.: Yale University Press, 2007.

Morrison, I., et al. "Vicarious Responses to Pain in Anterior Cingulate Cortex:

Is Empathy a Multisensory Issue?" *Cognitive, Affective, Behavioral Neuroscience* 4 (2004): 270–78.

Morson, Gary Saul. "The God of Onions: *The Brothers Karamazov* and the Mythic Prosaic." In R. L. Jackson, *A New Word on "The Brothers Karamazov,"* 107–24.

———. "Introductory Study: Dostoevsky's Great Experiment," introduction to *A Writer's Diary I: 1873–1876*, by Feodor Dostoevsky, 1–117. Translated by Kenneth Lantz. Evanston, Ill.: Northwestern University Press, 1993.

———. *Narrative and Freedom: The Shadows of Time*. New Haven, Conn.: Yale University Press, 1994.

———. "The Process of Ideological Becoming." In *Bakhtinian Perspectives in Language, Literacy, and Learning*, edited by Arnetha F. Fall and Sarah Warshauer Freedman, 317–31. Cambridge: Cambridge University Press, 2004.

———. "Verbal Pollution in *The Brothers Karamazov*." In *Critical Essays on Dostoevsky*, edited by Robin F. Miller, 234–42. Boston: G.K. Hall, 1986.

Morson, Gary Saul, and Caryl Emerson. *Mikhail Bakhtin: Creation of a Prosaics*. Stanford, Calif.: Stanford University Press, 1990.

Natov, Nadine. "The Ethical and Structural Significance of the Three Temptations in *The Brothers Karamazov*." *Dostoevsky Studies* 8 (1987): 3–43.

Nietzsche, Friedrich. *The Complete Works of Friedrich Nietzsche*. Edited by Oscar Levy. Translated by Horace B. Samuel. 18 vols. Edinburgh: T.N. Foulis, 1909–13.

———. *Nietzsche Werke: Kritische Gesamtaufgabe*. 9 vols. Edited by G. Colli and M. Montinari. Berlin: W. de Gruyter, 1967–2005.

Nikiforov, Vladimir. "First Philosophy as Philosophy of Individual *Postupok*." *Symposion* 4–6 (1999–2001): 61–105.

Nygren, Anders. *Agape and Eros*. Translated by Philip S. Watson. Chicago: University of Chicago Press, 1982.

Oakley, Barbara. *Cold-Blooded Kindness: Neuroquirks of a Codependent Killer, or Just Give Me a Shot at Loving You, Dear, and Other Reflections on Helping That Hurts*. Amherst, N.Y.: Prometheus Books, 2011.

Oakley, Barbara, Ariel Knafo, Guruprasad Madhavan, and David Sloan Wilson, eds. *Pathological Altruism*. Oxford: Oxford University Press, 2012.

Orwin, Donna Tussing. *Consequences of Consciousness: Turgenev, Dostoevsky, Tolstoy*. Stanford, Calif.: Stanford University Press, 2007.

Outka, Gene. *Agape: An Ethical Analysis*. New Haven, Conn.: Yale University Press, 1972.

Palmieri, Giovanni. "'The Author' according to Bakhtin . . . and Bakhtin the Author." In Shepherd, *The Contexts of Bakhtin: Philosophy, Authorship, Aesthetics*, 45–56.

Pattison, George. "Freedom's Dangerous Dialogue: Reading Dostoevsky and Kierkegaard Together." In Pattison and Thompson, *Dostoevsky and the Christian Tradition*, 237–56.

Pattison, George, and Diane Oenning Thompson, eds. *Dostoevsky and the Christian Tradition*. Cambridge: Cambridge University Press, 2001.

Perlina, Nina. "Mikhail Bakhtin and Martin Buber: Problems of Dialogic Imagination." *Studies in 20th Century Literature* 9, no. 1 (Fall 1984): 13–28.

———. *Varieties of Poetic Utterance: Quotation in "The Brothers Karamazov."* Lanham, Md.: University Press of America, 1985

Pletnev, R. "Serdtsem mudrye (O 'startsakh' u Dostoevskogo)." In Bem, *O Dostoevskom: Sbornik statei*, vol. 2:73–92.

Pollard, Rachel. *Dialogue and Desire: Mikhail Bakhtin and the Linguistic Turn in Psychotherapy*. London: Karnac Books, 2008.

Poole, Brian. "From Phenomenology to Dialogue: Max Scheler's Phenomenological Tradition and Mikhail Bakhtin's Development from 'Toward a Philosophy of the Act' to his Study of Dostoevsky." In *Bakhtin and Cultural Theory*, edited by Ken Hirschkop and David Shepherd, 109–35. 2nd ed. Manchester, Eng.: Manchester University Press, 2001.

Poole, Randal. "The Apophatic Bakhtin." In Felch and Contino, *Bakhtin and Religion: A Feeling for Faith*, 151–75.

Pyman, Avril. "Dostoevsky in the Prism of the Orthodox Semiosphere." In Pattison and Thompson, *Dostoevsky and the Christian Tradition*, 103–15.

Reed, Natalia. "The Philosophical Roots of Polyphony: A Dostoevskian Reading." In *Critical Essays on Mikhail Bakhtin*, edited by Caryl Emerson, 117–52. New York: G.K. Hall, 1999.

Rice, James L. "The Covert Design of *The Brothers Karamazov*: Alesha's Pathology and Dialectic." *Slavic Review* 68, no. 2 (Summer 2009): 355–75.

Rizzolatti, G., et al. "Premotor Cortex and the Recognition of Motor Actions." *Cognitive Brain Research* 3 (1996): 131–41.

Rosen, Nathan. "Ivan Karamazov on Killing the Father." In *"Die Brüder Karamazow": Dostojewskijs letzter Roman in heutiger Sicht: Elf Vorträge des IX Symposiums der Internationalen Dostojewskij-Gesellschaft*, edited by Horst-Jürgen Gerigk, 135–58. Dresden: Dresden University Press, 1997.

Ruttenburg, Nancy. *Dostoevsky's Democracy*. Princeton, N.J.: Princeton University Press, 2010.

———. "Dostoevsky's Estrangement." *Poetics Today* 26, no. 4 (Winter 2005): 719–51.

Sabo, B. M. "Compassion Fatigue and Nursing Work: Can We Accurately Capture the Consequences of Caring Work?" *International Journal of Nursing Practice* 12 (2006): 136–42.

Sander, Angelika. "Normative und descriptive Bedeutung des ordo amoris." In Bermes et al., *Vernunft und Gefühl: Schelers Phänomenologie des emotionalen Lebens*, 63–80.

Savkin, I. A. "Delo o Voskresenii." In Valitskaia and Isupov, *M.M. Bakhtin i filosofskaia kul'tura XX veka: Problemy Bakhtinologii*, vol. 2: 112–18.

Scheler, Max. *Formalism in Ethics and Non-Formal Ethics of Values*. 5th ed.

Translated by Manfred S. Frings and Roger L. Funk. Evanston, Ill.: Northwestern University Press, 1973.

———. *Gesammelte Werke*. Edited by Maria Scheler and Manfred Frings. 15 vols. Bern: Francke Verlag, 1954–97.

———. *The Nature of Sympathy*. Translated by Peter Heath. Introduction by W. Stark. New Haven, Conn.: Yale University Press, 1954.

———. *On the Eternal in Man*. Translated by Bernard Noble. London: SCM, 1960.

———. *Ressentiment*. Edited by Lewis A. Coser. Translated by William W. Holdheim. New York: Free Press of Glencoe, 1961.

Schlossberger, Matthias. "Das Mitgefühl als Gefühl." In Bermes et al., *Vernunft und Gefühl: Schelers Phänomenologie des emotionalen Lebens*, 39–50.

Schultze, Brigitte. *Der Dialog in F.M. Dostoevskijs "Idiot."* Munich: Verlag Otto Sagner, 1974.

Seeley, Frank. *From the Heyday of the Superfluous Man to Chekhov: Essays on 19th Century Russian Literature*. Nottingham, Eng.: Astra, 1994.

Shalamov, Varlam. *Kolyma Tales*. Translated by John Glad. New York: Penguin Books, 1994.

———. *Sobranie sochinenii v shesti tomakh*. Edited by I. P. Sirotinskaia. 6 vols. Moscow: Terra-knizhnyi klub, 2004–13.

Shanton, K., and A. I. Goldman. "Simulation Theory." *Wiley Interdisciplinary Reviews: Cognitive Science* 1, no. 4 (2010): 527–38.

Shchennikov, G. K. *Tselostnost' Dostoevskogo*. Ekaterinburg: Izdatel'stvo Ural'skogo Universiteta, 2001.

Shchittsova, T. V. *Sobytie v filosofii Bakhtina*. Minsk: I.P. Logvinov, 2002.

Shchyttsova, T. "Die Idee der 'antwortenden Subjektivität' im Werk von Søren Kierkegaard und Michail Bachtin." In *Diskurse der Personalität*, edited by A. Haardt and N. Plotnikov, 241–50. Paderborn: Fink, 2008.

Shepherd, David, ed. *The Contexts of Bakhtin: Philosophy, Authorship, Aesthetics*. Amsterdam: Harwood Academic, 1998.

Shestov, Lev. "Dostoevsky and Nietzsche: The Philosophy of Tragedy." In *Essays in Russian Literature: The Conservative View: Leontiev, Rozanov, Shestov*, edited by Spencer E. Roberts, 3–183. Athens: Ohio University Press, 1968.

Singer, T., et al. "Empathy for Pain Involves the Affective but Not Sensory Components of Pain." *Science* 303, no. 5661 (2004): 1157–62.

Slattery, Dennis Patrick. *"The Idiot," Dostoevsky's Fantastic Prince: A Phenomenological Approach*. New York: Peter Lang, 1983.

Soloviev, Vladimir. *Sobranie sochinenii Vladimira Sergeevicha Solov'eva*. 9 vols. St. Petersburg: Obshchestvennaia Pol'za, 1901–7.

Sontag, Susan. *Regarding the Pain of Others*. New York: Picador, 2003.

Spader, Peter H. *Scheler's Ethical Personalism: Its Logic, Development, and Promise*. New York: Fordham University Press, 2002.

Stanton, Leonard J. *The Optina Pustyn Monastery in the Russian Literary Imagination: Iconic Vision in Works by Dostoevsky, Gogol, Tolstoy, and Others*. New York: Peter Lang, 1995.

Starobinsky, Jean. "The Struggle with Legion." *New Literary History* 4 (1973): 331–56.

Stein, Edith. *The Collected Works of Edith Stein, Sister Teresa Benedicta of the Cross, Discalced Carmelite*. Vol. 3, *On the Problem of Empathy*. Translated by Waltraut Stein. Washington, D.C.: ICS Publications, 1989.

———. *Edith Steins Werke*. Vol. 6, *Welt und Person: Beitrag zum Christlichen Wahrheitsstreben*. Edited by L. Gelber. Freiburg: Verlag Herder, 1962.

Steinby, Liisa. "Hermann Cohen and Bakhtin's Early Aesthetics." *Studies in East European Thought* 63 (2011): 227–49.

Steiner, George. *Tolstoy or Dostoevsky: An Essay in the Old Criticism*. Chicago: University of Chicago Press, 1959.

Stepanian, Karen. *Iavlenie i dialog v romanakh F. M. Dostoevskogo*. St. Petersburg: Kniga, 2009.

———. "Iurodstvo i bezumie, smert i voskresenie, bytie i nebytie v romane 'Idiot.'" In Kasatkina, *Roman F.M. Dostoevskogo "Idiot": Sovremennoe sostoianie izucheniia*, 137–62.

Störring, Gustav. *Psychologie des menschlichen Gefühlslebens*. Bonn: Friedrich Cohen, 1916.

Stueber, K. *Rediscovering Empathy: Agency, Folk Psychology, and the Human Sciences*. Cambridge, Mass.: MIT Press, 2006.

Sugarman, Richard Ira. *Rancor against Time: The Phenomenology of "Ressentiment."* Hamburg: Felix Meiner Verlag, 1980.

Terras, Victor. *Reading Dostoevsky*. Madison: University of Wisconsin Press, 1998.

Thompson, Diane Oenning. *"The Brothers Karamazov" and the Poetics of Memory*. Cambridge: Cambridge University Press, 1991.

Tillich, Paul. *Love, Power, and Justice: Ontological Analyses and Ethical Applications*. New York: Geoffrey Cumberlege, Oxford University Press, 1954.

———. *Systematic Theology*. 3 vols. Chicago: University of Chicago Press, 1951–63.

Tokarzewski, Szymon. *Siedem lat katorgi: Pamiętniki 1846–1857*. 2nd ed. Warsaw: Gebethner and Wolff, 1918.

Tolstoy, Lev. *Sobranie sochinenii v dvadtsati dvukh tomakh*. Edited by M. B. Khrapchenko. 22 vols. Moscow: Khudozhestvennaia literatura, 1978–85.

Trofimov, Evgenii. "Obraz Myshkina v pervoi chasti romana 'Idiot.'" In Kasatkina, *Roman F.M. Dostoevskogo "Idiot": Sovremennoe sostoianie izucheniia*, 239–49.

Tudor, Steven. *Compassion and Remorse: Acknowledging the Suffering Other*. Leuven: Peeters, 2001.

Tunimanov, V. A. *Tvorchestvo Dostoevskogo: 1854–1862*. Leningrad: Nauka, 1980.

Uddin, L. Q., et al. "The Self and Social Cognition: The Role of Cortical Midline Structures and Mirror Neurons." *Trends in Cognitive Sciences* 11 (2007): 153–57.

Valitskaia, A. P., et al., eds. *Bakhtinologiia: Issledovaniia, perevody, publikatsii*. St Petersburg: Aleteia, 1995.

Valitskaia, A. P., and K. G. Isupov, eds. *M. M. Bakhtin i filosofskaia kul'tura XX veka: Problemy Bakhtinologii; Sbornik nauchnykh statei*. St. Petersburg: Rosskiiskii gosudarstvennyi pedagogicheskii universitet, 1991.

Van den Bercken, Wil. *Christian Fiction and Religious Realism in the Novels of Dostoevsky*. London: Anthem, 2011.

Vetlovskaia, V. E. *Roman F. M. Dostoevskogo "Brat'ia Karamazovy."* Saint Petersburg: Pushkinskii Dom, 2007.

Volkelt, Johannes. *Das ästhetische Bewutßsein; Prinzipielfragen der Ästhetik*. Munich: Beck, 1920.

Wall, Anthony. "Chatter, Babble, and Dialogue." In Shepherd, *The Contexts of Bakhtin: Philosophy, Authorship, Aesthetics*, 197–209. Amsterdam: Harwood Academic.

Wasiolek, Edward. *Dostoevsky: The Major Fiction*. Cambridge, Mass.: MIT Press, 1964.

Weisberg, Richard H. *The Failure of the Word: The Protagonist as Lawyer in Modern Fiction*. New Haven, Conn.: Yale University Press, 1984.

Williams, Rowan. *Dostoevsky: Language, Faith and Fiction*. Waco, Tex.: Baylor University Press, 2008.

Wyman, Alina. "Bakhtin and Scheler: Toward a Theory of Active Understanding." *Slavonic and East European Review* 86, no. 1 (2008): 58–89.

———. "Revisiting Early Bakhtin: Problematic Aspects of *Vzhivanie*." In *Proceedings of the XII International Bakhtin Conference, Jyvaskyla, July 18–22, 2005*, edited by Mika Lahteenmaki, Hannele Dufva, Sirpa Leppanen, and Piia Varis, 414–23. Jyvaskyla, Finland, 2006. CD-ROM.

———. "The Specter of Freedom: *Ressentiment* and Dostoevsky's *Notes from Underground*." *Studies in East European Thought* 59 (2007): 119–40.

Young, Sarah. *Dostoevsky's "The Idiot" and the Ethical Foundation of Narrative: Reading, Narrating, Scripting*. London: Anthem, 2004.

Zenkovsky, V. V. "Fedor Pavlovich Karamazov." In Bem, *O Dostoevskom: Sbornik statei pod redaktsiei A.L. Bema*, vol. 2: 93–114.

Zhang, Wei. "Person und Selbstgefühl im phänomenologischen Personalismus Max Schelers." *Studia Phaenomenologica* 11 (2011): 265–84.

Index